starting out in methods and statistics for psychology
a hands-on guide to doing research

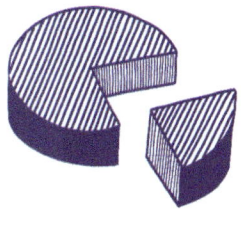

starting out in methods and statistics for psychology

a hands-on guide to doing research

Victoria Bourne

OXFORD
UNIVERSITY PRESS

Great Clarendon Street, Oxford, OX2 6DP,
United Kingdom

Oxford University Press is a department of the University of Oxford.
It furthers the University's objective of excellence in research, scholarship,
and education by publishing worldwide. Oxford is a registered trade mark of
Oxford University Press in the UK and in certain other countries

© Oxford University Press 2017

The moral rights of the author have been asserted

First Edition 2017

Impression: **4**

All rights reserved. No part of this publication may be reproduced, stored in
a retrieval system, or transmitted, in any form or by any means, without the
prior permission in writing of Oxford University Press, or as expressly permitted
by law, by licence or under terms agreed with the appropriate reprographics
rights organization. Enquiries concerning reproduction outside the scope of the
above should be sent to the Rights Department, Oxford University Press, at the
address above

You must not circulate this work in any other form
and you must impose this same condition on any acquirer

Published in the United States of America by Oxford University Press
198 Madison Avenue, New York, NY 10016, United States of America

British Library Cataloguing in Publication Data

Data available

Library of Congress Control Number: 2016963297

ISBN 978-0-19-875333-9

Printed in Great Britain by
CPI Group (UK) Ltd, Croydon, CR0 YY

Links to third party websites are provided by Oxford in good faith and
for information only. Oxford disclaims any responsibility for the materials
contained in any third party website referenced in this work.

For my family.

About this book

I have always loved teaching and doing psychological research. It can be quite challenging to convince a lecture theatre of around two hundred keen, new undergraduate students that research methodology and statistical analysis is the most exciting thing they will do during their degree, but I truly believe that it is. If you are interested in psychology, then you are interested in research, and what could possibly be more exciting than actually doing the thing that you are interested in?

I think it is really important that psychological research is learned as a complete process in which students are active participants. That is, I think the whole point of teaching this is to create confident and independent researchers. Doing successful research is a long process where a number of stages have to be completed. So often the emphasis is placed on just learning about methodology and statistics, often taught separately. I think methods and statistics only make sense when taught together, in a fully integrated way, and this is what I have aimed for this this book.

Although methods and statistics are core aspects of a good piece of psychological research, they do not make a complete piece of research on their own. Research also involves finding and understanding published research, a healthy dose of critical thinking, considering ethical issues and applying for ethical approval. That is before you really get into the methods and statistics part of research. With all this done, you then need to clearly present your research, and do a bit more critical thinking. I have endeavoured to cover all aspects of doing a simple piece of psychological research in this book, from the very first spark of an idea through to presenting well thought through findings. By putting all of the component parts into one book, I hope that you will feel more confident in completing your own research project.

I strongly believe that the best way to learn something is to do it, and therefore if you want to learn how to do psychological research, you need to get your hands dirty and actually do it! Reading about the theory of research certainly has its place in the learning process, but if you can actually design your own study that comes from some spark of inspiration you had, and you can analyse real data that you collected, then that learning is far more active and effective. Throughout this book I have tried to discuss research issues in a very practical way, often drawing on my own research experiences and frustrations, and the study questions at the end of each chapter are intended to get you thinking like a researcher.

Finally, I'm keenly aware that many students find statistics boring at best and terrifying at worst! I started my psychology degree with some statistics anxiety, and now I spend much of my professional life doing and teaching statistics. Perhaps unusually, I firmly believe that the best way to deal with any maths anxiety is to learn statistics through calculating everything by hand. Don't avoid it, tackle and conquer it. If approached in the right way, the maths side of statistics really does not need to be intimidating and complicated. In fact, understanding what is going on behind the equations is a massive advantage for understanding research findings, and therefore I only teach the basics of statistics through hand calculations. Besides, as you will learn in this book, statistics is all about cake. How could cake be intimidating and complicated?

Research is fun, exciting, and dynamic, and I hope that once you have finished with this book, you will agree with me. Even just a little! Research is also imperfect, and it is quite likely that this book is too. For any errors or typos that slipped though, I apologise. Most likely those parts were written on chocolate-free days!

Victoria Bourne
Department of Psychology
Royal Holloway, University of London

Acknowledgements

My first thanks must go to the hundreds of students who I have taught over the past few years. Each year I learn a little more about how to teach methodology and statistics, and I hope that each year I get a little better at making all this stuff fun, exhilarating, and accessible. Thank you for not judging me too harshly for my over excitement in stats lectures, and even more thanks for sometimes joining in! I couldn't run my courses successfully without my team of amazing lab tutors, both past and present, who help to put it all into practice. Thank you to all of you. Particular thanks to Danijela Serbic who is a really fantastic teacher and has been an invaluable sounding board for all things methods and statistics teaching related. Huge thanks also to Alana James who provides balance in my teaching life by bringing the qualitative to my quantitative! Thank you for taking the time to help me frame and put together the qualitative chapter in this book.

Massive, massive thanks to Martha Bailes, who has been so much more than an editor! Over the past two years she has really helped to shape this book and has kept me on track with our shared love of colour coded Excel sheets. Our chocolate choices might differ greatly, but it really has been great fun and I've laughed so much during our review phone calls. I will miss our Friday morning chats! Thank you for guiding me so attentively and patiently through this process.

Thank you to the reviewers who have read drafts of chapters at various stages throughout the writing process. There are a number of places in the book where I have added or changed things that were generously suggested by anonymous reviewers. If you would care to de-anonymise yourself at any time, I will gladly show my appreciation with chocolate! Thanks also to Rachel Nesbit and Sweta Gupta who went through this book with a fine toothcomb to check for accuracy.

Two people have really shaped my career. Graham Hole taught me statistics when I was an undergraduate, and then supervised my PhD. If anyone is to blame for my over enthusiastic love for teaching statistics, it is certainly Graham. More recently, Patrick Leman has really supported my 'unique' approach to teaching methods and statistics, giving me the confidence to push ahead with ideas that others might have written off as bonkers. He also strongly encouraged me to approach publishers with my idea for a textbook that would be similarly 'unique'. So, Patrick, this book is your fault!

Dawn Watling has been my constant source of academic support and empathy for more years than I care to remember! We started off teaching statistics together as PhD students, cementing a friendship and a geeky mutual adoration of statistics that survives to this day. Far too often I need to bounce ideas around, and Dawn is always my first port of call. I cannot say thank you enough, for letting me borrow your brain so frequently, for hiding my chocolate stash in your office (I have no self-control!), and for the constant supply of coffee and pain au chocolat.

Finally, to the two most important people in my life; my husband Mat and our daughter Elizabeth. To Mat, thank you so much, and in so many ways, for the support you always give me. So much of what I do would be impossible without you. But thank you in particular for the evening when I tentatively said 'I think I'd like to write a methods and statistics textbook' and you replied with 'I know, go for it' rather than 'Are you crazy?!' When I started working on this book I was pregnant with Elizabeth, and as I write this she is soon to turn two years old. I'm sure every parent thinks their child is the smartest, funniest, and cutest on the planet, but mine really is! She counts everything in sight and is obsessed with chocolate cake. Perhaps it is in the genes?

Brief contents

About this book	vi
Acknowledgements	viii
About the book	xxi
About the online resources	xxiii

PART ONE Introduction

1.	An overview of how to do research	3
2.	How to design a psychological research study: the basics of methodology	21
3.	How to find, read, write, and think about research papers	43
4.	Qualitative methods in psychological research	68
5.	The basics of statistical analysis	82

PART TWO Experimental design

6.	How to design an experiment	113
7.	How can I tell if scores differ between two groups? Independent *t* test	129
8.	How can I tell if scores differ between two conditions? Repeated *t* test	142
9.	How can I tell if scores differ between three or more groups? One-way independent measures ANOVA	153

PART THREE Correlational design

10.	How to design a correlational study	171
11.	How can I tell if two variables are correlated? Pearson's correlation	180
12.	How can I tell if one variable can predict another? Simple linear regression	192

PART FOUR Non-parametric statistics

13.	When and why might I need to use non-parametric statistics?	207
14.	Do my data fit the expected frequencies? Chi squared	219

BRIEF CONTENTS

15. **Are there differences between groups or conditions? Mann-Whitney *U* and Wilcoxon signed rank tests** — 231
16. **Is there a relationship between two variables? Spearman's correlation** — 247

PART FIVE **Beyond the basics**

17. **Which statistical test should I use?** — 259
18. **Moving beyond the basics of research and analysis: how do I understand more complicated research designs?** — 266

Glossary — 294
Appendix 1 Statistical symbols and conventions — 301
Appendix 2 Area under the normal curve (z scores) — 303
Appendix 3 Critical values tables — 309
Appendix 4 Short answers for study questions and additional datasets — 319
Index — 335

Detailed contents

About this book — vi
Acknowledgements — viii
About the book — xxi
About the online resources — xxiii

PART ONE Introduction

1. An overview of how to do research — 3

Research and statistics in psychology — 3
The research process — 5
  How it all begins — 5
  Testing new ideas or replicating old findings? — 5
  A study in chocolate: a quick overview of how research works — 6
Hypothesis testing and the scientific method in psychological research — 7
  Null hypothesis significance testing (NHST) — 7
  The alternative hypothesis: one-tailed and two-tailed hypotheses — 8
  The scientific method — 9
Ethics in psychological research — 10
  Informed consent and debriefing — 11
  Deception — 13
  Protecting participants from potential harm — 14
  Right to withdraw — 14
  Anonymity and confidentiality — 15
  Additional considerations when working with vulnerable groups — 15
  Designing ethical research and applying for ethical approval — 16
  Running and writing up an ethical study — 17
Study questions — 18
References — 19
Wider reading — 19

2. How to design a psychological research study: the basics of methodology — 21

Introduction — 21
Measuring Variables — 21
  Operationalising variables: defining what you are measuring — 22
  Types of variables and data you can collect — 22
  Parametric and non-parametric analysis — 24

DETAILED CONTENTS

Confounding variables	25
Categorical research designs: looking at frequencies within categories	28
Experimental research designs: comparing groups or conditions	29
Correlational research designs: looking at relationships between variables	30
Validity and reliability in research design	31
Construct validity	32
Internal validity	33
External validity	33
Ecological validity	33
Inter-rater reliability	34
Test-retest reliability	35
Internal consistency	35
Selecting and recruiting participants	37
Random sampling	37
Systematic sampling	38
Stratified sampling	38
Volunteer and opportunity sampling	38
How to run a psychological research study	39
Study questions	40
Wider reading	42
3. How to find, read, write, and think about research papers	**43**
How is a psychological research paper structured?	43
Title	44
Abstract	44
Introduction	44
Methods	46
Results	48
Discussion	50
References	52
Appendices	53
Writing a psychological research paper	53
Psychological research reports: the hourglass	54
Presenting psychological research: what are the standards for presenting research?	55
Writing style	55
Presenting statistics	56
Referencing	57
Finding psychological research papers	60
What psychological research should you trust, and where can you find it?	60
Hints and tips to help you find psychological research	62
Thinking critically: how good is this research?	64
How is research published? The publishing process	65
Study questions	66
Wider reading	67

4. Qualitative methods in psychological research — 68

Introduction — 68

Comparing qualitative and quantitative methods — 68
- Framing research questions — 70
- Sources of data for qualitative analysis — 70

Methodological issues when running qualitative studies — 71
- Sampling for qualitative research — 71
- Validity and reliability in qualitative research — 71
- Ethics and qualitative research — 71

What types of qualitative analysis are there? — 72
- Thematic Analysis — 72
- Grounded Theory — 73
- Interpretative Phenomenological Analysis — 73
- Discourse Analysis — 74

An overview of Thematic Analysis — 74
- Phase 1: Familiarise yourself with the data — 76
- Phase 2: Generate initial codes — 76
- Phase 3: Search for themes — 77
- Phase 4: Review the themes — 77
- Phase 5: Defining and naming themes — 78
- Phase 6: Produce the report — 78

Pluralism and mixed methods in psychological research — 79

Study questions — 80

Wider Reading — 80

5. The basics of statistical analysis — 82

Introduction — 82

Roughly where is the middle score in my dataset? Descriptive statistics: central tendency — 83
- Calculating the mode — 83
- Calculating the median — 84
- Calculating the mean — 84
- Which average should you use? — 86

Roughly how spread out are the scores in my dataset? Descriptive statistics: dispersion — 86
- Understanding variability: an example — 86
- Calculating the range — 89
- Calculating the variance and standard deviation — 89
- Thinking about dispersion in data — 91

Distributions in datasets — 92
- What happens if your data are not normally distributed? — 93

z scores — 95
- What can z scores be used for? Comparing studies — 95
- What can z scores be used for? Looking at scores and distributions — 95

DETAILED CONTENTS

z score problem 1	97
z score problem 2	97
z score problem 3	98
z score problem 4	98
z score problem 5	98
How are z scores relevant to the rest of psychological statistics?	99
Inferential statistics: what is significance?	99
Understanding possible outcomes in hypothesis testing	100
Statistical significance and p values	101
What are the problems with p values?	103
Significance, between and within group variability	103
The importance of your sample size and degrees of freedom	103
Presenting descriptive and inferential statistics	105
Study questions	107
Additional dataset	107
Wider reading	108
Example paper using this statistic	108

PART TWO Experimental design

6. How to design an experiment — 113

Introduction	113
Describing your variables: what do you manipulate and what do you measure?	113
What happens if you cannot manipulate your independent variable?	114
What is the difference between independent and repeated measures designs?	115
Independent measures design	115
Repeated measures design	116
Longitudinal and cross-sectional designs	116
What other decisions do you need to make when designing an experiment?	117
The impact of the type of experimental design on analysing your data	118
How many different conditions would you like with your experimental design?	119
Avoiding common pitfalls in experimental design: dealing with confounding variables	120
Randomising participants	120
Matching participants	121
Counterbalancing	121
Avoiding common pitfalls in experimental design: random variability and bias	122
Double blind design	123
Looking experimentally at treatments and interventions	123
Intervention experiments and repeated measures	124
Using control groups	124
Randomised control trials	124

	One-tailed or two? Devising hypotheses for an experimental design	125
	One- and two-tailed hypotheses and the normal distribution	126
	Analysing your experimental data	127
	Study questions	127
	Wider reading	128
7.	**How can I tell if scores differ between two groups? Independent *t* test**	**129**
	Introduction	129
	The logic behind the independent *t* test: understanding where variability comes from	130
	How does the independent *t* test work?	131
	Calculating and interpreting an independent *t* test: a worked example	132
	Is the independent *t* test significant?	135
	Interpreting and writing up an independent *t* test	137
	Are *p* values enough? Effect sizes for the independent *t* test	138
	Study questions	139
	Additional dataset	140
	Are p values enough? An additional exercise	140
	Example paper using this statistic	141
8.	**How can I tell if scores differ between two conditions? Repeated *t* test**	**142**
	Introduction	142
	The logic behind the repeated *t* test: understanding where variability comes from	142
	How does the repeated *t* test work?	144
	Calculating and interpreting a repeated *t* test: a worked example	145
	Is the repeated *t* test significant?	147
	Interpreting and writing up a repeated *t* test	148
	Are *p* values enough? Effect sizes for the repeated *t* test	149
	Study questions	150
	Additional dataset	150
	Are p values enough? An additional exercise	151
	Example paper using this statistic	151
9.	**How can I tell if scores differ between three or more groups? One-way independent measures ANOVA**	**153**
	Introduction	153
	Why not just run lots of *t* tests? Understanding familywise error	153
	The logic behind the ANOVA	154
	Stage one: calculate the Sums of Squares (SS)	156
	Stage two: calculate the degrees of freedom (df)	157

Stage three: calculate the Mean Squares (MS)	157
Stage four: calculate the *F* ratio	157
Calculating and interpreting an ANOVA: a worked example	158
Stage one revisited: calculate the Sums of Squares (SS)	159
Stage two revisited: calculate the degrees of freedom (df)	160
Stage three revisited: calculate the Mean Squares (MS)	160
Stage four revisited: calculate the *F* ratio	161
The ANOVA summary table	161
Is the ANOVA significant?	162
Interpreting and writing up an ANOVA	163
A problem with interpreting ANOVAs	163
Are *p* values enough? Effect sizes for the ANOVA	164
Thinking more widely about ANOVAs	165
Study questions	165
Additional dataset	166
Are p values enough? An additional exercise	166
Example paper using this statistic	167

PART THREE Correlational design

10. How to design a correlational study	**171**
Introduction	171
What kinds of relationships can we find with a correlation?	171
Positive relationships	172
Negative relationships	172
No relationship	172
Relationships and hypotheses	172
What kinds of variables can we use in a correlational study?	173
Continuous variables and the correlation motto	173
Categorical variables: a common pitfall	173
Correlation does not imply causation	175
Confounding variables in correlational designs	175
What to do with confounding variables	176
Using correlational designs to form predictive models	177
Linear regression	177
Study questions	178
Wider reading	179
11. How can I tell if two variables are correlated? Pearson's correlation	**180**
Introduction	180
The logic behind a Pearson's correlation: understanding the role of variability	181
What does the Pearson's correlation do?	183

	Calculating and interpreting a Pearson's correlation: a worked example	184
	Is the Pearson's correlation significant?	186
	Interpreting and writing up a Pearson's correlation	188
	Are *p* values enough? Effect sizes for Pearson's correlation	188
	Which variables can't you use for a Pearson's correlation?	189
	Study questions	189
	Additional dataset	190
	Are p values enough? An additional exercise	191
	Example paper using this statistic	191
12.	**How can I tell if one variable can predict another? Simple linear regression**	**192**
	Introduction	192
	Regression models: a note about terminology	193
	Linear regression and the line of best fit	193
	Drawing the line of best fit: slope and intercept	193
	Building a predictive model	194
	Working through a regression analysis: looking at delayed gratification	197
	How much variance is explained? The R^2 statistic	197
	Calculating the slope and intercept	199
	Writing up a regression analysis	201
	Are *p* values enough? Effect sizes for linear regression	201
	Study questions	202
	Additional dataset	203
	Are p values enough? An additional exercise	204
	Example paper using this statistic	204

PART FOUR Non-parametric statistics

13.	**When and why might I need to use non-parametric statistics?**	**207**
	Introduction	207
	What are the assumptions of parametric analyses?	207
	Assumption 1: Independence of observations	208
	Assumption 2: Variables are measured at interval or ratio level	209
	Assumption 3: Data are (roughly) normally distributed	210
	Assumption 4: Homogeneity of variance	211
	How do I know if I have violated the parametric assumptions?	212
	How do I know if my data are normally distributed?	212
	How do I know if I've violated the homogeneity of variance assumption?	214
	How do non-parametric tests work?	214
	What are the non-parametric equivalents of the parametric tests we have learned?	216
	Interpreting non-parametric statistics with descriptive statistics	216
	Are non-parametric statistics really needed?	216

DETAILED CONTENTS

Study questions	217
Wider reading	218

14. Do my data fit the expected frequencies? Chi squared — 219

Introduction	219
Chi squared and the goodness of fit	219
Different designs and the chi squared test of association	220
Calculating and interpreting a chi squared goodness of fit: a worked example	221
Is the chi squared goodness of fit analysis significant?	223
Interpreting and writing up a chi squared goodness of fit	224
Calculating and interpreting a chi squared test of association: analysing more than one variable	225
Is the chi squared test of association analysis significant?	227
Interpreting and writing up a chi squared test of association	227
Are there any assumptions for using the chi squared test?	228
How is the chi squared analysis typically used in psychological research?	228
Study questions	229
Additional dataset	229
Example paper using this statistic	230

15. Are there differences between groups or conditions? Mann-Whitney U and Wilcoxon signed rank tests — 231

Introduction	231
Mann-Whitney U test (two independent groups)	232
The logic behind the Mann-Whitney U test	233
Calculating and interpreting a Mann-Whitney U test: a worked example	234
Wilcoxon signed rank test (two repeated conditions)	238
The logic behind the Wilcoxon signed rank test	239
Calculating and interpreting a Wilcoxon signed rank test: a worked example	240
Non-parametric tests of difference with large samples: z scores	242
Study questions	243
Additional dataset for Mann-Whitney U	244
Additional dataset for Wilcoxon signed rank	245
Example papers using these statistics	245

16. Is there a relationship between two variables? Spearman's correlation — 247

Introduction	247
The problem of Spearman's correlation and tied ranks	247
Calculating and interpreting a Spearman's correlation: a worked example	250
Is the Spearman's correlation significant?	252
Interpreting and writing up a Spearman's correlation	253

Study questions	254
Additional dataset	254
Example paper using this statistic	255

PART FIVE Beyond the basics

17. Which statistical test should I use? — 259

Introduction	259
What type of research design did you use?	259
Questions to ask yourself if you used a categorical design	260
Questions to ask yourself if you used an experimental design	262
Questions to ask yourself if you used a correlational design	263
Which test next?	264
Study questions	264
Wider reading	265

18. Moving beyond the basics of research and analysis: how do I understand more complicated research designs? — 266

Getting to grips with published research: the basics	266
Getting to grips with published research: advanced experimental designs	267
Breaking down a significant effect in an ANOVA	268
Comparing three or more conditions in a repeated design: one-way repeated measures ANOVA	269
Analysing multiple independent variables: factorial ANOVAs	272
Analysing confound variables in an experimental design: analysis of covariance (ANCOVA)	277
Getting to grips with published research: advanced correlational designs	278
Controlling for a control variable in a correlation analysis: partial correlation	278
Analysing multiple predictor variables in a regression model: multiple regression	279
Using categorical predictors in a regression model: regression with categorical variables	281
How can regression models become more complex? Complex regression models	282
Using regression to predict binary outcome variables: logistic regression	283
Looking for groups of similar variables within a larger dataset: factor analysis	283
Presenting findings from complex analyses: graphing data	285
Getting to grips with published research: issues and debates in statistical analysis	286
Significance: are p values really any good?	287
Is there an alternative to the p value? Effect sizes	287
Detecting an effect: power analysis	290
Statistics and the variability cake: a lesson to take away	291
Study questions	291
Example paper using advanced statistical techniques	292
Wider reading and additional resources	293

DETAILED CONTENTS

Glossary	294
Appendix 1 Statistical symbols and conventions	301
Appendix 2 Area under the normal curve (z scores)	303
Appendix 3 Critical values tables	309
Appendix 4 Short answers for study questions and additional datasets	319
Index	335

About the book

Starting Out in Methods and Statistics for Psychology: a Hands-on Guide to Doing Research and its accompanying online resources contain many learning features to help you to build your understanding of research methods and statistics in psychology. This section explains how to use these features.

In this chapter you will learn...
- Why research and statistics are so important for psychology
- The process behind running a research project
- How to develop hypotheses and hypothesis testing
- How to design and conduct ethical research

Learning outcomes

Each chapter begins with a set of learning outcomes to show you what you can expect to learn and to provide a road map of what is to follow.

Calculating and interpreting a chi square A worked example

In this first analysis, we will look at the simple handedness dat 18 left handed participants and 82 right handed participants. distribution of handedness differs from what we would random handed and half right handed participants. To do this, we ne frequencies, which we would expect to have occurred by rando these values to the actual observed frequencies. The greater th served and expected frequencies, the larger the calculated chi

Worked examples

The chapters that focus on the individual statistical tests (7, 8, 9, 11, 12, 14, 15 and 16) all include complete worked examples which walk you through the hand calculations step-by-step, explain how to work out whether your findings are significant, and show you how to interpret and write up your test results. You will also be shown how to calculate the appropriate effect size for the statistic in *Are p values enough?*

Study questions

1. Four different labs have run a study looking at whether there ar number of friends that children aged 8 years old report having. statistics and *p* values below, complete the table to summarise t

Lab	Boys		Girls		Significance	Is the analysis significant? What is the chance of a Type I Error?
	Mean	SD	Mean	SD	*p*	

Study questions

Study questions help you to check your understanding of the chapter and to practice what you have learned. They highlight the important elements in the chapter, and often emphasise the integration between methods and statistics. Short answers are provided in Appendix 4 at the end of the book, and full answers can be found in the online resources which accompany the book.

Additional datasets

Additional datasets appear at the end of each statistics chapter to give you another opportunity to consolidate and practice what you have covered in that chapter. You will also be encouraged to calculate the appropriate effect size for this dataset in an additional exercise *Are p values enough?* Again, brief answers to the questions here are provided in Appendix 4 at the end of the book, and fully worked example answers can be found online.

Wider reading and example papers

Each chapter lists and describes sources of further information so that you can find out more about the material you have just covered. For the more methodological chapters, the wider reading may be a more advanced textbook or a review paper. For the qualitative methods chapter and the statistical chapters, the wider reading will be an example paper that uses the analytical method(s) from that chapter to show you how the analysis can be used and written up within psychological research. A critical commentary is included for each to guide further study.

How to run this analysis in SPSS

All of the statistics chapters conclude with a boxed feature pointing you to a screencast showing you how to use SPSS to calculate the statistic you have just worked through.

Glossary of statistical terms

Research methodology and statistical analysis can sometimes feel a little like learning a new language, and the new terminology and symbols can be confusing, so a glossary is provided to help build your understanding and will be useful for revision. In addition, you can find statistical symbols and conventions in Appendix 1.

Statistical tables

Statistical tables in Appendix 3 enable you to look up the critical values you will need to help you determine whether the different statistics you will calculate are (statistically) significant.

About the online resources

Online resources are available to accompany this book. They are free of charge and designed to maximise your learning experience.

online resources
www.oup.com/uk/bourne/

Please note that lecturer resources are available only to registered adopters of the textbook. To register, simply visit www.oup.com/uk/bourne/ and follow the appropriate links.

Student resources are openly available to all, without registration.

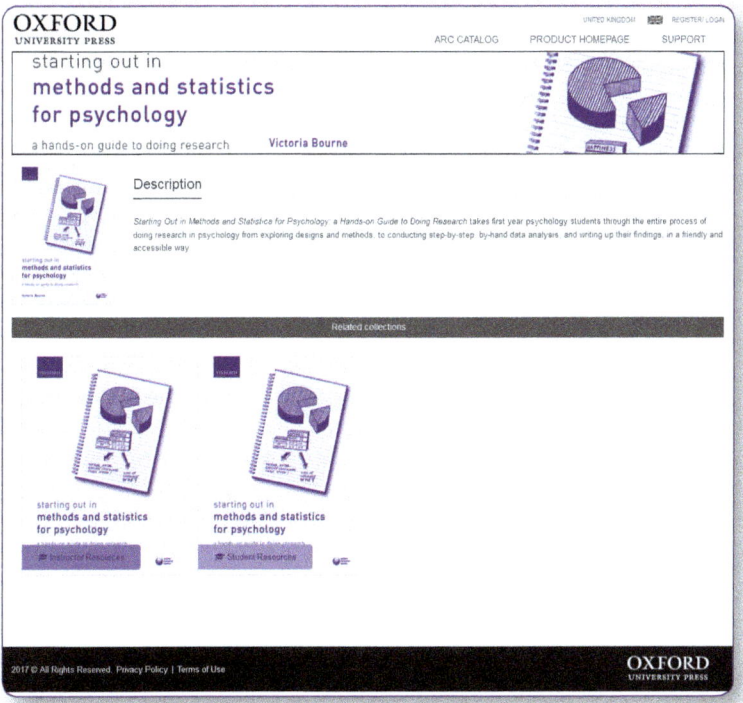

For students

A numeracy skills quiz to help identify your strengths and weaknesses

Some students worry about the maths needed to calculate statistics but the level of maths needed is not as high as you might think. To help clarify what you need to know, this online numeracy skills quiz covers all of the areas of maths you will need to understand the statistics in the text. It has been created to help you identify your strengths and those areas to be strengthened. You will also find recommendations for external websites that might help you to build your maths skills.

Example lab reports

Annotated example lab reports are available to guide you when writing your own lab reports. You will find an example of a "good" lab report written according to APA guidelines, and a "bad" lab report created to illustrate the common mistakes people make when writing their reports.

Example ethics application forms

Example ethics forms are provided to show you what to expect and to help you complete your own ethics applications. Each institution will have its own forms and guidelines, but the forms provided should familiarise you with some general principles.

Full answers to the in-text study questions

These supplement the short answers to study questions provided in Appendix 4. You can check the details of your workings and solutions here to ensure you have understood each step of the calculations.

Full calculations for effect sizes within chapters

Fully worked calculations are provided for the effect sizes covered in chapters 7, 8, 9, 11, and 12.

SPSS screencasts

SPSS screencasts are provided for each of the statistics you have learned how to calculate in the book. These show you how to use SPSS to run each statistical test and interpret the output, and use the same datasets you used for the hand calculations so you can see that whichever approach you use gives you the same results.

Links to papers and websites

A series of annotated links, organised by chapter, enables you to build your understanding by seeing research methods and statistical analysis in real, current research.

For registered adopters of the book

Worksheets with additional datasets

The online worksheets provide the opportunity for students to consolidate and practice what they have learned for each type of analysis they have covered in the text. These can be used to monitor students' understanding and progress during the term, or in formal assessment at the end of the course.

Fully worked answers to worksheets

Worked answers can be given to students so that they can check the details of their workings and solutions to ensure they have understood each step of the calculations.

Test bank

This customisable resource contains 10 questions per chapter with answers and feedback, plus five additional questions related to the worksheets provided on this part of the website.

Figures and tables from the book, ready to download

Lecturers can find the artwork and tables from the book online in ready-to-download format. These can be used for lectures without charge (but not for commercial purposes without specific permission).

PowerPoint® slides

A suite of customisable PowerPoint® slides has been included for use in lecture presentations. Arranged by chapter, these slides may also be used as handouts in class. These slides include animated solutions to the hand calculations so that you can talk students through these, step-by-step, in class.

Part 1
Introduction

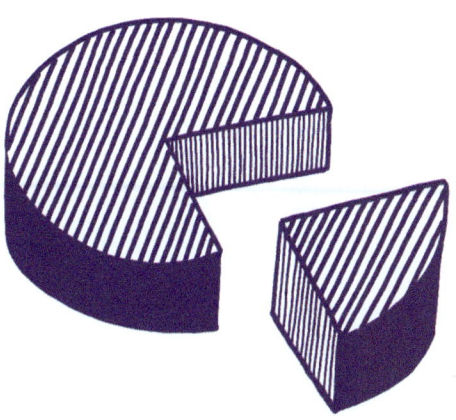

1 An overview of how to do research

In this chapter you will learn ...
- Why research and statistics are so important for psychology
- The process behind running a research project
- How to develop hypotheses and hypothesis testing
- How to design and conduct ethical research

Research and statistics in psychology

Psychology is a discipline that is almost entirely driven by research. All of our psychological knowledge comes from research studies. Therefore, being able to understand research methods and statistics is fundamental to understanding psychology. The majority of undergraduate psychology degrees in the UK are accredited by the British Psychological Society (BPS). This has two important implications for psychology students. First, it means that when you graduate you can be eligible, subject to certain criteria, for Graduate Membership of the BPS. This is essential for certain psychological postgraduate studies and careers. Second, it guides much of the curriculum of your studies.

The BPS curriculum sets out core areas of psychology that must be covered in any BPS accredited degree, and these include Cognitive Psychology, Biological Psychology, Developmental Psychology, Social Psychology, and Individual Differences. One key thing is that all of our existing knowledge of psychology comes from research into these different areas, as you can see in Figure 1.1. We know that eyewitness memory is fallible, we know which part of the brain processes faces, we know how children learn by observing others, we know how group biases occur, and we know that Cognitive Behavioural Therapy is an effective treatment for a range of clinical psychological conditions purely as a result of psychological research. Having a strong understanding of psychological research methods and statistical analysis provides you with a key skill for understanding all of psychology. Therefore the skills you gain will also be vital in helping you to understand and do well in all of your other academic psychology modules, as they are all based on research!

The BPS also outlines the key areas of research skills that are essential for all undergraduate psychology students to learn. This includes understanding how different research methodologies are used within psychology, how to use the appropriate statistical tests to analyse quantitative datasets, and how to use qualitative approaches to analyse and interpret text based datasets. It also specifies that students should be able to present and think critically about research. All of these different aspects of research skills are covered in this book.

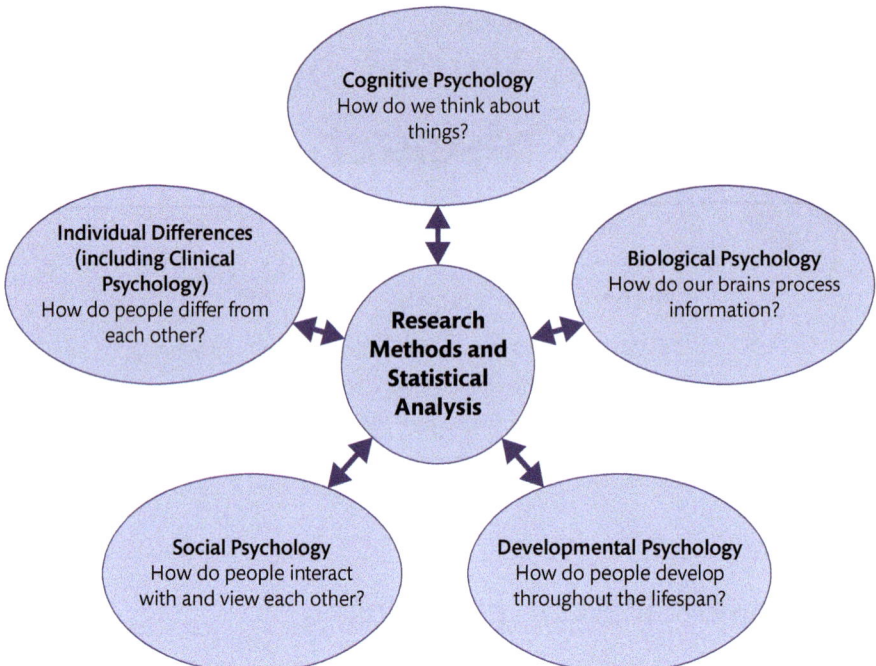

Figure 1.1: Core areas of psychology within the British Psychological Society curriculum.

Whilst reading and learning about psychological research is interesting, it cannot compare to the thrill of doing your own research. When you develop a research question that fascinates you, you design a study to test it, you collect data from participants and then you finally do the appropriate analysis to see what you found out—now that is exciting! For that moment you are the only person on the planet with this new insight into psychological processes, and you have discovered something novel. Through a typical undergraduate psychology degree you will complete training in how to conduct psychological research, and this will culminate in you completing an independent research project in your final year. Doing (and passing) this research project is a fundamental part of being eligible for Graduate Membership of the BPS, and it is also often the part of their degree that students enjoy the most.

If this isn't enough to convince you that psychological research is the best and most exciting part of being a psychology student, then it might also be interesting to know that the research component of a psychology degree could be the thing most likely to get you a job after graduation! Through studying psychological research methods you can develop the ability to think critically and problem solve; the ability to review literature and develop projects; the ability to handle and present data; the ability to communicate clearly and use various computer programmes; and the ability to work both independently and as part of a team. These are the key skills on your CV that will make you look attractive to employers.

Hopefully I've managed to convince you that research methods and statistics will be the most exciting and the most useful part of your psychology degree. So let's now start learning the basics of how to do psychological research.

The research process

When you are aiming to do high quality psychological research, one of the key things is to be systematic. There is a relatively standard process that you go through for each research project that you complete, which runs from initially reading around your area of interest through to writing up and presenting the findings of your own research. In this book you will be taken through every single stage of the research process, which you can see in Figure 1.2, with the aim of giving you a strong grounding in the basics of how to do psychological research. As well as giving you lots of hints and tips for the practicalities of doing research, you will also learn the 'why' behind the methods and statistics.

How it all begins

Research starts with an initial idea, something that sparks your imagination. Why is it that people experience language difficulties after a stroke? How do children seem to intuitively be able to use touch screen technology at such a young age? What happens to criminals after they take part in a rehabilitation programme? Are people happier after eating white chocolate or milk chocolate? There is loads and loads of psychological research out there, hundreds of thousands of published research papers, so the very first stage in the research process is to find and select any relevant papers, read them, and bring together all of the existing research in the area. This will help you to develop and form your own research study.

Testing new ideas or replicating old findings?

Psychological research falls into two broad categories: novel research ideas and **replications**. For academics who publish their research in journals, there has been a great deal of emphasis on producing novel research with new research findings, and therefore the majority of the

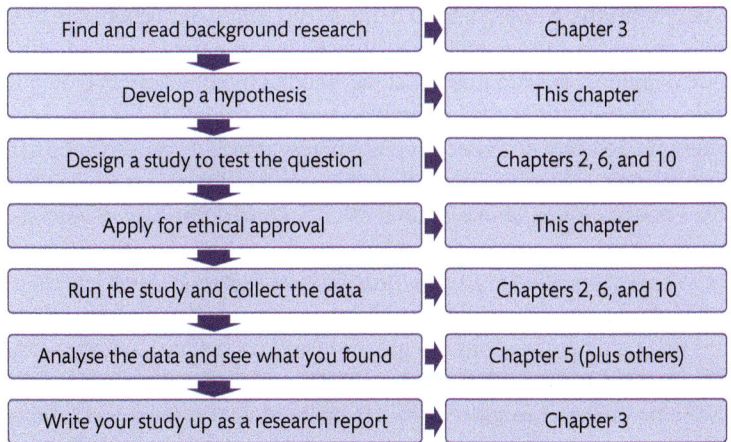

Figure 1.2: The research process, and its coverage within this book.

published research addresses individual and unique research questions. However, replicating previously published findings is also an important aspect of psychological research. The clearest way to show that a finding is robust is for an entirely different research lab to run exactly the same study, and find exactly the same results. Unfortunately, for quite a long time replication studies have rarely been published in favour of publishing new and novel studies, but the importance of replication has been discussed a great deal by psychologists recently, and there is a new drive to examine and publish and replicate psychological studies. Some of the findings are very controversial and there have been failures to replicate some well-known findings. To find out more about the current 'replication (or reproducibility) debate' in psychological research, take a look at the wider suggested reading at the end of this chapter.

A study in chocolate: a quick overview of how research works

Let's think about how research works in practice. Imagine that I want to conduct a piece of psychological research looking at happiness after eating different types of chocolate. I would first need to search for, find, and read the existing published research in this area. If I am to design and run a research study, it is essential to fully understand the previous work on this topic so that I can be confident of asking relevant and new questions. I would also need to think critically about the methodology and findings of the previous research. No piece of research is perfect, and therefore it is important to think about the strengths and weaknesses of previous research to help me design a rigorous piece of research. How to think critically about research is covered in Chapter 3. With a clear idea of the previous research, I would then develop my **hypothesis**, or predicted findings from my study, and we will be discussing how to do this in the next section of this chapter. For my chocolate study, I predict that participants will be happier after eating milk chocolate than after eating white chocolate. This is my hypothesis, or prediction.

Now I would need to design my study, thinking carefully about which methodological approach I should take, what stimuli and materials to create, which participants should be recruited and how to recruit them. In Chapter 2, I give an overview of some of the key issues to consider when designing a study, and then later in the book there are further chapters, which go into more specific detail on particular study designs. For my chocolate study, I want to run an experiment where I will give half of my participants white chocolate to eat, and the other half milk chocolate. Immediately after they have eaten the chocolate, I will give them a standardised happiness questionnaire that has been frequently used in previous research.

When designing your study, it is important to not just think about your needs as a researcher to design an elegant and effective piece of research, but you also need to think about your participants and the possible impact that being involved in your study will have on them. Therefore, you need to think about various **ethical considerations** in your study design, and you have to gain ethical approval from an appropriate body (usually a University board) before you can collect any data at all. This process is explained in detail later in this chapter, but for my chocolate study there are no unethical elements and approval has been granted.

This means that I am now ready to run my study and collect my data. With your data collected, we can move on to the really exciting stage of the research process. We need to analyse the data to see whether you can support your hypothesis. At this stage, I will find out whether people really are happier after eating milk chocolate than after eating white chocolate. Each methodological approach has its own set of statistics that can be used to analyse your data,

HYPOTHESIS TESTING AND THE SCIENTIFIC METHOD IN PSYCHOLOGICAL RESEARCH

and you can see an overview of this in Chapters 2 and 17. Using the appropriate method of statistical analysis (an independent measures *t* test in this case, covered in Chapter 7), I find that participants who ate the milk chocolate were significantly happier than the participants who ate white chocolate. We will discuss what 'significance' actually means in Chapter 5.

Finally, you need to write up your study in a lab report, which should be structured and read a little like a published piece of research. How to do this is covered in Chapter 3. Remember, also, that in addition to accurately and clearly presenting your research question, methodology and findings, you should constantly be thinking critically about your research, considering how to improve your study and thinking about what further research needs to be done to address the remaining unanswered questions. And then the whole research cycle starts again with your next study!

Hypothesis testing and the scientific method in psychological research

A key principle that underlies psychological research is **hypothesis** testing. Simply put, a hypothesis sets out your predicted findings, on the basis of having reviewed the previous research in the area. Your hypothesis, or prediction, is usually based on some form of **theory**. A theory is an explanation of a particular behaviour or phenomenon. For example, Social Learning Theory, initially proposed by Bandura (1977), suggests that children learn behaviours through the observation of other people's behaviours. In Bandura's Bobo doll experiment (Bandura, Ross, & Ross, 1961), which was designed to test Social Learning Theory, children observed adults being physically and verbally aggressive towards a doll. On the basis of Social Learning Theory, it was hypothesised (or predicted) that children would be more aggressive towards the doll if they had observed an adult being aggressive towards it than if they had not observed an adult being aggressive towards it.

Thinking back to my chocolate experiment, there is a theory that the chemical phenylethylalanine can create feelings of excitement and may have anti-depressant effects. Chocolate contains phenylethylalanine, and therefore I could predict that participants will be happier after eating milk chocolate, which contains phenylethylalanine, than after eating white chocolate, which does not contain phenylethylalanine.

Theories and hypotheses can work in an almost cyclical way, which you can see in Figure 1.3. When designing a study you look at the current theories, and on the basis of this you develop your hypothesis. Once you have conducted your study and analysed your data, your findings might allow you to further develop and refine the current theory. You might then test this newly developed theory with another research study, which will have a hypothesis, and so on. This is how research and psychological knowledge constantly progresses and develops.

Null hypothesis significance testing (NHST)

Whilst a clearly developed hypothesis is important for framing any research that you conduct, the hypothesis also forms a fundamental part of the analysis of your data. For many years the analysis of data collected in psychological research projects has taken the statistical

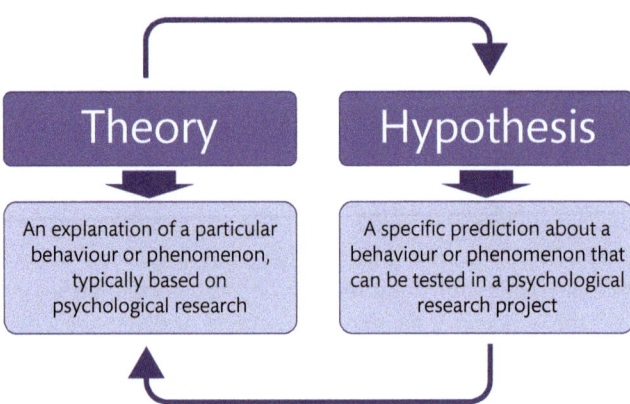

Figure 1.3: Theories and hypotheses in psychological research.

approach of **null hypothesis significance testing** (NHST). Essentially, when you design a study you have a prediction, and you then want to analyse your data to see whether your prediction can be supported, or not. **Statistical significance** tells you the chances that your findings occurred by random chance, or whether there is something more meaningful going on in the data.

First, it is important to understand the different types of hypotheses that you can develop when you run a research project. You can see a summary of these in Figure 1.4. Let's start with the null hypothesis that is so central to NHST. The null hypothesis, sometimes signified as H_0, is the hypothesis of no effect. If we think back to my chocolate and happiness study, a null hypothesis might be: *There will be no difference in happiness ratings after eating white chocolate and milk chocolate.*

The **null hypothesis** is important in significance testing as the statistical analyses are aiming to determine whether the data that have been collect support the null hypothesis, or whether the null hypothesis can be rejected. When we find significant effects we can reject the null hypothesis in favour of an alternative hypothesis: a hypothesis whereby we find some kind of significant effect.

The alternative hypothesis: one-tailed and two-tailed hypotheses

The **alternative hypothesis**, sometimes signified as H_1, is when you predict that there will be an effect within your data. However, there are actually two different types of alternative hypotheses: a **one-tailed hypothesis** and a **two-tailed hypothesis**. With both of these you would be predicting that you will find effects in your data, but in slightly different ways. A two-tailed hypothesis would predict that effects will be found, but without specifying the potential direction of those effects. So it might predict that two groups differ, but it would not predict which group would have the higher scores. For example, in my chocolate study, I could have the following two-tailed hypothesis: *Happiness ratings will differ between participants eating white chocolate and milk chocolate.*

A one-tailed hypothesis is far more specific about the effects that it predicts as it includes the direction of the predicted findings, such as which group would have higher scores. If I

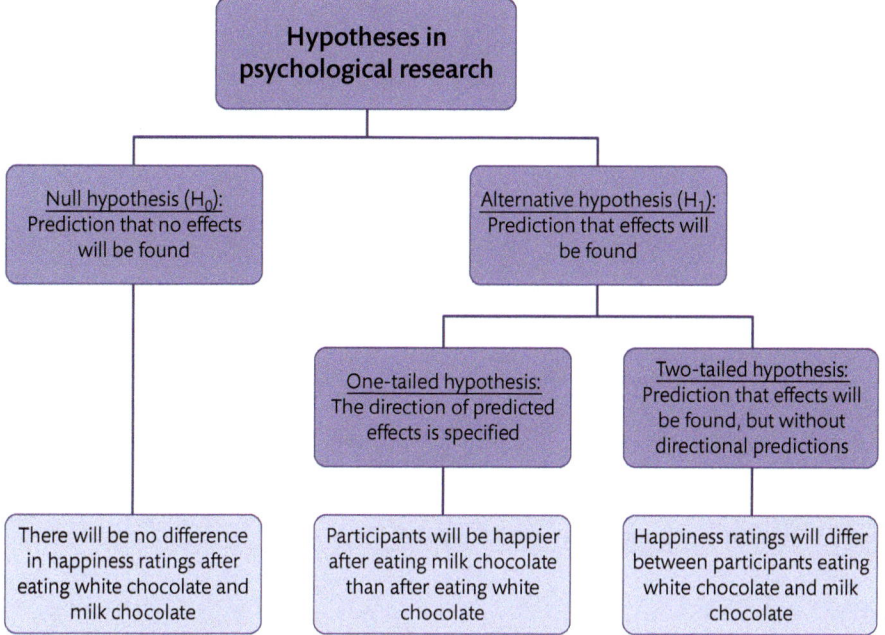

Figure 1.4: Developing hypotheses for psychological research.

have a one-tailed hypothesis for my chocolate study, I might predict something like this: *Participants will be happier after eating milk chocolate than after eating white chocolate.*

You should develop your hypothesis after having reviewed all of the relevant research literature, but before collecting and analysing your data. Very importantly, whether to have a one-tailed or two-tailed hypothesis should be based entirely on the findings of the research that you review. You need to think carefully about the previous research findings, how these relate to your own research question and design, and what you predict you will find on the basis of this. To have a one-tailed hypothesis, you would need to have a strong reason for expecting to find the directional effect that you predict.

As we move through this book and learn more about research design and statistical testing, we will return to the issue of NHST and really importantly, how this relates to significance. We will come back to this in Chapter 5, when we will discuss what significance really means, and how it relates to our acceptance, or rejection, of the null hypothesis. However, although gaining a significant result is often viewed as the outcome to aim for when doing psychological research, it is necessary to bear in mind that NHST has been criticised in recent years. As a result, tests of statistical significance tend to be presented together with **effect sizes**. We will also be talking about effect sizes more in Chapter 5.

The scientific method

Hypothesis testing forms a part of the **scientific method**, which is a way of conducting research, in a number of stages that end up forming a cyclical process. This empirical method,

An overview of how to do research

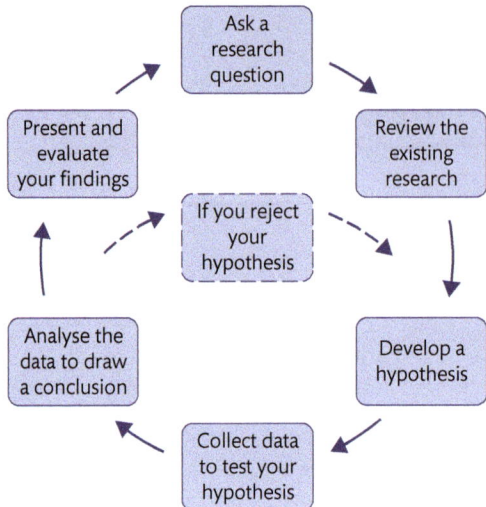

Figure 1.5: The scientific method in psychological research.

which you can see in Figure 1.5, really just outlines the research process that you will go through each time you conduct a piece of research.

You ask a research question and then review the existing research to develop a hypothesis. Using the appropriate methodological approach, you then run a study to collect data and you analyse the data. Your findings will lead you to either accept your hypothesis (you were right) or to reject your hypothesis (you were wrong). If you accept your hypothesis you then present and consider your findings, leading to the development of further research questions. However, if you reject your hypothesis then you may need to go back and re-develop a new hypothesis, which you can then test. Either way, the scientific method is a cyclical one, which means that research is never finished!

There are important aspects of the scientific method; it must be **testable** and it must be **falsifiable**. Testable means that it must be possible to make observations (or collect data) that allow you to test your hypothesis. Falsifiable means that it must be possible to find enough evidence against your predictions that, ultimately, your theory and hypotheses need to be either revised or totally disposed of. These are important aspects to take into consideration when developing a research study and a hypothesis. A good hypothesis must always be both testable and falsifiable. Taking this systematic approach to psychological research allows us to constantly move forward and gain a greater understanding of how we think, feel and behave.

Ethics in psychological research

An overarching principle of all psychological research is that any study we run should be ethical. That is that the safety and rights of the participant should be considered and respected, and that the behaviour of the researcher should be honest, considerate, and professional. In the UK we follow the ethical guidelines of the BPS; however the guidelines of the American

Psychological Association (APA) are very similar. Links to both of the guidelines are given in the Wider Reading of this chapter.

There are a few fundamental guidelines that steer psychological research, and it is really important to bear these in mind when designing a psychological study. However, the responsibility for designing and conducting ethical research is not something that is ever taken on by an individual person. Most psychology departments will have an Ethics Committee, and all psychological research projects have to gain approval from the committee before any participants can be recruited. The role of the Ethics Committee is vital as it provides reassurance to both the researcher and the participant that all of the ethical guidelines have been fully considered and that the study is deemed ethical by a group of people that are independent of the research team.

In the next few sections we will discuss the key principles of ethical research, and some of the difficulties that you might encounter when designing and running a psychological study.

Informed consent and debriefing

The first point in the ethical guidelines is **informed consent**. This actually splits into two separate and very important issues. First, participants must give their signed consent to participate in a study. You cannot just drag someone off of the street and force them to take part in your project! Second, that consent must be informed, which means that they must have a very good idea of what you will be asking them to do. Consenting to take part in a study when you have no idea what will be asked of you would really not be a good idea. We need to ensure that participants have a reasonable and accurate idea of what we are asking them to do before they consent to participate. For example, there is a huge difference between completing questionnaires for ten minutes and taking part in a brain scanning experiment that involves completing complex cognitive tasks for two hours. Some people might be more than happy to participate in one of those studies, but not the other. Therefore, it is really important to give participants a fair idea of what you will be asking them to do, why this piece of research is important and necessary, and for how long they will be doing it.

This information should be given to the participant in a written information sheet, and they should be able to read it and ask any questions that they have before signing a form to show their consent to participate. The signed consent form is then kept by the researcher, whilst the participant should keep the information sheet.

How 'informed' should consent be?

Informed consent sounds very straightforward and obvious, but it can actually be somewhat more complex than it sounds. First of all, how 'informed' should informed consent be? You absolutely need to give participants a fair idea of what you will be asking them to do, but you need to be careful of telling them too much and potentially influencing their behaviour. For example, if I were running a study on the effects of alcohol on emotional memory, the following information might bias participants' responses: *In this study you will be given some alcohol to drink, and you will then be asked to read some emotional stories. We will then ask you questions about the positive and negative emotional content of the story as we expect you to remember the negative emotional content more than the positive emotional content after drinking alcohol.* Participants who have read this passage now might pay more attention to the negative aspects of the study, and therefore they are likely to remember more of the negative emotional content.

One way to avoid influencing their behaviour is to tell them about the aims of the study, but not the expected outcomes. This information might be more appropriate to ensure that participants can give fully informed consent, without influencing their behaviour: *In this study you will be given some alcohol to drink, and you will then be asked to read some stories. We will then ask you some questions about the content of the stories.* In this version I am clearly telling the participants what they are consenting to participate in, but without any additional details that might influence their behaviour during their study.

The importance of voluntary consent

Another aspect of informed consent is that it must be voluntary, however this can be quite difficult to really achieve and researchers often debate what counts as 'voluntary' and what counts as coercion or bribery to participate. For example, does a participant voluntarily participate in a study if they are paid cash, or given a gift of chocolate, or entered into a raffle, or if they gain some form of course credit? You could argue that participation is only truly voluntary if there is no 'incentive' given. However, if no incentives were ever given, then it is likely that far fewer people would participate in research, and those who did would be a very distinct and self-selecting group of altruistic people!

When don't you need informed consent?

It can also be difficult to gain informed consent in some studies. For example, in observational research the aim is to observe people behaving naturally. If you first gain informed consent, might they behave differently as they know they are being observed? The general guidance here is that if you are observing people in an environment where they would expect to be observed, and if you are not manipulating their behaviour in anyway, then informed consent in advance of the study is not necessary. So observing how two people interact in a coffee shop without informed consent would be acceptable, but observing them in their dining room by peeking through their window would not!

The importance of debriefing

Having gained informed consent before a participant participates in a study, it is then important to fully debrief them after they have finished all of the tasks that they have been given to fully explain what they were asked to do, why they were asked to do it, and to explain the aims and expected findings of the study. **Debriefing** can be done verbally, but it is usually good to provide participants with a written debriefing sheet that they can read in their own time. Here you can give more information about exactly why you asked them to do the things that you did and what you are expecting to find from the study. It can also be helpful to give them your contact details on the debriefing form in case they have any questions about the study at a later date.

Deception

We should never deceive the participants in our study, but **deception** is another ethical principle that initially sounds simple, but can actually be quite difficult to define. This picks up on some of the issues that we have already discussed around informed consent. Clearly it is wrong to tell participants complete lies about the study we are asking them to take part in, but is it okay to withhold some of the information about the study in order to preserve its integrity?

There are actually two types of deception, and it is important to think about which type you would be committing if there is any element of deception in your design. **Passive deception** is when you simply do not reveal all of the details about your study, just in case giving them too much information influences their behaviour, like in the alcohol and emotional memory example earlier. In contrast, **active deception** is when you willingly mislead participants. For example, you might tell them they will be drinking grape juice, when they are actually drinking wine.

Passive deception is usually acceptable, but active deception is far trickier. In some designs, however, it might be impossible to address your research question without some level of active deception. Imagine that we want to look at how people respond to unexpected emergency situations. We might want to get them into the lab under the pretence of doing something very straightforward and boring, but then create an emergency situation. If we tell them all about the emergency situation in the informed consent sheet then the research will be totally useless as the emergency situation will no longer be unexpected. This research question could only be answered with some active deception, so how is it possible to run this study ethically?

The key thing to remember is that all research studies are approved by an Ethics Committee, and in your application you will be asked to highlight any possible ethical issues and how you will deal with them. This is a really important point; it is possible to make some minor 'unethical' decisions in your study design, but you need to really think through how you can protect your participants and make the study as ethical as possible. This is usually achieved through a strict debriefing procedure, sometimes followed up by additional suggestions of support or advice for the participant. If the Ethics Committee feels that the contingencies that you have in place address any possible flouting of the ethical code, then your study may be granted ethical approval.

You will often find that this is the case with ethics. Ideally you will design a study that is perfectly ethical and raises no issues at all. But if you can only ask your research question with some minor contraventions of the ethical guidelines, then you need to have a clear plan in place within the design of your study to ensure that participants are protected and treated well.

For example, in the unexpected emergency example, you might want to pre-screen participants before they take part in your study to make sure none have actually been in a traumatic emergency experience. If anyone reports having been in an emergency situation, such as a fire or road traffic accident, then you would not include them in your study as it might be upsetting and psychologically damaging for them to participate. You could also include some advice to participants in the debriefing document, such as websites or guidance to visit their GP if they experience any lasting negative effects from participating in the study.

Protecting participants from potential harm

We should also strive to ensure that participants are not exposed to harm in any way when participating in our research. **Potential harm** does not just mean physical harm. It also includes potential psychological harm, such as causing anxiety or negatively impacting on self-esteem. However, similarly to deception, it can sometimes be difficult to do psychological research with absolutely no risk of harm to participants. We research some controversial, sensitive and emotive topics that would be impossible to investigate with absolutely no risk of upsetting our participants.

One thing to be careful of here is commenting on how people have performed in the study, and participants often do ask about this. If a participant has performed poorly, then telling them this could be quite upsetting. For example, if you are working with older adults, they may be anxious about whether their memory is starting to decline. Therefore, telling them that they have done badly on a memory test could be very upsetting for them.

Again, we need to think carefully about whether there is any potential harm within our design. If there is, first we need to minimise it as much as possible. For example, if we are running a study about bereavement, then we should write our informed consent sheet and select our materials to be as sensitive as possible to the potential upset that participants could experience. We should also give participants a fair warning of the topic of the research project when we advertise the study, during the recruitment process, and in the informed consent sheet. Participants need to be fully aware that they are participating in a study on bereavement, not discover that halfway through completing a questionnaire.

A well thought through debriefing is also essential if there is any potential harm to participants. It is important to explain that they could feel upset after taking part in the study so that they are fully aware. You should also give pointers to where they might find appropriate ongoing support, just in case there are any lasting negative consequences from participating. For example, you might advise participants to visit their GP, or you could give them links to some bereavement websites.

Right to withdraw

Participants must have the **right to withdraw** from the study at any time they choose. You are not allowed to compel them to continue participating against their wishes. This must be made very clear to participants in the informed consent sheet. An important aspect of the right to withdraw is that participants must be able to withdraw without any cost to themselves. This means that if you have told the participant that they will be paid £10 or given a bar of chocolate for participating, you must still give this to them, even if they choose to withdraw before completing the study.

One thing to think about is how participants might communicate that they wish to withdraw, as some participants might feel uncomfortable saying that they want to stop participating. This might be particularly difficult with participants from vulnerable groups, such as children. It is therefore important to think about providing participants with a clear and easy way of letting you know that they wish to withdraw. For example, between different phases of the study, you could ask them verbally if they are happy to continue.

Anonymity and confidentiality

When we do psychological research we can ask participants for personal and sometimes sensitive information. In order for them to feel comfortable answering your questions and completing your tasks, it is really important that they are aware of the ethical principles of **anonymity** and **confidentiality**. Anonymity means data are collected and stored in such a way that individual participants cannot be specifically identified. For example, you would not ask for a participant's name and store this within the data file that you analyse. With confidentiality, it may be possible for the researcher to identify a particular individual, but this information is stored securely and never made available to anyone outside of the research team. For example, you might store a participant's name and email address if you will need to get in touch with them at a later date, but the data file should be secured with a password that is only known to members of the research team.

All of the data that you collect should ideally be stored without names or any identifying information. Instead, participants are usually given a unique participant code, which will be their ID for the duration of the study and in the storing and analysis of any data. The data should also be used in such a way that individuals could never be identified.

It is also important to establish that all of the data provided are entirely confidential and will not be shared with anyone outside of the research team. However, it is important to consider whether there are any potential limits to confidentiality within your design. For example, if you are doing research in forensic psychology and a participant tells you that they have committed a crime, are they still entitled to confidentiality? Or what if you are running a brain scanning study and you identify a brain tumour in a participant, should you share that information, and if so, with whom?

Again, it is really important to think through any potential situations where anonymity and/or confidentiality may need to be broken. If this is a possibility then you should think through strategies for dealing with it, include this in your ethics application and in your consent form too so that the participant is fully aware of the limits on confidentiality and anonymity in your design. For example, if you are running a brain scanning study, you might raise the possibility of identifying tumours in the study, and give the participant different options for how that should be dealt with, such as informing their GP.

Additional considerations when working with vulnerable groups

If you are working with vulnerable groups, such as children, older adults, or clinical groups, you need to be even more cautious when you evaluate the ethics of your research design. It might be necessary to add in some additional safeguards to ensure that your participants are fully protected. Often researchers working with vulnerable groups ensure they have a current DBS (Disclosure Barring Service) check, which identifies any criminal convictions that a researcher may have. Often schools or carers will ask researchers to have a current DBS check, showing that they have no criminal convictions, before they have any contact with participants.

With informed consent, is it possible for a vulnerable participant to really give informed consent? If not, who should be consenting to their participation? If you are doing research with children in schools, then you will also need to gain consent from the parents, and probably the head teacher too. If you are working with patients who have dementia, then you may need to gain additional informed consent from their next of kin or health care professional.

You may need to provide a more explicit mechanism for withdrawing from the study. For example, if you are collecting data in schools then children usually are not allowed to withdraw from a class. So how can you make it clear to them that they can withdraw from the study at any time, and how should they indicate that they wish to withdraw?

Designing ethical research and applying for ethical approval

Designing an ethical study can be a bit of a balancing act. This is acknowledged in the BPS Code of Human Research Ethics, where they raise a cost-benefit type of approach to the decision making around ethics. Any possible risk, or cost, to the participant needs to be weighed up in relation to the possible benefits that could emerge from your study. You want to ensure that you run an ethical study where the participant gives fully informed consent, they understand their right to withdraw from the study, there is no deception or risk of harm, there is full anonymity and confidentiality, and they are fully debriefed after participating. However, as we have discussed, it is not always possible to conduct psychological research without a slight contravention to the ethical guidelines.

The really important thing is to think through the implications of your design, be clear about any potential ethical issues within your design, and have a contingency plan in place to deal with any possible issues. This is where the role of the Ethics Committee is vital, as they provide the objective and independent assessment of your design and the safeguards that you have in place. With ethical approval you can be confident that you will be treating your participants ethically.

Three of the key elements that really help you to ensure that your study is ethical are clearly written participant information sheets, consent forms and debriefing sheets. This way the participant is well informed about the research they will be a part of before the study (information sheet), they give consent to participate (consent form) and the purposes of the research are clearly explained after participating (debriefing sheet). In Box 1.1 there is a summary of the key information to be included in each to help you ensure that your study is ethical. Putting together an ethics application and gaining ethical approval can be a time-consuming practice, and sometimes an Ethics Committee will ask you to make some changes to your application before granting approval. However, it really is a fundamental aspect of conducting a good piece of psychological research that protects both the researcher and the participants in the study, so it is worth allowing plenty of time to work on this.

Box **1.1**: A summary of the information to be included in the Participant Information Sheet, Consent Form and Debriefing Sheet.

Participant information sheet

- Title of the project
- Aims of the project and the reasons why the research is necessary

- Summary of what participant's will be asked to do
- Statement about anonymity and confidentiality
- Statement about participation being voluntary and the right to withdraw
- Information about any possible risks, or that there are none
- Statement that ethical approval has been granted, and by whom
- Contact details for the researchers

Consent form
- Title of the project
- Statements of confirmation, each of which has a 'Yes/No' response
  - Confirmation that the study and its aims have been explained
  - Confirmation that they have been able to ask questions about the study
  - Confirmation that they are aware they can withdraw from the study at any time
  - Confirmation that they agree to participate in the study
- Participant's name, signature and date

Debriefing sheet
- Title of the project
- Aims of the project. This can be more detailed than in the 'Participant Information Sheet'
- Expected findings from the study
- If there was potential risk, an explanation of this, and how to reduce possible lasting effects
- Contact details for the researchers
- Say 'Thank you' to the participant

Running and writing up an ethical study

One important thing to bear in mind is that ethics is not just about the design of your study and applying for ethical approval. You need to think about ethics all the way through the research process, from thinking about your initial research question, through to writing up your research study. Some areas of research may be controversial, such as looking at issues around race or sexuality, and therefore you need to think carefully about how you frame your entire study, the predictions and the design. Once you have gained ethical approval, you still need to ensure that your research is ethical right the way through running the study, analysing the data and writing up your findings.

You might also want to think about the ethics of who actually runs the research project, as some methods may require higher levels of competency in order to maintain an ethical approach. For example, a simple questionnaire study could be run by pretty much anyone with a basic training in how to conduct psychological research. However, if you wanted to run a negative mood induction study where you aim to make participants miserable by playing them depressing music and asking them to read negative sentences about themselves, then the researcher needs to have far more experience in order to maintain an ethically run study and deal with any difficulties that may arise. Before running any study, really think through whether you are fully equipped to run the study and cope with potential problems that could occur.

When you start collecting data, remember that every participant needs to be treated in exactly the same way. You need to allow them time to read the information sheet, answer any questions they have, bear in mind their comfort and safety throughout the study, debrief them fully, giving them ample opportunity to ask any questions, and finally, if any participant gets in touch after having participated, then you should respond to them in a timely manner. With the first few participants it is easy to pay attention to running your study ethically, but it is important to ensure that you give the same level of ethical attention to your fiftieth and five hundredth participants! It is also easy to let some of these elements of ethical procedure slip if you are including friends as participants, so always keep in mind that all participants should be treated in the same way. This also applies to how you recruit your participants, and whilst it is fine to ask friends to participate in your study, be careful not to coerce friends into participating.

You should also think about the ethics of how you handle and analyse your data. Remember the importance of confidentiality and anonymity when storing, analysing, and reporting your data. When analysing your data, you should also ensure that you do not participate in any unethical practices, such as removing participants without good reason, for example, if their results do not match your expectations! Finally, when writing up your research, the piece of work must be your own. Issues regarding plagiarism and academic dishonesty are issues of ethics, so make sure that the work you present is entirely your own, and that if the work and ideas of others are included, you credit them appropriately. The institution you are studying at should have some clear policies regarding academic dishonesty, and most places provide training for their students to help them understand what academic dishonesty is and how to avoid it. If you have any questions or queries about academic dishonesty, one of your lecturers should be able to give you some advice and guidance.

Study questions

1. For this question, you will need to develop some hypotheses. Below are three different research questions that could be addressed in a psychological research project. For each of the research questions, suggest a hypothesis for the predicted findings of the study. The specific type of hypothesis that you should develop is given after the research question. Take a look back at Figure 1.4 to revise these different hypotheses.

    1.1 Are there differences in people's satisfaction with life, depending on whether they have a pet or not? Develop a two-tailed hypothesis.

    1.2 Are there differences in people's levels of general anxiety depending on whether they classify themselves as having spider phobia or not? Develop a null hypothesis.

    1.3 Are there differences in people's IQ depending on whether they are currently studying for a psychology degree or another subject? Develop a one-tailed hypothesis.

2. A researcher wants to run a study looking at bullying in children aged 11–13 years old. They explain the study to children before asking them to sign a consent form. During the study

ETHICS IN PSYCHOLOGICAL RESEARCH

children are first asked to tell the researcher about a time that they have been bullied and to identify who their bully was. This is because in the second phase of the project they are planning to talk to children who are bullies to identify possible reasons why they bully. In order to collect as much data as possible they very strongly encourage all children to answer all of their questions, even if it makes them feel uncomfortable. At the end of the study the researchers speak to each class to debrief them about the aims and expected findings of the research study. Imagine that you are on the ethics committee that is asked to evaluate this study. For each of the ethical considerations (listed below), comment on whether you feel the study is ethical, and if not, why?

   2.1 Informed consent

   2.2 Deception

   2.3 Protecting participants from harm

   2.4 Right to withdraw

   2.5 Anonymity and confidentiality

   2.6 Debriefing

3. Earlier in this chapter I described a study I could run looking at happiness after eating white chocolate or milk chocolate (A Study in Chocolate). Prepare an ethics application for this study, with the following three documents listed below. For this task, it might be helpful to check back on Box 1.6. for the essential information to include, or take a look at the examples in the online resources.

   3.1 A participant information sheet

   3.2 A consent form

   3.3 A debriefing sheet.

References

Bandura, A. (1977). *Social Learning Theory*. Englewood Cliffs, NJ: Prentice Hall.

Bandura, A., Ross, D. & Ross, S.A. (1961). Transmission of aggression through imitation of aggressive models. *Journal of Abnormal and Social Psychology, 63,* 575–82.

Wider reading

Resources from the BPS:

www.bps.org.uk
   This is the main BPS website, where you can find out lots of information about becoming a psychologist.

www.bps.org.uk/what-we-do/membership/graduate-member-mbpss/graduate-member-mbpss
   Here is where you can find out more about becoming a Graduate Member of the BPS.

www.bps.org.uk/what-we-do/ethics-standards/ethics-standards
   The ethical guidelines of the BPS can be found here.

http://digest.bps.org.uk/
   The BPS Research Digest is a blog that reports on recently published psychological research. It is a great way to keep up to date with the latest developments.

http://www.apa.org/ethics/code/
   The APA ethical guidelines are very similar to the BPS guidelines, but you can find the APA ethical information here.

Open Science Collaboration. (2015). Estimating the reproducibility of psychological science. *Science, 349*(6251), aac4716.
   If you are interested in finding out more about the reproducibility debate in psychological research, this is a great paper to read.

For full answers to study questions, and to explore a range of other materials, including an example ethics application form, visit the online resources that accompany this book:
www.oup.com/uk/bourne/

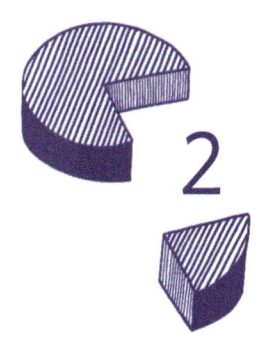

2 How to design a psychological research study: the basics of methodology

In this chapter you will learn...

- The types of variables that you can define and measure in psychological research
- The different types of research designs that are used in psychological research
- How to consider different elements of validity and reliability within a research design
- Different methods of sampling to recruit participants to a research study

Introduction

Designing a psychological research study involves making lots of decisions. These decisions will largely have been framed by the research question you ask, and the methods that you use to collect your data will determine the way in which you choose to analyse that data and interpret the findings. In this chapter we will cover the basics of how to design a methodologically rigorous piece of psychological research: which type of methodological approach you should take, what you should measure, how you ensure that you measure what you are intending to measure, and how you select the participants in your study. Some of these issues can seem a little abstract and theoretical, so through this chapter we will design a study that looks at chocolate addiction, as well as discussing some other relevant research examples along the way.

Measuring variables

When you conduct any piece of psychological research you will be identifying key **variables** that you are interested in and that you want to measure. A variable is something that can be measured or manipulated. For example, you might want to measure your participant's age, intelligence, memory, happiness, or how often they eat chocolate. You might also want to manipulate variables. For example, you might manipulate whether participants are given white or milk chocolate, or you might allocate them to a placebo or a treatment group. When you are designing a psychological research study, one of the first things you need to do is clearly define the variables that you are interested in and the **data** that you will collect. In quantitative research, the data are the actual numbers that make up the information that you collect. For example, you might have participants with the ages of 21, 18, and 24 years old, or they might eat chocolate 1, 6, or 28 times a week. These numbers are the data that have been collected.

Operationalising variables: defining what you are measuring

When you design a psychological research study of any type, you need to clearly define the variables that you will be measuring. This is called **operationalising** your variables, and this needs to be done across all types of research design. Operationalising a variable is more than clearly naming it; you need to clearly define how it will be measured. So how can you get a score that represents that variable?

For example, if I am interested in chocolate addiction, there are various ways I could operationalise this variable. First, I would need to define what I mean by chocolate addiction, which is an uncontrollable compulsion to eat chocolate. I could then use a questionnaire to measure how addicted a participant is, I could record the number of times per week a participant eats chocolate, or I could give a participant two chocolates, ask them to wait as long as possible between eating the first and the second chocolate, and then record the number of minutes that the participant waits before they eat the second chocolate. As another example, I might operationalise 'happiness' as the number of times a participant smiles over the course of an hour, or a score on a happiness questionnaire. Alternatively, I might take blood samples from participants and measure levels of the neurochemical dopamine, which is associated with happiness. In this situation I would operationalise happiness as having higher levels of dopamine.

There is usually not a single correct way to operationalise a variable, so there are often a number of different ways a variable can be operationalised. In the happiness example, recording the number of smiles in an hour or measuring dopamine levels are very different but equally good ways of operationalising the variable. However, which method of operationalisation you choose will have a big impact on how you design your study, your results, and the way that you interpret your findings, so it is important to think through the implications of the way that you choose to measure your variables.

Types of variables and data you can collect

There are various types of data that you can collect in psychological research studies, and different types of variables are used in the different types of research design that you will be introduced to later in this chapter. You can see a summary of the different types of quantitative data, data that are made up of numbers, which can be collected in Box 2.1.

MEASURING VARIABLES

> **Box 2.1:** Types of quantitative data that can be collected in psychological research studies.
>
> ### Nominal (categorical) data
> - Frequency of belonging to a 'category'
> - Example: Handedness, classed as left, right, or mixed handed?
>
> ### Ordinal (continuous) data
> - Clear order to data, but distance between points may vary
> - Example: Place in a race, 1st, 2nd, 3rd place etc. …
>
> ### Interval (continuous) data
> - Order to data points, fixed distance between points and negative values
> - Example: Temperature, 1° is always the same, –ive temps. possible
>
> ### Ratio (continuous) data
> - Order to data points, fixed distance between points **no** negative values
> - Example: Height, cm is same at all heights, no negative heights

Nominal data

A very simple type of data is **nominal data**, which are also sometimes called **categorical** or **frequency** data. Nominal data records the number of participants that belong to each category, and any kind of variable where you define a number of categories and then count the number of participants that belong in each category will give you nominal data. There can be any number of categories within a nominal variable. Examples of nominal variables could be the outcome of a driving test (pass or fail), degree subject (psychology, history or physics), clinical diagnosis (anxiety, depression, or psychosis) or verdict at a trial (guilty or innocent). You can think about nominal data as being a bit like label data, i.e. each person can have a label that determines which group they belong to. So a participant would be given either the label of, for example, 'guilty' or 'innocent'.

Ordinal data

Ordinal data exist on a continuum in that you collect data with a range of scores from lower scores through to higher scores where the numbers exist in a clear order. However, the key defining characteristic of ordinal data is that the 'distance' between each number can differ. The easiest example of ordinal data is where people are placed in a race. Imagine that we have ten participants and they take place in a race. The data that we collect will be whether they came in first place (a score of 1), second place (a score of 2), third place (a score of 3), and so on through to the person in last place (a score of 10). You can see that we are clearly collecting numerical data that exist in a logical order.

However, whilst ordinal data might exist in a clear order, the distance between each number can be variable. For example, the race might have been really close between first and second place, there might just be a couple of second's difference in their finish time, and therefore the distance between the numbers 1 and 2 is very small. But there could have then been a large gap before the person in third place crossed the finish line. They might not have crossed the line until twenty minutes later, and therefore the distance between the numbers 2 and 3 is quite large.

Another example of ordinal data could be rank scores. You could give participants a list of five different types of chocolate and ask them to rank order them according to which they prefer, from 1 being their favourite through to 5 being their least favourite. It might be that one participant only really likes one type of chocolate, and then there will be a large distance between their scores of 1 and 2, but the distances between the scores of 2 through to 5 will be very small as they are all quite comparably disliked.

Interval data

Interval data are also continuous in nature, but with these data the distance between each number is always exactly the same. Importantly the numbers can be either positive or negative. One of the simplest examples of interval data is temperature, as measured on the Celsius scale. When temperature is measured, one degree is always the same. As such, the difference between one degree and two degrees is the same amount of increasing warmth as is the difference between eleven degrees and twelve degrees. Negative temperatures are also possible on the Celsius scale, and again, the difference between minus one and minus two degrees would be the same amount of difference.

Another example of interval data that is more relevant to psychology can be the measurement of handedness. A participant completes a questionnaire that asks various questions about which hand they would use to do various tasks, such as writing, brushing their teeth, or opening a box. The final scores run from −42 through to + 42, where negative values indicate left handedness and positive values indicate right handedness. These values exist on a continuum, with the same distance between each number, and negative values are possible, and therefore these handedness scores are a good example of interval data.

Ratio data

Ratio data are very similar to interval data in that the distance between each number is the same, but the key difference is that negative numbers are not possible with ratio data. Height is a great example of this. If you measure someone's height in cm, then each cm is the same amount no matter how tall or short the person is. Importantly though, it is impossible to have a negative value for someone's height!

Many of the variables that we measure in psychological studies are ratio data. Intelligence, reaction times and memory scores are all very often used in research, and all are ratio data as the distance between each number is always the same, and negative values are not possible.

Parametric and non-parametric analysis

The type of variables that you measure and the data that you collect really determine the types of statistical analyses that you can conduct. One of the decisions that you will need to make is whether you can use a **parametric** or **non-parametric** analysis. Parametric analyses are usually seen as the 'gold standard' and preferred method of statistical analysis in psychological research, however they can only be used under certain circumstances.

If you look back at Box 2.1 you can see that there are four different types of quantitative data that can be collected. Nominal and ordinal data are analysed using non-parametric methods, whereas interval and ratio data can be analysed using parametric approaches. Non-parametric statistics are covered in Part 4 of this book. In Chapter 13 I explain in lots of detail why non-parametric statistics are needed, when to use them, and how they work. Interval and ratio variables provide parametric data, and therefore are often seen as preferable. All of the statistics covered in Parts 2 and 3 of this book are parametric. Where possible you should aim to design a study that can be analysed using parametric analyses. So, for example, try to design a study that collects either interval or ratio data rather than ordinal data.

Confounding variables

When designing a psychological research study, or even when reading about psychological research, it is important to always bear in mind potential **confounding variables**. Essentially, a confounding variable is one that you are not particularly interested in for the key aims of your study, but the confounding variable might still inadvertently explain some of your findings, or your lack of findings!

My favourite example comes from the finding that there is a strong relationship between ice cream sales and the number of shark attacks that occur each year in Australia. The more ice cream that is sold, the more shark attacks there are. Now, it is very unlikely that there is a direct and causal relationship between these two variables (unless sharks are partial to ice cream and, with their very keen sense of smell, they can detect the smell in swimmers and find it difficult to resist!). However, there are other variables that could help to explain this relationship. The temperature, for example, would be a likely confounding variable in this study. It can explain the relationship as people are more likely to buy ice cream when it is hot, and people are also more likely to swim in the sea when it is hot.

Confounding variables and co-variables in psychological research

In psychological research, if a researcher suspects that there might be a confounding variable within their design, it is possible to measure and control for in the statistical analyses. As soon as you measure a confounding variable it becomes a **co-variable**, sometimes also known as a **control variable**, **extraneous variable**, or **mediating variable**. Co-variables are usually variables where we already know from previous research that this variable is likely to explain a significant amount of the effects that we are interested in. However, we do not want to actually look at these effects, we want to ignore them and then see whether what we are doing has any additional effect, over and above the co-variable.

A great example of this is the use of reading age as a co-variable in developmental research. If you are conducting a research study on social anxiety in children, you might ask children to complete social anxiety questionnaires. However, their reading age could explain some of the variability in their scores. If a child finds it difficult to read the questionnaire, then they might misunderstand some of the questions and not give the correct answer, whereas a child that is very skilled at reading will give far more accurate answers. This could mean that the measurement of younger children's social anxiety is inaccurate, as the children do not clearly understand the questionnaire, whereas the measurement of older children's social anxiety may be more accurate. In this situation, is it really fair to compare social anxiety between older and younger children? And if you did find a difference between these two groups, could you be confident that it was a result of the two groups being different physical ages, or might the difference be the result of the co-variable of reading age?

Another good example is sex differences in the recognition of emotional facial expressions (e.g. whether males and females differ in recognizing recognizing whether a person is happy, sad, or angry). There is a lot of previous research showing that females are better at these kinds of tasks than males. As a result, some of the research in this area now controls for these possible sex differences in their research. Imagine that we want to compare the ability to recognise facial emotion between people who have been diagnosed with clinical depression and people who have no clinical diagnosis. We know that sex differences in emotional face recognition exist, however we are not really interested in them and we don't want these effects to overshadow the effects that we are actually interested in. We might therefore try to control for the co-variable of the participants' sex, and this way we can see the possible difference between the two groups of participants more clearly.

Selecting and thinking about co-variables

When you are designing a psychological study it is important to try to think of any possible co-variables. These should be well justified from your reading of the previous relevant research. So you cannot simply pick out a whole load of co-variables that you think might possibly be relevant. The selection of co-variables should be strongly theoretically justified (e.g. research has shown significant sex differences) and you should keep the number of co-variables measured to a minimum, usually no more than one or two.

When you are thinking about potential co-variables, it is important to be very clear about the exact way in which you think it might influence your study. For example, say you are running study looking at how well people remember a list of written words. Whether a participant speaks English as their first language could be a possible co-variable as a person who speaks English as their second (or third, or tenth!) language may not perform as well in the memory task if they are not as proficient as native speakers. If you are collecting data in a university with a high proportion of international students, then this could be a very important co-variable to consider within your design. However, if you are collecting data at a university that recruits the vast majority of their students from native English speaking backgrounds, then the co-variable is unlikely to really have much impact on the findings. So when thinking about co-variables, try to think about both what might be theoretically important, but also what is practically likely to influence the findings of your actual study.

There are some quite sophisticated ways of dealing with co-variables in your statistical analyses (known as statistically controlling for co-variables), but these are beyond the scope of this book. The methodological issues surrounding the inclusion of co-variables in experimental and correlational designs are slightly different, and each of these is discussed in greater detail in the relevant later chapters (Chapter 6 for experimental designs and Chapter 10 for correlational designs).

Different designs for different questions

Roughly speaking, there are three key types of research design that are used within psychological research: **categorical**, **experimental** and **correlational** designs. For the purposes of this chapter we simply want to understand the key features that define each type of approach and how they differ, but each method is described in far greater detail in later chapters in this book (Chapters 6 and 10). One really important point is that each methodological approach is associated with specific methods of analysis, which you can see in Figure 2.1. For this reason, it is always important to think about research design and statistical analysis at the same time when you are developing a piece of psychological research. For example, if you know that you want to use an experimental design, then you will need to use one of the methods of analysis that is covered in Part 2 of this book. When you are designing a study, before you collect any data at all, you should know exactly how you are going to analyse your data. This makes the whole research process far easier and smoother.

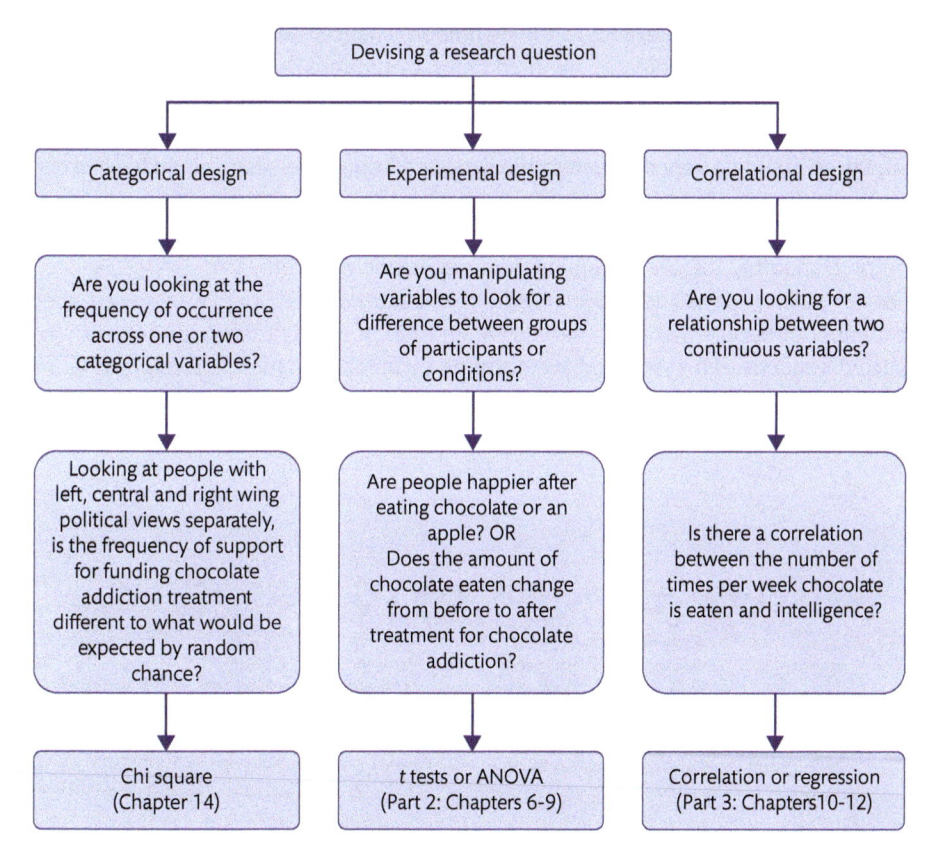

Figure 2.1: Different research designs in psychological research.

Categorical research designs: looking at frequencies within categories

Categorical research designs are very simple, although they are probably the least frequently used of the three key methodological approaches. The idea here is that you are interested in the frequency at which participants 'belong' to particular categories. For example, you might be interested in whether people class their political views as 'left wing', 'centre' or 'right wing'. You would collect data that tells you the number of participants who belong to each of these three categories. The easiest way to think about this type of research design is to imagine big banners, each of which has the name of one of the categories on it. You ask each of the participants in your study to go and stand under the banner that describes the category they belong to: left, centre or right. You can look at two separate categorical variables within one study. So you might look at political views in association with whether people are 'pro' or 'anti' providing funding to treat people with chocolate addiction. You would now have six different categories that people could belong to, across two separate variables: political views (three categories) and view of supporting chocolate addiction treatment (two categories). You can see the banners and participants within each category in Figure 2.2.

The logic behind the analysis of categorical designs is to look at the number of people within each category, or the observed frequency, and to see whether this differs from the frequency that you would expect to see by random chance. Take, for example, the tossing of a coin. If you tossed a coin one hundred times, by random chance you would expect the result to be 'heads' about fifty times and 'tails' about fifty times. If you tossed the coin one hundred times and got 'heads' sixteen times and 'tails' eighty four times, then these observed frequencies would be very different to the expected frequencies that should have occurred by random chance. This might suggest that there is either something suspicious about the coin, or about the person tossing the coin. Either way, the coin tossing result is certainly not occurring randomly, there is something more systematic going on.

For our political views and chocolate addiction treatment, we would want to see whether the number of people that we observed within each of the six categories differs from the expected frequencies that should have occurred by random chance. You can read far more about categorical designs, including how to analyse these data using a **chi square test**, in Chapter 14 of this book.

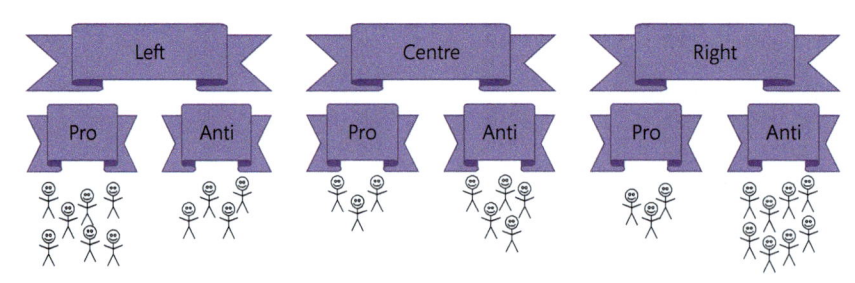

Figure 2.2: Participants in a categorical research design.

Experimental research designs: comparing groups or conditions

When you conduct an experimental piece of psychological research, the key idea is that you want to experimentally **manipulate** something, and see whether it has an effect on something else. For example, I might manipulate whether I give participants an apple or a bar of chocolate to eat. I could then ask them to complete a questionnaire that measures how happy they are. With this design I would be manipulating the type of food given to participants and expecting it to have an effect on their happiness.

In an experimental design, the thing that you manipulate is called the **independent variable**, and the thing that you measure and expect to be affected by the independent variable is called the **dependent variable**. So, in our design the type of food given is the independent variable and the happiness score is the dependent variable. You can see this design in Figure 2.3. I would then want to analyse the happiness scores to see which group of participants were happier; the ones who ate an apple or the ones who ate a bar of chocolate. Importantly, this type of experimental design is an **independent measures design** that has two separate groups of people: the apple eaters and the chocolate eaters.

Repeated experimental designs: testing one set of participants multiple times

A slightly different type of experimental design might include just one set of participants, and test them multiple times. In a **repeated design**, the independent variable would determine what differs each time the participants are tested, and you would expect this difference across testing times to cause scores to differ. For example, I might want to examine whether an intervention I have developed to treat chocolate addiction could reduce the amount of chocolate that people eat. In this design my dependent variable is the amount of chocolate that participants report eating, and I expect this to vary depending on whether I collect these

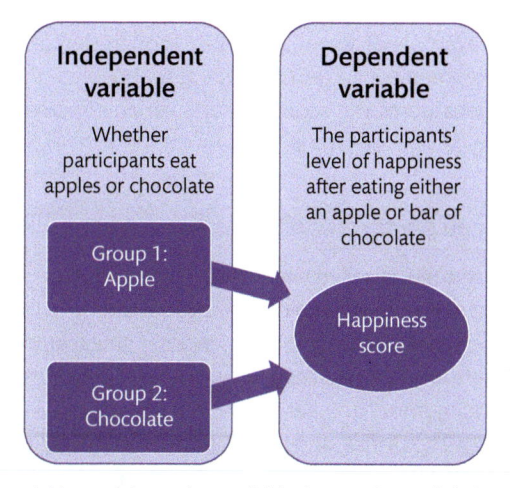

Figure 2.3: Independent variables and dependent variables in experimental designs.

data before or after the chocolate addiction treatment, which is the independent variable. I would analyse these data to see whether the amount of chocolate eaten was significantly higher before the addiction treatment than afterwards.

Designing experimental studies

Of course, designing experiments is a little more complicated than this, and the whole of Part 2 of this book is dedicated to experimental approaches to psychological research. Chapter 6 tells you all about how to design an experimental piece of research, and then the various ways that you can analyse the data that you collect in an experiment are covered in Chapters 7 to 9.

One really important point to bear in mind is that experimental designs are the *only* type of psychological study that can be used to explore whether one thing 'causes' another. So, if you are interested in **causality** in psychological research, then an experimental design is what you need.

Correlational research designs: looking at relationships between variables

Correlational designs are very different from experimental designs in that nothing is experimentally manipulated. Instead, you simply measure different things, and see if there is any kind of relationship between them. These variables have to be continuous scores, so ordinal, interval or ratio data, ranging from low numbers through to high numbers and with lots of numbers between high and low. Good examples of these are things like age, height, or intelligence.

In a correlational study you measure naturally occurring continuous variables and then look at the relationship between them. For example, I could ask participants how many times a week they eat chocolate and also measure their intelligence. Both of these are continuous variables. I could then look at the type of relationship between the two variables. It might be that the more intelligent people are, the more chocolate they eat. This would be a positive relationship, because as the scores on one variable increase, so do the scores on the other variable. You can see an example of how this might look on the left of Figure 2.4. Alternatively, it could be that the more intelligent a person is the less chocolate they eat. This would be a negative relationship, because as the scores on one variable increase, scores on the other variable decrease. This type of relationship is shown on the right of Figure 2.4.

Continuous variables and the correlation motto

The term '**correlation**' is often misused when research findings are presented in the media. A correlation can only occur between two continuous variables. To check whether a 'correlation' can really be a correlation, try saying this sentence ... *As the scores on one variable increase, scores on the other variable increase/decrease.* For example, if you were told that there is a correlation between age and memory in older adults, you could say ... As age increases, memory decreases. This sentence makes sense, and therefore the finding really does represent a correlation, and a negative correlation, between age and memory. Now imagine that you are told that there is a correlation between a person's memory and their degree subject (psychology or physics). Try putting this into the sentence ... As memory scores increase, a person's degree

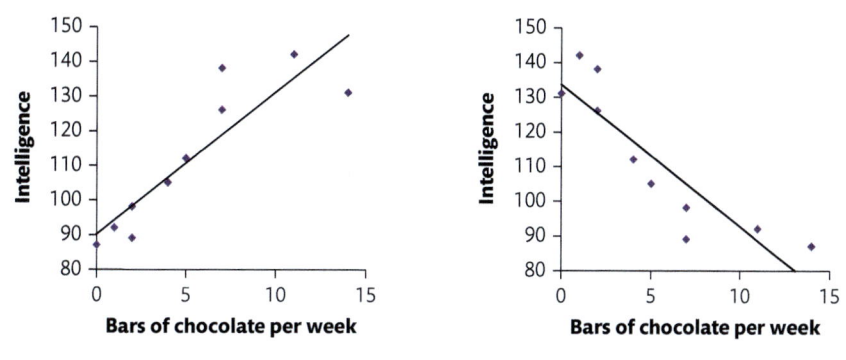

Figure 2.4: Correlational design showing a positive relationship (left) and a negative relationship (right).

subject ... ?! A person's degree choice is a nominal variable, in this example representing two categories, and therefore it doesn't work in a correlational design. Both variables must be continuous, so ordinal, interval, or ratio variables.

Correlation does not imply causation

Another important point to always remember when thinking about correlational designs is the mantra of 'correlation does not imply causation'. So just because two variables are highly correlated, you cannot assume that one of the variable causes the other. For example, there may be a strong correlation between the amount of chocolate that someone eats and how happy they are, but does this really mean that one of these variables causes the other? Does eating chocolate make you happy? Or could it be that being happy causes you to eat more chocolate? The only way to determine causality is with an experimental design. If we wanted to know whether eating chocolate causes you to be happy, we would need to run an experiment like the one summarised in Figure 2.3.

Part 3 of this book is devoted to the design and analysis of correlational studies. As with experimental designs, there are a large number of factors to take into account when designing a correlational study, and these are discussed in much more detail in Chapter 10. There are then two key methods of analysis that you can use if you have designed a correlational study. You can simply look at whether there is a positive or a negative relationship between variables using a correlation analysis (covered in Chapter 11), or you could actually look at whether one variable can predict another using a linear regression analysis (covered in Chapter 12). With this type of analysis, you could ask whether the number of bars of chocolate eaten per week can predict a participant's intelligence score!

Validity and reliability in research design

When designing a psychological research study, it is important to aim for a study that has both validity and reliability. **Validity** is achieved when you are measuring what you aim to measure, whereas **reliability** concerns being able to measure it in a consistent way, which you can see in Figure 2.5. If we return to our chocolate addiction study, there isn't an existing chocolate

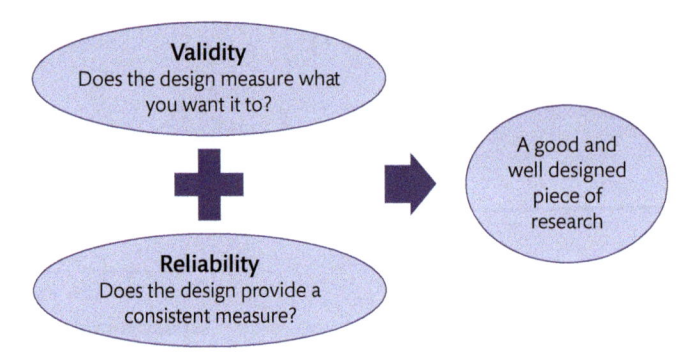

Figure 2.5: Validity and reliability in psychological research.

addiction questionnaire and therefore I need to develop my own new scale, the Chocolate Addiction Scale (CAS). Before using the CAS in a study, I would need to run a pilot study to establish that the scale is both valid and reliable. So, does the scale really measure chocolate addiction, and does it provide consistent scores for each participant?

Construct validity

Construct validity relates to whether your measurement is measuring what you think it should. The first stage of this it to ensure that you have a clear definition of the variable you will be measuring: that you have clearly *operationalised* it, as described earlier in this chapter. For our CAS, we would need to be clear about how we define both chocolate and addiction. So, chocolate refers to a sweet food or drink that contains cocoa, and addiction is a strong compulsion to consume a substance. Therefore, in attempting to measure chocolate addiction with our CAS, we are attempting to measure a variable that represents a strong compulsion to consume sweet food or drink that contains cocoa.

Construct validity comprises three different elements. **Content validity**: Does it measure all of the possible parts of the variable that you are measuring? **Convergent validity**: Is your variable measure correlated with other measures of the same (or very similar) thing? **Discriminant (or divergent) validity**: Is your variable measure not correlated with other unrelated measures?

Thinking about our CAS, we would need to ensure that there were items within the questionnaire that reflect all of the different components of chocolate addiction that we are interested in measuring to ensure that we have content validity. To assess whether the CAS has convergent and discriminant validity, we would need to collect some additional data. For convergent validity, we would need to think of some other variables that we might expect to be highly correlated with chocolate addiction. For example, the number of times per week that a person eats chocolate might be a good variable, as you would expect people with high scores on the CAS to eat chocolate more frequently. Therefore, if the two variables are highly correlated, this would confirm the convergent validity of the CAS. For discriminant validity, we would need to think of some other variables that we would not expect to be correlated with chocolate addiction, for example, the number of cups of tea that a person drinks each day. This is unlikely to be correlated with scores on the CAS.

Internal validity

Internal and external validity (below) relate a little more generally to your study design. **Internal validity** is all about whether your study is designed and run in such a way that no other variables could possibly explain your findings. For example, are there any other possible variables that might explain your findings? Earlier in this chapter we talked about confounding variables. Is there a possible confounding variable that could explain the results of the study? It is important to think carefully about internal validity if you want to be able to draw any valid conclusions about the findings of your study. You want to be confident that any findings are the result of the manipulation and/or measurement of the variables that you are interested in, and not the result of any other possible unmeasured confounding variables.

Alternatively, are there any biases in sampling (which we will talk about in the next section of this chapter) or participant withdrawal? Were the participants selected in a way that was random and fair, or was a specific kind of participant selected, which means that the findings might be biased and only relate to that particular kind of person? Similarly, if the participants are motivated to behave in a particular way that could influence the findings? To avoid this, it is really important to think carefully about the information that you give people before they participate in your study so that they are not biased in anyway. Are the researchers behaving and running the study in a totally unbiased manner? Finally, if you have participants in different conditions, such as in an independent experimental design, are they recruited and treated in exactly the same way, or are their differences across the conditions that might explain the findings?

External validity

External validity relates to whether the findings of the study can be generalised beyond the sample that has been tested. For example, can the findings be generalised to other groups of people or other situations? One of the strongest sources of external validity is when findings are replicated by others. If researchers from a different lab can use the same methodology with an entirely different group of participants and find the same results, then it is likely that the methods have strong external validity.

Ecological validity

Another aspect of validity that is sometimes talked about is **ecological validity**. A study has ecological validity if the methodology allows for the conclusions of the research to be extrapolated to the real world. Whereas external validity is about generalizing the findings to other groups of people or people tested in different labs, the issue with ecological validity is more to do with whether the findings are relevant if applied to a 'real word issue'. Has the study been designed to ensure that the findings can be extrapolated from the lab to the real world? A good example of a study where ecological validity would be an issue is research on jury behaviours in murder trials. Whilst a study might be really well designed, can the findings really have ecological validity if the study is run in the lab and the trial is hypothetical, rather than dealing with the murder of a real person, in a real court room, and a decision that will have a massive impact on the accused?

Thinking back to our chocolate addiction study, there are various precautions we can take to ensure the internal validity of our study. First, we would need to think carefully about how we recruit participants to the study. Recruiting through the Facebook 'Chocoholics Anonymous' page would seriously threaten the internal validity of our study, so we would be better to recruit our participants from a cohort of undergraduate psychology students. When running the study, we would also protect the internal validity of the study by ensuring that the researchers know nothing about the chocolate consumption of the participants whilst actually collecting the data. That way we can be certain that there are no intentional or unintentional biases in the researcher's behaviour. It is likely that our study will have good external validity if the questionnaire is designed to very generally ask about chocolate addiction, and we can check this by asking another research lab to replicate our findings.

Inter-rater reliability

Inter-rater reliability is an issue when multiple people are scoring the data collected in a research study. If multiple people are scoring data that is then all analysed together, it is really important to ensure that they are all scoring the data in exactly the same way. If the scoring systems vary, then this could have massive implications for the findings of the research. Additionally, if there are any researcher biases, or if they have different motivations, then the data could be scored quite differently by the researchers and this could lead to lower levels of inter-rater reliability. For example, you might have two people coding the data, the researcher in charge of the project and a paid research assistant. It is possible that the researcher in charge of the project could be biased in the way that they score the data as they have certain expectations about what they will find. The paid research assistant might not have these expectations, so they may be more objective in their coding.

Various statistics have been developed to analyse whether inter-rater reliability has been achieved within a study. This is done by taking a subset of the data that needs to be coded, often around 10% of the full dataset, getting everyone to do all of the scoring, and then running statistics to determine whether the researchers coding are in agreement with each other, or whether there are differences across the researchers.

In our chocolate addiction questionnaire, we have the following open ended question: How do you feel when you do not have access to chocolate? The data collected is qualitative (so it is based on words rather than numbers) and very open ended, so it would be important to put some safeguards in place to try to maximise inter-rater reliability in our study. We could address this before the coding (or scoring) occurs by establishing a clear coding (or scoring) scheme that is used by all of the people who are coding the data. We might develop a scoring scale to quantify whether the feelings reported are positive or negative, with scores ranging from −5 (very negative), through 0 (neutral) to +5 (very positive). For example, a response of 'Miserable, I just keep thinking about chocolate' might be given a score of −4, whereas a response of 'ok, it is kind of nice to not have easy access to chocolate' could be scored +2. We could then ask all of the researchers to code a subset of the questionnaires and we would then analyse the data to check that the data were similar across all of the people. As long as the analyses come out well, we can be confident that we have inter-rater reliability and that our collected data is reliable.

Test-retest reliability

If we develop a new measure, it is important to know that the scores provided by the measure would be the same, or at least very similar, if a person were to complete the measure at two different time points. This is **test-retest reliability**. If we use the same measure with the same person, in the same way at two different time points where there have been no experimental manipulations and all of the testing conditions are identical, then the data collected should be comparable. As with inter-rater reliability, there are statistics that tell you whether the scores gained at the two time points are similar or not.

When developing our CAS, test-retest reliability is definitely something that we would want to look at. To do this we would ask a group of participants to complete the CAS twice, one week apart. We would then run the statistics to see whether the two sets of responses are highly related (you will be learning more about this method of analysis in Chapter 11 of this book). If they are, then we can be confident that the CAS will provide us with reliably consistent scores about participant's addiction to chocolate.

Internal consistency

Internal consistency looks at whether the responses to items within a measure receive similar scores. If a questionnaire has twenty items that are all supposed to be measuring the same thing, then scores should be very similar across all twenty items, showing internal consistency to the measure. Again, statistics can be used to determine whether a measure has internal consistency.

Internal consistency and Cronbach's alpha

The most frequently used statistic here is **Cronbach's alpha**. The logic behind this test is that if you divide the items within a measure into two halves, the scores in each of the two halves should be similar if all of the items are measuring the same thing. For example, imagine a happiness questionnaire with six questions, scored from 1 through to 5 with higher scores indicating that a person is very happy. If I divided the questionnaire randomly into two sets of three questions, the responses in one half of the questions should be very similar to the responses in the other half of the questions. If they are, then it seems that both halves are measuring a similar thing, happiness, and getting similar responses. If the responses are very different in the two halves, then the questions might be asking about different things. This is **split-half reliability**. Cronbach's alpha goes a little further and does this for every possible way of dividing the items in half, which you can see in Figure 2.6. The alpha statistic then provides a measure of internal consistency across all possible versions of these split halves.

Cronbach's alpha: what the numbers tell you

Cronbach's alpha goes from 0–1, with higher values representing greater levels of internal consistency. Generally, Cronbach's alpha should be at least .7 to represent an 'acceptable' level of internal consistency, as you can see in Figure 2.7. When developing a scale or questionnaire, if the internal consistency was deemed to be questionable, or worse, then you would look at all of the items in the questionnaire and try to work out which are the 'less

HOW TO DESIGN A PSYCHOLOGICAL RESEARCH STUDY

Split half: Set 1				Split half: Set 2			Split half comparison
1	2	3	vs.	4	5	6	Comparison 1
1	2	4	vs.	3	5	6	Comparison 2
1	2	5	vs.	3	4	6	Comparison 3
1	2	6	vs.	3	4	5	Comparison 4
1	3	4	vs.	2	5	6	Comparison 5
1	3	5	vs.	2	4	6	Comparison 6
1	3	6	vs.	2	4	5	Comparison 7
1	4	5	vs.	2	3	6	Comparison 8
1	4	6	vs.	2	3	5	Comparison 9
1	5	6	vs.	2	3	4	Comparison 10

All comparisons combine to calculate Cronbach's alpha

Figure 2.6: Using the split half method to calculate Cronbach's alpha to examine internal consistency in a questionnaire with six items.

reliable' items. It could be that the item is poorly written and participants are therefore giving random responses, or the item could be clearly written but asking about something different to the other items within the scale.

There may also be a problem if the alpha is too high, such as .95 or higher. This is because it means that all of the questions are getting near identical responses, and therefore the questions might be near identical. The aim is to have a number of different questions that tap into the same underlying 'thing', such as happiness. But the questions do need to be different. So if Cronbach's alpha is very close to 1, this suggests that the questions might be too similar. Consequently, you want Cronbach's alpha to be high, but not perfect.

Cronbach's alpha	Internal consistency
≥ .9	Excellent
.8 - .9	Good
.7 - .8	Acceptable
.6 - .7	Questionable
.5 - .6	Poor
< .5	Unacceptable

Figure 2.7: Standards for defining the internal consistency using Cronbach's alpha.

Often when developing a new questionnaire a researcher has to go through a few versions of it until internal consistency is gained. Returning to our CAS, imagine it was designed to have two separate scales: lack of control over consumption (e.g. can't say no to chocolate when offered) and emotional consequences of chocolate eating (e.g. guilt). Each scale has ten questions and after asking one hundred people to complete it we run Cronbach's alpha on each scale separately. The lack of control scale has poor internal consistency, whereas the emotional scale has good internal consistency. We might then want to look at the questions in the lack of control scale to see if any of the individual questions seem quite different to the others, as this might be the question that reduces the internal reliability of the scale.

Selecting and recruiting participants

When we decide to run a psychological study, it is usually because we want to understand something about people quite generally, because we want to understand something about the entire **population**. The population is the entire group of people that you are interested in. If you are interested in something quite specific, such as study skills in psychology students in the UK, then your population is made up of every single psychology student in the UK. If you are interested in something more general, such as whether people are happier after eating white or milk chocolate, then the population is far less clearly defined, and could really encompass the entire population of the planet! However, we are never going to be able to test the entire population of the planet, and it is even quite rare to be able to test an entire very specific population, so we just have to make do with a small **sample** of people from within that population. We then hope that our sample somehow reflects the overall population, and if we find something within our sample then we might infer that it is also true in the general population, as you can see in Figure 2.8. The question then is, how do you select your sample to best reflect the population that you are aiming to study?

Random sampling

In **random sampling** the sample is chosen from everyone in the relevant population entirely by random chance. For example, each person in the population might be allocated a number, and then a random number generator can be used to randomly select out a smaller sample from the larger population. Whilst this method is great for providing a truly unbiased sample, it can be difficult to achieve in practice unless you actually have access to the entire population. Imagine that you want to conduct a study involving children with an Autistic Spectrum Disorder (ASD). It is virtually impossible to have access to all children who have

Sample	Population
All of the participants that we collect data from in our study	All of the possible people that could have been included in our study

We study a sample in the hope that from our findings we can *infer* something about the entire population!

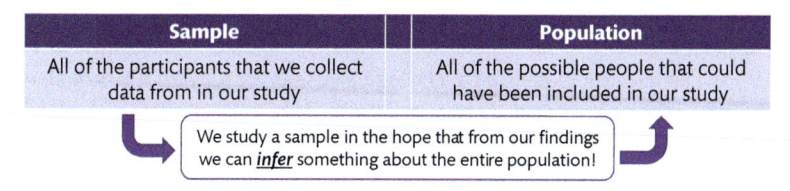

Figure 2.8: Conducting research with a sample to reflect a population.

ASD, and therefore recruiting from this population using random sampling is not going to be possible. However, if your aim is to understand why students choose to study psychology at a particular university, random sampling could be possible. I could give each student a different number and then use a random number generator to pick out a sample to test. Whilst random sampling is great to aim for in theory, it can be very difficult to achieve in practice.

Systematic sampling

There is a fair amount of overlap between random sampling and **systematic sampling**. Both work by initially allocating numbers to the entire relevant population, but with systematic sampling the sample is selected from the population by recruiting every Nth person. For example, the population could be numbered from 1 to 1000, and we then select every fifth person to recruit to our study. So we would approach the people with numbers 5, 10, 15, 20, 25, and so on, until we had recruited a large enough sample. If we were running the project about why students pick a particular psychology programme, then we could perhaps use their student ID codes, put them all in order, and then recruit every fourth participant to our study. As with random sampling, systematic sampling can be difficult to achieve in some situations.

Stratified sampling

Stratified sampling can be very helpful when the population that we are aiming to recruit from has specific characteristics or subgroups that we wish to reflect within our sample. To make stratified sampling work, you need to have some understanding of the population you are looking at, and their typical characteristics. For example, let's go back to our study about why psychology students pick a particular university to study at. We know that about 80% of psychology students are female, so we would want our sample to reflect this. Therefore, if we want to recruit 100 participants to our sample, using stratified sampling we would recruit 80 females and 20 males to our study. With stratified sampling we can be more confident that our sample really does reflect the population that we are interested in. However, if you don't already have a clear idea of the makeup of your population, this method can be problematic.

Volunteer and opportunity sampling

In practice, much of psychological research actually uses either **volunteer sampling** or **opportunity sampling**. With volunteer sampling the researcher simply advertises their study, and individuals volunteer to participate in a self-selecting way. Whilst this can be a relatively easy way to recruit participants, there is a risk that the sample could be biased towards participants with a particularly keen interest in the topic being investigated. For example, if I advertise to recruit people to participate in one of my chocolate studies (the advert would say 'Would you like to participate in a psychological research study about chocolate?'), there is a chance that I might be more likely to recruit people that like chocolate than people who do not like chocolate. With opportunity sampling, the researcher more actively approaches people to be participants in their study, however this method could be quite biased, both in terms of who the researcher approaches and who then offers to participate.

How to run a psychological research study

In this chapter we have discussed a large number of design elements that need to be considered when running a psychological study. To illustrate how these all come together, let's think about how we might design a study to look at chocolate addiction. I am specifically interested in whether people who are addicted to chocolate are more intelligent. This is suitable for a correlational design as I could say the sentence ... 'As the extent of chocolate addiction increases, intelligence increases/decreases'. To look at this relationship, I need to measure two continuous variables, one that measures chocolate addiction and one that measures intelligence. When I design this study I thoroughly review the existing research in this area, and on the basis of this I might predict that we will find a positive relationship; so, the more addicted to chocolate a person is, the more intelligent they are.

Now that I have decided on my basic research design, I need to operationalise my two variables, remembering that they both need to be continuous (interval or ratio ideally) variables. Chocolate addition will be measured by a newly developed questionnaire that I have designed specifically for the purposes of this study. With this measure higher scores will reflect a greater addiction to chocolate. Intelligence will be measured using a very widely and well-validated existing measure called Raven's Progressive Matrices.[1] This is a measure of non-verbal reasoning and higher scores indicate higher levels of non-verbal reasoning, which is a key component of intelligence.

I also want to think about some potential co-variables in my study that could influence my findings. A potential co-variable could be whether a participant generally has an addictive type of personality. If they do, then it could be that being more of an addictive person generally is correlated with intelligence, rather than it being specifically anything to do with an addiction to chocolate. To measure this I will use the Addiction Scale from a very frequently used personality questionnaire (the Eysenck Personality Questionnaire-Revised). For this scale, higher scores indicate a more addictive personality. I could then use these co-variable scores within my statistical analysis to control for any possible effects of having a generally addictive personality.

With my variables clearly operationalised, I need to think about reliability and validity within my design. Raven's Progressive Matrices and the Addiction Scale have both been really well considered in previous published research and there is lots of evidence that they are both valid and reliable, so I am confident in using those measures. For my Chocolate Addiction Scale (CAS), however, given that I have developed it especially for this study, I do need to collect some additional data to ensure that it is both a valid and reliable measure of chocolate addiction. If it lacks any aspect of validity or reliability, then I might not be so convinced by the findings of my study.

To consider convergent validity (whether it is correlated with similar measures) I would also ask participants to report how frequently they eat chocolate and for divergent validity (whether it is not correlated with dissimilar measures) I would ask participants how many

---

[1] True story—I am a total genius if you measure my intelligence using Raven's Progressive Matrices. I get every single item in the test correct. But only if you present the stimuli to me upside down. I spent over a year working on a research project looking at cognitive decline in older adults, and Raven's was one of the tests we used. So every day I sat opposite someone whilst they completed the test, meaning I looked at it upside down!

cups of tea they drink a day. If the CAS is positively and significantly correlated with chocolate eating frequency, then this would be evidence for convergent validity, and if it is not correlated with tea consumption, then this would be evidence for divergent validity. I would ensure internal validity by making sure that the participants do not know that the study is about chocolate addiction before providing any data (they will just be told it is about eating habits) and the researchers will not have access to the participants' CAS scores until after all of the data have been collected.

There is one open ended question in the CAS, which needs to be scored by researchers. We discussed this question earlier in this chapter when discussing inter-rater reliability: How do you feel when you do not have access to chocolate? Therefore I will develop a clear coding system prior to any analysis, and I will test for inter-rater reliability by asking two researchers to independently code 10% of the questionnaires and we will analyse the data to ensure that there is consistency in their coding. For the quantitative part of the CAS, I will examine test-retest reliability by asking participants to complete the CAS twice, with a months' delay in between these two testing time points. I will then look at whether the two sets of responses are correlated. If they are, then I can be confident that the CAS has test-retest reliability. Finally, I will look at internal consistency using Cronbach's alpha.

To recruit participants I will use opportunity sampling from the cohort of psychology students that are currently enrolled in the department where I work. Normally I offer a bar of chocolate to each participant to thank them for taking the time to participate in my study. However this would not be appropriate for my chocolate addiction study as it could bias my sample. People who love chocolate might be keen to participate, and those who hate chocolate might avoid my study. Therefore, giving participants chocolate might lead to me only recruiting participants with a chocolate addiction. I want to ensure that I get a good balance of participants who both love and loathe chocolate, so for this study I will give participants £5.00 to thank them for their involvement in my research study.

Now that we have a beautifully designed study that is methodologically rigorous we need to apply for ethical approval, which we discussed towards the end of Chapter 1. Once ethical approval has been granted we can collect the data. With all of the data collected we can run the appropriate statistical test and see whether there is a significant positive correlation between intelligence and chocolate addiction. How to do this analysis is covered in later chapters, but hopefully you now feel confident in how to think about some of the methodological issues that come up in a very simple psychological research study.

Study questions

For these study questions you will need to work on some simple tasks about research methodology, all based around the following research question: How are cognitive abilities influenced if a child attends a nursery before two years of age?

1. Design three simple studies to address the research question outlined above. For each one I've given you some hints and tips to help you create a very simple psychological study.
    1.1 Categorical design: For this study you should have two categorical variables. Remember that these types of variables should allow for you to collect frequency data. I have

designed the first categorical variable for you: Did the child attend a nursery before the age of two years old? Yes or no. Think of a second variable that you could look at along with the variable I have designed. This variable should have two or three categories to help keep the design nice and simple. Remember that you need to somehow evaluate each child's cognitive ability in later life. You might also find it helpful to look back at Figure 2.1 to help you with this task.

1.2 Experimental design: This experiment should be very simple; it is easy to over-complicate things with an experimental design. You need to design an experimental study, thinking about what will be your *independent variable* and what will be your *dependent variable*. Keep things simple with your independent variable by only having two conditions, so you want to compare two different groups of participants in this design. Your dependent variable should be a continuous score (either an interval or ratio variable) that you expect to differ between the two groups. Looking at Figure 2.1 might be helpful for this task.

1.3 Correlational design: Again, keep this study very simple by selecting two continuous and naturally occurring variables to measure that you think will somehow be related. It can be helpful to think about whether you would expect a positive or a negative relationship from this pair of variables. Look back at Figure 2.1 to help you think about how the relationship might look in your study.

2. For this question, I want you to think in more detail about your correlational design from study question 1.3. You will have designed the study so that you measure two continuous variables.

    2.1 Operationalise both of these variables. How will you define each of these variables so that you can collect measurable data?

    2.2 Think of two possible confounding variables for your design. For each one, suggest how you think the confounding variable might influence your findings and how you could measure it and turn it into a co-variable.

3. Pick one of the variables that you operationalised in study question 2.1, and suggest how you would ensure that your design was both valid and reliable for the following:

    3.1 Convergent validity
    3.2 Divergent validity
    3.3 Internal validity
    3.4 Inter-rater reliability (only needed if there is subjective coding required for your measure)
    3.5 Test-retest reliability
    3.6 Internal consistency

4. What method of sampling will you use, and why?

The research outline for these study questions was inspired by this paper, which showed that children who spend more time in nursery day care before the age of two years perform better in cognitive tests at age four years.

Barnes, J., & Melhuish, E. C. (2016). Amount and timing of group-based childcare from birth and cognitive development at 51 months: A UK study. *International Journal of Behavioural Development*. DOI 10.1177/0165025416635756

Wider reading

Breakwell, G. M., Smith, J. A. and Wright, D. B., eds., 2012. *Research Methods in Psychology: 4th edition*. Sage.
> This book is a great resource that covers a wide range of psychological research methods, including both qualitative and quantitative approaches. It is an edited book, so each chapter is written by a different person who is an expert in the area of methodological design that they are writing about. It is a slightly advanced textbook, but a great place to find out more about the complexities of designing a piece of psychological research.

Lewis, K., Elam, K., Sellers, R., Rhoades, K., Jones, R. B., Thapar, A., & Thapar, A. (2013). The Depression Impairment Scale for Parents (DISP): A new scale for the measurement of impairment in depressed parents. *Psychiatry Research, 210*, 1184–1190.

Gould, C. E., Segal, D. L., Yochim, B. P., Pachana, N. A., Byrne, G. J., & Beaudreau, S. A. (2014). Measuring anxiety in late life: A psychometric examination of the Geriatric Anxiety Inventory and Geriatric Anxiety Scale. *Journal of Anxiety Disorders, 28*, 804–811.

Calvo-Francés, F. (2016). Internet Abusive Use Questionnaire: Psychometric properties. *Computers in Human Behaviour, 59*, 187–194.
> Reliability and validity are often examined in published research papers that are reporting on the development of questionnaire scales. The three papers above all do this in slightly different ways. Some of the statistics that they report are beyond the level that we are covering in this book, but they have quite clear subtitles within the results section that should help you to pick out the key sections that relate to reliability and validity.

For full answers to study questions, and to explore a range of other materials, including examples of good and bad lab reports, visit the online resources at:
www.oup.com/uk/bourne/

3 How to find, read, write, and think about research papers

> **In this chapter you will learn . . .**
> - How psychological research papers are structured and the key information contained within each section of a paper
> - The style in which a psychological research paper should be written and presented
> - How to find published psychological research
> - How to think critically about psychological research: both the research published by academics and your own research studies

At the very beginning of this book I talked a great deal about how central research is to being a psychologist. Almost everything you learn in a psychology degree will come from published research, and you will also be learning to design, run, analyse and write up your own research projects. In this chapter we will be talking in detail about how to find, read, write and think critically about psychological research. These are absolutely essential skills for any psychologist, and they will be useful across all of your studies for your entire degree.

How is a psychological research paper structured?

The way that psychological research papers are structured and formatted is determined by the American Psychological Association (APA) standards. These apply to both published research papers and lab reports that are written by psychology students. In many ways this makes both reading and writing about psychological research far easier. There are set sections, always presented in the same order, for you to read or write, and broadly the same information should always be presented in each section, although you may occasionally see papers published that deviate from these conventions. It is also important to check the requirements that your institution might have for writing up research reports, as your lecturer might ask you to do things in a slightly different way for educational purposes. You can see the main sections in Table 3.1, and each of these will now be explained in more detail. There is also an example research report within the online resources for this book, which has lots of notes attached, explaining some of the conventions and giving hints and tips for when you

Table 3.1: The structure of a psychological research report, following APA standards.

Title	Title (about 10-15 words)
Abstract	Overall summary of your study
Introduction	What do we know? Why is your study needed?
Methods	What did you do in your study?
Results	What did you find?
Discussion	Interpretation, critique, and future directions
References	What previous research do you cite?
Appendices	Materials to aid understanding of methods/results

write about your own research project. The APA guidelines cover a huge number of conventions that guide how psychological research is published, and this chapter identifies the key aspects. However, if you wish to find out more about the APA style, there is a great website included in the Wider Reading of this chapter.

Title

The title should be a very concise overview of the research that is presented in the paper. Sometimes a title focuses on the aims of the study (e.g., Can chocolate make people happier? An experimental examination) or alternatively it might focus on the key findings (e.g., Chocolate makes people happier, but only when eating milk chocolate). Try to ensure that the title is very specific to the study that has been conducted, and to achieve this think about the key variables that have been measured and the key findings. Titles should be very short, usually about 10–15 words, although the APA suggest that a title should be no more than 12 words. You should avoid any acronyms in a title, unless they are ones that are instantly recognisable without explanation, such as fMRI.

Abstract

The **abstract** is a short summary of the entire research report. It is usually about 150–250 words in length. One of the most important things with the abstract is to make sure that it is a balanced summary of the report, so the introduction, methods, results, and discussion should each be summarised in just one or two sentences. When I write an abstract I sometimes print it up, although you could also easily do it onscreen too, and then use four different coloured highlighter pens to identify the summaries of each of the four key sections. If there is approximately the same amount of each colour, then the abstract is well balanced. Although the abstract is right at the beginning of the report, I tend to write it last. After I have written the full research report it is far easier to identify and pick out the key information that needs to be included in the abstract.

Introduction

The **introduction** is usually quite a substantial part of a psychological research report. The key aim is to review the previous research that has led to the study that is being presented, and to justify the rationale and design of your study. The first paragraph of the introduction typically sets the broad context of the study, and the final sentence of this paragraph often tells the reader what the overall aim is of the study that is being presented.

Having given the reader an idea of what the introduction will build towards, the majority of the Introduction should then summarise and consider the previous research that has been published and why it is relevant to understanding your own study. It is really important that this is very focused on leading to and justifying your own piece of research. For every piece of research that is presented in the Introduction, try to think about the following:

1. *Why is this piece of research relevant to justifying your own research study?* This could either be theoretical relevance or methodological relevance. Another way to think about this is to consider why the reader needs to know about this study to understand your own study.

2. *What are the key methods and findings that are relevant to your own research study?* It is important to clearly and concisely summarise the methodology and results of previous research, but really think about what aspects are necessary to understand the need for and design of your research study. Some research will need explaining in more detail than others. For example, the key piece of research within the area is likely to need more attention and detail and could take one or two paragraphs to explain, whereas a paper that justifies one of your methodological decisions might just need a sentence or two.

3. *What is wrong with the previously published research?* No piece of research is perfect (more on this later in this chapter!), and you do need to use your critical thinking skills in the Introduction. Remember that psychological research is usually novel (unless you are doing an explicit replication study). When you present a relevant piece of research in your Introduction, you need to be clear how your own research is novel and different to the previous research. Are there some elements of the previous research that were not ideal, and how will your study improve upon it? For example, was there a sampling bias, or a potential issue with the reliability of a questionnaire they used? It is important to highlight these weaknesses, but it is vital to then link these to your own design as these will justify your study. For example, you will improve the sample by ensuring that it is balanced according to sex, or you will use a different questionnaire that has been found to be more reliable.

The final paragraph of the Introduction should draw together the key points and weaknesses of the previous research that you have reviewed, and this should be used to explain and justify the need for your own study. You would then finish this paragraph off with your **hypotheses**, or predictions. To revise how to develop these, take a look back at Chapter 1. Your hypotheses should be the very last thing that you include in your Introduction.

Importantly, you need to really think about whether you have two-tailed and open ended hypotheses (e.g., Happiness ratings will differ between participants eating white chocolate and milk chocolate) or whether you will have one-tailed and directional hypotheses (e.g., Participants will be happier after eating milk chocolate than after eating white chocolate). Which type of hypothesis you decide to use should build on the previous research that you have reviewed in the introduction. If your study is very novel and there is little previous research that is directly related to it, then a two-tailed hypothesis would be most appropriate. Alternatively, if the previous research is relevant but the findings have been very contradictory, then a two-tailed hypothesis would again be appropriate. However, if the previous research clearly finds results in a particular direction, then it would be better to develop a one-tailed hypothesis.

Methods

The **methods** section is where you describe the participants in your study, and the methodology that you used. It is typically divided into four subsections: participants, materials, procedure, and design. It is important to get the level of detail right in the methods section. You need to give the reader enough information so that they could replicate your study by recruiting similar participants and using the same materials and procedures. However, you don't want to go into too much detail, so only include information that is essential to the design of your study. For example, it doesn't really matter that your study was run on a Tuesday, that it happened in room 16 on the 9th floor, or that participants completed the questionnaires with a purple sparkly pen.

In published research you will sometimes see a slightly different structure within the methods section, particularly in more complex research designs. For example, if a study uses a number of questionnaires, the author might decide not to use separate materials and procedure sections, but instead might have separate sections for each questionnaire, and to combine the information that would normally go into the materials and procedures sections within each questionnaire section. You might also sometimes see the design section presented as a design and analysis strategy, and this can be presented straight after the participants, or as the final section in the methods. If you look at neuroimaging studies, they also often structure their methods section differently. When you write a paper, you should normally aim for the traditional structure, but it can be adapted if you think the information would be presented in a clearer manner (and if your course tutor agrees!).

Participants

In this section you want to describe your **participants** and how you recruited them. Key pieces of information to include about your participants are: the number of participants, the number and/or percentage of males and females, and statistics about the age of participants, usually the mean and standard deviation, but sometimes also the range. If you have participants in different conditions that are determined by simple descriptive characteristics (e.g. age, sex, eye colour), you would need to give information about the groups. You should say how many participants were in each condition, and you would usually give the key participant information, such as age and sex distribution, for the entire sample and then for the participants in each condition separately. However, if participants are allocated to different conditions on the basis of an experimental manipulation, you would explain how you allocated participants to each condition within the procedure sub-section that comes later in the methods.

You should also tell the reader about any additional relevant information that helps to describe your sample. For example, if you were doing a study on reading ability, you might want to record and report the number of years of full time education for the participants. Or, if handedness were relevant, you could include the number of left and right handers and perhaps the statistics for strength of handedness gained from a handedness questionnaire.

The method of recruitment used should also be mentioned (you can revise these in Chapter 2), and whether there was any form of reimbursement for their participation. For example, were they paid, and if so, how much? Where they entered into a prize draw by participating, or were all participants given chocolate as a token? Did they take part to gain some form of course credit? You should also report where you recruited them from. For example, was the study advertised with posters around the Psychology Department, or through an email list of people interested in taking part in psychological studies?

At the end of the participants section is also where you normally tell the reader that you had **ethical approval** for the study. As well as explicitly stating that ethical approval was granted, you should also say who gave this approval. Usually it is a Departmental Ethics Committee, but it might also be a University level committee, or an NHS board.

Materials

In this section you need to describe all of the **materials** that you used in the study. Remember here that the reader needs enough information to exactly replicate the methodology, but be careful not to give any unnecessary information. This is the section of the methods where it can be easy to give too much information.

Your materials should be described in enough detail that the reader can replicate your study. If you are using materials that have been used and published previously, for example a personality questionnaire or a neuropsychological test, then you should include a reference to the original source that used this material. That way the reader can easily find out more about it, if they wish to do so. If there is any published data on the reliability and validity of that measure, such as a Cronbach's alpha (see Chapter 2 to revise what this is), then this can also be added in this section.

If you developed your own new materials -perhaps you developed a memory test, a happiness questionnaire, or you created photographic facial stimuli -then you need to describe these in enough detail that another person could recreate them. It can sometimes be useful to put newly developed materials into the appendix of a research report.

Whether you use existing materials, or you develop your own, you need to give a good level of detail. For example, if you developed a questionnaire, you should note how many items it had, what type of responses participants were asked to give, whether there were subscales within the questionnaire, and perhaps include an example item or two. If you were developing a face recognition task, then you would note how many different faces were used, whether they were used repeatedly or just once, the size of the facial stimuli, whether they were presented in greyscale or colour, how long they were presented for, etc.

You should also clearly describe the scores that are gained through the methodology, and if any computations were needed to calculate final scores. It is also important to give the reader an idea of what 'high scores' and 'low scores' mean, and if relevant, what are the minimum and maximum possible scores. If you were using a questionnaire, you might say something like 'Scores were summed across the twenty items giving scores ranging from 20-100, where higher scores indicate being happier'. For the face recognition example, you might look at both speed of responding and accuracy, and then you could say something like 'From the ten trials in each condition, mean reaction times and the percentage of correct responses were calculated.' In this example, it is quite clear that smaller reaction times are faster and that higher percentages are more accurate, so some people might not explain that explicitly, but others might.

Procedure

Within the **procedure** you should describe the order in which participants completed the different components of the study, the length of time they were given to complete tasks (if limited) and any specific instructions given to participants. If you have participants in different conditions as a result of an experimental manipulation, you can explain in this section the method that you used to allocate participants to conditions, so how you decided which condition each participant should be in. You can also provide information in this section about the ethical running of the study (e.g. informed consent and debriefing) and anything relevant to special ethical considerations, such as how you dealt with deception or potential risk within the debriefing.

Design (and Analysis)

In this section you need to clearly specify the **design** that you used (e.g., experimental or correlational). You might sometimes see that the design section also includes the analysis strategy, making it design and analysis. If you do this, this is where you should explain how you analysed the data. This should not simply involve stating the statistical test used. You need to explain each of the variables analysed and give any of the relevant details for the type of statistical analysis that you used. The exact details here will depend of the method of analysis that you will be reporting, and the whole of Chapter 17 is devoted to explaining how you select and describe the right statistical test.

Results

The structure of a **results** section differs slightly according to the type of statistical analysis that you have run, and for this reason the way in which each test result is presented is covered within each statistical chapter. However, there are some things that should be common across all results sections. First, there is a particular way of presenting each statistic, which is set out by the APA standards. This will be clearly set out for each statistic within the relevant chapter.

As we will find out later in this book, statistics fall into two key types: **descriptive statistics** (e.g. the average score) and **inferential statistics** (e.g. the significance results). In Chapter 5 you will learn far more about these two different types of statistic, and what each tells you. It is really important to report both descriptive and inferential statistics, and to use them together to help the reader to understand the findings of your analysis. It is sometimes tempting to present and discuss each type of statistic separately, but you should integrate these together, as it is by using both types of statistic that we get the fullest understanding of our findings.

If a result is significant, it is important to not just state that you have a significant finding, but to also interpret the *direction* of the significant finding. You interpret the direction by using the descriptive statistics. For example, if you find that happiness differs significantly between participants eating white and milk chocolate, *which* group has the significantly higher scores? Whilst finding a significant result is important, without knowing the direction of that significant finding, it actually tells you very little. The directional interpretation really tells you what is going on.

HOW IS A PSYCHOLOGICAL RESEARCH PAPER STRUCTURED?

If a result is not significant, you still need to present the full statistics in APA format, but there is no need to write about and interpret the direction. You do, however, still need to present the relevant descriptive statistics, just do not talk about them as if they are showing anything significant or directional. It is important to still have the descriptives there as the reader might want an idea of what the sample is like, or how that compares to other samples in published papers.

This can be particularly important to help with critical thinking about the paper. For example, imagine a study was run on some aspect of intelligence, but did not have significant findings. It would be helpful to know the average intelligence of the sample. Do they have a similar level of intelligence to previously published research? Or are they far less or far more intelligent? If your sample seems very different from previously researched samples, then this could perhaps explain why the results unexpectedly differed. We will talk more about critical thinking later in this chapter.

Descriptive statistics might be presented within the text of the results section, or they could be presented in a table or graph. You can see examples of these three different ways in Figure 3.1. Any of these three ways is usually fine, but you need to bear in mind two important things. First, you should only present the descriptive statistics once. Whether it is in the text, a table, or a graph is fine, but do not repeat any of the information you give in the results. Second, you should present them in the clearest manner possible. If the study is quite simple and you do not have too many descriptives to report, it can be easiest to present them in the text. However, if the study is a little more complicated and you have quite a few numbers to present, then a table or graph can be a clearer method of presentation.

Whilst on the topic of tables and graphs, or figures as they tend to be called in psychological papers, it is important to number each one (e.g., Table 1, Figure 4; tables and figures are numbered separately) and to write a short table or figure legend that describes what is presented in it (e.g. 'Descriptive statistics for males and females separately'). This is usually just a short sentence. For a figure the legend is presented below the image, but for a table it is presented above. You should also tell the reader when it is appropriate to look at the table or figure, for example, by saying 'see Table 2 for the descriptive statistics'. If you don't tell the reader to look at it, then they are likely to not look at it! If you look through this book you will see lots of examples of figure numbering, figure legends, and references to figures within the text.

"Males had a mean score of 15.6 (SD = 1.7) and females had a mean score of 16.5 (SD = 1.4)"

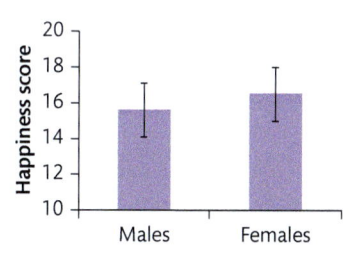

Figure 3: Mean happiness scores (±1 SD) for males and females separately.

Table 2: Descriptive statistics showing happiness scores as a function of sex.

	Males	Females
Mean	15.6	16.5
SD	1.7	1.4

Figure 3.1: Examples of how to present descriptive statistics within a results section, but remember to just pick one way to present them. (SD refers to the standard deviation, a measure of dispersion that we will talk about a lot in Chapter 5.)

As I just mentioned, when a finding is significant you should use the descriptives to interpret the direction of the finding, but when a finding is not significant you should still present the descriptives, but you should not interpret them. An easy way to achieve this is to just present the descriptive statistics in a table, and refer the reader to the table at the relevant point in your results section. This way the reader can see the information, but you avoid the possibility of discussing them in a way that suggests you found something when you didn't!

Discussion

In the same way that an introduction tends to follow a similar structure, so should the **discussion**. The first paragraph must summarise the findings and then relate them back to the hypotheses. If the study is very simple, then this paragraph would just reiterate the findings, whereas in more complex studies this paragraph would pick out and highlight the most important findings. You should not include any of the actual statistics or numbers within this summary though, just a simple written explanation of the key findings to emerge from the analyses.

This paragraph is also where you would consider whether your findings support your hypotheses, or not. It is fine for your results to contradict your predictions, and this can actually make the discussion far more interesting to write as you have far more to think about and examine. So don't be tempted to go back and revise your hypotheses to match your findings!

Having clearly summarised your findings, you now need to discuss how these relate to the findings of the previous relevant research that you discussed in the introduction. Do your findings support the findings of previous research? If so, what are the implications of this? For example, what has your study added to the existing knowledge of this area of research? Or, do your findings contradict the previous evidence in this field of research? If they do, then you need to consider why they might have differed. How did your study differ from the previous research, and might these differences have contributed to the contradictory results? For example, was your sample different, or did you use different stimuli, or a different timing within your procedure? Again, it is totally fine for your findings to contradict the previous research, but you need to give good consideration to explaining why this might have been the case.

Next, you need to critique your own study. You can mention the strengths of your research, but it is more important to fully consider the weaknesses and limitations. Try to avoid discussing more superficial criticisms. One way to think about this is to consider whether your critique could be applied to most psychological research (e.g. the participants were all psychology students, and therefore may have had a special insight into the study). Whilst these may be valid criticisms of psychological research more generally, you need to think about issues that are more specific to your actual design. For example, is the way that you sampled the participants really unbiased? Or, were the materials that you selected really appropriate, or could you have picked a better validated questionnaire, or a better quality set of facial images?

It is really important that you do not simply list a whole load of things that were possibly wrong about your study. Instead you should select a few fundamental critique points and then discuss them fully. First, you should clearly identify what the potential problem with your design is. Then you need to explain exactly how this might have influenced your findings. If a critical issue does not potentially explain something in your findings, then it may not be such a strong point and you might want to consider including other aspects in your critique instead.

There are various ways that a critical point, an aspect of your design that you choose to critique, might have influenced your findings. Say, for example, that you failed to find any significant results. Might the critical point explain your lack of findings? Or, might the opposite be true? Could your findings have been exaggerated as a result of the critical point? If you have participants in different conditions, you might also want to think about whether any of your design elements differed between the groups. This is likely to provide a strong critical point. For example, if you are looking at alcohol consumption in males and females and you collect the data in a pub at 10.30 pm on a Friday night, you are likely to find quite high levels of alcohol consumption. However, these higher scores are likely to be the same for both males and females as they all will have had a few drinks already. So although it might have been a bad methodological design to collect your data at that time in a pub, it is not likely to explain any difference between males and females. However, if the critical point that you are trying to make is likely to have caused over-inflation in one group, but not in the other, then this is a big problem! Particularly if you find significantly higher scores in the group that has been influenced by the over-inflation. For example, if you tested all the females at 5.00 pm and the males at 10.30 pm, finding that the males had consumed more alcohol than females is unlikely to reflect anything meaningful. Instead it is more likely to be a result of the methodological flaw of testing females at the beginning of the night before having drunk much, and testing males at the end of the night when they are likely to have had a few drinks.

Ideally, you will also back up your ideas with research. This might not always be available, but where possible you should include this. It will add credibility to your argument. For example, if you were to criticise the questionnaire that you used, then previous research showing that it lacks validity or reliability would make your argument far stronger than you just claiming it. You might then need to justify why you picked this questionnaire, even though it was lacking in validity or reliability. By this point you will have clearly identified the problem, considered how it could have influenced your findings, and this would be backed up with research. You now need to suggest how you could improve the study in any future projects, and also how the findings might differ as a result of this re-design. Alternatively, you might feel that the results wouldn't change. You can see a summary and an example of how to work through a critique point in Box 3.1. In this example, the personality trait of extraversion is suggested as a possible unmeasured **confounding variable** within the design.

You should finish off your discussion with a paragraph that highlights the key findings and issues to emerge from your piece of research, and to suggest future directions for this project. Now, when I say 'future directions', try not to think too far into the future or too broadly. It can be tempting to extrapolate from your findings to some major world issue that it could have implications for, potentially, at some point, in the very distant future. Whilst it can be exciting to think about how your research could increase eye witness accuracy, improve diagnosis for Alzheimer's disease or encourage greater donations to charities, you need to think in a more focused way. What would be the next study or two that you might run? What could be the next issue to be tackled as a result of your research?

That is your discussion written, however I just want to address one question that my students often ask me: Is it ok to use new references in the discussion, or can I only use references

> **Box 3.1:** How to structure and discuss a weakness of your study in the discussion of a research report.
>
> Discussing a weaknesses of your own study ...
> - Identify and explain a single issue relating to your study.
> - Explain *exactly* how this might have influenced your findings (e.g., were the effects overestimated or underestimated?). Use research to support this.
> - Consider alternative ways of designing the study to overcome weaknesses.
> - Suggest how the findings might change as a result of this re-design.
>
> A practical example of how to do this ...
> - A possible limitation of this study is that the sample was unbalanced according to the sex of the participants, with 85% females and 15% males.
> - This could be problematic as females have been found to have significantly higher levels of extraversion than males (Schmitt, Realo, Varacek, & Allik, 2008). It is therefore possible that the findings of this study could have been overestimated as a result of having a highly extraverted sample.
> - In future research it would be important to recruit a more balanced sample.
> - This could lead to a smaller difference being found between the two conditions, which would be more consistent with previous research.

that I have used in the introduction? I'm not sure where this idea comes from, but I am often asked this question.

The short answer is that it is totally fine to include new references in the discussion. Your introduction should (effectively) be written before you collect and analyse your data, and therefore how could you possibly know which references will be relevant to explain and critique your findings when you have no idea what your findings are yet? However, there is one aspect of the discussion where you should absolutely not be using new references: the section where you discuss your findings in relation to the previous relevant and similar research. If the research is relevant and similar, then it should be in your introduction! Bringing in new literature at this point means that you have gaps in your review of the relevant literature in your introduction. Other than with this caveat, it is acceptable, and in fact necessary, to include references in your discussion that you have not included elsewhere in your paper.

References

The **references** list is where you give the details of all the research you have discussed in your research report. It is really important that this is complete and accurate. Imagine that the reader finds out about a really interesting piece of research from your introduction, or that they disagree with the way that you have interpreted the results of a study and they would like to go back and check it. With a complete and accurate references list, they can simply look up the full details of the paper, and then read it for themselves.

Importantly, the references list should include every single source that you include in you research report. This is likely to mainly be journal articles, but it could also be a textbook or website. However, it is not a list of everything you read to prepare for writing the report. If you read twenty papers when writing up the lab report, but only actually mention fifteen of them through the report, then the five that you read but did not cite do not go in the references list. It should only include sources that you have both read and cited.

The way that you present the references is determined by strict APA rules, which may seem very picky, but they are important to learn as a psychologist. These are discussed in far more detail later in this chapter. The references list should be presented in APA format, with the references presented in alphabetic order, and it should start on a fresh page, immediately after the discussion.

Appendices

Finally, you may need to include some **appendices**. The general rule is that you should avoid appendices where possible, but they can be helpful to help the reader to understand the methodology of your study, and sometimes the analyses. If you have used tables or figures to present the findings of your statistical analyses, these do not belong in the appendices as they are fundamental to understanding your findings. Only supplemental tables and figures would go into an appendix. If your methods are based on previously published materials, such as a well-established questionnaire or set of photographic facial stimuli, then you should just give the reference to the previously published work in your methods section. You wouldn't need an appendix in this case as the reader can simply go to the originally published source and get any additional information that they want from there.

However, if you have developed your own materials, it may be helpful to include an appendix. Ideally you can explain your materials and procedure clearly enough in the methods that the reader could replicate your study from simply reading your paper. But if this would not be possible, for example if you developed your own brand new questionnaire, then you should include the additional information, such as a full copy of your questionnaire, in an appendix. Remember to refer to the appendix at the relevant point in the methods section so that the reader knows it is there and to look at it, and if you have multiple appendices they should be referred to alphabetically using capital letters. For example, you might say: 'The full questionnaire can be found in Appendix A'.

Writing a psychological research paper

Whilst a psychological research paper is very clearly compartmentalised into different sections, each of which presents different information, it is important to think of your report as one big piece of work, where each section flows into the next. The introduction should present the previous research in a way that builds towards the justification and hypotheses for your specific study, you then describe how you ran this study in the methods and what you found in the results, before considering your findings in the discussion. In particular, think about your hypothesis and how this runs right through your report. If you have a one-tailed hypotheses, then the research you review in your introduction should clearly justify a directional prediction, your data should be analysed in an appropriate way, and the interpretation of your findings in your discussion should reflect the directional prediction that you proposed in the introduction, even if your findings do not support your hypotheses.

For example, if I am writing up my study comparing happiness after eating white and milk chocolate, then I will review all of the existing literature in my introduction. However, there is relatively little research in this area, and the findings are quite inconsistent, therefore I develop a two-tailed hypothesis and analyse the data appropriately (you will learn how to do this for each statistical analysis within the later statistical chapters). Unfortunately I find no significant difference in happiness between people who have eaten white and milk chocolate. When I summarise my findings in the discussion, I need to acknowledge that the statistical analyses did not support my predicted findings, and consider why this might have happened.

Psychological research reports: the hourglass

I've often heard the structure of a psychological research report described as an hourglass. I'm not sure where this description first came from, but it really is a nice analogy, and you can see it in Figure 3.2. The report starts broadly, becomes narrower, and then becomes broader again towards the end. The introduction starts with the broad research question of interest, narrows down to the specifically relevant previous research, and finishes off specifically talking about the design and predictions of your study. The methods and results are the narrowest sections, and both concentrate specifically on your own study. The discussion then starts still quite narrow, simply describing and then explaining the findings of your study, it then becomes broader in thinking critically about your study and findings, and finishes up by broadly thinking about what needs to be done next.

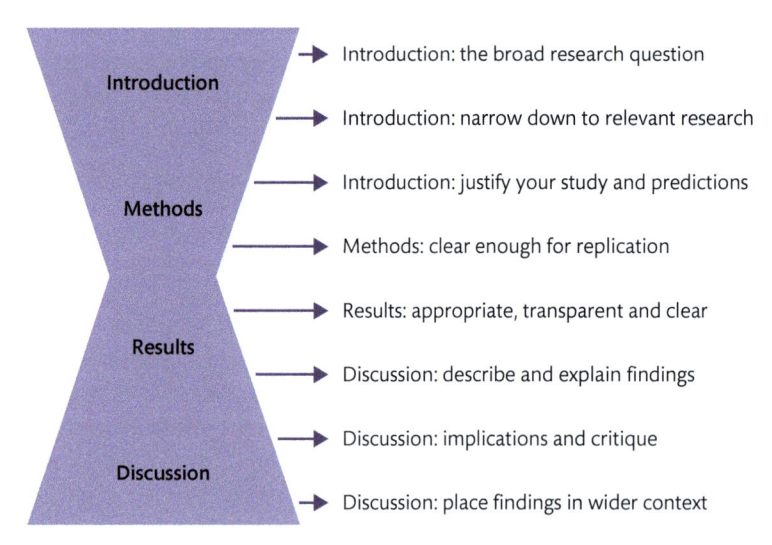

Figure 3.2: Viewing a research report as an hourglass.

Presenting psychological research: What are the standards for presenting research?

Many of the current standards for conducting and presenting psychological research are determined by the American Psychological Association (APA). The APA set the expectations in terms of the ethics of research, the presentation of research papers, formatting of statistical analyses, and the referencing of other sources of information in all psychological research. In the previous section of this chapter I described what should be included within each section, but the APA also has broader considerations that relate to the style of writing that should be used across the entire research report. These are summarised in here, and you can also take a look at the example Lab Report in the online resources to see it all in practice.

Writing style

When you are writing a psychological research report, you should aim to write in short and scientific sentences. A lab report is not the place for flowery or journalistic language. You want to be concise, clear and to the point. The best way to get to grips with the style of writing is to read plenty of published pieces of research. You are aiming to write and present your own research in the same way as the research that is conducted and published by academics (quite possibly the academics who teach you!).

In terms of writing style, the APA generally suggest that you should avoid using the first person, but if you read published research, you will see that this is not always the case. You will very rarely see 'I' being used, and you should avoid using 'I' in a lab report. However, the use of 'we' or 'our' is becoming increasingly acceptable in published research, though try to use them only when describing quite factual aspects of your paper, such as your design. It is still usually best to avoid personalising any critical opinions that you present. It can be particularly helpful to talk about 'our research' in the discussion when you are comparing your findings to the previous research, otherwise it can get confusing whose research you are talking about.

The majority of the report should be written in the past tense. So the introduction might note that 'Smith found ...', the methods that 'Participants were shown ...', and the results that 'There was a significant difference ...' However the discussion tends to be written in the present tense e.g. 'Our findings suggest ...'

The APA also has clear guidance on how to discuss the people that are involved in your research. They should always be referred to as participants. Older research typically involved 'subjects', but the APA now recommends that you avoid this terminology, although you do still see it in publications sometimes. Referring to the people who volunteer to take part in your study as 'subjects' makes them seem like they are passively being subjected to the methods you use. However, especially with stringent ethical approval and informed consent, it is now true that volunteers are more like active participants in research studies.

I have put together a list of hints and tips to help you write in a style that is appropriate for psychological research reports, which you can see in Table 3.2. It is also good to avoid using quotes from other sources, unless they are really essential. Generally, it is better to explain something in your own words than to rely on the words of another person—in particular, if you are writing a research report for a coursework assessment, the reader (or marker) needs

Table 3.2: Hints and tips for writing psychological research reports.

The hint ...	What not to write ...	What to write ...
Avoid too many acronyms, try to only use established and recognised acronym, and avoid very similar ones	The RTs to the EFR stimuli were slower than to the EFD stimuli ...	Reaction times were slower in the emotional face recognition task than in the discrimination task ...
Avoid using contractions	Participants hadn't been involved in previous studies ...	Participants had not been involved in previous studies ...
Do not start sentences with a number	150 participants were recruited ...	One hundred and fifty participants ...
Never, ever claim that something has been 'proved'	Our study proved ...	Our findings suggest ...
Do not claim that statistical analyses are 'insignificant'	The difference between conditions was insignificant ...	The difference between conditions was not significant ...
Avoid anthropomorphizing your study (i.e., giving it human traits)	This study found ...	The analyses showed ...

to know that you really understand the content of your report. Relying too heavily on quotes can give the impression that you do not understand the content well enough to explain it in your own words. You might notice that you rarely see quotes in published research. If it is absolutely essential to include a quote, you must put quotation marks around it, and give the page number/s that the quote was taken from, along with the reference.

Presenting statistics

The final area of APA convention that you will need to learn for writing research reports is how to present the results of your statistical analyses. Descriptive statistics, such as the **mean** and **standard deviation** could be presented within the written text, in a table or figure, and they should be presented to two decimal places. The mean is signified with an italicised M (i.e. *M*) and the standard deviation with an italicised SD (i.e. *SD*).

For the tests of **statistical significance**, the exact specifications vary depending on the statistic that is being presented, and in each statistical chapter in this text the APA format is explained. However, they usually do work in roughly the same way, and you can see this in Figure 3.3. You start with a letter that represents the statistical test that you have calculated and this should be italicised. This is followed by the degrees of freedom presented within brackets. The degrees of freedom are either calculated from the number of participants in the study, or the number of conditions within the design. You then have an equals sign and give the calculated statistic value. This should be presented to two decimal places and followed by a comma. Finally you give the ***p* value**, the number that tells you about the significance of the analysis, and this should be presented to three decimal places. The *p* should be italicised. As we will be calculating all of the statistics by hand in this book, we will always be reporting a significant result with *p* values less than (<) a particular value, for example *p* < .050. In published research you are far more likely to see exact *p* values reported, where *p* = .XXX.

$$\textit{statistic } (df) = X.XX, p < .XXX$$

- The type of analysis calculated is signified by a letter (e.g., *r* or *F*) which is italicised
- Degrees of freedom (df) are shown in brackets.
- The calculated value of the statistic is presented to two decimal places
- The *p* value is presented to three decimal places and the "*p*" is italicised.

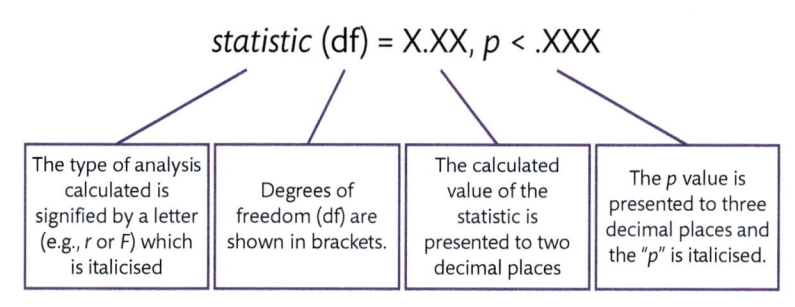

Figure 3.3: APA convention for presenting the findings of a test of statistical significance.

It can sometimes be a bit confusing as to whether a number should have a leading zero, which is a number 0 before the decimal place for numbers less than 1. For example, should you report 0.12 or .12? The rule here is that it depends on whether numbers greater than 1 are possible. If it is possible to have numbers greater than 1, then there should always be a leading 0 (i.e., 0.12). However, if it is impossible to have a number greater than 1, then a leading zero is not needed (i.e., .12). In each chapter, where I show you how to present the statistical analysis, whether or not a leading zero is needed will be made very clear, but they are never needed for *p* values.

Referencing

When you are writing about, or citing, the research conducted by others, there are certain conventions that you need to follow. As noted before, these are set by the APA, and you need to follow these referencing guides strictly. There are many different sources of information that you could cite within a research report. Mainly you will (or should) be citing previously published research papers, so for this section I will concentrate on how you accurately reference these using APA style. However, if you need to cite a different source, such as a website or online video, then check out the Wider Reading at the end of this chapter.

Referencing within the text of a psychological research report

What should you be referencing in the body of your research report? The simple answer is anything that you have read and referred to in your report. This could be either a **primary source**, a paper that you have actually read, or a **secondary source**, a paper that you have not actually read, but which you read about within another paper. The way that you refer to primary and secondary sources is slightly different. These are summarised, with examples, in Table 3.3. You should only ever use the author's surname within the text of your report. Never use their first name or their initials. You also need to give the year in which the paper was published. This is really important as most researchers have a number of publications, so the year allows the reader to identify the exact piece of research that you are referring to.

It is really important that you cite secondary sources accurately, and that you are honest about when you have actually read a source (i.e. a primary source) and when you have read about a piece of research within another source (i.e. a secondary source). Whilst it might be tempting to treat all references as primary sources, this could be a big mistake. If you were

Table 3.3: Citing primary and secondary sources in a psychological research report.

Who do you want to cite?	How to cite them ... (Different methods shown)	Extra things to note ...
Primary source: one author	Jones (2015) found that ...	Only ever use the author's surname
	... higher levels of accuracy (Jones, 2015)	Have a comma after their surname and before the year
Primary source: two authors	Smith and Jones (2014) developed new stimuli ..	When citing names in the sentence, use 'and'
	... newly developed stimuli (Smith & Jones, 2014)	When citing names in brackets, use '&'
Primary source: 3-5 authors	Johnson, Smith, Harris and Jones (2010) examined ...	For the first citation, give all authors names
	... a significant difference was found (Johnson et al., 2010)	For subsequent citations, use 'et al.' (note the full stop after the al.)
Primary source: 6 + authors	Samuels et al. (2008) considered the role of ...	Use 'et al.' from the first citation
Secondary source	Smith (2012, cited in Jones, 2016) examined the use of ...	Use 'cited in' and then give the reference you have actually read
	... has been found (Smith, 2012, cited in Jones, 2016)	Do not use brackets around the date within brackets. Use commas.

to do this, you would be relying on the author of the paper that you are reading having presented the research they talk about (i.e. the secondary source) accurately and fully. What happens if they misinterpreted or misunderstood the secondary source? If you present this source as if you have read it, then the person reading and marking your work will think you didn't understand the previous research. If you are clear that you read about it somewhere else, then they will know that it might be the author of the primary source that made the mistake. With your accurate referencing, they could actually go to the source and check where the mistake came from.

Referencing at the end of a psychological research report

We have already talked a little bit earlier in this chapter about the references list that you must include at the end of your research report. It should contain all of the sources that you have both read and included in your report. Thinking about how this works for secondary sources, if you take the example from Table 3.3, you would include Jones (2016) in the references list as you have actually read that source. You would not include Smith (2012) in the references list as you did not read that paper. By accurately using 'cited in' within the text of the report, the reader knows that you read about the Smith (2012) research in the Jones (2016) paper, and they can find the full reference for this in your references section if they wish to look into either paper in more detail.

There are strict conventions, again set by the APA, that determine how to present your references at the end of your report. You can see this summarised in Figure 3.4. You can find this information on the front page of any published research paper, or if you are online the

Alexander, E. S. & Onwuegbuzie, A. J. (2007). Academic procrastination and the role of hope as a coping strategy. *Personality and Individual Differences, 42,* 1301–1310. doi:10.1016/j.paid.2006.10.008

Annotations on the reference:
- Surname then their initials (not full name)
- Before last author, include an ampersand (not "and")
- Year of publication (in brackets) followed by a full stop
- Article title (use sentence case for title)
- Journal title (italicised and each word capitalised)
- Volume number (italicised)
- Start and end page numbers followed by a full stop
- Digital object identifier (DOI) presented as doi:xxx

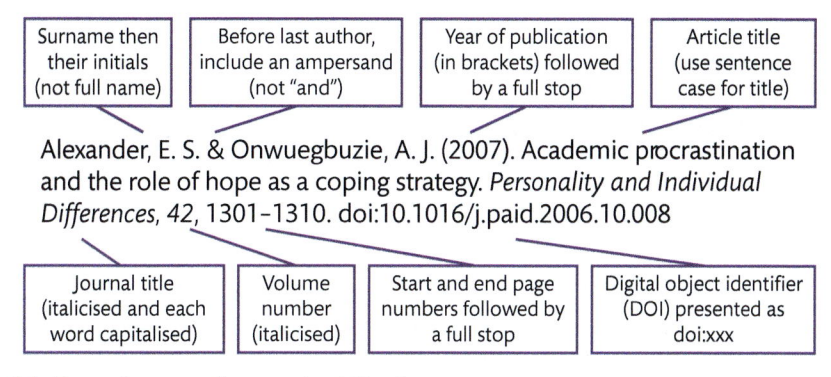

Figure 3.4: How to format a reference using APA style.

information is usually at the very top of the page. Although referencing is determined by the APA, their requirements are updated every few years and this means that their requirements do change from time to time. One example of this is the issue number, which used to be a requirement, and was given in brackets after the volume number, but is no longer included. However, it is still included in many journals and you are likely to see it quite often in older papers, or even in some more recently published research.

Another relatively recent change is the introduction of Digital Object Identifiers (DOIs) for almost all published research papers, which you can see included in Figure 3.4. Nowadays the vast majority of journals publish research papers online, often in advance of the paper volumes coming out. The DOIs are unique identifying codes for each published paper that allow people to identify papers more easily online, particularly if they come out online far in advance of the official publication in a paper volume that you can hold in your hands. A DOI starts with '10.' and then has some random looking string of numbers and letters. DOIs were introduced in 2000, so anything published before then does not have a DOI, and not all journals started using them immediately. However, if a journal article does have a DOI, you can add this to the end of the reference. Indeed, the latest version of the APA Publication Manual suggests that you do so, but it is taking a while for this to become universally applied in journals.

You can put the references together and into APA format by just typing it all in and doing the formatting yourself, but this can be time consuming, fiddly, irritating, and it is easy to make mistakes. There are numerous ways that you can make this whole process far easier and quicker. You can do the referencing within Word, under the References tab, or there are dedicated programmes, such as Endnote, to which most universities have access.

Some people compile their references list as they are writing their report. Each time they cite a paper they add it to the references list. Others wait until they have finished writing the whole report, and they then put the references list together. Either way is fine, and which way you do it depends on your own way of working. I tend to put the references list together after having totally finished writing, just in case I end up removing any references when I cut down my inevitably over-long paper!

Once you have all the references recorded, they need to be listed in alphabetical order. The easiest way to make sure you have done this, assuming you are using Word to write your report, is to select all of the references and then click on the button that has A and Z, with a downwards arrow. If you have multiple references from a single author, you should list these in chronological order, with the oldest paper first. If you have multiple references from multiple authors where the first author is always the same, then you list them alphabetically according to the second author's surname.

Finding psychological research papers

One of the most exciting things about studying psychology is that it is a dynamic and current subject. Every day there are major advances in our understanding of the way we think and behave, and when you study psychology you will be learning about this research and conducting your own research. Whilst it is exciting that psychological research is constantly advancing, this does mean that you need to keep looking for the latest research for any assignment. Why rely on research that is twenty or thirty years old, when you could be looking at research that has been published in the past few months? No matter how good a textbook is, they are slightly out of date from the first day they come out. Therefore, when you are doing your own research, it is important to know how to access the latest psychological research to support your own and which research you should trust and include in your report.

It is also important to use primary sources, so the actual research papers, as much as you can. Whilst it can be tempting to rely heavily on secondary sources, such as textbooks or articles that provide a review of an area of research, this can really limit your research. First, you end up using just one source a great deal, and second you are reliant on both the breadth of their own literature review and their interpretation of the research that they review. What if they did not include a large section of published research that is highly relevant to your topic of interest? You would be missing out on some research findings that are potentially highly relevant to your own piece of research. Or, what if they misinterpreted some of the research that they review? That misinterpretation would carry forward into your own research report. Wherever possible, always aim to read the actual research papers that you write about in your research report.

What psychological research should you trust, and where can you find it?

There are many, many different ways of finding psychological research, and you can see these summarised in Figure 3.5. Each method has its own advantages and disadvantages. Possibly the simplest way is to use Google, or any other search engine, type in a few relevant keywords and see what comes up. Whilst this method is very simple and it could return some high quality psychological research papers, you risk finding a whole load of websites that discuss research in an unverified and potentially inaccurate manner. This is really not the type of evidence that you want to be using in a piece of academic work. You may think that Wikipedia is a more reliable source, after all it looks and reads like an encyclopaedia, but this should also be avoided. Anyone can add information to Wikipedia, and there are many examples of people adding false or malicious information to pages. Go to any Wikipedia page and click on the 'View history' tab at the top of the page. Here you can see the number of edits that are made, and you can often see possible vandalism occurring and being fixed. Again, is this the kind of information that you really want to be citing in your academic work?

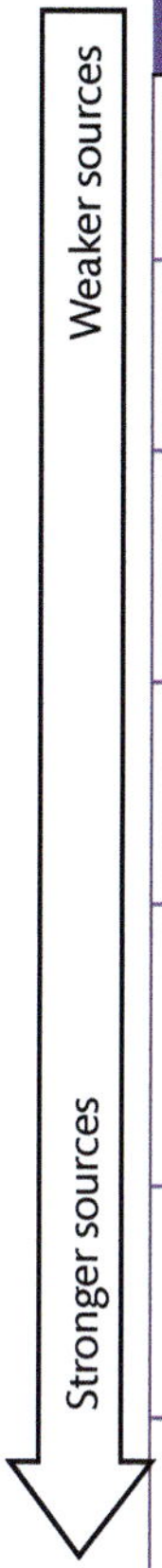

FINDING PSYCHOLOGICAL RESEARCH PAPERS

Source	Advantages	Disadvantages
Google	✓ Free to access and easy to use	✗ Anyone can upload information ✗ Quality/accuracy is not checked by an independent expert in the field
Wikipedia	✓ Free to access and easy to use ✓ Can be helpful for very simple facts, but always verify information	✗ Anyone can contribute to a wiki ✗ Often contains errors or omissions ✗ Constantly changing and updated
Google Scholar	✓ Free to access ✓ Gives easy links to PDFs where they are available	✗ Searching difficult and unclear ✗ Can give unreliable sources (e.g., student essays, non-reviewed research)
PubMed	✓ Free to access ✓ Search facilities easy and logical ✓ Links to publisher website (PDFs)	✗ Not all journals are indexed, and this search engine is mainly for medical research, so sources may be missed
PsychInfo	✓ Search engine is quite flexible with a range of options to select between ✓ Links to institutional access for PDFs	✗ Can only access it if the institution you are at subscribes (it is quite expensive!) ✗ Not all journals indexed by PsychInfo
Science Direct Scopus	✓ Free to access, but for abstracts only ✓ Easy access to full text, but only with an institutional subscription.	✗ Can only access full text and PDFs if you have an institutional subscription ✗ Search facilities relatively limited
Web of Knowledge	✓ Sophisticated and flexible search engine ✓ Only indexes peer reviewed sources, so any information you find can be trusted ✓ Links to publisher website (PDFs)	✗ As with PsychInfo, you need an institutional subscription to access WoK

(Weaker sources → Stronger sources)

Figure 3.5: Different ways of finding psychological research, and the advantages and disadvantages of each one.

When you search for psychological research, you really want to use a source that will only return to you pieces of published psychological academic work that you can trust and use with confidence. There are a number of different search services that will allow you to do this, and you can see some of these in Figure 3.5. Which ones you can and should use might vary according to the university you are studying at, as many of them cost a great deal to subscribe to. Google Scholar is free to use, however it can return some potentially unreliable sources (e.g. unpublished student work), and the search functionality is not too sophisticated and not always useful. PubMed is also freely available to use and only indexes, or includes, properly published research, but it focuses on more medical research, so some sources of psychological research are not included.

Indexing services such as PsychInfo, Science Direct, and Web of Knowledge are probably the most reliable sources when searching for psychological research, and I would strongly recommend only using these when you are searching for psychological research. However you will need to access these through your institution's library pages to access their full functionality. All of these work in similar ways: by entering information such as keywords, author names, and dates of publication into a search engine. You then get a big long list of 'hits', which are pieces of published research that match your criteria.

Within these searches you are usually only given the abstract of the paper, the short summary that is always given at the beginning of a paper. From this you need to decide whether the paper is relevant enough for you to want to read the full research paper. Psychological research papers are published in journals, and many of them charge the reader to access the full paper. Most universities pay subscription fees to the vast majority of the journals, so as long as you access the papers through your institutional library website or if your computer is connected to your institution's network, you should be able to access most psychological research papers without having to pay.

Hints and tips to help you find psychological research

Exactly how you search for psychological research varies slightly according to the indexing service that you use. Most university library services provide training on how to use each individual service, but there are some hints and tips that will help to you find the psychological research that you need to include in your own psychological research reports. If you simply take the keywords from the topic of your assignment, and stick them into the search engine, then you are likely to only find a small amount of the relevant research. There are a number of techniques you can use to help widen your search, which you can see in Table 3.4.

When you are searching for psychological research, you want to follow a systematic process to ensure that you find as much of the relevant research as possible. This process is summarised in Figure 3.6. First, you need to brainstorm as many different keywords as possible, and then think about how you can combine these to maximise the possible number of hits that you get. You can see some examples of these at the bottom of Table 3.4. You may need to run a few different searches to be confident that you have found a sufficient amount of the relevant published research.

Once you have run a search in one of the suggested indexing services, you will have a large number of potentially relevant papers. But not all will be of interest to you, so you need to work through the list and identify the papers that you might be interested in reading and using for your piece of work. As mentioned earlier, you are likely to only see the abstract summary of the paper, so using this you should decide whether the paper is relevant enough for you to look for and access the full paper. For example, does a paper build on the theory that you are interested in, or do they use the same questionnaire that you plan to use, or have they conducted research on the same key variables?

If you find a highly relevant paper, you could use this to look for more related research. Every published piece of research will cite a large number of older research papers in their introductions and discussions. It is quite possible that some of these could be relevant for your own work. You can usually find all of the papers that are listed in the references section of a paper at the click of a button that will say something like 'cited references'. One difficulty with this strategy is that you are always moving backwards in time and looking at older resources. Remember that psychology is a contemporary subject and research is published every day, so you want to ensure you are also looking for the most recently published relevant research.

FINDING PSYCHOLOGICAL RESEARCH PAPERS

Table 3.4: Techniques to help with searching for psychological research papers.

Hints for searching for papers		Example searches
*	The asterisk wildcard can be added to the end of partial words and will return all words that start with the same initial string of letters.	**recogni*** Will return sources including the keywords: recognition, recognise, recognize, recognised, recognized, recognising, recognizing, etc.
OR	Will allow you to search for two alternative terms. They usually need to be contained within brackets and must be capitalised.	**(emotion OR expression)** Will return sources including either 'emotion' or 'expression' keywords.
AND	Will return only sources that contain all of the keywords. Again, they usually need to be contained within brackets and must be capitalised.	**(development AND facial)** Will return sources including *both* 'development' *and* 'facial' keywords.
" "	If phrases are contained within speech marks, the search will only return that exact phrase.	**"emotional expression recognition"** Will return sources only if they contain this exact phrase, with these three words, spelt in this way, and written in this order.
Examples of combining search techniques:		Emoti* AND recogni* (ageing OR aging) AND "cognitive decline"

Most of the searching index services allow you to see a list of all the more recently published papers that have cited the paper you are interested in, and there will be a button called something like 'Citing Articles' that will show you all of these.

Having searched for all of the relevant previous research, identified the most highly relevant sources and located the PDFs of the full papers, you will be ready to read about this research and use it in your own work. Remember, though, how important it is to always think critically about psychological research.

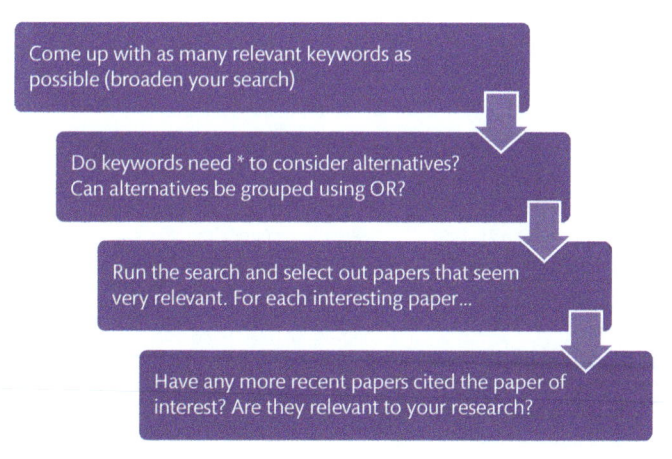

Figure 3.6: The suggested process for searching for published psychological research papers.

Thinking critically: how good is this research?

It is really important to acknowledge that no research is ever perfect. This is true for all research, from the research that you will conduct as a student through to the research that is published by top professors in the best journals. Being able to think critically about research is a vital skill to develop, both for understanding the research of others, but also to critique and evaluate your own work. When you are writing about your own research, or reading about the research of others, try to look at the list of questions in Table 3.5. In the left hand panel are ten key questions to try to answer when reading the published research of others. These questions can help to guide your reading and understanding of a piece of research. In the right hand panel are some questions to prompt your critical analysis of the research. With this crib sheet you should be able to tackle understanding and criticizing any piece of published research, but you can also try to answer these questions for your own research reports to help strengthen and develop your own research skills.

Thinking critically about design: potential confounds

In Chapter 2 we discussed various aspects of methodological design that you should think about when critically evaluating a piece of research. Potential confounding variables that are not measured within the design are often discussed when critiquing a paper. In psychological research there are often many confounding variables, and whilst researchers may strive to measure and control for some co-variables, there are often unmeasured confounds that could have influenced the findings of a piece of research. What additional confounds do you think could be relevant within the design? It is important not to simply list a whole lot of potential confounds, but instead think carefully about just one or two that could be

Table 3.5: Key questions to ask yourself when thinking critically about psychological research.

Reading psychological research	Thinking critically about research
1. What is the most important previous work presented in the introduction? 2. What are the main hypotheses? 3. Why is this research important? 4. How is this research novel and new? 5. Did the researchers use appropriate measurements and procedures? 6. What type of research design was used? 7. What were the variables in the study? 8. What were the key findings of the research and statistical analyses? 9. Do the statistical findings justify the authors' conclusions? 10. What are the limitations, and do they make you believe or trust the researchers' findings less?	Think about the introduction: • Does the previous research justify the current study? Are the predictions logical? • Are any major areas of previous research not included or misinterpreted? Think about the methods and results: • How good are the methods? Are they valid and reliable? Are there better alternatives and why? • Do you agree with the method of analysis and the interpretation of the results? Think about the discussion: • Are results explained in terms of previous research? • Are the effects of possible confounds considered? • Can criticism of the methods (e.g. selection of participant/materials) explain findings?

relevant and really consider how these might have influenced the findings of the research study.

Thinking critically about design: validity and reliability

Validity and reliability are key issues to consider when thinking critically about research. Can the materials used in the design of the study be criticised for lacking construct validity or might there be a problem with inter-rater reliability? You might also want to consider the sample that was recruited and the way in which participants were recruited. Be careful here though as much psychological research is conducted using opportunity sampling from undergraduate psychology students. Try to think about whether this is really likely to impact on the findings of the research. For example, if the sample comprises 80% females, is there a well-documented sex difference in the psychological process that is being studied? If there is then the results could have been biased by this sampling. If there isn't, then it is unlikely the results would have been affected and this point would be a weaker critique point.

Think critically about your critique!

We have already considered how to think through the logic of a critique point earlier in this chapter when we talked about how to consider a weakness of your own research in the discussion section of a research report. The guide on how to do this in Box 3.1 is an excellent way to frame and guide your critical thinking about the research of others, as well as your own research. A really important point is to not just identify a critical point (e.g., the questionnaire lacks internal consistency, the sample was biased, age could be a confound), but to fully consider exactly how it might influence the findings of the research. Remember that no research is perfect, and that each piece of research should propose and lead onto the next study. Therefore critical thinking should not just be about critiquing a study, but about using this to further develop the research that is done within the area of research.

How is research published? The publishing process

I've said a couple of time through this chapter that, when you are writing a psychological research report, you should be aiming to write something that looks like and has the style of a published piece of psychological research. Through a psychology degree, academics are aiming to develop students into researchers, and this culminates with the final year research project. Sometimes these projects can be published, and therefore it is not unfeasible that your own research could be published one day.

As a student, once you have finished writing your research report that is pretty much the end of the process. However, published research has to go through far more before it appears in print. All published research first has to go through the **peer review** process. Once the paper has been written it is submitted to a journal that publishes research in the general area of interest. The editor of the journal then reads the paper and decides whether it fits within the general scope of the journal. If it doesn't then the paper is rejected and sent back to the author. They might then try to submit the paper for publication at a different journal.

If the editor decides that the topic of the paper is suitable, then they will ask two or three academics, who are experts in that area of research, to review the paper. Each reviewer will read the paper very critically and will produce a report, which can be anything from one paragraph to several pages, which highlights the strengths and potential weakness of the paper. This is where they really use all the critical thinking skills we have discussed in this chapter! They also give the editor a recommendation regarding the publication of the paper: accept with no revisions (this very, very rarely happens), accept with minor revisions (only very occasionally happens), revise and resubmit, or reject with no option for resubmission.

The editor then looks at the paper, the reviews and the recommendations of the reviewers, and makes their own decision regarding the paper. If resubmission is an option, then the author must revise their paper to the satisfaction of the reviewers, and write a letter explaining exactly how they have revised their manuscript and how this addresses the reviewers' concerns. Once the paper has been resubmitted the same reviewers usually look at the manuscript a second time and decide whether it is ready for publication, whether some further revisions are needed, or whether it should be rejected.

You can therefore see that the published research you read about has been through many rounds of revision and improvement in response to the critical thinking of other academics. Yet, still, published research is not perfect. This is really important to bear in mind when you read and think about research. There is no such thing as a 'perfect' piece of research. The important thing is that you design the study in such a way that you have the strongest methodology you can develop, you analyse the data appropriately, you report it accurately and completely, and you should show an awareness of the limitations of your research and the implications of these weakness for your findings. If you achieve all of these, then you should feel quite confident in your skills as a researcher, and this is what we are aiming to achieve in this book!

Study questions

1. You need to search for literature to write up a research report on colour perception in babies. Suggest three different combined search techniques that you could use to conduct this literature search. You might find it helpful to look back at Table 3.4 when completing this task.
2. You have conducted a study looking at cognitive decline in two groups of older adults. One group regularly use supplements that are supposed to help maintain cognitive abilities, whereas the other group do not use them. A possible criticism of the study is that the two groups could differ in terms of their level of education, but you did not collect these data. Using the suggested structure in Box 3.1, write a paragraph to discuss this weakness.
3. Below is a short references list that contains three papers on the psychological aspects of studying. For each one, identify the errors in APA citation formatting.
    3.1 Cassady, Jerrell. C. (2004). The influence of cognitive test anxiety across the learning-testing cycle. *Learning and instruction*, *14(6)*, 569–592.
    3.2 Moneta, G. B., Spada, M. M., & Rost, F. M. (July, 2007). Approaches to studying when preparing for final exams as a function of coping strategies. *Personality and Individual Differences*, *43(1)*, 191.

3.3 Komarraju, M., Ramsey, A., and Rinella, V. (2013). Cognitive and non-cognitive predictors of college readiness and performance: Role of academic discipline. <u>Learning and Individual Differences</u>, *24*, 103–109.

Wider reading

Publication Manual of the American Psychological Association (6th ed.) (2010). Washington, D.C.: American Psychological Association.
The key source for writing up psychological research papers is the APA publication manual. However, it is written more for academics who wish to publish their research, and therefore it is rarely actually used by students. If you are particularly interested in taking a look at it, then the reference is below. A far more digestible way to find out about the APA recommendations is to take a look at their APA style website, where there is lots of information available: www.apastyle.org

Braun, V., & Clarke, V. (2013). *Successful qualitative research: A practical guide for beginners*. Sage.
The conventions for writing up a qualitative research report can be somewhat different to the overview provided in this chapter. To find out more about writing qualitative reports, you can take a look at Chapter 13 of this book:

http://researchtheheadlines.org/
Unless you are studying psychology, you are most likely to find out about psychological research through journalistic reports, either online, in newspapers or magazines. Unfortunately very few journalists are properly trained in how to read and think critically about research, and therefore these reports are often inaccurate. This is an excellent website that looks at research that is discussed in the media and compares the reports to the actual published work. Reading these pieces is an excellent way of further developing your critical thinking skills, and the site has a really helpful section of 'How To' tips.

http://io9.com/i-fooled-millions-into-thinking-chocolate-helps-weight-1707251800
This has to be my favourite tale of psychological research ever. In 2015 there was a massive amount of press attention, all around the world, on a study that provided evidence that eating chocolate helps you to lose weight. Yup, slimming by eating chocolate! Unfortunately the whole thing was a hoax. Yes, a research study was conducted, significant results were found and it was published, but it was intentionally and horrifically flawed in many ways. The aim was to highlight some of the issues that occur with the conducting of research and the representation of research in the media. It is a great illustration of why you should always have your critical thinking cap on, and don't blindly trust the reported findings of research projects. You can read all about how they did it on their website.

For full answers to study questions, and to explore a range of other materials, including examples of good and bad lab reports, visit the online resources at:
www.oup.com/uk/bourne/

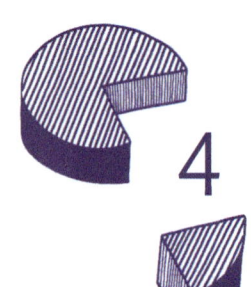

4 Qualitative methods in psychological research

> **In this chapter you will learn...**
> - How qualitative and quantitative approaches to research are both similar and different
> - Methodological issues to consider when conducting a qualitative research study
> - The main types of qualitative analysis and when to use each one
> - How to conduct a simple Thematic Analysis

Introduction

The majority of this book, and a great deal of psychological research, is quantitative in nature. When we design a piece of **quantitative research** we aim to collect and analyse numeric data to help us understand psychological processes. Although quantitative methods are frequently used, it is really important to remember they are not the only approaches to understanding psychological phenomena. **Qualitative methods** move away from the strict use of only numbers as a form of data, and instead consider and analyse rich qualitative datasets that mainly contain words, such as interviews or online forum discussions. In the past, qualitative and quantitative approaches have been set up as vastly differing approaches that are in opposition to each other. Luckily most psychological researchers nowadays see the two types of psychological research design as complementary. Each approach allows us to ask questions about psychological processes in a different way, and there are a growing number of researchers who now combine both qualitative and quantitative methods within a single research study to gain a fuller understanding of the issues they are interested in.

Comparing qualitative and quantitative methods

Qualitative and quantitative research take quite different approaches in a number of ways, and you can see these summarised in Figure 4.1. Qualitative research is far more exploratory and open-ended than quantitative research. It tends to ask and explore questions, rather than test specific variables and hypotheses. It is **naturalistic**, in that it aims to understand psychological phenomena in a naturally occurring setting, whereas quantitative research tends to

COMPARING QUALITATIVE AND QUANTITATIVE METHODS

Qualitative research	Quantitative research
Naturalistic	Manipulative
Inductive	Deductive
Subjective	Objective
Research questions	Hypothesis testing
Mainly word based data	Numeric data

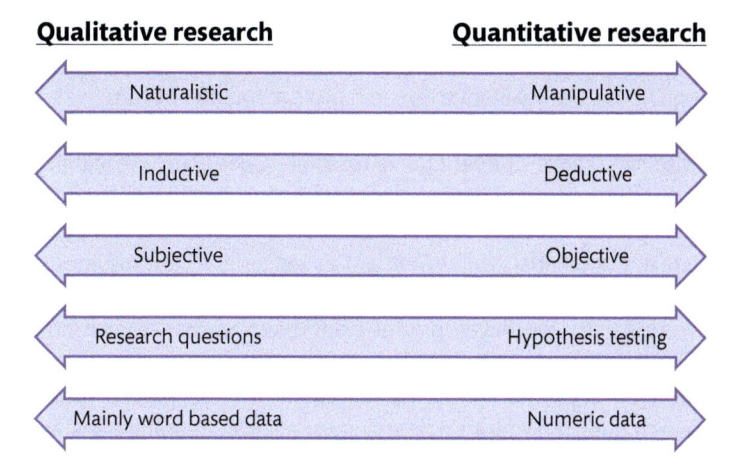

Figure 4.1: Highlighting the different approaches of qualitative and quantitative research.

manipulate psychological phenomena in order to further understand them. Qualitative research is also **inductive** (or bottom up) in nature. This means that the collection and analysis of the qualitative data occurs before the development of possible explanations of constructs or the generation of a theory about psychological processes. This is in complete contrast to quantitative research, which is **deductive** (or top down) in nature. This means that the research process begins with the development of a theory, uses this theory to specify a prediction and then the data are used to either reject the hypothesis or not. **Subjective** meanings are also important within qualitative research, either in terms of understanding the views of participants or the researcher's interpretation.

Qualitative research can be used to answer a wide range of questions about psychological processes, and it provides a high quality understanding of some topics that cannot be understood using quantitative methods. Having said that, as it is far more exploratory and open ended, it can be helpful during the earlier phases of quantitative research that aim to understand a particular phenomenon. One of the ways in which qualitative studies can be used is to generate theories. These theories might subsequently be explored with qualitative or quantitative methods. Qualitative research can also be used to provide a more detailed examination of phenomena identified in quantitative research. For example, a quantitative piece of research might provide some interesting numeric data, but to really understand why some people gain higher scores whilst others have lower scores, a qualitative study might be necessary.

Both qualitative and quantitative methods are essential to having a fuller understanding of the way that people think, feel, and behave. Each has its own advantages and disadvantages. The most important thing is to select the most appropriate method to address the area of research that you are interested in. Neither is better or worse than the other (although some people try to argue that they are!), but rather each is uniquely suited to different areas of psychological research. Mixed methods, used in studies where both qualitative and quantitative approaches are used, are becoming far more frequently used in contemporary psychological research, and it is perhaps in combining these two complementary approaches that we can best understand psychological phenomena.

Framing research questions

When you design and run a qualitative research project you first need to clearly define your **research question**. A qualitative research question is very different to the **hypothesis** that you would devise for a piece of quantitative research. Quantitative research occurs within the process of hypothesis testing. On the basis of previous research and theories you design a study, with carefully defined variables, to test a very specific hypothesis or prediction, collect the numeric data and then analyse it. Whether you get a significant result or not will determine whether you accept or reject your hypothesis.

In qualitative research, you develop a research question that is far more open-ended than that which will be explored through the qualitative design. There is no specific hypothesis or prediction, but a phenomenon that you wish to investigate and understand. The qualitative research question should still be quite specific in defining the aims of the study. The question often starts with 'how' or 'what' and should clearly identify the issue that is being explored.

For example, imagine that we are interested in why some people make more charitable donations than others. If I were to design a quantitative study I might ask participants how much they donate to charity each year and then ask them to complete a standardised selflessness questionnaire. I could then look at whether there is a correlation between these two variables, and I might predict that there will be a positive correlation, whereby people who are more selfless will donate more money to charity. In contrast, if I were to design a qualitative study, I might decide to collect data from charity workers who are heavily involved in fundraising in order to explore the research question: Why do they think that some people donate more to charities than others?

Sources of data for qualitative analysis

When you conduct qualitative research, there are a wide range of sources from which you can gather data. With methods such as **interviews**, **focus groups** or **observational studies** you actively collect your own dataset. In contrast, qualitative analyses can also be conducted on pre-existing datasets, such as online forums, social media, newspaper and magazine articles, or historical records.

Interviews are the most frequently used method within qualitative research, and they can be either **semi-structured** or **unstructured**. Of these two types of interview, the semi-structured interview is the more common. With a semi-structured interview the researcher has a small set of questions, clearly related to the research question, that they can use to guide the interview. However, it is important to note that it is a guide that does not have to be rigidly followed. It is possible to skip questions, change the order in which questions are asked, or to ask additional questions if a participant raises something particularly interesting or unexpected. In contrast, the unstructured interview has no pre-defined questions, just broad topics that the researcher wishes to discuss. You may also occasionally come across structured interview, where the questions are set and there is no deviation from the planned questions. These interviews are less frequent in psychological research, but are used quite commonly in market research.

Methodological issues when running qualitative studies

When you design and run a qualitative psychological study, many of the methodological issues are similar to those that you will encounter in quantitative studies, such as those outlined in Chapter 2. However, there are some key issues to highlight that can be particularly important to bear in mind when designing and running a qualitative study.

Sampling for qualitative research

Qualitative research studies tend to have smaller samples than quantitative studies, and therefore your method of sampling is particularly important. For example, you need to pay close attention to the way in which you recruit your sample. Qualitative research can be concerned with quite small and specific populations of participants (e.g. nurses working in a children's hospital, people recently divorced), so you need to ensure that the way in which you select your sample accurately reflects the population of interest. As a result, sampling for qualitative studies is often purposive, in that it actively aims to recruit particular types of participants. This is in contrast to sampling for quantitative studies, which aims to recruit participants that are more broadly representative of a wider population.

Validity and reliability in qualitative research

You also need to think carefully about how to ensure both **validity** and **reliability** within a qualitative design. We discussed a range of issues around validity and reliability in Chapter 2, so you might find it helpful to look back at that section to revise the key issues. Qualitative analysis is interpretative and therefore subjective in nature, however a qualitative researcher should aim to accurately reflect the data that they are analysing to maintain validity. It is important, though, that the researcher acknowledges that there are individual biases that can influence their analysis and interpretation of a qualitative dataset. Qualitative analysis can be somewhat messy, and there is no correct solution, but it is important to strive for an accurate analysis of what participants have said. One way to help with this issue is to have more than one person analysing the qualitative data, but then you need to think about inter-rater reliability (whether the different researchers are analysing the data in the same way) and consider how you can evaluate this within a qualitative design.

Ethics and qualitative research

Finally, the same **ethical guidelines** apply to both quantitative and qualitative research. We discussed these in detail in Chapter 1 if you need a quick recap. For either approach you should be thinking about how to conduct an ethical study when designing the study, when collecting all of your data, and when analysing and presenting your findings. However, with qualitative research there are some issues that you should pay particular attention to. If your project is in relation to a sensitive topic, then when collecting data you need to be constantly vigilant that every participant is protected from any **possible harm**.

For example, imagine you are conducting an unstructured interview on women's safety on university campuses. Every question you ask is likely to differ and to not be planned in advance, and therefore it is possible that a question could be upsetting if one of your participants has had a bad experience. You would then need to think very carefully about the next question you ask and how to word it. If you are working with participants in a group setting, such as with a focus group, you need to pay close attention to the dynamic and interactions between participants in case one participant upsets another. For example, you could be running focus groups about attitudes towards immigration, but within the group you have one participant who is an immigrant and another who has strong opinions against immigration. A qualitative researcher really needs to think on their feet when collecting data to ensure that participants are treated ethically. For this reason the data collection for qualitative research on sensitive topics would usually only be conducted by quite experienced qualitative researchers.

It is also important to think about **confidentiality** and how to maintain the **anonymity** of the participants in a qualitative piece of research. When qualitative research is written up, it is important to include sample quotations from the collected data. In many qualitative publications, when it is necessary to distinguish between different participants, each person is typically referred to by their initials or using a pseudonym. However, you also need to think carefully about the quotes that you select and whether the information that they contain might contain potentially identifying information. This is particularly important if your research is interested in a very small, specific and easily identifiable population. For example, if you have selected your sample from first year psychology students at a particular university, and all of this information is given in the methods of the paper, giving a quote from a participant who you identify as 'the only gay male in the first year' would identify that participant without actually naming them.

What types of qualitative analysis are there?

There are a number of different qualitative methodologies that can be adopted to analyse the data collected from a qualitative study. Broadly speaking, they all take a similar approach in that they consider all of the data available, and then synthesise it to identify the key categories and themes to emerge. For each type of analysis, there is an example of a published piece of research that has used that method of analysis in the Wider Reading for this chapter. These are explained within each of the following sections.

Thematic Analysis

Thematic Analysis is one of the key qualitative approaches to data analysis, and it focuses on identifying and analysing the themes within a dataset. A theme is a recurring issue that is identified from within the entire dataset. There are six key phases to conducting a Thematic Analysis, and these are very clearly explained in a paper by Braun and Clarke (2006), which you will find in the Wider Reading section of this chapter. Through a process of interpretation, analysis and refinement, the researcher identifies themes within a qualitative dataset. An example of how to conduct a Thematic Analysis is given later in this chapter.

Attard and Coulson (2012) used Thematic Analysis to consider the ways in which individuals with Parkinson's disease communicate with each other online. Their analysis identified six different themes within the communications, three of which were positive and three were negative. The positive themes were around sharing information and experiences, gaining support from a peer group, and aiding positive thinking. The negative themes came from a lack of responses, sometimes due to symptoms preventing the use of the forum, members leaving the forum, and misunderstandings.

Grounded Theory

Grounded Theory is similar to Thematic Analysis in that it attempts to draw out themes (also sometimes called categories in Grounded Theory) from the qualitative dataset, but the approach is somewhat different. The aim is to use the emerging themes to develop a theory. Importantly Grounded Theory occurs over multiple iterations of data collection and analysis to fully understand the emerging themes and to guide the development of the theory. For example, a theme may emerge that the researcher wants to find out more about, so they might conduct a second interview with the participants or they could interview a new set of participants to explore this further. They repeat the cycle of data collection and analysis until all of the themes have been exhausted and they can derive a clear theory from their analysis.

Grounded Theory was used by Lovell (2016) to examine how parents from low income families receive and understand information about child health and nutrition. They initially interviewed parents from sixteen different families, but importantly, whilst they were analysing the data they conducted follow-up interviews to gain further insight and clarification. They identified one key theme of culture and context, and within that there were a number of themes, such as parental values (e.g. viewing food as a symbol of love) and parental engagement (e.g. evaluating whether to trust information).

Interpretative Phenomenological Analysis

Interpretative Phenomenological Analysis (IPA) is rather more focused than both Thematic Analysis and Grounded Theory in that it concentrates on understanding the particular experiences of a particular group of participants, in relation to a particular phenomenon. Whereas Thematic Analysis aims more broadly to describe the themes within the qualitative dataset, IPA is far more interpretative, often including fewer participants, but examining their data in greater depth. As such IPA is primarily concerned with exploring how individuals perceive and make sense of situations. Consequently it is usually interested in recruiting a sample from a small and very specific population. IPA is often used in clinical and health psychology research, to understand the experiences of, for example, a particular group of patients who are receiving the same experimental treatment at a particular clinic. The analysis itself still focuses on identifying themes within the dataset, but the way in which they are extracted and interpreted always concentrates on understanding the individual's subjective experience.

IPA was used by Epstein and Ogden (2005) to look at GPs' views towards the treatment of obesity. Using semi-structured interviews, data were collected from 130 GPs who all worked for the same inner London Trust. An overarching theme within the discussion surrounded responsibility, and whether the main responsibility was on the patient, as GPs feel, or on the medical professionals, as patients feel. The differing views on who is responsible for their obesity were identified as being a key sourceof conflict between GPs and patients, and possible ways of dealing with this conflict were identified by the GPs.

Discourse Analysis

Discourse Analysis differs from the previous qualitative approaches in that it is interested in more than just the spoken words that a participant uses, instead it examines the way people communicate, either in written or spoken form. In addition to analysing the words used, it analyses a wide range of 'discourse markers' such as pauses in speech, umm's and ahh's, or changes in intonation (e.g. getting louder). Discourse Analysis is also concerned with the way that language is used when people are communicating with each other and the verbal and non-verbal interactions that occur, such as turn taking and interactions. As such, it aims to identify how individuals construct meaning through examining their communications with others.

McKinney (2014) used Discourse Analysis to examine interactions within foster families. They observed two families over four months and then used Discourse Analysis to understand the interactions between individuals. In the analysis of these interactions, it was concluded that were different definitions of 'winners' (e.g. doing well at a school test) and 'losers' (e.g. doing badly at a school test) between the foster child and the family that they were living with. This then led to misunderstandings, frustration and conflict.

An overview of Thematic Analysis

Thematic Analysis (TA) is one of the core qualitative methods, and it is also relatively simple and straightforward, so in this section we will run through a brief example of how to conduct a Thematic Analysis. Luckily there is a fantastic paper that really clearly sets out one approach to Thematic Analysis, how to do it, and some of the difficulties that you can encounter when doing a TA. This paper, by Braun and Clarke (2006) is in the Wider Reading of this chapter and well worth a read if you are interested in learning more about Thematic Analysis.

For this example we will be using a Thematic Analysis to examine two short extracts from fictional interviews with students. The research question is: How do students approach academics for support during their studies? The excerpts are in response to the question 'Can you tell me about a time you asked an academic a question when preparing to write an essay?' and you can see them in Figure 4.2. It important to note that you would usually conduct a Thematic Analysis across a number of participants and their responses to a number of questions. So this example is really just a brief illustration of the key stages of how to conduct a Thematic Analysis.

To conduct a Thematic Analysis you need to go through six different phases, as outlined by Braun and Clarke (2006). You can see each of these phases in Figure 4.3, and we will work our way through each of these phases now. Before doing so, it is important to briefly mention the importance of reflexivity throughout the analysis process. That is, that it is important to always be aware of how the researcher, and their interactions with the participants, may influence the analysis. To avoid this, some researchers keep a reflexive journal whilst they are analysing the data to keep a record of any possible times in the analysis process where bias might have occurred.

AN OVERVIEW OF THEMATIC ANALYSIS

Excerpt 1
Oh, I often ask questions. I want to make sure that, you know, I totally get everything before I start writing. Normally I email. It's easier than trying to get to an office hour, and the answer is written down so I can go back to it. I don't like using the forums. What if I'm asking a really stupid question? If I still don't get things I might go to an office hour. Like for the last lab report, I just couldn't get the analysis so I needed to show the lecturer my calculations.

Excerpt 2
I don't! Some people do seem to ask loads of questions, you know, the geeks that queue up to speak to the lecturer at the end of a class? I'm not with that crowd. Rather grab a coffee after a lecture to wake up properly. The deadline is on a Monday so I usually start on it over the weekend, and my lecturers never check their email then. I could go on the forums, but then I'll look like the idiot who left it until the last minute. Besides, I usually get it enough to do a decent enough assignment. I've not failed anything yet anyway!

Figure 4.2: Two excerpts from a semi-structured interview to be analysed using Thematic Analysis.

Phase 1: Familiarise yourself with the data
Transcribe your data (if necessary), read through the data and make any initial notes

⬇

Phase 2: Generate initial codes
Highlight interesting features systematically and identify initial codes

⬇

Phase 3: Search for themes
Group codes together within broader themes

⬇

Phase 4: Review the themes
Refine themes by looking back at your data, codes and themes

⬇

Phase 5: Define and name themes
Give each theme a clear, short and easy to understand name

⬇

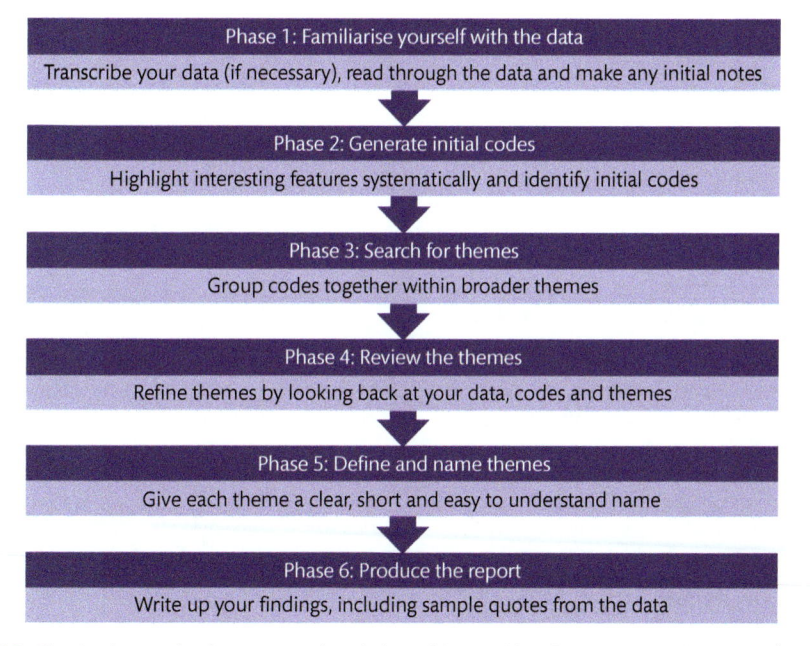

Phase 6: Produce the report
Write up your findings, including sample quotes from the data

Figure 4.3: The six phases of a Thematic Analysis (adapted from Table 1 from Braun & Clarke, 2006).

Phase 1: Familiarise yourself with the data

You will need your data in an easy format to read and work with. If you are working with existing text data, such as from newspaper articles or online forums, the data will already be in an easy format for you to analyse. However, if you have recorded the data from focus groups or interviews, then you will first need to transcribe your data. It is really important that this is done as accurately as possible, and you can include nonverbal aspects, such as pauses or coughs. There are different ways of identifying these within a transcript, and some of these conventions are explained in the paper by Bailey in the Wider Reading of this chapter. Once the data have been transcribed it is useful to listen back through the audio files to check the accuracy of the transcription. You should then read through the data, possibly a number of times, until you feel comfortably familiar with it. It can also be helpful to make some initial notes during this phase. You can see the transcriptions of the two experts that we will be analysing in Figure 4.2.

Phase 2: Generate initial codes

Once you are familiar with your data, you need to identify some initial **codes** within the data. These codes should identify key things that are raised within the text. An easy way to do this is to simply highlight the interesting elements, and then describe them, as simply as you can (whilst always keeping in mind that you are approaching this as a psychologist presenting research to other psychologists). In Table 4.1 you can see some initial interesting comments from the excerpts underlined in the left hand column, and the codes described in the right hand column. The way that each individual researcher identifies the codes within the data can

Table 4.1: Generating initial codes in a Thematic Analysis.

Oh, I <u>often</u> ask questions. I want to make sure that, you know, I totally get everything <u>before I start writing</u>.	Often asks for help Planning in advance
Normally I <u>email</u>. It's easier than trying to get to an office hour, and the <u>answer is written down so I can go back to it</u>.	Preferred method of approach—email Able to revisit answer
I <u>don't like using the forums</u>. What if I'm <u>asking a really stupid question?</u>	Prefer anonymity Fear of negative perceptions by peers, looking 'stupid'
If I still don't get things I might go to an <u>office hour</u>. Like for the last lab report, I just couldn't get the analysis so I needed to show the lecturer my calculations.	Office hour as a last resort
I don't! <u>Some people</u> do seem to ask loads of questions, you know, <u>the geeks</u> that queue up to speak to the lecturer at the end of a class?	Group norms Negative perception of help seekers
<u>I'm not with that crowd</u>. Rather grab a coffee after a lecture to wake up properly. The deadline is on a Monday so I usually <u>start on it over the weekend</u>, and my lecturers <u>never check their email then</u>. I could go on the forums, but then <u>I'll look like the idiot</u> who left it until the last minute. Besides, I usually get it enough to do a decent enough assignment.	Identifying different social groups Last minute preparation style Help seeking doesn't work last minute Fear of negative perceptions by peers, being an 'idiot'
I've <u>not failed anything yet</u> anyway!	Impact on grades

differ, so you may identify different codes within the text, or you may label them differently to how I have. Remember that the codes are just ways of identifying key information within the transcript. In the next phase of the analysis these will be analysed and combined to develop the emerging themes within this dataset.

Phase 3: Search for themes

With the initial codes all generated, you now need to look through them all and try to identify some common **themes** across them. You can group together the initial codes and show how they link to the themes with an initial thematic map, like the one in Figure 4.4. Remember to bear in mind the research question that you are trying to address when identifying these codes. All of the initial codes should be included within this map, even if they seem irrelevant. You will refine the themes in the next phase of the analysis. It can also be helpful to identify subthemes within each theme if there are some codes that seem to belong together.

In this initial thematic map there seems to be two interlinked themes around the social aspects of the student's attitudes towards approaching academics for support. There is then a separate theme that is more about different studying styles and the impact that these can have on the student's studying and grades.

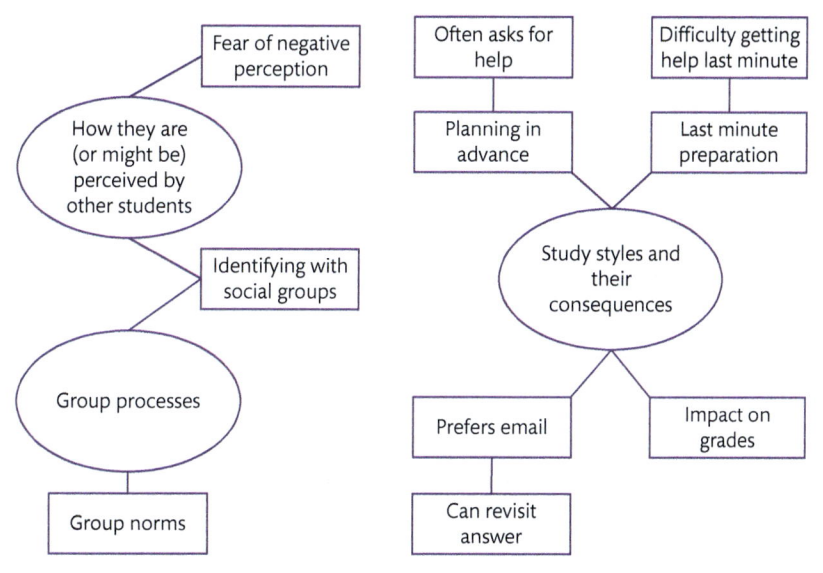

Figure 4.4: Initial thematic map showing the codes (in squares) linked to different initial themes (in circles).

Phase 4: Review the themes

You now need to review your themes and sub-themes, which you can do by re-reading the data and looking at your codes and themes within the initial thematic map. At this stage you might want to combine similar themes, remove themes that do not have enough data to

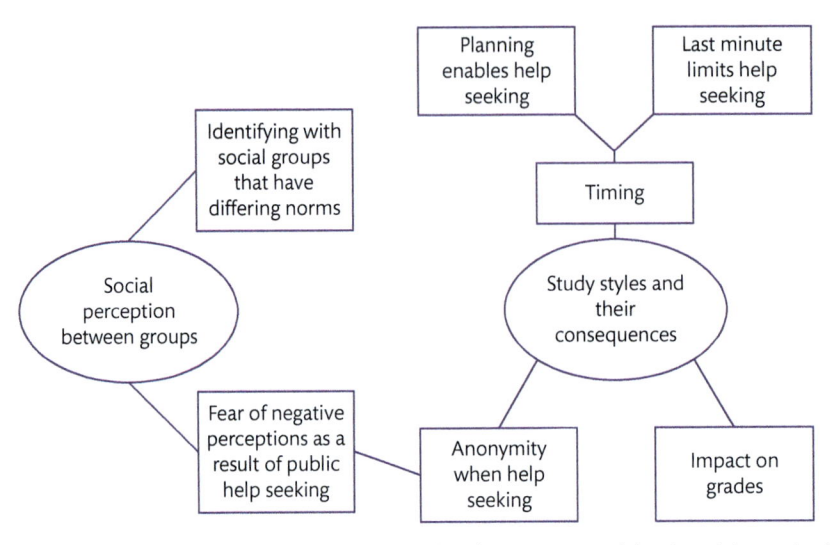

Figure 4.5: Developed thematic map showing developed codes in squares and developed themes in circles.

support them, or change the names of themes to better reflect the raw data. You can see the final thematic map for our data in Figure 4.5.

In this final map I have removed some of the codes that did not occur frequently across the entire dataset, such as having difficulty getting help at the last minute. I have combined the two more socially-oriented themes into one overarching theme as the social aspects of seeking support came up quite frequently, but in an overlapping way that made it difficult to clearly distinguish two different social elements. Impact on grades was a recurring theme, both with positive and negative elements, and there were clearly two different approaches that linked to help-seeking as a result of timing: preparing in advance and asking for help and advice, or last minute work that precludes the option of asking for additional help. One element seemed to link the two themes which was a desire to ask for support in an anonymous way. This had both study style and social perception aspects.

Phase 5: Defining and naming themes

Now that you have clearly identified the themes and sub-themes that have emerged from your data, you need to name them, define them and make it clear how each of the themes are distinct. The name of each one should be a clear and concise representation of the themes that you drew out of the data. You should also select out some quotes to illustrate each theme and sub-theme. In Table 4.2 you can see two quotes for each theme, selected from the two excerpts, that I feel clearly represent the two themes.

Phase 6: Produce the report

Once the Thematic Analysis is complete and you have identified the themes and sub-themes within your data you are ready to write up your report. In your report you need to clearly

Table 4.2: Illustrative quotes for each of the themes to have emerged from a Thematic Analysis.

Theme	Illustrative quotes
Social perception between groups	'I don't like using the forums. What if I'm asking a really stupid question?'
	'Some people do seem to ask loads of questions, you know, the geeks that queue up to speak to the lecturer at the end of a class? I'm not with that crowd.'
Study styles and their consequences	'I want to make sure that, you know, I totally get everything before I start writing.'
	'The deadline is on a Monday so I usually start on it over the weekend, and my lecturers never check their email then.'

explain the themes and sub-themes that you found within your data, in response to your research question. Your analysis should be supported by quotes to provide evidence for your identified themes and sub-themes.

Pluralism and mixed methods in psychological research

Analytical pluralism is an increasingly used approach in contemporary qualitative psychological research. The idea is to apply multiple analytical approaches to a single dataset in order to gain a range of perspectives on a question. Typically different qualitative approaches to data analysis are adopted, for example, Grounded Theory and IPA could be used to analyse a set of focus group transcripts about how people feel about the amount of chocolate that they eat and their experiences of trying to reduce their consumption.

The key way in which pluralism differs from mixed methods is that the multiple analyses that are conducted in a pluralistic study occur simultaneously, looking at one set of data in different ways and then attempting to integrate those findings. Additionally, pluralistic research tends to use multiple qualitative methods, although it can combine both qualitative and quantitative approaches. In contrast, **mixed methods** tend to be more sequential. So the research occurs in phases, one phase before the other, and each phase takes a different approach.

Intervention studies, studies that examine a treatment or attempt to change some form of behaviour, are an easy way to think about mixed methods approaches. Imagine that we want to develop an intervention to help chocolate addicts stop consuming chocolate. First we might run some focus groups with self-confessed chocoholics and analyse the data with a qualitative method to identify the key issues that drive the addiction and prevent people from easily 'quitting'.

From this an intervention can be developed, and the efficacy of the intervention could be evaluated experimentally with the collection of quantitative data before and after people take part in the intervention. For example, we could record the number of bars of chocolate eaten per day before and after the intervention and analyse the quantitative data to see whether there is a significant reduction in the amount of chocolate eaten.

An additional qualitative phase could also be added to this study to further examine why the intervention was more effective for some participants, and less effective for others. Using the quantitative data, we could classify people as either showing no reduction in chocolate consumption (intervention not effective) or showing a reduction in chocolate consumption (intervention effective). We could then run separate focus groups with each group, and analyse the data qualitatively with a view to understanding the different factors that determine why the intervention was effective for some people but not for others.

With this qualitative analysis we could further refine our intervention to treat chocolate addiction, and evaluate it with another quantitative experimental study. And so on, and so on, through repeated cycles of research using both qualitative and quantitative approaches, until chocolate addiction is finally cured forever!

Study questions

A researcher is interested in how athletes competing in the women's 100 metres race in the Paralympic Games prepare psychologically just before competing. There is very little known about this topic as the vast majority of the previous work has not looked at Paralympic competitors, and has typically only included male participants.

1. Imagine that you were to examine this research area in two different ways: as a quantitative piece of research and as a separate qualitative piece of research.
    1.1. Develop a hypothesis that you could test using a quantitative approach.
    1.2. Develop a research question that you could explore using a qualitative approach.
2. Which qualitative approach would you use to analyse the data collected in this study, and why is this particular approach most appropriate?
3. How would you ensure that this qualitative study was methodologically rigorous? In particular, think about and comment on:
    3.1 The representativeness of the sample
    3.2 Reliability and validity
    3.3 Ethical considerations

Wider reading

If you are interested in finding out more about qualitative research and analysis, then these are good starting points for further reading:

Madill, A. & Gough, B. (2008). Qualitative research and its place in psychological science. *Psychological Methods*, 13, 254–271.
   This is a really interesting paper that discusses the role of qualitative research within psychology as a scientific discipline, and includes some interesting consideration of the relative contributions of qualitative and quantitative approaches.

Smith, J. A. (Ed.). (2015). *Qualitative Psychology: A Practical Guide to Research Methods*. Sage.
   This is a good general textbook on qualitative approaches to psychological research.

Braun, V., & Clarke, V. (2006). Using thematic analysis in psychology. *Qualitative Research in Psychology*, *3*, 77–101.
    This paper gives a really clear overview of how to conduct Thematic Analysis and is the key guide to using this method.

Bailey, J. (2008) First steps in qualitative data analysis: transcribing. *Family Practice*; *25*, 127–131.
    If you want to transcribe some data, this is a very clear and simple guide, including information on how to code non-verbal information.

In this chapter we briefly discussed four different methods of qualitative analysis. The papers below show how each of these methods are used and presented in published research.

Attard, A., & Coulson, N. S. (2012). A thematic analysis of patient communication in Parkinson's disease online support group discussion forums. *Computers in Human Behavior*, *28*, 500–506.
    Thematic Analysis.

Lovell, J. (2016). How parents process child health and nutrition information: A grounded theory model. *Appetite*, *97*, 138–145.
    Grounded Theory.

Epstein, L., & Ogden, J. (2005). A qualitative study of GPs' views of treating obesity. *British Journal of General Practice*, *55*, 750–754.
    Interpretative Phenomenological Analysis.

McKinney, J. (2014). Speaking of self: 'Winners' and 'losers' in therapeutic foster care. *Children and Youth Services Review*, *39*, 84–90.
    Discourse Analysis.

For full answers to study questions, and to explore a range of other materials, visit the online resources at: **www.oup.com/uk/bourne/**

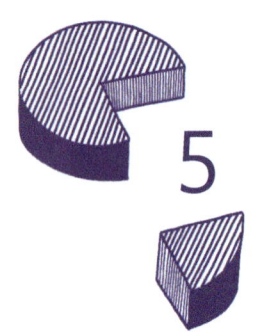

5 The basics of statistical analysis

> **In this chapter you will learn . . .**
> - The difference between descriptive and inferential statistics
> - How to calculate and interpret measures of central tendency and dispersion
> - How to calculate z scores and use them to solve problems
> - What significance really means and what a p value really represents
> - The difference sources of variability within a dataset, and how this relates to significance

Introduction

Once you have designed and run your psychological study you will have collected lots of data. The next stage in the research process is doing something with that data so that you can understand what you have found. You will need to use the data to ask yourself questions such as: Did the study work? Are my hypotheses supported or not? To start making sense of your data and to answer these questions, you will need to analyse your data.

If you are taking a quantitative approach, this is the time you'll be getting to grips with your statistical analysis. Often this stage of the research process is seen as the scariest and most boring, but it is actually the most exciting part of doing research. Remember that statistics are just a tool for psychologists to understand what they have found in their research. This is when you discover what you have found out after all of the hard work of designing and running a study!

Broadly speaking, statistical analyses fall into two families: descriptive statistics and inferential statistics. **Descriptive statistics** give you basic descriptions of what is going on in the data you collected, roughly speaking, what the '**central tendency**' is and how much '**dispersion**' there is in the dataset. In other words, approximately where the middle score is in your dataset (the average) and how spread out the data points are around this (the dispersion). **Inferential statistics** tell you if there is a significant finding in your dataset. We will come back to what **significance** actually means later in this chapter. Sometimes descriptive and inferential statistics are treated as two totally separate ways of analysing your data, but actually they are best used in combination as each will tell you something different about your data.

As you will find out in the next section of this chapter, descriptive statistics (averages and dispersion) are very interesting and useful statistics. However, much of our interpretation of data is formed by whether our findings are 'significant', which comes from inferential statistics. It is really important for any researcher to really understand what a significant result actually tells us, and we will consider this later in this chapter.

Roughly where is the middle score in my dataset? Descriptive statistics: central tendency

If we have a large amount of data, we are likely to want to simplify lots of numbers and summarise them in one number that describes the whole dataset—for example, in one number that represents approximately where the 'middle' is: the central tendency of the dataset. Central tendency includes a few different ways of calculating the 'average' score. If we ask eleven people to complete a memory task where they are asked to recall fifteen words, what is the average memory score?

Although we might often talk about 'the' average, we can actually calculate three different measures of central tendency: **mode**, **median** and **mean**. Here are the memory scores that for the eleven participants that took part in our study: 6 12 3 4 5 10 1 15 7 2 1. We will now summarise these using each of the three types of average.

Calculating the mode

The *mode* is the simplest of the 'averages'. The modal value is simply the most frequently occurring value in the dataset. A value that occurs more often than any other must be meaningful and interesting, right?

The easiest way to work out the mode is to record how often each of the possible scores in our dataset appears (see Figure 5.1), i.e. record its frequency. The score which occurs the most often—that is, with the highest frequency—is the mode. When we do this for our memory data, only one value occurred more than once, a score of 1, which was achieved by two of the participants. Therefore the mode for our analysis is 1.

However, you might think that this is not particularly representative of our dataset. There are lots of scores, ranging from 1 through to 15, and although 1 is the most frequent score, it could be argued that it is not representative of the dataset! This is one of the criticisms of the mode as a measure of central tendency.

Another problem with using the mode as a measure of central tendency is that it is very possible to have more than one modal value in a dataset. If we had a twelfth participant, and they remembered 15 words, we would now have two modal values: 1 and 15. This means the dataset is **bimodal**, and it makes it quite difficult to interpret and understand what you have

Calculating the mode:

Score	1	2	3	4	5	6	7	8	9	10	11	12	13	14	15
Frequency	2	1	1	1	1	1	1	0	0	1	0	1	0	0	1

Figure 5.1: Calculating the modal value of a dataset. The score of 1 (circled in the figure) is the most frequently occurring score, and therefore the modal value.

Calculating the median

The median is a slightly more common measure of central tendency. This type of average tells you what the middle score in a dataset is. To determine this value, order your data from the smallest value through to the largest value and then find which score is right in the middle. In our memory data we have eleven scores, so when the scores are placed in order from the lowest to the highest, the middle score will be the sixth value, which you can see in Figure 5.2. From this dataset, we can see that the median value is 5.

Calculating the median:

| Scores in order from lowest to highest | 1 | 1 | 2 | 3 | 4 | 5 | 6 | 7 | 10 | 12 | 15 |

Five smaller memory scores ← | → Five larger memory scores

Middle score: Median

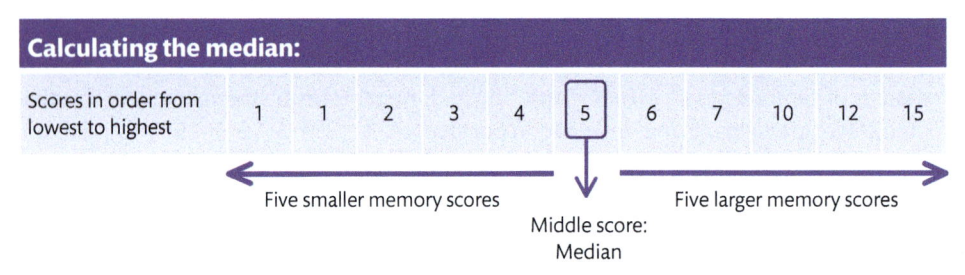

Figure 5.2: Calculating the median value of a dataset.

One of the biggest advantages of the median is that it is not influenced by outlying scores or skewed distributions (I will be talking more about these a little later in this chapter). Say you are running a reaction time study and you collect five reaction times, measured in milliseconds. Here are the data: 150 ms, 323 ms, 114 ms, 237 ms, and 828 ms. It is clear that one reaction time is far larger than the others—perhaps the participant needed to sneeze during that trial! If this data point were included in our calculation of the measure of central tendency it could greatly distort our findings. We will return to this issue again when we discuss the mean statistic.

Although the median does have this great advantage, there are some disadvantages too. In particular, it relies only on one participant's score, and therefore it may not be seen as a true reflection of the entire dataset. For this reason it may also fluctuate a great deal between different studies. It is also less relevant to some of the tests of statistical significance, such as *t* tests and correlations, which we will talk about later in this book. However, the median is really useful when you have ordinal data or need to run non-parametric tests, and this is the measure of tendency that you should be using for any non-parametric analyses that you run. These approaches are covered in Part 4 of this book.

If your dataset has an even number of data points, then there will be no middle score that represents the median. Instead, you should look at the middle two values, and calculate the mean of these to give you the median. How to calculate the mean is covered next.

Calculating the mean

When people talk about the 'average', they are usually referring to the mean value. Although the mean is the most commonly presented average, we may use any of the three averages, so

Calculating the mean:

Step 1:	Sum (∑) all the scores	1 + 1 + 2 + 3 + 4 + 5 + 6 + 7 + 10 + 12 + 15 = 66
Step 2:	Divide the sum by the number of scores	66 / 11 = 6
		$\bar{x} = 6$

Equation to calculate the mean:

$$\bar{x} = \frac{\sum x}{N}$$

Figure 5.3: Calculating the mean value of a dataset.

it is always important to be clear which measure of central tendency you are calculating, presenting and discussing. The mean is represented by the symbol $\bar{x}$, and is pronounced 'x bar'.

The mean is calculated in two stages and you can see the equation in Figure 5.3. Firstly the scores are added up, or summed. The action of summing (adding up) a set of values is shown as $\sum$ in equations, which is pronounced 'sigma'. You then divide this summed score by the total number of individual scores, which is represented by the symbol N in equations. Let's return to our memory data. Figure 5.3 shows that the mean of these data is 6.

Although the mean is the most frequently used 'average' in psychological research, and it is used with interval or ratio data alongside most parametric analyses, there are still problems with this statistic that you need to bear in mind. One big advantage of the mean over the median is that all of the values in the dataset are included. Therefore, the mean might be more representative. However, the fact that all data points are included also brings with it disadvantages. Why is this? Well, if one of those values is markedly different from the rest (an outlying or extreme score) it can really influence the calculated mean, as you can see in Figure 5.4. A very

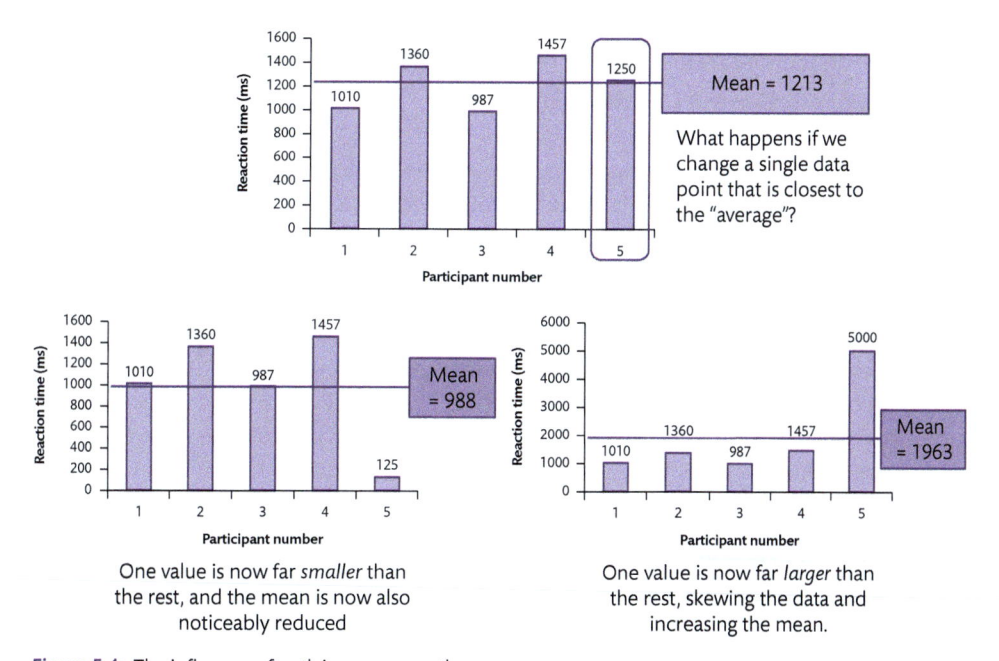

What happens if we change a single data point that is closest to the "average"?

One value is now far *smaller* than the rest, and the mean is now also noticeably reduced

One value is now far *larger* than the rest, skewing the data and increasing the mean.

Figure 5.4: The influence of outlying scores on the mean.

high outlying score might artificially increase the calculated mean (see Figure 5.4 bottom right); whereas a very low outlying score might artificially decrease it (see Figure 5.4 bottom left). If you have outliers, your mean value may not be representative, and it could be better to use the median value instead, as this is unaffected by extreme scores.

Which average should you use?

If you are trying to summarise a dataset, which type of average should you use? As we noted earlier, the mean is most frequently reported measure of central tendency, and is most likely the statistic that you should present. However, always bear in mind the advantages and disadvantages of each measure, which you can see summarised in Table 5.1, and use the central tendency statistic that best suits your needs.

Table 5.1: Advantages and disadvantages of different measures of central tendency.

	Advantages	Disadvantages
Mode	• Simple to explain and easy to calculate!	• Can have more than one mode: bimodal (2 modes) or multimodal (3+ modes) • May not be representative
Median	• Unaffected by outlying scores • Unaffected by skewed distributions	• Can fluctuate across samples • Less helpful with parametric statistics
Mean	• Calculated from every data point, so represents whole sample • Resistant to differences across samples	• Very influenced by any extreme or outlying scores as calculated from every data point!

Roughly how spread out are the scores in my dataset? Descriptive statistics: dispersion

We now know that when we see an average value, we need to consider which type of average we're looking at. Often people place a great deal of importance on understanding the central tendency within their dataset, but this is only part of getting to grips with our data. We also need to consider what the dispersion around the average is. In other words, how widely spread around the average are the raw data points?

Not only does understanding dispersion help us to make sense of our data but, as I will explain below, it is also one of the most fundamentally important concepts that runs through almost all of psychological statistics. Understanding the variability in our data is exactly what statistical analysis is trying to achieve. Therefore, this section is possibly the most important part of the book!

Understanding variability: an example

Imagine that we want to know whether caffeine improves our memory. We have two groups of participants: one is our experimental group and they are given a large mug of caffeinated coffee; the other group are our control group and they are given an equally large mug of

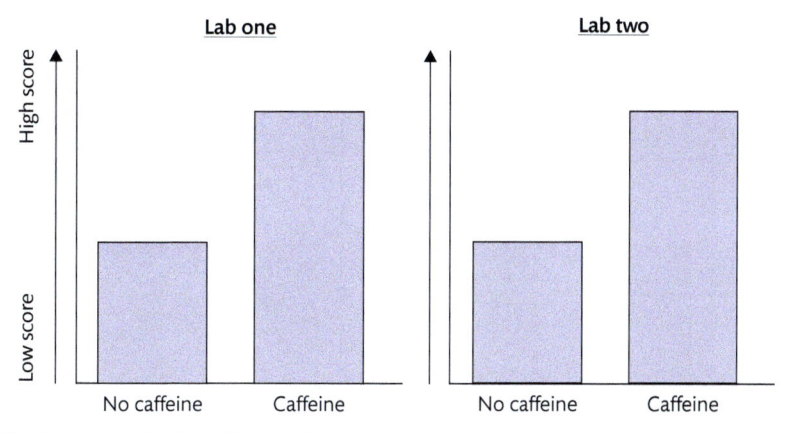

Figure 5.5: Mean scores for the caffeine and memory experiment from two different labs.

coffee, but it is decaffeinated. After drinking the coffee, all of the participants are shown a picture of a busy high street scene for 10 minutes and then given a memory test: a list of twenty different objects that may or may not have been in the scene. They then have to decide whether they saw the object or not. The scores range from 0 (totally rubbish) through to 20 (perfect performance). Two different and independent labs run the study in exactly the same way. You can see the data they collected in Figure 5.5.

Looking at these two graphs, it seems that each lab found exactly the same thing. The control group, who had the decaffeinated coffee, had a mean memory score of 8. In contrast, the experimental group, who had the caffeinated coffee, had a higher memory score of 16. Excellent! We have a clear finding that your memory is improved after drinking caffeinated coffee. Because the experiment was run twice, each time in a completely independent lab, and found exactly the same thing we can be even more confident that our experiment worked.

But can we really be so confident about our findings? After all, we know that mean values only tell us the central tendency of the data collected. This central tendency is very important as a summary of the memory scores in each group, but is there anything else that we might be able to find out about the data we collected that might be both important and informative? Let's look at exactly the same graphs again in Figure 5.6, but this time also plotting the raw data points, the actual memory score for each participant.

Different sources of variability: between and within

We can now see that each lab found something very different. In Lab 1, there was very little variability in the data. All of the participants in the decaffeinated (control) group had a memory score of around 8. They all performed in a very similar way. If we look at the participants in the caffeinated (experimental) group, again, they all had very similar scores of around 16 and there was little variability in the data. This is fantastically beautiful data and exactly the kind of data that every researcher would love to collect (although real data is never this perfect!):

- **Within** each group there is little variability: participants within each of the conditions all have similar memory scores.

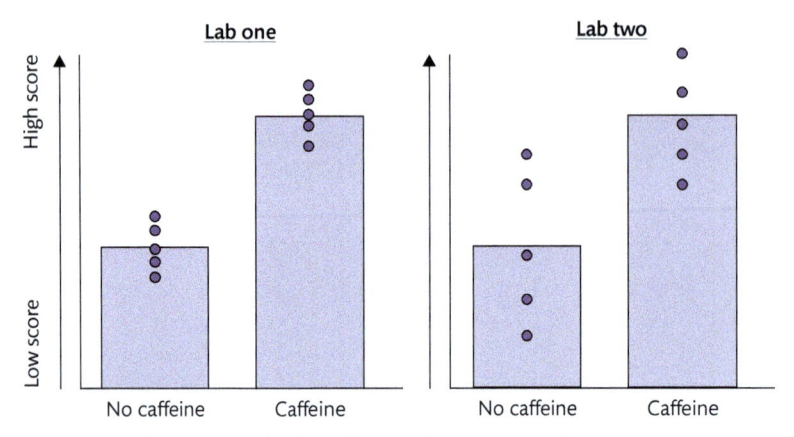

Figure 5.6: Raw data and mean scores for the caffeine and memory experiment.

- **Between** the two groups there is lots of variability. Importantly, there is clearly a big difference in memory scores between the two groups of participants tested in Lab 1. You can easily see that the memory scores in the decaffeinated group are much lower than in the caffeinated group. The experiment was obviously a huge success! Having a caffeinated drink clearly improves memory.

However, if we then look at the raw data collected in Lab 2, we would probably draw very different conclusions about how well the experiment worked:

- *Within* each group there is a huge amount of variability: some participants have very high memory scores whereas others have much lower memory scores. This really isn't what a researcher wants to see in their data. A good manipulation should influence all participants in the same way.
- *Between* the two groups there is a lack of variability, which a researcher would find quite worrying. There is a huge overlap in memory scores between the two groups. Notice that some of the top scoring participants in the decaffeinated group actually have higher memory scores than those in the caffeinated group.

On the basis of the data collected by Lab 2, how confident would you be that caffeine improves memory? Even though the mean memory scores are identical in the two studies, the dispersion of the data means that you would draw very different conclusions from the two studies.

Imagine that we conducted a different experiment, one with far more serious consequences. Imagine that we are doing medical research and that we are looking at a potential new treatment for cancer. We would want that treatment to have a very consistent effect on all of the patients in our study. If some patients had a great deal of improvement, some showed a small improvement and others no change at all, how confident would we be about the effectiveness of this drug treatment for cancer? We would want all patients to respond to the treatment in a very similar way and for there to be a clear difference between the group who received the new treatment and those who did not. In short, we would want our data to look like the data collected by Lab 1 and definitely not like the data collected in Lab 2.

ROUGHLY HOW SPREAD OUT ARE THE SCORES IN MY DATASET?

The moral to this story is that there will always be variability in data. That is not a bad thing. People are different and respond differently to different things. What is very important in psychological research is that we understand the nature of that variability and consider its implications, which is where both the central tendency and the dispersion of the data we collect come in. Never be happy to just look at the average. *Always ask yourself: 'Ah yes, but how widely are the data spread around that average?'*

Calculating the range

The simplest way of summarizing the dispersion of a dataset is to calculate the **range**. The value of the range is simply the largest value in your dataset minus the smallest value in your dataset. As can be seen in Figure 5.7, the range for our memory data is 14. Whilst the range can be informative, it sometimes simply tells you the range of possible scores in the scale you are measuring, so it only tells you the difference between the highest possible value (15) and the lowest possible value (1). It therefore is sensitive to any outlying, or extreme, scores in your dataset.

Calculating the range:

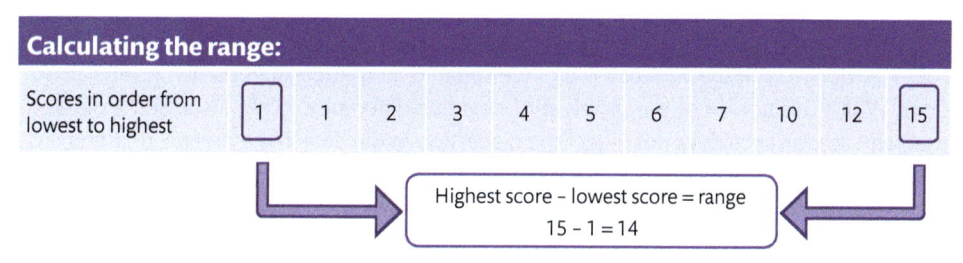

Scores in order from lowest to highest: 1, 1, 2, 3, 4, 5, 6, 7, 10, 12, 15

Highest score – lowest score = range
15 – 1 = 14

Figure 5.7: Calculating the range of a dataset.

Calculating the variance and standard deviation

Although the range is very simple and can be informative, it is not the most useful or widely used measure of dispersion. In psychological research, we are far more likely to calculate and talk about the **standard deviation** of a set of data. The standard deviation is closely related to the mean. It tells you how much the raw scores tend to deviate, or vary, from the mean. A small standard deviation means that the raw scores deviate very little from the mean (little within group variability, as shown in Lab 1 in the caffeine and memory example). In contrast, a large standard deviation means that the raw scores deviate a great deal from the mean (lots of within group variability, as shown in Lab 2 in the earlier example).

You can calculate the variance, which is the first stage of calculating standard deviation, like this:

1. The first thing we need to do is to calculate the difference between each raw score (x) and the mean score ($\bar{x}$). For the memory data we already know that the mean score is 6 and we use that to calculate the difference, $x-\bar{x}$, for each participant in Figure 5.8. We now know how much each participant's score differs from the mean. However, we would like just one value to represent the dispersion of the dataset. Consequently these difference scores need to be combined somehow.

2. We cannot simply add them up as there are both positive and negative values, and if we did add these together they would cancel each other out. To resolve this problem we can square each of these values to give positive numbers (when you square a negative number, you get a positive number).
3. Once that has been done, we can now add, or sum (Σ), all these difference scores. This gives us an overall measure of how much dispersion there is within the dataset.
4. We now divide this by the number of participants minus 1 (*N*-1). As we have eleven data points, this would give us 11–1 = 10. When we divide 214 by 10, we get 21.4. This value is the **variance** (see Figure 5.8, bottom left).

Note that there are actually two versions of this equation. One uses *N*-1, whereas the other just uses *N*. The difference between the two is whether you are testing the entire population, or just a smaller sample from the population. The population statistic uses *N*, whereas the sample statistic uses *N*-1. Given that we rarely test the entire population in psychological research, the version of the standard deviation that we tend to use is the sample, where we divide by *N*-1.

Although the variance is not often reported in psychological research papers, it is actually one of the most important statistics and is used in many of the more complex inferential statistics that we will be considering in later chapters.

One problem with the variance is that we squared all of the values earlier in the calculations. Whilst this got rid of the problem of negative difference scores, it caused a different problem: the variance does not reflect the dispersion in the data in the original unit of measurement as the differences were increased by squaring.

For example, the participant who had a memory score of 2 had a difference score of –4, meaning that they scored 4 below the mean. When this value was squared, it increased to 16. This is great as we got rid of that annoying negative sign, but the value of 16 no longer reflects the actual difference between the mean score and that participant's score. If we wanted this score to reflect the actual score, we could take the square root of the value, which would get us back to a number that reflected the actual difference ($\sqrt{16}$ = 4).

This is exactly what we do to the variance score to calculate the standard deviation; it is simply the square root of the variance. So for our memory data, we just calculate the square root of 21.4, the variance we previously calculated, giving us a standard deviation for the memory dataset of 4.63 (see Figure 5.8, bottom right).

Calculating the variance and standard deviation

Raw scores (x)	1	1	2	3	4	5	6	7	10	12	15
Raw score – mean ($x - \bar{x}$)	–5	–5	–4	–3	–2	–1	0	+1	+4	+6	+9
$(x - \bar{x})^2$	25	25	16	9	4	1	0	1	16	36	81
$\Sigma(x - \bar{x})^2$	25 + 25 + 16 + 9 + 4 + 1 + 0 + 1 + 16 + 36 + 81 = 214										

$$\frac{\Sigma(x - \bar{x})^2}{N-1} \quad 214 / (11-1) = 21.4 \qquad \sqrt{\frac{\Sigma(x - \bar{x})^2}{N-1}} \quad \sqrt{21.4} = 4.63$$

Variance   Standard deviation

Figure 5.8: Calculating the variance and standard deviation for a dataset.

Thinking about dispersion in data

We are now able to summarise the dispersion of our data in three different ways: the range, variance, and standard deviation. But before we move on, I would like to remind you how very important dispersion is within a dataset. Remember that understanding the patterns of variability within a dataset is the most important aspect of truly understanding what you have found. If you look again at the beginning of this section, I talk about two types of variability in a dataset: the variability *within* conditions, and the variability *between* conditions. When we calculate the standard deviation we are looking at the dispersion of scores around the mean *within* one group of participants, or *within* one condition.

There is always going to be variability within a dataset, and the aim of our statistical analyses is to understand where the variability comes from. Is it simply random variability, or is something more meaningful going on? Typically, we are looking for small amounts of variability *within* a condition, showing that all of our participants performed in a similar way (as they did in Lab 1 in the caffeine example). If the *within* variability is large, then this means that there is lots of random and unexplained variability in the dataset. For example, there could be individual differences or measurement error.

On the other hand, we are usually looking for large differences *between* our conditions. In both of the labs that ran the caffeine studies there were quite large differences in mean memory score between the caffeine and the control conditions.

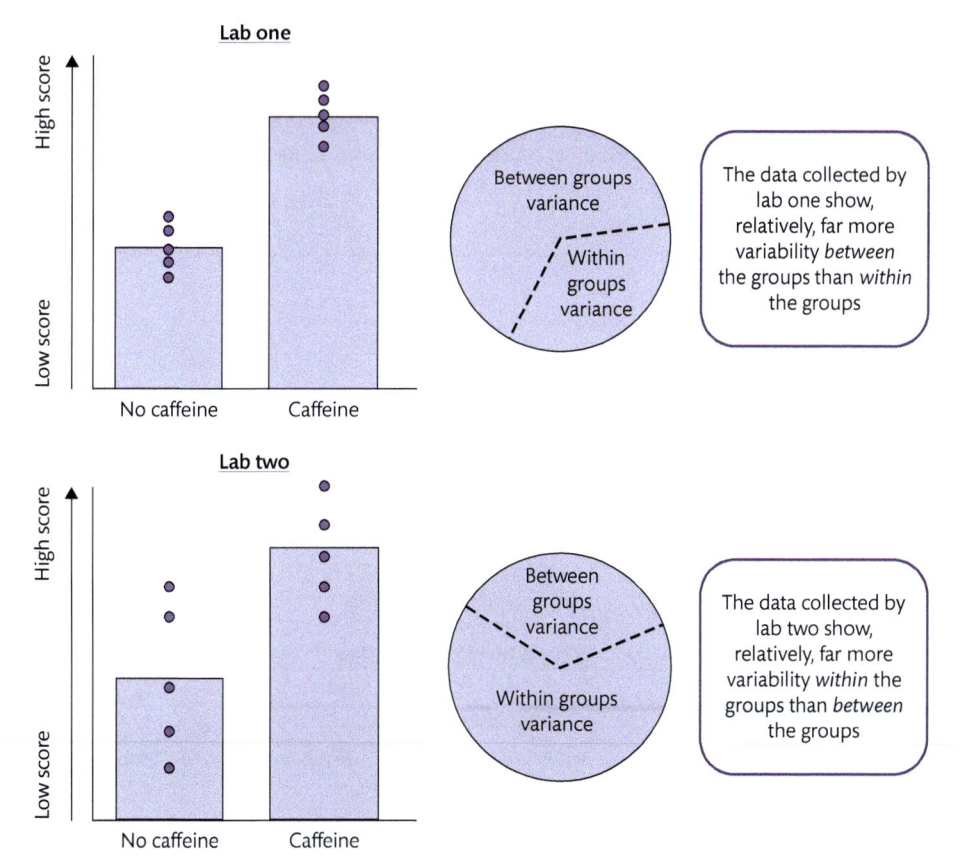

Figure 5.9: Summary of within group and between group variability, as represented by slices of a cake.

THE BASICS OF STATISTICAL ANALYSIS

One really important thing to think about is how much *within* group variability there is in relation to the variability *between* groups. Imagine that your dataset is represented by a cake, and that that cake represents all of the variability in your dataset. What you want to know is how much of the cake represents the *within* group variability, and how much represents the *between* group variability. It is really the ratio between these two types of variability that is interesting for our statistical analysis.

If you look at Figure 5.9 you will see how the two different types of variability are represented through the cake analogy. We will be returning to this analogy frequently throughout this book, and indeed, again later in this chapter.

Distributions in datasets

When we collect a set of data, we would generally expect those data to be normally distributed (this is a **parametric assumption**, which is talked about in great detail in Chapter 13). A normally distributed dataset is one where most people have a roughly average score, and the dispersion around this central tendency is symmetrical. You can see an example of the **normal distribution** curve in Figure 5.10, which is also sometimes called a bell curve.

The normal distribution graph shows the frequency with which scores occur. The **x-axis** (the horizontal axis) shows the possible scores gained by participants and the **y-axis** (the vertical axis) shows the frequency of these scores. If you were to imagine that these were IQs, you would see that the most frequently occurring IQs are quite average and in the centre of the possible IQ scores. There are some quite low IQ scores and some quite high IQ scores, but there is a similar number of these more extreme scores, so the data distribution is symmetric.

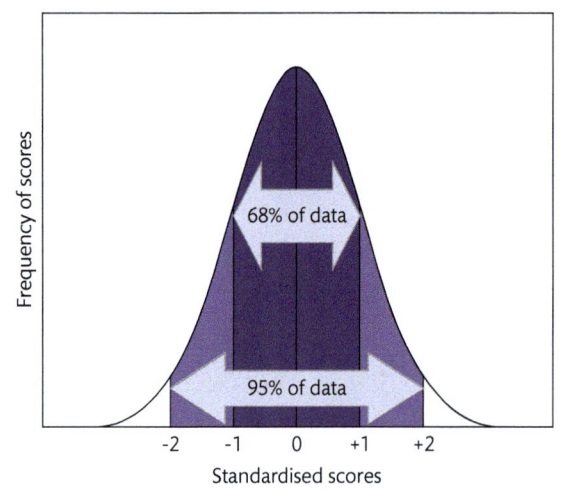

Figure 5.10: A normal distribution curve, showing the percentage of data points that would be expected to fall between ±1 standard deviation and between ±2 standard deviations.

Throughout statistical analysis the distribution of a dataset is really important, and a perfect normal distribution curve, or a **standard normal distribution**, is described as having a mean of 0 and a standard deviation of 1. If you look again at Figure 5.10, you can see that the mean value, right in the centre of the x-axis, is 0. If a dataset is normally distributed, then the mean, mode and median are usually the same, or at least very, very similar.

The boundaries of one and two standard deviations are then shown around this mean value. If a dataset is normally distributed, then you would expect about 68% of the data to fall within one standard deviation of the mean and about 95% of the data to fall within two standard deviations of the mean. Therefore, if we measured the IQ of 100 participants and calculated the mean and standard deviation, we would expect about 68 of those participants to have an IQ score between one standard deviation below the mean and one standard deviation above the mean, and we would also expect about 95 of those participants to have an IQ score between two standard deviations below the mean and two standard deviations above the mean. This also means that we would expect two or three people with extremely low IQ scores, lower than the mean minus two standard deviations, and we would expect two or three people with extremely high IQ scores, higher than the mean plus two standard deviations.

What happens if your data are not normally distributed?

Unfortunately data are not always normally distributed, and this can have serious implications for our statistical analyses as many methods work on the assumption that the data will be normally distributed. A more detailed explanation of this, and of what you can do if your data are not normally distributed is given in Chapter 13, but for now I just want to show some of the more frequently occurring **non-normal distributions** that can occur in datasets.

In Figure 5.11 you can see the normal distribution at the top of the figure. Below this are four different examples of non-normal distributions. In the middle row you can see datasets that have **skewness**, which is that they are not symmetrically distributed. In these datasets you might expect the mean, mode and median to vary a great deal. In the bottom row you can see datasets that have **kurtosis**, which refers to the 'peakiness' of the dataset. In these datasets the data are still symmetrically distributed, and you would expect the mean, mode and median to be similar, but the dispersion within these datasets is far from normal.

Skewness

Looking again at the skewed distributions in Figure 5.11, they show positive and negative skew in the data. Very importantly, the positive or negative skew label applies to where the 'tail' of the distribution is (not the 'bump'). So the example on the left shows **positive skew**, as the tail is towards the higher end of the scale scores. An example of this kind of data might be reaction times, where most of the data points show similar reaction times, but there may be a few outlying and long reaction times, perhaps where people have had a lapse in attention.

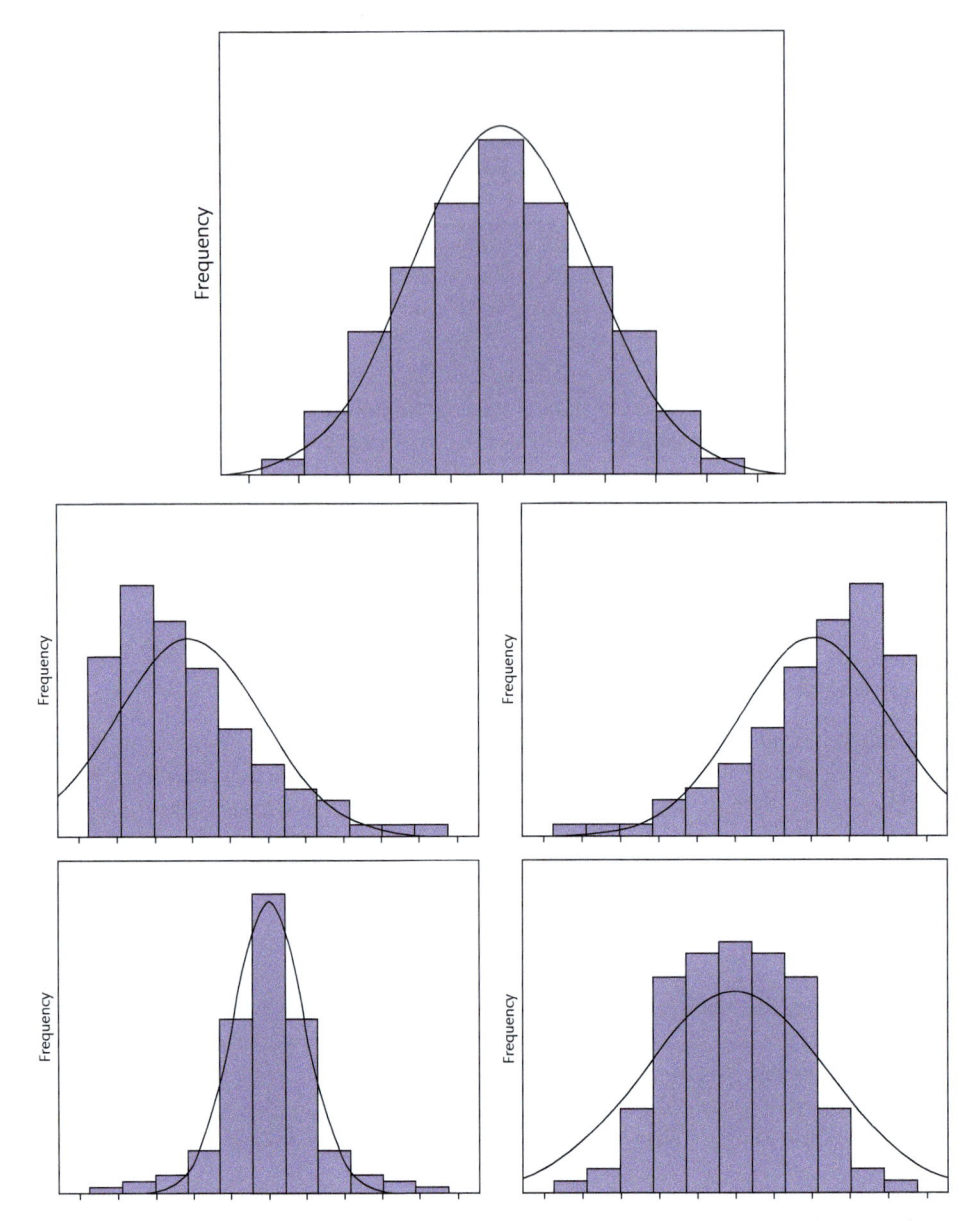

Figure 5.11: The normal distribution (top) and examples of data showing positive skewness (middle left), negative skewness (middle right), a leptokurtic distribution (bottom left) and a platykurtic distribution (bottom right).

Therefore the small number of long reaction times 'skew' the data more into the positive end than would occur without these outliers. The example on the right shows **negative skew**, as the tail is towards the lower end of the scale scores. This data might represent test scores where most of the children did very well on a test, but a small number did very badly and gained very low scores.

Kurtosis

An alternative way in which a distribution can be non-normal is as a result of kurtosis, or the 'peakiness' of a distribution. In the kurtosis examples, shown at the bottom of Figure 5.11, most of the participants gained a score that was roughly average, but the distributions around the mean differ greatly. The graph on the left shows a **leptokurtic distribution** where there is very little variability around the mean. Most of the participants here gained a very 'average' score. In contrast, the graph on the right shows a **platykurtic distribution** where there are very wide ranging scores around the mean, but this wide variability is symmetric.

z scores

z scores are standardised scores that are often used in research as they allow us to make easy comparisons between datasets collected in different labs. These scores do assume that the data are normally distributed though, and so they are standardised. This means that they will have a mean of 0 and a standard deviation of 1, just like the standard normal distribution curve. The z score equation is shown in Equation 5.1. The x represents the raw score from an individual participant, the $\bar{x}$ represents the mean of the dataset, and the SD represents the standard deviation for the dataset. Using z scores there are two types of questions that we can ask:

$$z = \frac{x - \bar{x}}{SD}$$

Equation 5.1: Equation for the z score.

What can z scores be used for? Comparing studies

We know how the normal distribution works, and z scores are based on the normal distribution. Therefore, we can use Equation 5.1 to convert any score to a standardised z score, as long as we know the mean and standard deviation of the dataset from which the score we want to convert comes. For our IQ example, we might want to know how many standard deviations away from the mean a particular participant's score is. This could be particularly useful if we want to compare scores across different measures or studies. Imagine we have data from two different studies, using two different measures of IQ that provide totally different scores. Looking at their raw scores, it would be difficult to directly compare two scores. On one intelligence scale a score of 10 could be a very, very low score, whereas on another scale a score of 10 could be the maximum possible score. If these were both converted to standardised z scores, we could compare these scores.

What can z scores be used for? Looking at scores and distributions

Again, we know how the normal distribution works, and we know how many people we would expect to 'fall' under each part of the curve. If you look back at Figure 5.10, remember that we would expect 68% of the sample to have scores between ±1 SD of the mean. That means, if we had a sample of 100 people, we would expect 68 people to have scores between ±1 SD

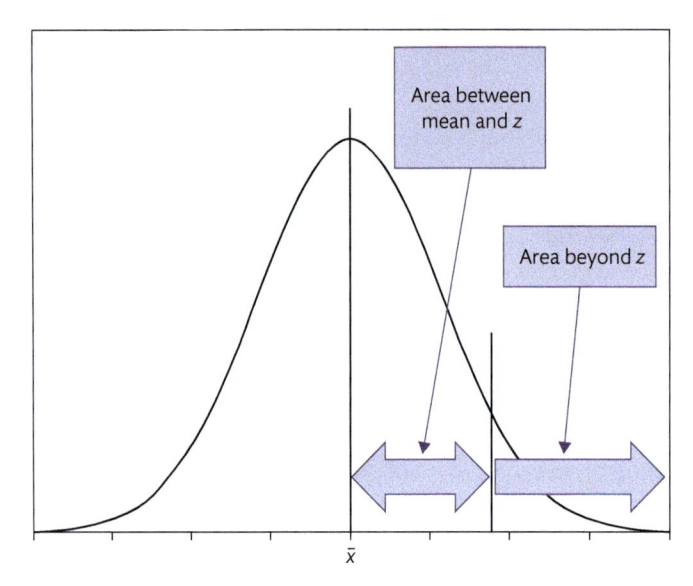

Figure 5.12: Looking up the area under the curve using z scores.

of the mean, 16 people to have scores greater than the mean plus 1 SD, and 16 people to have scores less than the mean minus 1 SD.

If we extend this logic, we can calculate how many participants we would expect to score above or below a particular score, or even how many we would expect to fall between two particular scores. We achieve this with the help of a look up table, which can be found in the appendices of this book, but a quick look at Figure 5.12. will show you the logic behind the table. It contains three columns, the first is the z score (as you would have calculated it from the first type of problem explained above). The second column tells you the proportion of the sample that you would expect to have scores between the mean value and your z score. The third column tells you the proportion of the sample that you would expect to have scores greater than your z score.

Remember that for the normal distribution we have a mean of 0, so we would expect half (50%) of our sample to score above that value, and half (50%) to score below that value. If you go to the table and look up the row for a z score of 0, the value is 0 for the area between mean and z, and 0.5 for the area beyond z. These values are proportions, so you can simply convert them to percentages by multiplying them by 100. So this information tells you that 50% (0.5 * 100 = 50) of your sample would be expected to score above the mean value. This is exactly what we would expect!

Let's try another example. According to the normal distribution we would expect 68% of the sample to fall within ±1 SD of the mean, so we can look up a z score of 1 in the table. This gives us a value of 0.3413 between the mean and plus 1 SD. Because the normal distribution curve is symmetric, we know that there will be another 0.3413 between the mean and minus 1 SD. So in total, between minus 1 SD and plus 1 SD around the mean, we would expect the proportion of the sample to be 0.6826 (0.3413 + 0.3143 = 0.6826). If we convert this to a percentage (0.6826 * 100 = 68.26), we can see that 68% of our sample would be expected to get scores between ±1 SD around the mean.

One more example using the normal distribution and standardised values. We expect 95% of the sample to gain scores between ±1.96 standard deviations around the mean, so around 2.5% of the sample should get scores above the mean plus 1.96 SD and around 2.5% of the sample should get scores below the mean minus 1.96 SD. If we go to the table and look up the area beyond z for a z score of 1.96, you can see that it is 0.0250. If you convert this to a percentage (0.0250 * 100 = 2.5), you can see that you would expect around 2.5% of the sample to score above the mean plus 1.96 SD.

When using the table, remember that it is symmetric. So if you need to ask what percentage of the sample would score below 1 SD beneath the mean, this is exactly the same value as the percentage that would score above the mean plus 1 SD.

Below there are five different problems that can be solved using z scores. For these problems, imagine we have a set of IQ scores from 100 participants. IQ data are usually normally distributed, and you would expect these data to have a mean of 100 and a standard deviation of 15. The first two are problems of the first type described above, where we use z scores to calculate standardised scores. The next three are problems of the second type described above, where we use z scores to calculate the expected proportion (or percentage) of participants that would score above, below or between specific scores. You can see these represented in Figure 5.13.

z score problem 1

If a participant has an IQ of 132, how many standard deviations away from the mean is their IQ score? This is the simplest of questions to answer. We have the raw IQ score from the participant, which is 132, and we know that the IQ scores have a mean of 100 and a SD of 15. We can then enter these values into the z score equation . . . $z = (132-100)/15$, which gives us $z = 2.13$. This tells us that the participant's score is 2.13 standard deviations above the mean. If the z score we calculated were negative, then their score would be below the mean.

z score problem 2

I'd like to compare the scores of a participant using two different intelligence scales. A participant in our study, Bert, gained an IQ score of 97. He had previously taken part in another intelligence study and we want to compare his scores, but the other study used a different intelligence test that measures intelligence on a totally different scale. In the previous study the mean was 52, the SD was 4.5 and Bert got a score of 57.

Which intelligence test did Bert do better on? To answer this question, we need to calculate the standardised z score for each of the intelligence scales:

- Our study: $(97-100)/15 = -0.20$
- Previous study: $(57-52)/4.5 = 1.11$

This shows us that Bert's IQ was 0.2 standard deviations *below* the mean in our study, whereas it was 1.11 standard deviations *above* the mean in the previous study. Therefore, Bert gained a far higher intelligence score in the previous study.

THE BASICS OF STATISTICAL ANALYSIS

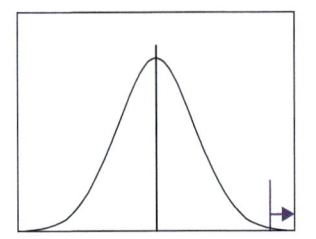

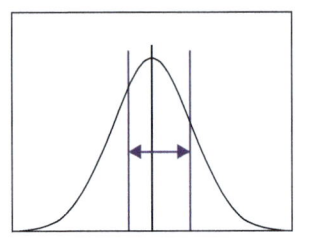

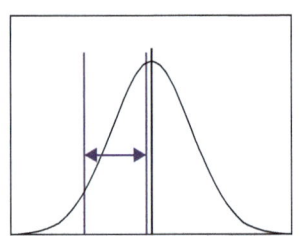

Figure 5.13: Graphics representing problems 3 (left), 4 (middle), and 5 (right).

z score problem 3

What proportion (or percentage) of participants would I expect to have IQ scores greater than 142? The first thing we need to do is calculate the z score for a score of 142, which is 2.8 ((142 − 100)/15 = 2.8). If you now go to the table, you need to look up the area beyond z (so the proportion of the sample scoring more than 142) for a z score of 2.8. If you look at Figure 5.13 left, you can see this represented graphically. This gives us a value of 0.0026, which we can convert to a percentage by multiplying it by 100. We can therefore say that we would expect around 0.26% of a sample to have an IQ score greater than 142.

z score problem 4

What proportion (or number) of participants would I expect to have IQ scores between 94 and 111? We start by calculating the standardised z score for each of the values, giving us z scores of −0.4 ((94 − 100)/15 = −0.4) and 0.73 ((111−100)/15 = 0.73). Notice that the first value is a negative z score, meaning that this score is below the mean, whereas the second value is positive, meaning it is above the mean.

Next we need to work out the area beneath the curve between the z scores of −0.4 and 0.73. There are various ways you could do this, but start by thinking about (or drawing) the normal distribution curve, plotting where the two z scores are and shade the area we are looking for. You can see this in Figure 5.13, middle. I would calculate this by looking at the area between the mean and −0.4 and then looking at the area between the mean and 0.73, and finish up by adding these together.

Looking at the table, the area between the mean and −0.4 (you can just ignore the sign for looking it up, so just look for the 0.40 row) gives a proportion of 0.1554 and the area between the mean and 0.73 gives a proportion of 0.2673. If we add these together we can see the area beneath the curve between −0.4 and 0.73, which is 0.4227 (0.1554 + 0.2673 = 0.4227). Converted to a percentage, this shows that we would expect about 42% of participants to have IQ scores between 94 and 111.

z score problem 5

What proportion (or number) of participants would I expect to have IQ scores between 87 and 98? This problem has a similar logic to the previous question, but this time the two values do not fall either side of the mean, they will both fall beneath the mean, so on the same side of the distribution curve. You can see the area we are looking for in Figure 5.13, right. To work this out I will first calculate the proportion that you would expect to score below 98, then calculate the proportion you would expect to score below 87, and then look at the difference between them. There are other ways you could do this, and all should give you the same result.

First I will calculate the *z* score for the value of 98 ((98−100)/15) = −0.13) and look up the area beyond *z* for this value, which is 0.4483. This means that we would expect around 44.8% of the sample to have an IQ score below 98. Second, I will calculate the *z* score for the value of 87 ((87−100)/15) = −0.87) and look up the area beyond *z* for this value, which is 0.1922. This means that we would expect around 19.2% of the sample to have an IQ score below 87.

Finally, to answer the question we want to take the percentage that would score below 98 and subtract from this the percentage that would score below 87 (44.8 −19.2 = 25.6). We can therefore conclude that around 25.6% of a sample would be expected to get an IQ score between 87 and 98.

How are z scores relevant to the rest of psychological statistics?

If you take a look back towards the beginning of this section on *z* scores, we spent a while considering what percentage of our sample we would expect to fall within ± 2 SD around the mean, assuming that the distribution is normal. We would typically expect around 95% of our sample to fall within these boundaries, leaving 5% of our sample being more extreme scores. This 5% is really important in the statistical analyses used in psychological research, and we will find out why in the next section of this chapter.

Inferential statistics: What is significance?

In the vast majority of psychological research papers, within the results section the authors will explain whether their analyses were statistically **significant** or not. First, let us explore what this term really means. If we go back to our caffeine and memory example we could ask: how big does the difference in memory score between the decaffeinated and caffeinated conditions have to be for us to say that something interesting has really happened? Although the average, or mean, memory scores in the two groups *look* different, are they different enough to be *significantly* different? Significant findings are often presented as a factual finding that proves the researcher correct. In our example, we could say that memory was significantly better after having a caffeinated coffee, giving us proof that caffeine improves your memory. The problem is that a significant result tells you no such thing. *You can never 100% prove anything through statistics*. So what does significance really mean and what does it tell us about our dataset?

The first thing to understand is why tests of statistical significance are called **inferential statistics**. We think that drinking caffeine will improve memory, but to entirely prove this you would need to test the entire population of the planet. Given that this is impossible, we will just include a small sample of representative participants in our study. We might then *infer* that whatever we find in our sample echoes what occurs in the entire population (see Figure 5.14)

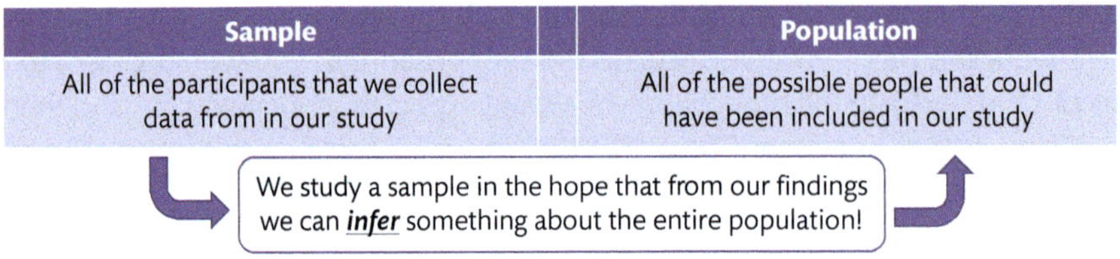

THE BASICS OF STATISTICAL ANALYSIS

Sample	Population
All of the participants that we collect data from in our study	All of the possible people that could have been included in our study

We study a sample in the hope that from our findings we can *infer* something about the entire population!

Figure 5.14: Understanding inferential statistics, moving from a sample to the population.

This is what statistical significance tells us: How confident are you that what you found in your small sample of participants reflects what is really occurring in the entire population?

When you design a study you will develop a hypothesis on the basis of an existing theory or some previous research. For the caffeine study, we may have had a prediction that memory would be better after having a caffeinated drink than after having a decaffeinated drink. This would be our **experimental hypothesis** or **alternative hypothesis** (H_1), our hypothesis that something will happen in our experiment, to cause a difference between the two groups of participants. Alternatively, we might predict that there will be no difference in memory score between the two groups. This would be our **null hypothesis** (H_0), our hypothesis of nothing happening. If you remember back to Chapter 1, our statistical analyses are framed by **Null Hypothesis Significance Testing** (NHST), and as such we technically aim to test whether our null hypothesis is true or not.

Whatever the outcome of our research one of the hypotheses will be supported by the data collected from our sample of participants. Either we find evidence in support of our experimental hypothesis (H_1) or we find no such evidence (H_0). The same thing holds true when thinking about whether the effect exists in the entire population. It may be that the effect really does exist, supporting the experimental hypothesis, or maybe it actually doesn't exist, supporting the null hypothesis. Figure 5.15 shows how we have four possible outcomes in a research study.

Understanding possible outcomes in hypothesis testing

The ideal outcome of a study is that we find something in our sample that exists at the population level (bottom right outcome in Figure 5.15). This would be a 'correct decision' as we

		Result of your statistical analysis (sample)	
		Accept H_0 (No effect)	Accept H_1 (Find effect)
Truth in the real world (population)	Accept H_0 (No effect)	Correct decision ✓	Type I error ✗
	Accept H_1 (Find effect)	Type II error ✗	Correct decision ✓

Figure 5.15: Possible outcomes in hypothesis testing.

would have found something that occurs in the real world and we can be confident of our findings. The alternative type of 'correct decision' would occur if we failed to find anything in our sample because nothing occurs in the population (top left outcome in Figure 5.15). The other two outcomes, however, are not as good because both mean that we have made a mistake.

Type II errors

A **Type II Error** (bottom left outcome in Figure 5.15.) occurs when our experiment has found nothing and we supported the null hypothesis, but in the real world there really was an effect and the experimental hypothesis should have been supported. This is a bit like finding a false negative effect; your study didn't find anything, and you incorrectly accept the null hypothesis, but it missed out on finding the real effect that does exist. If you are the researcher who dedicated the past few months of their life to conducting this research, this is very frustrating! At this point you can go back to the drawing board, try to work out why the experiment failed and figure out how you can run a different kind of experiment that will find the effect that you know exists in the population.

Type I errors

A **Type I Error** (top right outcome in Figure 5.15) is often viewed as the mistake that no researcher wants to make, and it is exactly what we are trying to avoid as researchers. This is when you find an effect in your study and you can support the experimental hypothesis, but where there really is no such effect in the population. This would be a false positive, where you incorrectly reject the null hypothesis and instead falsely accept the alternative hypothesis. For some reason your findings are just random and spurious; more importantly though, they are wrong. Imagine that you are conducting medical research. If you were to commit a Type I Error, it is possible that the medication you are studying would go forward for more testing. This would waste valuable resources. Worse still, the medication could be trialled on people who are ill based on the assumption that the finding from your study was real.

Statistical significance and *p* values

In any kind of research, we want to minimise our chances of committing a Type I Error. This is where statistical significance becomes relevant. For any statistical test, you end up with a *p* value. The p stands for probability and tells us the *probability that we made a Type I Error*. Think about trying to determine whether two groups of participants have different scores or not, say comparing a caffeine using group and a no caffeine group. What is the largest difference that you could find between the two groups that you think would still not be large enough to represent a true difference? This **critical value** is what your data will be compared to. The *p* value tells you the probability of finding a difference at least as big as, if not bigger, than this critical value.

If at the end of our study we conduct a statistical analysis that gives us a *p* value of .050, we could convert this into a percentage (*p* value * 100). This would tell us that there was a 5% chance of us having made a Type I Error. For example, in the medical study, we could say that there was only a 5% chance of us having mistakenly rejected the null hypothesis and found an effect that does not really exist.

So, our inferential statistics tell us the probability of us committing a Type I Error, essentially how likely we are to have made a mistake in our analysis. Put another way, we are determining the chance that we found something in our sample that does not exist out there in the real world. The next obvious question is how risky are we willing to be? Because we cannot test every person on the planet there will always be a chance of making a mistake. For every piece of research, there is a chance of making a Type I Error, even if this chance is very tiny. The smaller our Type I Error the better, so we are always aiming for a small p value. But how small does our p value need to be for us to confidently conclude that our findings are significant?

The alpha level

The criterion used to determine how risky we can be is called the **alpha level** (α). In psychological research we use α = .050 (this comes from the normal distribution curve that we saw in Figure 5.10, so from the 5% outside of the 95% that fall within plus or minus two standard deviations around the mean). That is, we are willing to accept up to a 5% chance of us making a Type I Error. We want no more than a 5% chance that what we might claim to have found in our sample does not exist out there in the real world. This means that, when we run a test of statistical significance, a p value equal to or less than .050 ($p \leq .050$) gives us a significant result.

Although the most frequently used alpha level is .050, this is not always the case. In some areas of research you may want either a stricter or a more forgiving alpha level. For example, in medical research you would want to be really certain that the findings of your study exist in the real world and you would only be willing to accept a small chance of committing a Type I Error. In this case you might want to adopt an alpha level of .010 (or even .001). This would mean that you would limit your chances of making a Type I Error to 1% (or 0.1%). In contrast, if you were conducting some exploratory research, you might be happy to have a more lenient alpha level of .10 and risk up to a 10% chance of not being able to extrapolate your findings to the real world (see Table 5.2).

A note about reporting p values

Throughout this book we will be looking at p values, typically reporting significant results where $p < .050$, $p < .001$, or other p values. When you read published research papers, you

Table 5.2: Linking alpha levels with p values: what is significant?

Outcome of your statistical analysis		Alpha level (α) that you are aiming for		
p value	Probability of Type I Error (%)	.050	.010	.001
.100	10%	Not significant ✗	Not significant ✗	Not significant ✗
.050	5%	Significant ✓	Not significant ✗	Not significant ✗
.010	1%	Significant ✓	Significant ✓	Not significant ✗
.001	0.1%	Significant ✓	Significant ✓	Significant ✓

will more often see exact *p* values reported. Rather than reporting *p* < .050, you might see *p* = .048. The difference simply comes from whether the statistics are calculated by 'by hand' or using specialised computer programmes. In this book everything is done by hand, so we will only ever be reporting *p* values less than a particular alpha level. But when you read published research, or indeed later in your studies when you learn how to use statistical programmes, it is more usual, and preferable according APA guidelines, to report exact *p* values.

What are the problems with *p* values?

In recent years there has been quite a lot of criticism of the NHST approach, and this tends to focus on two different issues. First, the alpha value of .050 constitutes something of an arbitrary distinction between 'significant' and 'not significant' findings. Is there really such a big difference between .049 and .051? Some people view the *p* value as too blunt a tool for this reason, and instead feel that a more continuous measure of the magnitude of the effects that are detected within the dataset would be preferable. Second, NHST is greatly influenced by sample size. Essentially, the larger your sample, the smaller the difference or relationship that can be identified as statistically significant. This can lead to some quite strange outcomes where an analysis is significant, but the size of the difference is actually very, very small.

The alternative to NHST and the *p* value are **effect sizes**. These deal with both of the criticisms of *p* values as effect sizes exist on a continuum, identifying small, medium and large effects, and they are unaffected by sample size. Whilst some critics suggest that the use of *p* values should be replaced with the use of effect size, more often they are used together to help researchers understand their data and findings. Each of the statistical analyses in Parts 2 and 3 of this book are tests of statistical significance, but effect sizes are often used in conjunction with their *p* values to help gain a fuller understanding of the data; are the findings significant, and what is the size of that effect? Each of these chapters will finish with a section showing you how to calculate and report effect sizes along with the significance statistics. Effect sizes are not discussed in Part 4 (non-parametric statistics) as they are reported less frequently in published research and they are more complex conceptually than the effect sizes used for parametric statistics, but this will be discussed in more detail in Chapter 18.

Significance, between and within group variability

The cake analogy also relates strongly to whether our analyses are significant. If you look at Figure 5.16, you will see that the more *between* variability there is in the cake, the more likely it is that our findings will be significant. We will keep returning to the cake analogy throughout this book!

The importance of your sample size and degrees of freedom

One last factor that can greatly influence whether your analysis is significant or not is your **sample size**. Remember that when testing for statistical significance you are trying to infer something about the population from a sample. So you are testing a small number of people

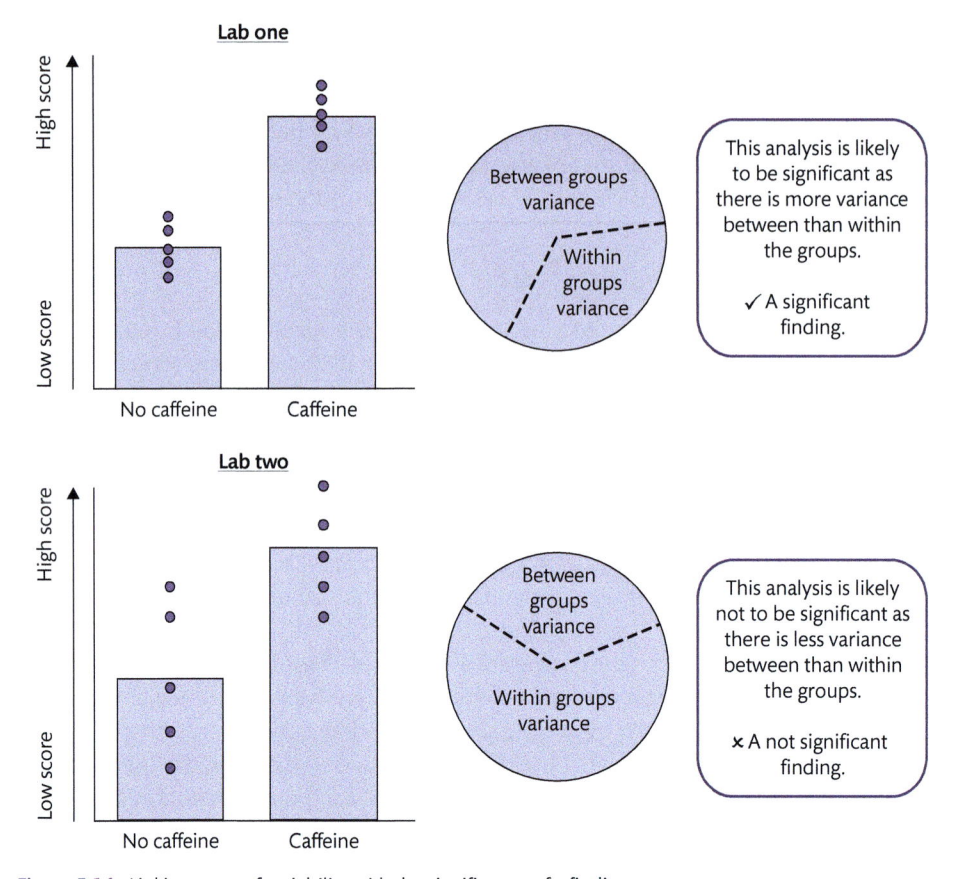

Figure 5.16: Linking types of variability with the significance of a finding.

and hoping to understand all people. Therefore, the larger your sample is, the more confident you can be that you can extrapolate your findings to the population as a whole.

One consequence of this is that how significant your findings are is adjusted according to your sample size. The bigger your sample is, the more likely they are to be representative of the population, and this is taken into account when working out the significance of a finding. This means that is can be 'easier' to find a significant effect with a larger sample. For example, to get a significant result with a sample of 10 participants, you would need a far bigger difference between conditions than you would if the study were run with 1,000 participants.

This is worked out in tests of statistical significance through the **degrees of freedom**. As you will see when we calculate each statistic, the degrees of freedom are used to 'look up' whether the analysis is significant or not. The more degrees of freedom you have, the smaller the effect that you need to find to be able to claim a significant result with no more than a 5% chance of a Type I Error.

The degrees of freedom (df) are usually based on the number of participants in the sample, although they can be calculated in some analyses from the number of conditions. When calculating the df, we often subtract one from the N to make the analysis slightly more conservative, thereby helping to avoid committing a Type I Error.

Presenting descriptive and inferential statistics

At the beginning of this chapter, I said that it was best to use both descriptive statistics and inferential statistics together to fully understand your dataset. Most researchers are desperate to find out whether their findings are significant or not, but you should not stop here for your celebrations! It is great that you have a significant finding, but what does that mean? With our caffeine example, we would know that the memory scores are significantly different between the two groups. But which group has a significantly higher memory score? Inferential statistics will tell you if you have found something significant, but they tell you nothing about the *direction* of your findings. In other words, they will tell you that there is a significant difference between the groups, but not how big this difference is or which group has the significantly higher score.

For that, we need the descriptive statistics. In our caffeine and memory example, the descriptive statistics showed that people in the decaffeinated group had an average memory score of around 8, whereas participants in the caffeinated group had an average memory score of around 16. We could therefore conclude that individuals who have consumed caffeine have significantly better memory performance than those who have not consumed caffeine.

Whenever you present analyses, try to really integrate the discussion of the descriptive and inferential statistics. For example, you might say ... *There was a significant difference between older and younger adults (t (34) = 3.2, p < .001), with older adults scoring significantly lower (mean = 4.6, SD = 1.2) than younger adults (mean = 7.8, SD = 0.9).* Here, you are using the descriptive statistics to help the reader understand what the significant effect actually shows.

It is sometimes tempting to present them separately; describing what is going on in the dataset, and then separately showing what is significant. However, this approach should be avoided for several reasons. First, this style requires far more words as you have to present each finding twice, going through the descriptive statistics and then the inferential statistics. Second, you may end up discussing what seems like an interesting difference in means from the descriptive statistics, but then go on to present that this difference is not actually significant. This can be confusing for the reader. If a difference is not significant you should not discuss the descriptive statistics as if it were.

To fully present the findings of a study, it is important to give the reader three pieces of information: the *central tendency* of your dataset (typically the mean scores), the *dispersion* of your dataset (typically the standard deviation), and the *significance* of any inferential statistics that you have run. Again, presenting these in an integrated manner is what you are aiming for. However, if you have a large dataset and quite a few descriptive statistics to present, it may be cumbersome to write all of them out in the text of the results section. To avoid this, you can present the descriptives in either a table *or* a graph. You should not present the data twice, so decide which you should use to best present your data. You should also follow some basic rules when making a table or graph for a psychological research paper, and the simplest is to follow the APA rules! However, a list of simple rules to follow together with examples are presented in Table 5.3.

THE BASICS OF STATISTICAL ANALYSIS

Table 5.3: A quick guide to presenting data in a results section.

	Do	Don't
Tables and figures	... Follow APA standards. ... Have a legend with a simple description of what is being shown in the table or figures. ... Refer to the table/figure within the main text of the results section. You need to tell the reader when to look at the relevant information! ... Be consistent in the formatting of tables and figures in a report. It can save confusion.	... Show information twice. Decide on the simplest and clearest way to present the information for the reader. ... Make information 'pretty'. You need to present findings clearly and accurately. Pretty elements can be distracting and distorting. Don't ... ... Format any tables or figures in colour. ... Use and 3D effects in graphs.
Tables	Present both means and standard deviations for descriptive statistics. ... Include a summary of inferential statistics if you have lots to present.	Overcomplicate the borders you use, but think carefully how you can use them to segment the information you present. ... Overcrowd a table. It may be better to use two.
Graphs (figures)	... Clearly label both the x-axis (horizontal) and y-axis (vertical). Tell the reader what you are presenting. ... Include unit of measurement on the y-axis. If you measure reaction times, are the data presented in milliseconds, seconds, minutes or hours? This could really change the conclusions drawn!	... Distort the y-axis. Think about the possible minimum and maximum scores you could have collected and use those. So if you present percentages, the y-axis should start at 0% and stop at 100%. Starting at 50% and stopping at 55% would really distort your findings!

Table One: Descriptive statistics (mean and SD) of happiness ratings after eating each chocolate type.

	Happiness (out of 10)	
	Mean	SD
White chocolate	3.6	1.6
Milk chocolate	8.9	1.2
Plain chocolate	6.2	2.5

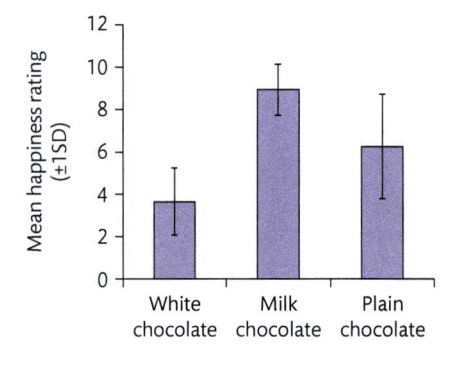

Figure One: Mean happiness ratings (±1 SD) after eating each chocolate type.

Figure 5.17: Examples of how to present descriptive statistics in tables and graphs.

The dataset created for this chapter was inspired by

Borota, D., Murray, E., Keceli, G., Chang, A., Watabe, J. M., Ly, M., . . . & Yassa, M. A. (2014). Post-study caffeine administration enhances memory consolidation in humans. *Nature Neuroscience*, 17, 201–203.

PRESENTING DESCRIPTIVE AND INFERENTIAL STATISTICS

Study questions

1. Four different labs have run a study looking at whether there are sex differences in the number of friends that children aged 8 years old report having. Looking at the descriptive statistics and *p* values below, complete the table to summarise the findings from each lab.

Lab	Boys Mean	Boys SD	Girls Mean	Girls SD	Significance *p*	Is the analysis significant? What is the chance of a Type I Error?	Which group has significantly more friends?	Comment on the variability in the dataset
1	7.8	1.3	9.2	2.6	.049			
2	6.1	1.6	6.5	1.2	.500			
3	6.8	3.5	5.2	2.9	.051			
4	8.3	2.3	10.6	1.9	.005			

2. Imagine that you have run a study looking at anxiety scores in two groups of participants: a control group and a clinical group who have been diagnosed with Generalised Anxiety Disorder.

    2.1. Think about the results that you predict, and on the basis of this draw a graph in a similar style to those shown in Figure 5.16. Think particularly about how much variability you would expect *between* the two groups, and how much variability you would expect *within* each of the two conditions.

    2.2. On the basis of your predicted findings and the graph that you have created, try to guess how that variability cake would be sliced up into within and between variability (similar to Figure 5.16) and whether you think there might be a significant difference in anxiety levels between the two groups.

3. A study has been run looking at levels of the personality trait 'extraversion' where the mean score was 48 and the standard deviation was 13.5. Using *z* scores, you are asked to calculate the percentage of the sample that you would expect to get extraversion scores between 32 and 45.

    3.1. Draw the normal distribution curve to show the area that you would be calculating.

    3.2. There are various ways you could calculate the area between the two scores. Try to work out as many different ways as you can.

Additional dataset

Below are some data on social anxiety, collected from questionnaires given to ten males and ten females. These scores range from 1 (low social anxiety) through to 20 (high social anxiety).

Males:	16	12	10	4	6	8	10	3	10	8
Females:	12	14	19	16	8	10	11	14	12	7

THE BASICS OF STATISTICAL ANALYSIS

Using these data, calculate the descriptive statistics to complete this table and then answer the three research questions.

	All participants	Males	Females
Mode			
Median			
Mean			
Range			
Variance			
Standard deviation			

1. Who is more socially anxious? Males or females? Provide statistics to support your answer.
2. Are social anxiety scores more varied for males or females? Again, provide statistics to support your answer.
3. Which sex has bimodal social anxiety scores?
4. Using the mean and SD that you just calculated for all of the participants, answer the following questions using z scores:
    4.1. If a participant had a social anxiety score of 8, how many SDs away from the mean is this score?
    4.2. What proportion of participants would you expect to score above 9.3?
    4.3. What percentage of would you expect to score between 10.9 and 12.9?

This dataset was inspired by

Sutterby, S. R., Bedwell, J. S., Passler, J. S., Deptula, A. E., & Mesa, F. (2012). Social anxiety and social cognition: The influence of sex. *Psychiatry Research, 197*, 242–245.

Wider reading

www.apastyle.org
   This is the website of the American Psychological Society, which sets the requirements for the presentation of psychological research. The website contains lots of helpful advice, as well as information about the APA Publication Manual. You are unlikely to actually need this manual, unless you wish to pursue Postgraduate studies, but if there is a copy in your library, it is well worth taking a look at it.

Wright, D., B. & Williams, S. (2003). How to produce a bad results section. *The Psychologist, 16*, 644–648.
   This is a very simple and tongue in cheek guide to writing a results section.

Example paper using this statistic

Crysel, L. C., Cook, C. L., Schember, T. O., & Webster, G. D. (2015). Harry Potter and the measures of personality: Extraverted Gryffindors, agreeable Hufflepuffs, clever Ravenclaws, and manipulative Slytherins. *Personality and Individual Differences, 83*, 174–179.

Most research papers include descriptive statistics, but they do vary in how they present them. In this paper, if you look at Table 1 on page 176, you can see the means and SDs clearly presented for each of the measures they included in their study. They also use the descriptives really nicely to show the direction of the differences, such as in Section 3.1, and their graphs are pretty good, although they haven't labelled their y-axis!!! Plus, this is generally a pretty cool paper to read . . .

> ### How to run these analyses in SPSS . . .
>
> If you would like to see how to run these analyses in SPSS, and to find other materials including a numeracy skills quiz and full answers to study questions, please go to the online resources: www.oup.com/uk/bourne/

Part 2
Experimental design

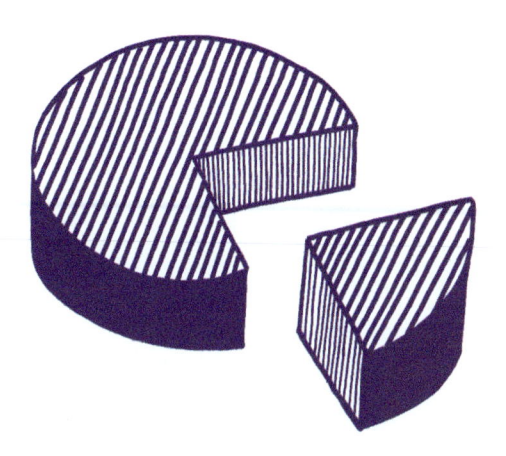

6 How to design an experiment

> **In this chapter you will learn . . .**
> - How to define the variables that you manipulate and measure in an experimental design
> - Different types of experimental design, and the advantages and disadvantages of each
> - How to avoid common pitfalls when designing experiments and how to design a methodologically rigorous experimental study

Introduction

One of the core methodologies used by researchers is **experimental design**. One of the key ideas with an experimental design is that you can look at causality. The idea here is very simple: you manipulate something (a variable) and see if this **manipulation** changes some kind of outcome measure. For example, you might manipulate whether participants' eat white chocolate (evil—I really don't like it, and it isn't really chocolate as it contains no cocoa powder) or milk chocolate (beautiful—always my preferred treat) and then measure each participant's happiness scores and see whether they differ according to the type of chocolate eaten. Are people happier after eating milk chocolate than after eating white chocolate? Or perhaps you are interested in emotional memory, so you show participants 10 happy faces and 10 sad faces, hence manipulating the emotional expression of the faces, you then give them a memory test and see whether they remember more of the happy faces or more of the sad faces. Are people better at remembering happy or sad faces?

Possibly the most difficult part of learning about experimental design is that it is crammed full of terminology. Even more annoyingly, there are multiple ways of saying exactly the same thing, which can make learning about experimental design far more complex than it really needs to be. In this chapter we will look at some of these basic issues in experimental design before going on to run the analyses in the next few chapters.

Describing your variables: what do you manipulate and what do you measure?

First thing: what is it that you want to manipulate? What are the different groups or conditions that you want to experimentally manipulate and then compare? This is your **independent variable**: the variable that you manipulate. Next, what is it that you want to measure? What

Table 6.1: Examples of independent variables and dependent variables.

	Independent variable	Dependent variable
	What you decide to manipulate before the participant goes IN to the lab	The score the participant provides that DEPENDS on your manipulation
Example 1	Type of chocolate eaten: white or milk	Happiness score
Example 2	Emotional expression: happy or sad	Number of faces remembered
Example 3	Treatment: placebo or 'genius' pill	Score on methodology exam

is the outcome score that you think might differ across your group or conditions? This is your **dependent variable**: the variable that you measure.

Distinguishing between your independent variable (IV) and your dependent variable (DV) can be one of the most difficult things when learning about experimental design (see Table 6.1). So try thinking about it in the following way... You are going to run an experiment and you have the lab all set up and ready for the first participant. What you are interested in is whether people differ in how happy they are after eating either white or milk chocolate. So when each participant arrives at the lab, you have to decide whether you will give them a bar of white chocolate or milk chocolate to eat. This is your **IN**dependent variable. What you decide to manipulate before the participant goes **IN**to the lab. So you give them their bar of chocolate and send them off into the lab to eat their chocolate and then diligently complete a questionnaire that will give you a score of how happy they are. This happiness score is your **DEPEND**ent variable the score that **DEPEND**s on your manipulation. So in this experiment, you manipulated the type of chocolate eaten by each participant, your IV, and measured how happy they were, your DV. Simple!

An important thing to remember is that the DV will always be a **continuous score**, so it must be **ordinal data**, **interval data**, or **ratio data**. To revise these you can take a look back at Chapter 2, but essentially it means that your DV should record numbers that exist on a continuum, from low through to high numbers. Good examples of potential DV scores are IQ, reaction time, accuracy of memory, score on an exam, or happiness score.

What happens if you cannot manipulate your independent variable?

OK, maybe it is not quite as simple as I made out. By definition, an experiment requires you to experimentally manipulate something: the IV. However, some things cannot be experimentally manipulated. Let's take two very simple examples; the sex of a person or the age of a person. Imagine we want to look at sex differences in intelligence. Are males more intelligent than females? We can't take each participant and experimentally manipulate whether they are male or female, that is pretty much already decided a long time before we started running our experiment. In a different study we are interested in whether older children are better at controlling their temper than younger children. Again, the age of a child is not something that we can experimentally manipulate and determine when each child turns up to the lab. Well, at least not until time travel is invented!

A core principle of experimental design is that the experimenter randomly allocates participants to conditions (random allocation is also sometimes known as random assignment, and we will talk about this in more detail later in this chapter). For example, if you are interested in how the type of chocolate you eat influences happiness, you need to make sure that you randomly allocate half of your participants to the white chocolate condition and half to your milk chocolate condition. This is really important to try to minimise the possibility of there being some kind of systematic difference between the two conditions, other than the type of chocolate that they eat, that might explain how happy they are.

But what happens if you can't experimentally manipulate what you are interested in? What if you want to look at differences between males and females, children aged three or six years old, mass murderers and non-murderers, patients with dementia and a control group? Fear not, you can still run your study, you just have what is called a **quasi-experimental design** instead. A quasi-experimental design simply means that you have a design where you cannot randomly allocate participants to the different groups of your IV.

One limitation of a quasi-experimental design is that is more difficult to establish causality, so where possible you should aim to randomly allocate participants to conditions and use a true experimental design. However, if it is only possible to conduct the research using a quasi-experimental design, such as looking at sex differences between males and females, then a quasi-experimental approach is a good and valid one. Just be careful of making any conclusions about causality if you use this type of design.

What is the difference between independent and repeated measures designs?

Now you know what your independent variable is, you know what you want to manipulate. Let's stick with the idea of giving our participants either white or milk chocolate. Now you have another big decision to make: **independent measures design** or **repeated measures design**? In everyday language, do you have separate groups of participants in each condition, an independent design, or do the participants repeat the experiment in each condition, a repeated design? This is one aspect of methodology where the terminology can vary between researchers, so the various terms that you might see are summarised in Figure 6.1.

Do you want to have two separate groups of participants, where one group has to eat white chocolate (surely this must be unethical?) and the other group has to eat milk chocolate? This would be an independent measures design, as you have independent participants in each condition. The alternative is to have just one group of participants and to ask them to complete the experiment twice, once when they eat white chocolate and once when they eat milk chocolate. This is a repeated measures design, as the participants repeat the experiment in each condition. Each has its own strengths and weaknesses, which we will discuss later in this chapter, so it is important to think carefully about which type of experimental design you will use.

Independent measures design

There are some designs where your decision is made for you by virtue of what you want to study. We just learned about quasi-experimental designs, where belonging to one particular

How to design an experiment

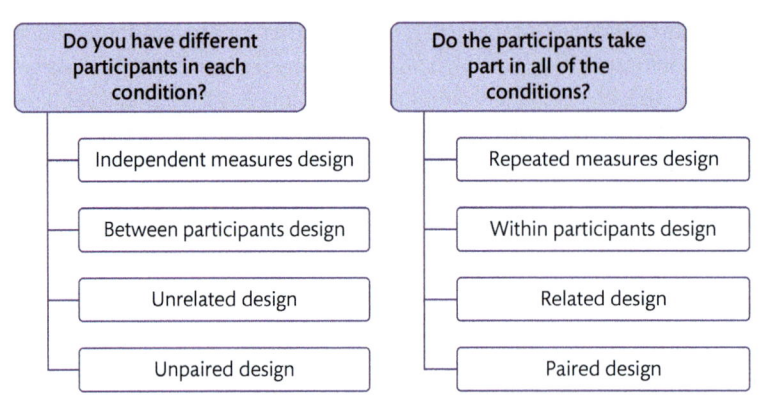

Figure 6.1: Different terminology used to describe independent and repeated measure designs.

condition or category is predetermined and cannot be randomly assigned by the researcher. For example, looking at sex differences will always be an independent measures design. Similarly, if you wanted to look at the differences between psychopaths and non-psychopaths, this would be an independent measures design. So sometimes, an independent measures design is the only option for you as a researcher.

Repeated measures design

In other pieces of research, a repeated measures design will be the obvious choice. Take, for example, any study that looks at the effectiveness on an intervention. Perhaps it is a new system for teaching children to read, or a new treatment for chocolate addiction. To really address these kinds of research questions, you need a repeated measures design so that you can see if scores *after* the intervention are significantly different from the scores *before* the intervention.

Repeated measures designs are often thought of as 'before' and 'after' designs, but there is actually far more that you can do with a repeated design, it is not just about repeating the same experiment at two different time points. It simply means that the participants take part in two conditions of the same IV. For example, in a study looking at face recognition you might show participants the faces of famous and unknown people and ask them whether they know who they are or not. This would be a repeated design, with the IV being face familiarity. Another example might be a memory experiment where participants were asked to learn two different lists of words, using a different memory technique for each one. Here the IV would be memory technique and participants would take part in both conditions, making it a repeated design. So always remember, repeated designs are about more than just 'before and after' designs, it is simply about the same participants taking part in multiple conditions within the IV.

Longitudinal and cross-sectional designs

When working in developmental research you will often hear people talking about **longitudinal designs** and **cross-sectional designs**. Essentially, these are just repeated and independent designs respectively. Longitudinal designs allow you to test the same group of participants repeatedly over time, so you can see how your participants change over time. However, it can be difficult to test participants over really long periods of time. If you wanted to look at cognitive aging from 60 years old through to 90 years old, the study would take 30 years! This is not usually realistic, so in this situation the researcher would be far more likely to use a cross-sectional design. This is an independent design, where different age groups would be compared. Often in developmental research the longitudinal design is seen as the gold standard, but where it is not possible a cross-sectional design can be just as effective.

What other decisions do you need to make when designing an experiment?

For some manipulations, there may not be an 'obvious' design, and then you need to start making some tough decisions as a researcher. Neither type of design is automatically better than the other; each has its own advantages and disadvantages, which are summarised in Figure 6.2 below.

As you will see, the advantage of one is generally a disadvantage of the other. So, for example, you might decide that an independent measures design is better in some ways, but that you are limited in terms of the number of research participants you have and therefore a repeated measures design is the way forward. In another example, you may want to run a repeated design experiment, but you worry about participants' performance improving or deteriorating from one condition to the other as a result of them completing the measures multiple times under different conditions. These are called **practice effects** (improvement) and **fatigue effects** (deterioration) and are discussed in detail later in this chapter. In the end it may be that an independent design works better for your needs.

When it is possible to run the experiment using either type of design, try weighing up the reasons for and against using each type of design. This is where your brain is your best research tool. Imagine discussing your ideas with your tutor or supervisor and arguing for the design you have chosen. How convincingly can you argue your case? Research is rarely,

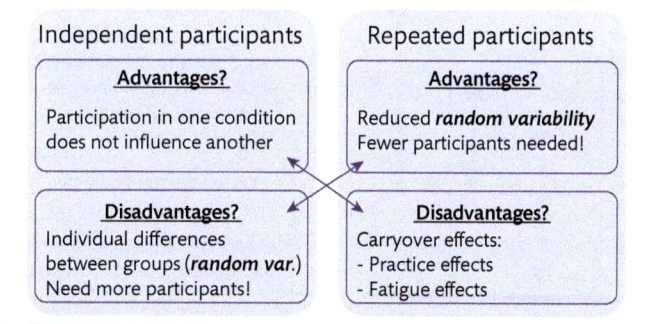

Independent participants	Repeated participants
Advantages? Participation in one condition does not influence another	**Advantages?** Reduced *random variability* Fewer participants needed!
Disadvantages? Individual differences between groups (*random var.*) Need more participants!	**Disadvantages?** Carryover effects: - Practice effects - Fatigue effects

Figure 6.2: Advantages and disadvantages of independent and repeated measures designs (see later in this chapter for a full explanation of practice and fatigue effects). You will notice that the advantages of one design are the disadvantages of the other, as represented by the arrows in the figure.

and quite possibly never, perfect. So the knowledge and skills you develop that allow you to make these decisions are an important part of being a psychological researcher. When you feel there are possible issues with your design, remember to consider these in your discussion when writing up your report. Why did you make the decisions you did? How might these decisions have influenced your findings? Would you expect to find something different if you had used the alternative design? Any limitations in your design just mean that you have more to talk about in your discussion!

The impact of the type of experimental design on analysing your data

The difference between a repeated and independent measures design also becomes important when thinking about how you will analyse your data as each design is analysed using a different statistical tool. At first sight you might think that the method of analysis would be the same in both designs; we're just comparing two groups right? Think back to Chapter 5 where we talked about understanding the variability in our data and the two different ways we can explain the variability in our scores. The variance that we want to see is the experimental variance, the variability in the data we have caused with our manipulation of the IV. However, there will always be some random variability in the data you collect.

If you look at Figure 6.3, you will see some fictional data for our simple design where our IV is the type of chocolate eaten and our DV is how happy the participants are after eating chocolate. First thing to look at is the overall difference between the two conditions. Here we can see that our participants were happier after eating milk chocolate than after eating white chocolate. This is our **experimental variance**, sometimes called the between variability, and we want loads of this. Unfortunately, our manipulation did not have exactly the same effect on all of the participants. In each of the conditions, some of the participants gained far higher (or lower) happiness scores than others. This is the **random variance**, also sometimes called the within, error or residual variance. This type of variability could have a number of different causes, but certainly not our manipulation of the IV, and we want as little of this type of variability as possible.

Random variance is a big problem in an experimental study. This is the left over, unexplainable junk that we really don't want to see. One possible source of random variability

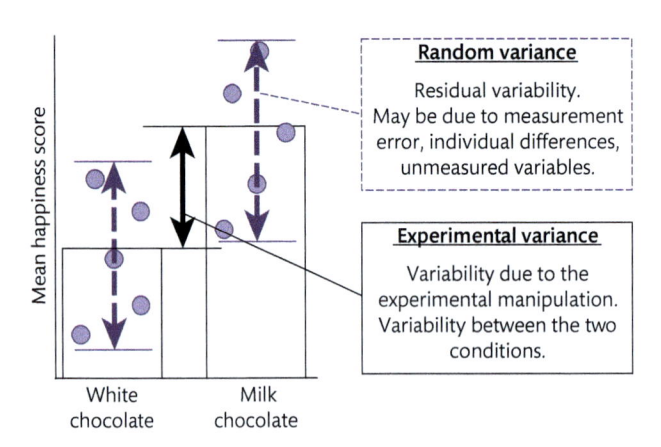

Figure 6.3: Graphic representation of random and experimental variance in a simple study.

is individual differences. People differ in terms of how happy they are, how much they like chocolate and the type of chocolate they would prefer to eat. This might cause a big methodological problem in an independent measures design. What if all the grumpy participants were in the white chocolate condition and all the happy participants were in the milk chocolate condition? Now our finding tells us nothing at all about our experimental manipulation of the type of chocolate eaten.

The possible effect of individual differences is one of the biggest methodological flaws in an independent measures design. How do you know whether the difference between the two conditions is the result of your manipulation of the IV, or some other coincidental difference? There are two ways around this problem. One is to use a repeated measures design. If you have the same participants repeating the experiment in both conditions, then differences between the conditions cannot be explained in terms of differences between the participants—they are the same people! The alternative method allows you to still use an independent measures design, but you try to ensure that the two separate groups of participants are as similar as possible. We could measure a number of additional variables and then try to match participants up across the two conditions.

For example, if we were forced to run our chocolate study as an independent measures design with twenty participants in each condition, we could match each participant in the white chocolate condition with one in the milk chocolate condition. We might ask all of the participants how happy they tend to be in life and how often they eat chocolate. We then pair up each participant in the white chocolate with a participant in the milk chocolate condition, and if we still find that people are happier after eating milk chocolate, we know that this cannot just be explained in terms of the happy chocoholics accidentally all ending up in the milk chocolate condition.

To take a more realistic example, **matching participants** is a really important methodological part of studies comparing clinical and non-clinical participants. Suppose we ran an experiment looking at semantic memory in patients with dementia and we wanted to compare their scores to a group of participants who do not have this condition. A well-matched design would probably ensure that each participant with dementia was matched with a participant without dementia of the same sex, roughly the same age and level of education. That way we can be confident that the lower scores in one group cannot simply be explained in terms of those participants being older, or less intelligent, than the other participants.

How many different conditions would you like with your experimental design?

All of the experimental designs that we have discussed so far have been very simple, and have only compared two groups or conditions. However, research is rarely this simple and far more complex designs are possible. You can compare more than two conditions, and technically you can compare as many as you want, although in practice researchers rarely have more than four of five conditions. It is also possible to manipulate more than one IV, but that gets a little more complicated (you can read more about these types of experimental designs in Chapter 18). Once you are comfortable with the simple experimental designs we cover in this part of the book, you can move onto Chapter 18 where I introduce you to some more complex experimental designs.

One thing to bear in mind when deciding how many conditions you will have is that it can change the type of analysis you will be doing. If you have a simple design with just two conditions you will need to analyse your data using a *t* test (covered in Chapters 7 and 8), whereas if you have three or more conditions you will need to run an Analysis of Variance, also known as an ANOVA (covered in Chapter 9). For more hints and tips on how to decide which method of analysis to use, try reading through Chapter 17, which guides you through this process in detail.

Avoiding common pitfalls in experimental design: dealing with confounding variables

You are now almost ready to design and run your own prize-winning psychological experiment, however there are a few final methodological bits and pieces to think about to ensure that your experiment really is amazing and methodologically rigorous. These issues sometimes seem irritating, petty and pedantic, but they are an important part of designing a methodologically rigorous experiment. As we will see, if you forget about these issues, it can be difficult to tell whether your findings are really due the manipulation that you think you have implemented, or whether they might have actually occurred due to some other reason. Thinking about these issues whilst designing your experiment can save a whole load of tears after you have run experiment it. These are also good points to bear in mind when reading and thinking critically about other people's research. Do the beautifully significant findings really show what the experimenter thinks they show?

We have already talked about one possible pitfall when we considered two experimental groups of independent participants differing on some kind of potentially measurable variable. The effect of differences between participants, when unmeasured, is a kind of **confounding variable**. If you measure and control for this variable, it becomes a **control variable** (sometimes also called a covariate). Confounds are variables that can be measured and may systematically explain some of the random variance within a design, and you can look back to Chapter 2 to read more about these if you need a quick reminder. It is really important to think about the potential confounds in your experiment when designing it. If you think there are potential confounds, then you can measure them as control variables and deal with them. You might choose to match participants to ensure that the groups don't differ according to that variable, or later in your research career you may choose to statistically control for this variability in the data (see Chapter 18 for more information on this).

For example, imagine that you want to run an experiment looking at two different memory techniques, but you know that intelligence (IQ) is a potential confound as people with higher IQs tend to have better memory. You want to design your study in such a way that you are confident that your findings reflect differences in memory ability, not differences in the IQ of participants. How can you design your experimental study to ensure that your findings reflect memory effects?

Randomising participants

We already talked briefly about **randomisation** earlier in this chapter when we discussed quasi-experimental designs. It's central to dealing effectively with potential confounds. A key principle within experimental design with an independent measures design is that participants should be randomly allocated to conditions. This means that if you are doing a study on curing chocolate addiction and you have a treatment group and a **placebo group** (a group who believes they are taking a treatment, but where the 'treatment' does not actually contain any active ingredient), you can't systematically put the most extreme chocoholics into one of the conditions. By ensuring you are totally random in allocating participants to different conditions you hope that the different groups will be as comparable as possible on all variables (age, IQ, happiness, chocoholicism, etc.). Therefore, if you conduct the memory experiment and find that the two groups differ significantly, you can be more confident that the difference is due to your manipulation of the IV (memory technique), rather than one group happening to be more intelligent than the other group.

There are many different ways to randomise. If you are giving participants ID codes, you could put all odd numbers in one condition and even numbers in the other condition. If you are using a computer programme, these can sometimes do the randomizing for you. The key thing is that you do not decide how to allocate participants on the basis of anything meaningful about them. You are aiming to have two groups that are as similar as possible.

Matching participants

In some experimental designs it is difficult or impossible to randomly allocate participants to conditions, for example if you have a quasi-experimental design. There are things you can do to try to help make the groups as similar as possible and reduce the effect of potential confounds. Say, for example, that you are looking at sex differences, obviously the two groups will differ in terms of being male and female, but you don't want them to differ in any other way. One way to achieve this is through **matching participants**. The idea here is that you match participants across the conditions on the basis of key variables that you think might be relevant.

For example, in the memory experiment, you might want the two groups to be the same in terms of age and IQ. Consequently, if you have a male participant who is 24 years old and has an IQ of 112, you will also recruit a female participant who is 24 years old and has a similar IQ of 115. This way, if you find a significant difference between males and females, you can be confident that the differences cannot be explained in terms of age or IQ.

You can also statistically analyse these variables to ensure that there is no significant difference between the groups on these variables. For example, if you wanted to compare the continuous scores of IQ across two groups, you could use an independent t test, which we will be covering in Chapter 7. To compare categorical variables, such as whether participants are male or female, then you could use a chi square, which is covered in Chapter 14 of this book. Remember that you would want these analyses to be not significant to show that the groups were comparable.

Counterbalancing

Counterbalancing is used with repeated measures designs only, and is probably best explained with another example. Say we are looking at differences in processing emotional words in an experiment with a repeated measures design. In a memory task participants look at individual words on a computer screen and have to decide whether each word is

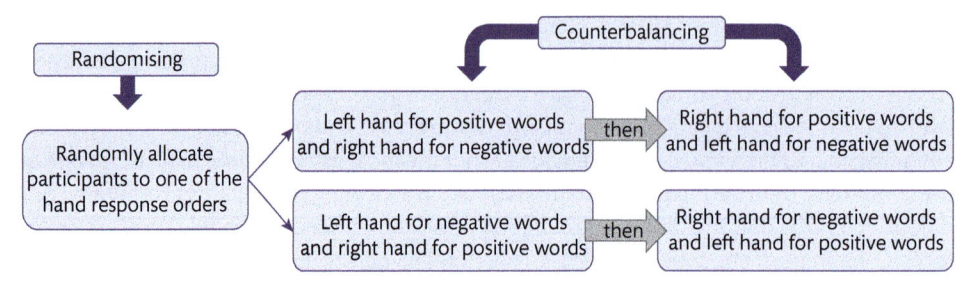

Figure 6.4: Using randomisation and counterbalancing in an experimental design.

a positive or negative emotional word. If they think it is positive they press a button with their right hand, if they think it is negative they press a button with their left hand. We find a fantastically huge significant difference: people are better at identifying positive words than negative words.

But wait, might there be a different explanation for our finding? The majority of people are right handed, so might our wonderful findings actually just show that most people tend to be better at responding to a stimulus with their right hand than with their left hand? This is where counterbalancing comes in. We don't always want the 'right hand' response to mean the same thing, and there are various safeguards we could use to avoid this possible issue messing up our whole experiment.

We could ask half of the participants to respond with the right hand for positive words and the left hand for negative words and the other half to respond with the left hand for positive and the right hand for negative words. As long as we are strictly following our random allocation to conditions rule, this should be OK. But there is still the chance that things could go wrong. It might be even better to have each participant use both methods of responding. So for the first half of the trials, a positive word is responded to with a right hand button press and a negative words is responded to with a left hand button press. In the second half of the trials this switches around the other way.

However, this is still not perfect, because all of the participants start and finish with the same responding pattern. What would be ideal would be for half of the participants to start with the right hand indicating positive words and to then switch to left hand responding halfway through the experiment. The other half would start with the left hand response and then switch to the right hand response. For an amazing experimental design we would also adopt randomisation to allocate participants to the two different hand responding orders. See Figure 6.4 for a simpler account of this fully counterbalanced and randomised design.

Avoiding common pitfalls in experimental design: random variability and bias

Essentially, what we are trying to do through randomisation and counterbalancing is reduce the chances of random variability explaining any differences between our conditions. Random variance can come from many sources, and in addition to measured control variables, it may also arise from **crossover or carryover effects**, such as *practice effects* or *fatigue* *effects*, which we mentioned earlier in this chapter. These two types of effects are, essentially, the opposite of each other. With practice effects participants may get better at the task the longer they do it for, whereas with fatigue effects they may get worse as they get tired or bored.

To deal with these kinds of issues it is really important to think about how many trials you might include in an experimental design. If participants are asked to look at emotive faces and identify the emotional expression on each one, how many faces should they have to look at during the experiment? You want to have quite a few trials to ensure that you have a good sized dataset, but you don't want to risk participants either getting too good at it (practice effects) or getting bored and stop trying (fatigue effects). This is where running a small **pilot study** can be helpful to help you get the balance right. A pilot study is a small scale version of your experiment, with just a few participants, where you can check whether your design is feasible. You can try running slightly different designs, and maybe even ask the participants their opinions on what you ask them to do.

Double blind design

Researchers and participants are quite an essential part of any experiment, but they can also be a source of bias in the design. If you think about the role of the researcher, there are various ways in which they could bias the design. They might bias it in the way that they design their study, select the materials or recruit participants. They may be biased in their method of randomizing and counterbalancing, or they may even be biased in the way that they treat participants during the study. Participants may also be biased, usually unconsciously, in the way they behave in response to having some idea (true or not) of what the experiment is about. These participant biases are known as **demand characteristics**.

One way in which experimenter and participant bias can be controlled is by using a **double blind design**. This means that neither the researcher nor the participant are aware of which condition or group they have been allocated to. This way the experimenter will treat all participants in the same way. Even if their intentions are honourable, if they know which condition a participant is in, they may unwittingly treat them differently. Similarly, if the participant doesn't know which group they are in they won't be able to try to respond in a particular way. Sometimes participants really want to 'help' the researcher to 'find the right result', and they can try to respond in what they think is 'the right way'. If they have no idea which condition they are in and how the responses are expected to be within that condition, then they can only respond in an honest and genuine manner.

Looking experimentally at treatments and interventions

Experimental designs are quite often used by researchers to evaluate a particular treatment or intervention. For example, you might want to see if a 'super genius' drug really does increase intelligence in comparison to a placebo. With these types of designs there are some additional considerations to take into account.

Intervention experiments and repeated measures

Intervention type experiments are almost always repeated measures. You measure participants' IQ at the beginning of the study, give them the 'super genius' drug, and then measure their IQ a second time. This way, if you find that their IQ increases, then you can conclude that this is as a result of the 'super genius' drug. But is it really this simple? With this result, is it possible that the increase in IQ could possibly result from the practice effects we discussed earlier in this chapter? Having already done the IQ test once, maybe they had a greater insight into how the test worked and because of this their score was higher the second time they completed the test?

One way that you could deal with this problem is to have two alternative versions of the same test. With two different versions you would hope that practice effects would be reduced. You could also counterbalance the order in which participants complete the two versions, just in case there are any differences between the two versions. So half of your participants would complete version A, take the 'super genius' drug, and then complete version B. The other half would complete version B first, take the drug and then complete version A. Obviously you would randomly allocate participants to each order too.

Using control groups

Another option might be to have a **control group**. If the increase in scores is due to practice effects, then it should happen even if participants haven't had the 'super genius' drug. In this design you would have two groups, with participants randomly allocated to each condition. One group would be the 'super genius' drug group, and the other would be your control group. You would expect there to be no increase in IQ in the control group when they were tested the second time, but an increase in the drug group. The next question is what makes an appropriate control condition? Should you give the control group nothing at all, or a placebo?

Randomised control trials

The gold standard of intervention studies is the **randomised control trial** (RCT). Whilst you are unlikely to have direct experience of being involved in an RCT as an undergraduate student, this is the experimental method used in most medical research that aims to evaluate the efficacy of new treatments. As such, you are likely to read about them when learning about clinical psychology, so it is helpful to know a little more about how they work and why they are so highly regarded.

RCTs are seen as the 'gold standard' for determining causality, such as the efficacy of a treatment, as they encompass many of the methodological strengths that we have discussed so far in this chapter. The basic design is a repeated measures longitudinal one. The participants complete the relevant measures, say a social anxiety questionnaire, they begin the new treatment, and then repeat the social anxiety questionnaire again after receiving the treatment for a certain period of time. Sometimes RCTs will include multiple measurements to assess the changes over time.

In addition to this basic design an RCT always includes a control group, and participants are randomly allocated to either the treatment group or the control group. In medical trials there is an ethical issue surrounding the control group in an RCT. These participants will have usually have a diagnosed condition, so it would be unethical to either give them no treatment or a placebo treatment. Therefore, in an RCT the control group usually has the current standard treatment. This way they are receiving the treatment that they would even if they were not participating in the trial, and by comparing a new treatment to the existing treatment the researchers can tell if the new treatment has any additional benefits over and above what patients currently receive.

The final methodological strength of the RCT is that it is a double blind procedure, so neither the researchers nor the participants know whether the participants are in the treatment condition or the control condition. By bringing together all of these methodological strengths, the RCT really is viewed as the ultimate rigorous experimental design.

Imagine that a researcher wants to examine whether a newly developed drug treatment is effective in alleviating the symptoms of social anxiety. If they were to conduct this study as an RCT, they would have two groups of patients, one given the current standard drug treatment for social anxiety and the other given the new drug therapy. Their levels of social anxiety are measured before and after taking part in the therapy, and neither the patients, nor the researchers collecting the data know whether the participants are taking the standard or the new drug. With this design, the researchers can see whether social anxiety improves as a result of taking the new drug, they can see whether in causes more improvement than the current treatment, and they can be sure that the results are not biased by either the participants or the researchers knowing which condition the patients have been allocated to.

One-tailed or two? Devising hypotheses for an experimental design

Once you have read all of the relevant background literature, designed your methodologically rigorous experiment and gained ethical approval, there is only one thing left to do before collecting data, and that is to devise your hypothesis. If you look back at Chapter 1 you can revise the different types of hypotheses that can be formed. We are aiming to reject our **null hypothesis**, which is our hypothesis of no difference. So if we were looking at whether there are sex differences in social anxiety, our hypothesis could be something like: Males and females will not differ significantly in terms of their levels of social anxiety.

Somewhat more interesting are hypotheses that predict differences between groups or conditions, the **alternative hypothesis**. There are two types of alternative hypotheses that we can form: a **one-tailed hypothesis** or a **two-tailed hypothesis**. A one-tailed hypothesis gives a directional prediction, where you specify within your prediction which group you think will score higher. For example, you might have a one-tailed hypothesis that females will have significantly higher social anxiety scores than males. A two-tailed hypothesis is one that predicts a difference between conditions, but does not specify the direction of that difference, or in other words it does not predict which condition will have the highest scores. For example, our two-tailed hypothesis may be that males and females will have significantly different levels of social anxiety.

It is really important that your hypothesis is based on a thorough review of the previous literature. If you wish to use a one-tailed hypothesis then there needs to be a very strong theoretical reason, reviewed in the introduction to your report, to justify this. As a result, unless you have a strong reason to have a directional prediction, then it is usually preferable to suggest a two-tailed hypothesis.

One- and two-tailed hypotheses and the normal distribution

It is worth taking a moment to explain why these different types of hypotheses are called one-tailed and two-tailed. If you remember, back in Chapter 5, we talked about the normal distribution curve and how we would expect 95% of our data to fall within ± two standard deviations around the mean. The normal distribution curve is shown at the top of Figure 6.5 Remember also that this 95% is important as it relates to significance testing and our criteria of wanting no more than a 5% chance that we have made a Type I Error (i.e. that we find a significant difference in our sample that does not really exist out there in the population).

If we have a one-tailed hypothesis we are predicting that our significant difference will be in a specific direction, so that the chance of making a mistake will all be at one end of the distribution.

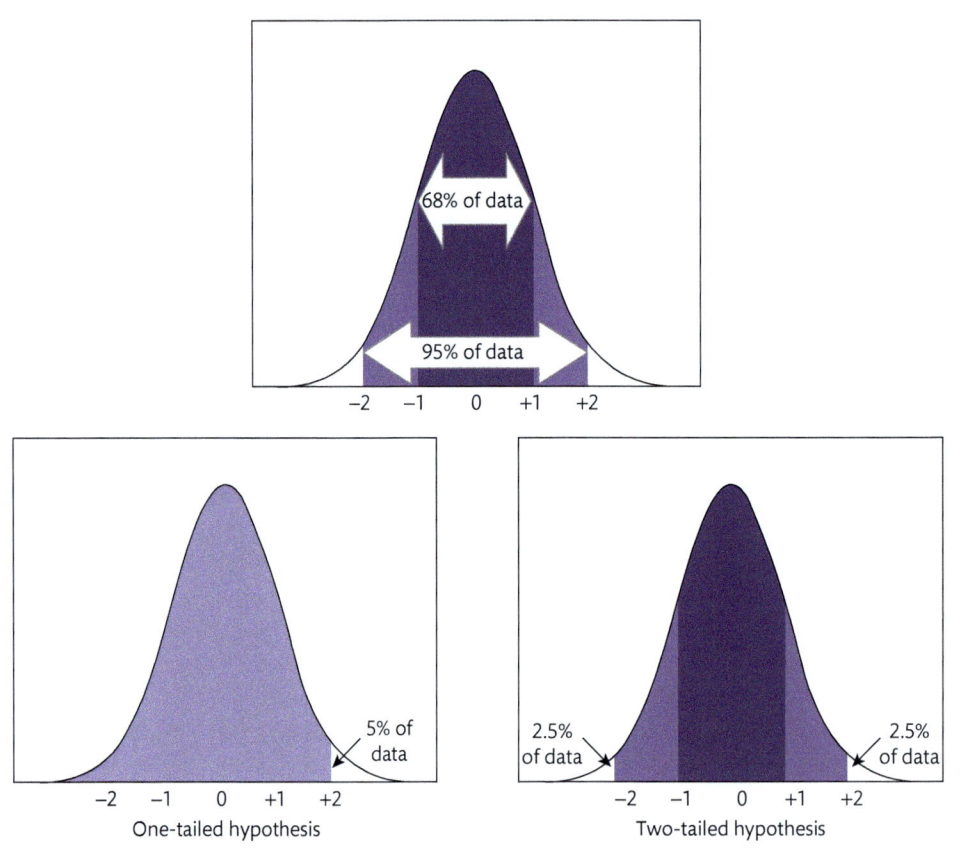

Figure 6.5: The top figure shows the normal distribution curve, bottom left shows the distribution when you have a one-tailed (or directional) hypothesis, and bottom right shows the distribution when you have a two-tailed (or non-directional) hypothesis.

This is shown in the bottom left graph in Figure 6.5. In contrast, with a two-tailed hypothesis, we are not specifying where the difference will be, so our chance of making a mistake is divided between the two ends of the distribution. This is shown in the bottom right graph in Figure 6.5.

This will become relevant in the next three chapters when we will be calculating the test statistics for experimental designs and looking up whether they are significant or not. How we do this differs according to whether your hypothesis is one-tailed or two-tailed, and your result may or may not be significant as a result of this decision. Consequently, it is really important to think carefully about your hypothesis and whether it should be one- or two-tailed. This decision should be based on the literature that you have reviewed in your Introduction.

If, for example, your Introduction clearly builds a case for females being more socially anxious than males, then you should have a one-tailed hypothesis. In contrast, if your introduction is full of discussion about how some researchers have found that males are more socially anxious whereas others have found that females are more socially anxious, then you should have a two-tailed hypothesis. Don't forget that your hypothesis should be clearly presented at the very end of your Introduction, before moving on to explain your methodology and presenting your results.

Analysing your experimental data

You can now design a methodologically fantastic experiment. Next you have to run your experiment and collect the data before you can get on to the really exciting bit, the statistics! Often people love the challenges of designing an experiment, love running the study and interacting with the participants, but hate the statistics that inevitably follow. As a self-confessed stats geek, my mission is to convince you that the statistics are actually the most exciting part of the research process. This is where you find out if all of your hard work has paid off and if your beautiful experiment resulted in fantastically interesting findings. This is where you find out if it worked. This is where you find out if your manipulation really did influence your dependent variable. This is where you discover something brand new about the way people think, feel or behave that no one else on this planet yet knows about. Surely as a psychological researcher, that has to be pretty exciting?

Study questions

In these study questions, you will need to answer different questions about three different experimental designs that are outlined here:

Experiment 1: A researcher is interested in whether there are differences in IQ between 12 year olds who are in state or private schools.

Experiment 2: A neuropsychologist has developed a new app to aid memory in patients with dementia. They ask them to complete a memory test (giving a score out of 50), ask them to use the app for one month and then they repeat the memory test.

Experiment 3: A researcher wants to see if mood improves after laughing. They randomly allocate participants to one of two conditions: comedy video or snooker video. Participants watch the video for ten minutes and then complete a questionnaire that provides a score out of 100 that represents whether they are in a good mood (high score) or bad mood (low score).

1. For each of the experiment outlines, identify the following design elements:
    1.1. What are the independent and dependent variables?
    1.2. Is the design experimental or quasi-experimental?
    1.3. Is the design independent or repeated measures?
    1.4. How many levels/conditions are there in the independent variable, and what are they?
2. Devise a hypothesis for each study, and be clear whether it is one- or two-tailed.
3. Each of the experiments described above potentially has some methodological flaws. First try to identify the flaws, and then redesign the experiment to improve it.

Wider reading

Charness, G., Gneezy, U., & Kuhn, M. A. (2012). Experimental methods: Between-subject and within-subject design. *Journal of Economic Behavior & Organization, 81*, 1–8.

This paper talks in detail about the advantages and disadvantages of independent (between) and repeated (within) experimental designs. They very nicely contrast the findings of studies addressing the same research questions with different experimental methodologies and look at when the findings are in agreement or disagreement. It really nicely highlights how design decisions can influence findings.

Kendall, J. (2003). Designing a research project: randomised controlled trials and their principles. *Emergency Medicine Journal, 20*, 164.

This paper goes into lots of detail about how to design a RCT study, the gold standard of experimental designs. It is written from a medical perspective, but all of the design principles are equally relevant for psychological research.

Zeelenberg, R., & Pecher, D. (2015). A method for simultaneously counterbalancing condition order and assignment of stimulus materials to conditions. *Behavior Research Methods, 47*, 127–133.

Counterbalancing is vital to a rigorous methodological design, but as designs get more complicated, so does the counterbalancing procedure. This paper goes into rather more complex designs than we have covered in this chapter, but it clearly explains the issues and has some great graphics to clearly make their point.

For full answers to study questions, and to explore a range of other materials, visit the online resources at: **www.oup.com/uk/bourne/**

7 How can I tell if scores differ between two groups? Independent *t* test

> **In this chapter you will learn . . .**
> - The logic behind the equation to calculate the *t* statistic
> - How to calculate an independent *t* test statistic
> - How to find out if your result is significant or not
> - How to interpret and write up an independent *t* test
> - How to calculate and interpret an effect size for an independent *t* test

Introduction

An **independent *t* test** is used when we want to compare two totally separate groups of participants, and we wish to see whether there is a **significant** difference in their scores (to revise what statistical significance really means, take a look back at Chapter 5). For example, we may want to see if psychology students and politics students differ significantly in intelligence, or whether dog owners and cat owners differ significantly in extraversion, or if people who have had caffeine do significantly better in a memory test than those who do not.

When we have this kind of a design, we must always remember to define our **independent variable** and our **dependent variable** (flip back to Chapter 6 if you need to revise these). In the first example above, the IV is whether the participant is studying psychology or politics and the DV is their intelligence. In the second example the IV is the type of pet they own and the DV is their extraversion. In the third example, the IV is whether they consumed caffeine or not and the DV is their memory score. Notice that all of the DV scores are continuous variables, and this is essential for a *t* test.

It is easy to assume that the independent *t* test works mainly by comparing the average, or mean, scores in the two conditions. However it is not quite as simple as that. If you remember back to Chapter 5 I spent ages going on about how important **variability** is and how it can come from different places. Remember that variability is the amount that your data spread out around the mean, so the larger the variance the more spread out your data are, where as a smaller variance comes from far more consistent scores with very little spread from the mean. Well, the concept of variance is fundamental for understanding how a *t* test works.

The logic behind the independent *t* test: understanding where variability comes from

In Chapter 5 I described a study where there were two groups of participants, one was not given any caffeine and the other was. They were then given a memory test. In this example the IV is whether participants were given caffeine or not and the DV is the memory score. The study is run in two separate labs, but following exactly the same design and procedure. If you take a look at the graphs on the left of Figure 7.1 you can see the data collected in each of the labs. Each of the dots on the graph represents a different person's memory score, or a different data point.

Both labs collected data that gave exactly the same **mean** scores in each condition, with participants in the caffeine conditions gaining greater memory scores than those in the control condition. If you were to simply compare means the result would be identical in both labs, but things would look very different if you were to calculate the *t* tests to look for significant differences. This is why it is so important to not just look at means, but to analyse the data using a *t* test. A significant result would only be found by Lab One. The data collected in Lab Two would not be significant, even though the means are identical. This is because the *t* test doesn't just look at the size of the difference between the two conditions, the **between groups variance** or **experimental variance**.

There is lots of variability in a dataset, but not all of it is the result of the experimental manipulation. There is also **within groups variance**, *or* **random variance**, in the dataset. You almost imagine all of the variability in the dataset as a 'variance cake', and what you need to do is to divide that up into two slices: within variance and between variance. You can see examples of the variance cake in Figure 7.1.

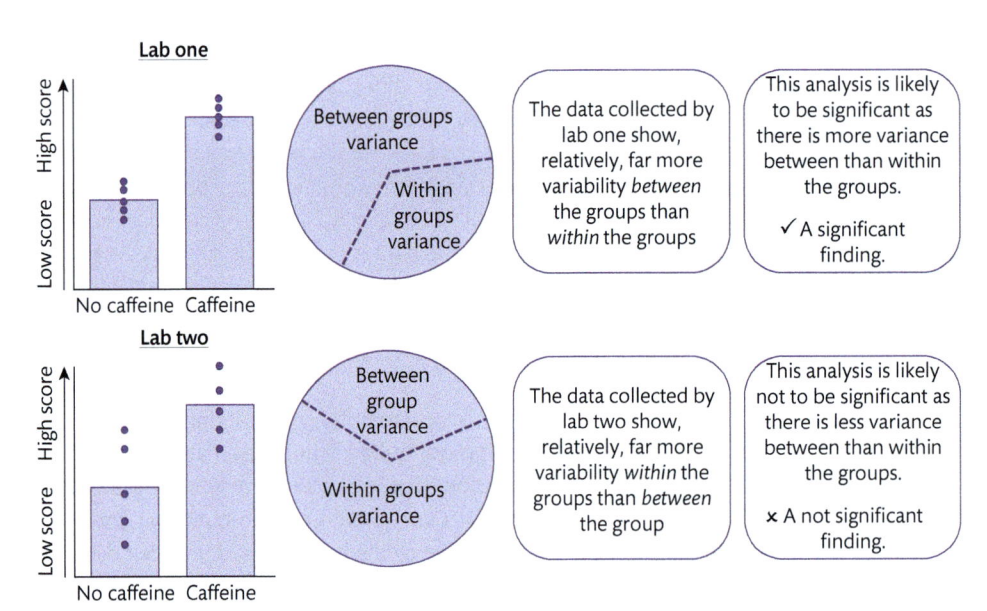

Figure 7.1: Understanding where variability comes from in an independent *t* test, and how it relates to significance.

If you look at the data collected by Lab One, the participants *within* each condition gained very similar memory scores and there is a clear difference in scores *between* the conditions. You want your data to look something like this, although real data rarely look as perfect as the data collected by Lab One! The caffeine manipulation influenced the participants in a very similar way. However, in Lab Two there is a lot of variability within the conditions. Some people had very high memory scores, whereas others had very low memory scores. There is not much consistency in scores *within* each condition and lots of overlap *between* the conditions.

Another way to think about these two types of variability is that the between groups variability represents the **experimental variance** between the groups that you, as a researcher, caused with your manipulation. Whereas the within groups variability represents the **random variance** that exists within each condition. To gain a significant finding you need to have more experimental variability than random variability.

How does the independent *t* test work?

A significant result arises when there is more variability *between* the conditions than *within* the conditions. The *t* test works by calculating the amount of variability between the two conditions (the difference between the mean scores in each condition) *and* the amount of variability within the conditions. If you take a look at Figure 7.2 you can see a simplified representation of the equation where the top part of the equation calculates the difference between the mean in each condition and the bottom part calculates the amount of variability within the conditions. We will look at the actual equation a little later in this chapter, and whilst it may look a little intimidating, it is actually just doing the same simple thing of enabling you to divide the explained variance between groups by the random variance within groups.

This means that, when you calculate the ***t* statistic**, you end up with a simple division sum. You can see some examples of this in Figure 7.3. The larger the top number, the greater the mean difference between conditions. The larger the bottom number, the greater the variability within conditions. You want there to be more variability between than within conditions, so ideally you are looking for a large value on the top part of the equation and a small value on the lower part. As such, the *t* statistic is actually a ratio of between (experimental) to within (random) variance. If the *t* statistic is calculated as 1, then there is exactly the same amount of between and random variance in the dataset. The larger the final calculated *t* statistic is, the

$$t = \frac{\text{between group variance}}{\text{within group variance}}$$

where the top (between group variance) represents the Difference between the two experimental conditions, and the bottom (within group variance) represents the Variability within the two experimental conditions.

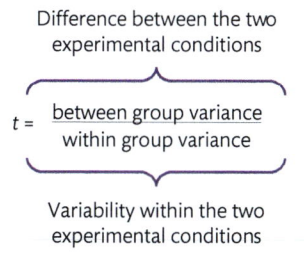

Figure 7.2: Simplified representation of the equation for the independent *t* test, showing where the calculations for between and within variance come from.

$$t = \frac{1.3}{2.6}$$

$t = 0.5$

More within group variance than between group variance.

✗ A not significant finding.

$$t = \frac{1.8}{1.6}$$

$t = 1.125$

Similar amounts of within group variance and between group variance.

✗ A not significant finding.

$$t = \frac{3.3}{1.1}$$

$t = 3$

More between group variance than within group variance.

✓ A significant finding.

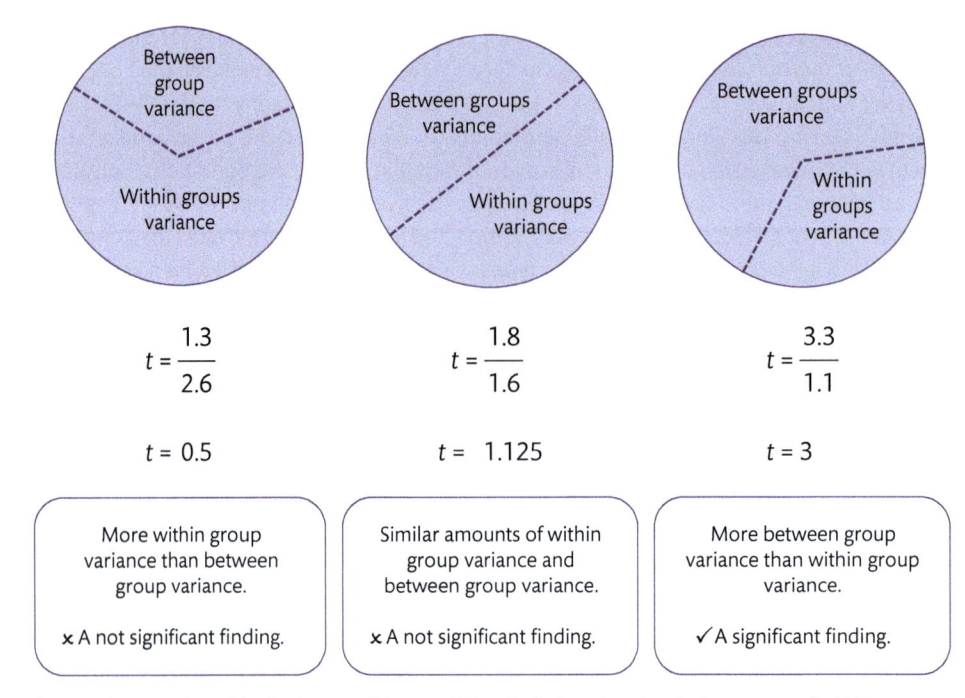

Figure 7.3: Examples of the final stage of the *t* statistic calculation, showing the between and within groups variance.

more likely you are to find a statistically significant difference between the two conditions. The threshold for deciding whether your analysis is significant or not depends on a few different things, and we will look at this in more detail later in this chapter.

In the next section of this chapter we will look at an example dataset and work through, step-by-step, how to calculate the *t* statistic, how to find out whether it is significant or not, and how to interpret and write up your findings. It is very important to note that there are various versions of the independent *t* test equation, and whilst they may look different, they all work in the same way (between groups variance divided by within groups variance) and they will all give you the same *t* value at the end.

Calculating and interpreting an independent *t* test: a worked example

It has been suggested that people are less liked if they tend to gossip about others. In this example dataset there are two separate groups of participants that are asked to read a vignette that describes a fictional person. The two vignettes are identical other than in the first condition the fictional person is clearly described as never gossiping about others, whereas in the second condition the fictional person is described as frequently gossiping about others. After reading the vignette participants are asked to rate how much they would like the person described on a scale of 1-10 where higher scores represent the person being more liked. These data are given in Table 7.1.

CALCULATING AND INTERPRETING AN INDEPENDENT t TEST

As a brief methodological aside, the example datasets that I have created are usually quite small to help make the calculations slightly easier and less time consuming to learn and practice. For example, in this chapter there are only five participants per condition. In an actual research project it is unlikely that such a small number of participants would be used. If you look at published real research, the numbers of participants are usually far higher. However, to keep things simple and because the analysis is being shown 'by hand' I've kept the number of participants in this example relatively small. If you run your own experiment, you should be aiming to have far more participants in each condition than five!

For this design the independent variable is whether the fictional person is described as a gossiper or not. This is an independent measures variable with two conditions: not a gossiper or a gossiper. The dependent variable is the rating of how much participants would like this person. Remember that before you start doing any data analysis, you need to clearly specify your hypothesis. Given that there is a great deal of previous research in this area, it would be sensible to have a one-tailed hypothesis: It is predicted that participants will 'like' people more if they do not gossip than if they do gossip.

Steps for calculating the independent t test:

Table 7.1: Raw data and the first steps of the calculation for the independent **t** test.

	Not a gossiper: Group 1		Gossiper: Group 2	
	Scores: x_1	Squared: x_1^2	Scores: x_2	Squared: x_2^2
	8	64	4	16
	6	36	6	36
	7	49	3	9
	9	81	5	25
	8	64	7	49
Total (Σ)	$\Sigma x_1 = 38$	$\Sigma x_1^2 = 294$	$\Sigma x_2 = 25$	$\Sigma x_2^2 = 135$
$(\Sigma x)^2$	$(\Sigma x_1)^2 = 1444$		$(\Sigma x_2)^2 = 625$	
Mean ($\bar{x}$)	$\bar{X}_1 = 7.6$		$\bar{X}_2 = 5$	
n	$n_1 = 5$		$n_2 = 5$	

1. Before calculating anything, note that the scores in the 'not a gossiper' condition are always referred to with the subscript of $_1$, and the scores in the 'gossiper' condition are referred to with a subscript of $_2$. So keep an eye on these to make sure you are looking at the values for the right condition!

2. First step is to take each raw score and square it to give you the values of x_1^2 in the third column of the table and x_2^2 in the final column of the table. So, for the first person in the 'not a gossiper' condition this is $8^2 = 64$ and for the first person in the 'gossiper' condition it is $4^2 = 16$.

3. Next, sum all four columns of data. These values can be seen in the row labelled 'Total (Σ)'. Remember that the symbol Σ, or sigma, means add up (or sum). This will give us four summed scores:

    3.a. The sum of the raw scores in the 'not a gossiper condition' ($\Sigma x_1 = 38$)

    3.b. The sum of the squared scores in the 'not a gossiper condition' ($\Sigma x_1^2 = 294$)

3.c. The sum of the raw scores in the 'gossiper condition' ($\sum x_2 = 25$)

3.d. The sum of the squared scores in the 'gossiper condition' ($\sum x_2^2 = 135$)

4. You now want to take the summed raw scores that you just calculated in 3a and 3c, and square these values, which you can see in the third row from the bottom:

   4.a. $(\sum x_1)^2 = 38^2 = 1444$

   4.b. $(\sum x_2)^2 = 25^2 = 625$

5. Next you simply need to count the number of participants (n) in each condition:

   5.a. $n_1 = 5$

   5.b. $n_2 = 5$

6. Now calculate the mean in each condition. Given that you have already summed the raw scores in 3.a and 3.c, you just need to divide each of these by the numbers of participants (n) in each condition:

   6.a. $\bar{X}_1 = 38/5 = 7.6$

   6.b. $\bar{X}_2 = 25/5 = 5$

With all of these values calculated, you have a large chunk of the numbers for the independent t test calculated. The next stage is to plug all of these into the equation. We've already talked broadly about how the equation works earlier in this chapter, and the equation is given in full in Equation 7.1. Before continuing with the calculations, it is worth taking a quick look at the equation to try to understand a little more about where the numbers are coming from.

The top half of the equation is very simple. Remember that the top half looks at the overall difference in scores between the two conditions. This is calculated very simply by calculating the mean ($\bar{X}$) in each condition, and then subtracting one from the other to see how big the overall difference is between the two conditions. The bigger this value is, the larger the difference between the two conditions is.

The lower part of the equation looks a little scarier, but remember what it is aiming to do. This part of the equation tells you how much overall variability there is within the dataset. You can see that each part of this lower section repeats twice, once for each condition (x_1 or n_1 and x_2 or n_2), and then adds these together. For example, see $(n_1-1) + (n_2-1)$. It is looking at the variability within each of the two conditions, and then adding these together to give an overall measure of random variance within the entire dataset.

Okay, let's get back to the equations and calculating the t value.

$$t = \frac{\bar{X}_1 - \bar{X}_2}{\sqrt{\frac{\left(\sum x_1^2 - \frac{(\sum x_1)^2}{n_1}\right) + \left(\sum x_2^2 - \frac{(\sum x_2)^2}{n_2}\right)}{(n_1 - 1) + (n_2 - 1)} * \left(\frac{1}{n_1} + \frac{1}{n_2}\right)}}$$

Equation 7.1: Equation for the independent t test.

7. Now take all of the values calculated in steps 2-6 above, and insert them into the equation.

$$t = \frac{7.6 - 5.0}{\sqrt{\frac{\left(294 - \frac{1444}{5}\right) + \left(135 - \frac{625}{5}\right)}{(5 - 1) + (5 - 1)} * \left(\frac{1}{5} + \frac{1}{5}\right)}}$$

CALCULATING AND INTERPRETING AN INDEPENDENT t TEST

8. Next calculate all four of the division sums that sit on the lower part of the equation.

$$t = \frac{7.6 - 5.0}{\sqrt{\frac{(294 - 288.8) + (135 - 125)}{(5-1) + (5-1)} * (0.2 + 0.2)}}$$

9. Then calculate the subtraction on the top part of the equation and the subtraction and addition sums within the brackets on the lower part of the equation.

$$t = \frac{2.6}{\sqrt{\frac{5.2 + 10}{4 + 4} * 0.4}}$$

10. Now complete the two addition sums on the lower part of the equation.

$$t = \frac{2.6}{\sqrt{\frac{15.2}{8} * 0.4}}$$

11. Then calculate the division on the lower part.

$$t = \frac{2.6}{\sqrt{1.9 * 0.4}}$$

12. Next complete the multiplication on the lower part.

$$t = \frac{2.6}{\sqrt{0.76}}$$

13. Now calculate the square root on the lower part.

$$t = \frac{2.6}{0.8717798}$$

14. Finally, calculate the division to compute the t statistic!

$$t = 2.98$$

Before moving on to look at whether this t statistic is significant or not, and interpreting what this means, I just want to look back at the figures we have in Step 13 of the calculations. Here we saw that $t = 2.6/0.8717798$. Remember that the value on the top part of the equation represents the between (or experimental) variance in the dataset (2.6), whereas the value on the bottom part represents the within (or random) variance (0.8717798). From just looking at these values we can see that there is far more experimental variance in the dataset than random variance. This means that our manipulation, so whether the vignette described some who did not or who did gossip, explains the majority of the variability in our dataset, which is good news for us!

Is the independent t test significant?

We now want to see whether our calculated t test is significant. Part of looking up significance involves looking at the **degrees of freedom** (df) within the design, which we talked about in detail in Chapter 5. For the independent *t* test, the df comes from the number of participants in the sample, by calculating the number of participants in each group separately, subtracting one from each, and then adding this together.

To look up the significance of our calculated *t* value, we need the critical values table (see Appendix 3), and the following four pieces of information:

1. Is the hypothesis one-tailed or two-tailed? We came up with a one-tailed hypothesis.
2. What is our **alpha** level? We will stick with the psychology standard of $\alpha = .050$.
3. What are our calculated degrees of freedom (df)? For an independent *t* test, they are:

   - df = $(n_1-1) + (n_2-1)$
   - df = $(5-1) + (5-1)$
   - df = 4 + 4
   - df = 8

4. What is our calculated *t* value? We just worked this out as $t = 2.98$

If you now take a look at Figure 7.4 you will see a part of the critical values table for the *t* statistic. Taking the information above, we can look for the correct column for a one-tailed test and an alpha of .050. We then look for the row for a df of 8, and we can see that the critical *t* value for our test is 1.860. Our calculated *t* statistic must be equal to or greater than this value to be significant. Given that out calculated value is 2.98, we have a significant finding!

Remember that the alpha level of .050 means that we have a 5% chance of having made a Type I Error assuming that the null hypothesis (of no difference) is true. So there is less than a 5% chance of us claiming to have found something meaningful that does not really exist. However, wouldn't it be great to be able to say that there is an even smaller chance of having

		Level of significance of a one-tailed test					
		$\alpha = .100$	$\alpha = .050$	$\alpha = .025$	$\alpha = .010$	$\alpha = .005$	$\alpha = .001$	$\alpha = .0005$
		Level of significance of a two-tailed test					
df		$\alpha = .200$	$\alpha = .100$	$\alpha = .050$	$\alpha = .020$	$\alpha = .010$	$\alpha = .002$	$\alpha = .001$
1		3.078	6.314	12.71	31.82	63.66	318.31	636.62
2		1.886	2.920	4.303	6.965	9.925	22.327	31.599
3		1.638	2.353	3.182	4.541	5.841	10.215	12.924
4		1.476	2.015	2.776	3.747	4.604	7.173	8.610
5		1.476	2.015	2.571	3.365	4.032	5.893	6.869
6		1.440	1.943	2.447	3.143	3.707	5.208	5.959
7		1.415	1.895	2.365	2.998	3.499	4.785	5.408
8		1.397	1.860	2.306	2.896	3.355	4.501	5.041
9		1.383	1.833	2.262	2.821	3.250	4.297	4.781
10		1.372	1.812	2.228	2.764	3.169	4.144	4.587

Figure 7.4: Section of the critical values table for the *t* statistic.

made a Type I Error? It is always good practice to report the smallest alpha level at which your calculated value is greater that the critical value.

If you continue to look along the df = 8 row, you will see that the critical value for α = .025 is 2.306, for α = .010 it is 2.896, and for α = .005 it is 3.355. Therefore, the smallest alpha value at which our calculated value is greater than the critical value is α = .010. This means that there is less than a 1% chance of having made a Type I Error, and we will use this value when we write up our test statistic.

What should you do with a negative t value?

All of the values in the *t* statistic critical values table are positive, but it is possible to get a negative *t* value. Whether the statistic is positive or negative simply depends on which condition you make condition 1, and which condition you make condition 2. In this example the no gossip condition was condition 1 and the gossip condition was condition 2, and we ended up with a positive *t* value as the scores were higher in condition 1 than in condition 2. We could have made the gossip condition into condition 1 and the no gossip condition into condition 2. If we had done that we would have had exactly the same *t* value, but it would have been negative as the scores in condition 1 would then have been lower than in condition 2.

The important point is that you can treat the critical values in the table as being either positive or negative. If you have a negative *t* statistic, you still want the calculated value to be more extreme than the critical value. So a critical value of 2.0 could be read as –2.0. If your calculated *t* statistic were –1.9 the analysis would not be significant as the calculated value is less extreme than the critical value. But if your calculated *t* statistic were –2.1 the analysis would be significant as the calculated value is more extreme than the critical value. This is illustrated in the number line example shown in Figure 7.5.

Interpreting and writing up an independent *t* test

When we write up an independent *t* test there are two important pieces of information to report: the inferential statistic (the *t* statistic) and the descriptive statistics (the means and standard deviations in each condition). Ideally the reporting of these will be combined so that you report your significant finding, and you then use the descriptives to show the direction of the effect by clearly stating which condition had the significantly higher scores. You use the means to help the reader to understand what the significant difference actually means.

The APA standard for reporting a *t* test is shown in Figure 7.6. We can get all of these values from our earlier calculations. Additionally we need the means and standard deviations for each condition. The means are already calculated in Table 7.1 and if you take a look back at

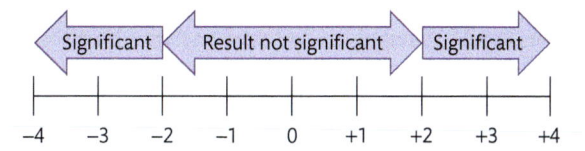

Figure 7.5: Interpreting the significance of negative calculated *t* values. In this example the critical value is 2.0, so any calculated *t* values from –1.9 through to +1.9 will not be significant.

$$t\,(df) = XX.XX, p < .XXX$$

- Tells you which statistic you calculated
  - Remember to use an italicised and lowercase "t"
- Tells you how many degrees of freedom there are
  - Calculated from the number of participants — this is different for independent and repeated designs.
- Tells you the statistic calculated value
  - This is the value that you calculate for your statistical analysis
- Tells you the significance (p value)
  - Report the smallest p value where your calculated value is larger than the critical value.

Interpret direction: Using the mean values in each condition, which group/condition had significantly higher scores?

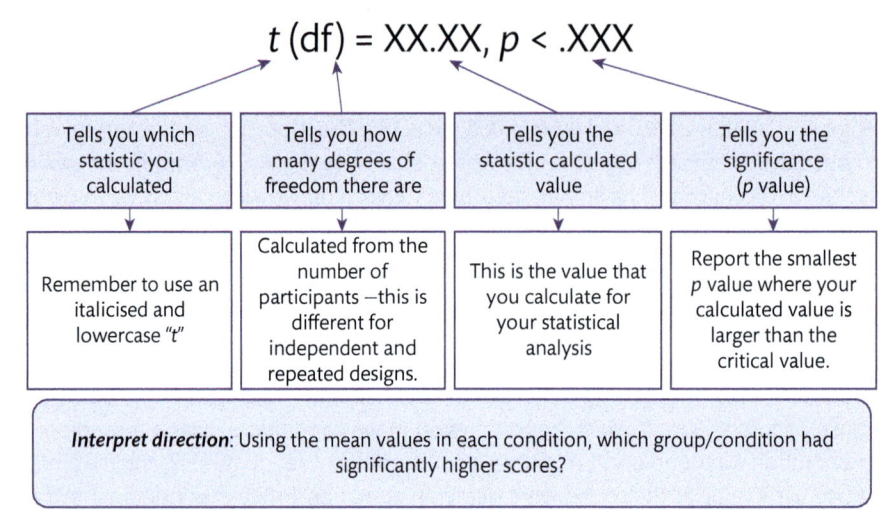

Figure 7.6: APA convention for reporting an independent t test.

Chapter 5 you can revise how to calculate the standard deviation. With all of this information collated, we could write up the results in the following way: There was a significant difference in likeability ratings ($t(8) = 2.98, p < .010$) with people who are described as not being gossipers being rated as more likeable (M = 7.6, SD = 1.1) than those who are described as being gossipers (M = 5.0, SD = 1.6).

Note, however, that you would phrase things slightly differently if your finding were not significant. You would still report the t statistic and the descriptives, but you would not include any interpretation of the descriptives that implied a difference in scores between the conditions. If we had found no significant difference, we might report this in the following way: There was no significant different in likeability ratings ($t(8) = 0.35, p > .050$) with similar likeability rating for people who are described as not being gossipers (M = 6.1, SD = 1.3) and those who are described as being gossipers (M = 5.8, SD = 1.4).

Are *p* values enough? Effect sizes for the independent *t* test

In Chapter 5 we discussed **effect sizes** and how some researchers choose to present them alongside *p* values. There are a number of different effect sizes that can be used with the independent *t* test, but the most frequently used is **Cohen's d**. Effect sizes are very different from *p* values in that they do not have a single criterion that defines 'significant' or 'not significant'. Instead you judge the size of the effect in a far more continuous way, with larger effect sizes indicating larger effects within the dataset. You can see the criteria that Cohen set for the *d* effect size on the left of Figure 7.7.

In the top right of Figure 7.7, you can see the equation for Cohen's *d*, although there are a few different versions of this equation that you might come across. It is quite simple, just using the means from each of the conditions ($\bar{x}_1$ for the first condition of not being a gossiper and $\bar{x}_2$ for the second condition of being a gossiper) and the standard deviations for each condition, which need to be squared (SD_1^2 being the squared standard deviation for condition one, and SD_2^2 being the squared standard deviation for condition two). In the middle right of Figure 7.7 you can see the values that we have already calculated entered into the equation, and the solution at the bottom of the figure. If you would like to see the fully worked solution for this calculation, then please take a look at the Effect Size document in the online resources.

Effect sizes are always written up and interpreted alongside the *p* value, as recommended by the APA, with the *d* statistic presented after the *p* value and an interpretation of the size of the effect. For the dataset analysed in this chapter, the write up might look something like this ... There was a significant difference in likeability ratings ($t(8) = 2.98$, $p < .010$, $d = 1.89$) with a large effect size. People who are described as not being gossipers being rated as more likeable ($M = 7.6$, $SD = 1.1$) than those who are described as being gossipers ($M = 5.0$, $SD = 1.6$)

Effect size	Interpretation
≥ 0.2	Small effect
≥ 0.5	Medium effect
≥ 0.8	Large effect

$$d = \frac{\bar{x}_1 - \bar{x}_2}{\sqrt{\frac{SD_1^2 + SD_2^2}{2}}}$$

$$d = \frac{7.6 - 5.0}{\sqrt{\frac{1.14^2 + 1.58^2}{2}}}$$

$$d = 1.887$$

Figure 7.7: Calculating and interpreting Cohen's *d* effect size for the independent *t* test.

The dataset created for this chapter was inspired by

Farley, S. (2011). Is gossip power? The inverse relationships between gossip, power, and likability. *European Journal of Social Psychology*, 41, 574–579.

Study questions

1. Two separate labs are asked to run the same study looking at sex differences in the personality trait agreeableness. Each of the labs report the following descriptive statistics:
   - Lab One—Males: $M = 46.3$, $SD = 3.6$; Females: $M = 50.1$, $SD = 3.9$.
   - Lab Two—Males: $M = 46.1$, $SD = 8.5$; Females: $M = 50.2$, $SD = 9.1$.

   Only one of the labs finds a significant difference. Which lab do you think found the significant difference, and why?

2. For each of the following *t* values and df, report the full results in APA format, giving the smallest α at which the finding would be significant, assuming that the researcher had a two-tailed hypothesis:

   2.1. $t(14) = 3.19$

   2.2. $t(25) = 2.55$

   2.3. $t(36) = 3.41$

3. The values below represent the final stage of calculations for the *t* statistic. For each, is there more random or explained variance within the dataset, and would you predict that the finding is likely to be significant or not?

   3.1. *t* = 2.1/4.8

   3.2. *t* = 1.6/1.4

   3.3. *t* = 5.7/1.9

Additional dataset

Some research has suggested that a serious head injury may actually increase an individual's satisfaction with life. In this dataset a researcher asked patients with either a mild or a serious head injury to rate their satisfaction with life, on a scale of 1–9 where higher scores indicate greater satisfaction with life (see Table 7.2).

Table 7.2: Raw data for the additional dataset.

Patients with a mild head injury	Patients with a serious head injury
2	6
3	4
5	5
3	6
2	3
1	5
5	6
3	4

1. What method of analysis will you use to analyse this dataset?
2. Suggest a suitable hypothesis for this analysis.
3. Calculate the *t* statistic and determine whether it is significant.
4. Interpret and write up your findings using APA standards.
5. What do you think is the greatest methodological limitation of this study, and how would you redesign the study to improve it?

Are *p* values enough? An additional exercise

Calculate Cohen's *d* effect size and integrate this analysis into your write up and interpretation from question 4 for the additional dataset above.

This dataset was inspired by

Jones, J., Haslam, S., Jetten, J., Williams, W., Morris, R., and Saroyan, S. (2011). That which doesn't kill us can make us stronger (and more satisfied with life): The contribution of personal and social changes to well-being after acquired brain injury. *Psychology and Health*, 26, 353–369.

Example paper using this statistic

Coyne, S. M., Ridge, R., Stevens, M., Callister, M., & Stockdale, L. (2012). Backbiting and bloodshed in books: Short-term effects of reading physical and relational aggression in literature. *British Journal of Social Psychology*, 51, 188–196.

In this paper there are two studies, both of which use independent measures *t* tests to compare separate groups of participants. They nicely report the descriptive statistics in with the inferential *t* test results to clearly show the direction of their findings.

> **How to run this analysis in SPSS...**
>
> If you would like to see how to run this analysis in SPSS, and to find other materials including full answers to study questions, please go to the online resources
> www.oup.com/uk/bourne/

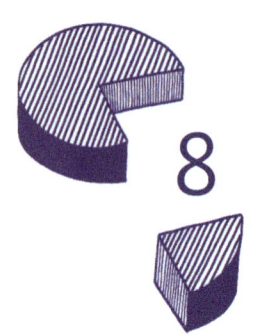

8 How can I tell if scores differ between two conditions? Repeated *t* test

> **In this chapter you will learn...**
> - The logic behind the equation to calculate the *t* statistic
> - How to calculate a repeated *t* test statistic
> - How to find out if your result is significant or not
> - How to interpret and write up an repeated *t* test
> - How to calculate and interpret an effect size for a repeated *t* test

Introduction

Now that you have mastered the independent *t* test, the **repeated *t* test** will be easy! The logic behind the test is the same, but the equation is far simpler. A repeated *t* test compares scores in two conditions where the participants are included in both conditions, so they complete the experiment twice under different circumstances. For example, we may want to evaluate children's reading ages before and after completing a new reading syllabus, or grumpiness scores after listening to Eurovision pop music or emo music.

You still need to define your **independent variable** (IV) and **dependent variable** (DV, remember this needs to be a continuous score). In the first example above, the IV would be time, so before or after completing the new reading syllabus, and the DV would be reading age. In the second example the IV would be the type of music listened to (Eurovision or emo) and the DV would be the grumpiness score.

The logic behind the repeated *t* test: understanding where variability comes from

The logic behind the repeated *t* test is exactly the same as for the independent *t* test. We are calculating the amount of **experimental (between) variance** and the amount of **random (within) variance**, and a significant result arises when the data are better explained by the experimental variance than by the random variance. Again, we are looking at the variance cake, and cutting it up to see how big the 'experimental' and 'random' slices of variability are. However, the repeated *t* test needs to be calculated in a very different way from the independent *t* test. This is because in an independent design you have two separate sets of participants, each providing one score within one condition. In a repeated design you have

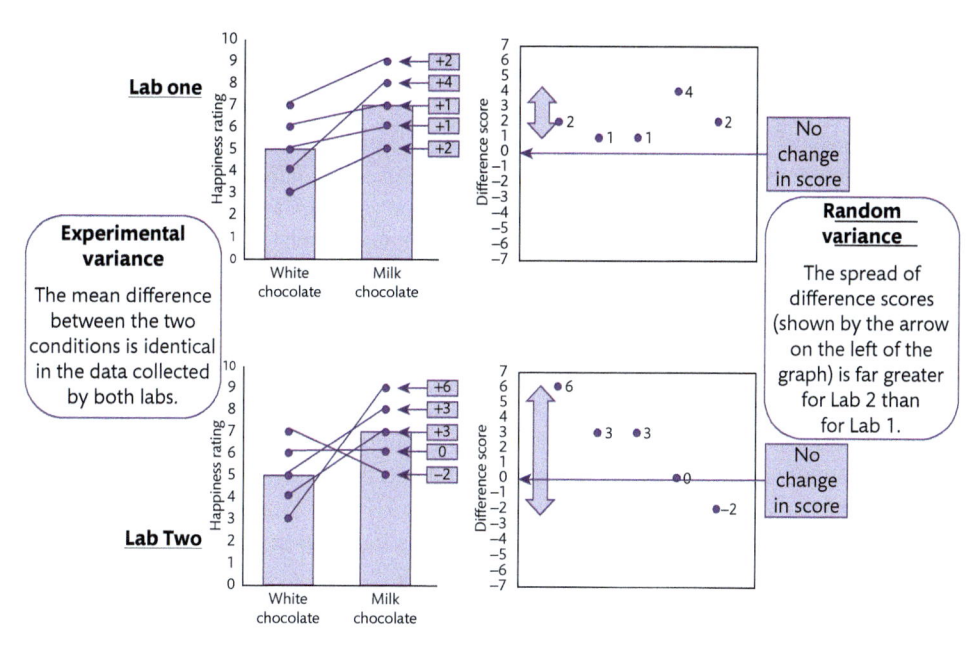

Figure 8.1: Understanding where the experimental and random variance come from in a repeated *t* test.

one set of participants who provide two data points, one for each condition. This makes a big difference to the way that you think about variance and calculate the *t* test.

Remember that the key thing in a repeated *t* test is that each participant provides two scores, one in each condition. This makes it possible to calculate a difference score to see how that individual person's score changes across the two conditions. In an independent *t* test each participant only contributes a score in one condition, so it is not possible to map scores onto each other between the two conditions. Consequently, looking at difference scores is fundamental to the repeated *t* test.

If you look at Figure 8.1, you can see the data collected by two separate labs for an experiment with identical designs. The IV was the type of chocolate eaten, with all participants taking part in two conditions, one where they eat white chocolate and one where they eat milk chocolate. The DV is their happiness rating immediately after eating each type of chocolate. The mean happiness ratings in each condition are exactly the same for both labs, a mean of 5 in the white chocolate condition and a mean of 7 in the milk chocolate condition. This mean difference between the two conditions (white chocolate and milk chocolate) represents the **experimental variance** in the dataset, and is identical for both labs.

Let's now look a little more at the raw data. If you look at the data collected by Lab One, shown top left in Figure 8.1, the top two data points show the data from one individual who had a happiness rating of 7 after white chocolate and a happiness rating of 9 after milk chocolate. Consequently, we can say that this individual's happiness was two points higher (+2) after milk chocolate than after white chocolate. Looking at the other participants, you can see positive difference scores of +4, +1, +1, and +2. So all of the participants showed an increase in happiness scores when the milk chocolate condition is compared to the white chocolate. Looking at the data collected in Lab Two, shown bottom left in Figure 8.1, you can see that there is far more variability in the difference scores between the two conditions, with difference scores of +6, +3, +3, 0, and −2.

HOW CAN I TELL IF SCORES DIFFER BETWEEN CONDITIONS?

Now we need to think a little more about the variability in these difference scores. The two graphs on the right of Figure 8.1 show the difference scores plotted, with a line across at 0, representing no change in happiness scores. For the data collected in Lab One, shown top right in Figure 8.1, you can see that there is relatively little variance in these difference scores, as shown in the arrow on the left of the graph. All of the difference scores are similar and positive values. In contrast, looking at the difference scores for the data collected by Lab Two, shown bottom right of Figure 8.1, you can see far more variability, with both positive and negative difference scores. The magnitude of this variability represents the **random variance** in the dataset.

How does the repeated *t* test work?

Essentially, the repeated *t* test does exactly the same thing as the independent *t* test: it looks at the ratio of variability between the experimental and random variance. If there is more experimental variance than random variance, as we see in the data collected by Lab One, then you are more likely to see a significant difference between the two conditions. However, if there is more random variance than experimental variance, as we see in the data collected by Lab Two, then you are more likely to find no significant difference between the two conditions.

The actual equation for the repeated *t* test is shown in Figure 8.2. As with the independent *t* test, there are a few different versions of the repeated *t* test equation, but they will all give you the same calculated *t* value. You might notice that the equation is far simpler than the independent *t* test equation. You might also notice that *d* comes up in a few places in the equation. The notation of *d* represents difference scores, so the values that we were looking at in Figure 8.1. The top part of the equation looks at the size of the difference between scores (*d*) but adding them up (remember that Σ means sum). As such, the top half of the equation represents the experimental variance between the two conditions.

$$t = \frac{\Sigma d}{\sqrt{\frac{(N * \Sigma d^2) - (\Sigma d)^2}{N - 1}}}$$

Top half of the *t* equation represents experimental variance

Bottom half of the *t* equation represents random variance

This analysis is likely to be significant as there is more experimental variance than random variance.

✓ A significant finding.

This analysis is likely not to be significant as there is less experimental variance than random variance

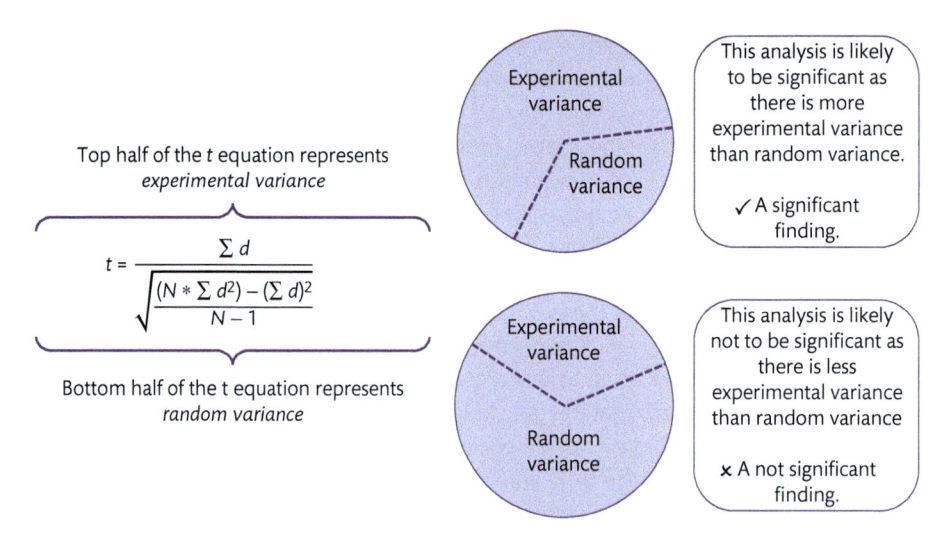

✗ A not significant finding.

Figure 8.2: The repeated *t* test equation and how this represents the different types of variability in a dataset.

The bottom half of the equation also looks at the difference (*d*) scores, but this lower section calculates the variance in these scores. Consequently, the larger the number is on the lower part of the equation, the more random variance there is in the dataset. Remember that the final stage of calculating the *t* statistic is to divide the experimental variance by the random variance. Effectively, you are calculating a ratio. A *t* value of 1 means that there is exactly the same amount of experimental and random variance in the dataset. The larger the *t* value, the more the dataset can be explained in terms of experimental variance.

It is also interesting to think about how using a repeated measures design fixes some of the methodological issues that can arise with confounding variables in an independent design. Remember that in an independent measures design you have totally different people in each of the two conditions, therefore, by complete chance you might have one group being far more intelligent, older, or shy (for example) than the other group. This means that the random variance within each group can vary greatly. In a repeated measures design you have just one group of participants who complete both conditions. Consequently, the intelligence, age and shyness of the participants in the two conditions will be identical, because they are exactly the same participants! This means that the random variance is likely to be far smaller within a repeated design than within an independent design.

We will now look at how to calculate the repeated *t* test statistic, how to work out whether your finding is significant or not, and how to explain and write about your findings.

Calculating and interpreting a repeated *t* test: a worked example

In this worked example we will be looking at whether mindfulness training (paying attention to your feelings and thoughts in the current moment) can reduce the amount of chocolate that an individual eats. Eight self-confessed chocolate addicts are recruited as participants. They report how many bars of chocolate they eat before starting the mindfulness training and then complete a mindfulness exercise every day for a month. They then report the number of chocolate bars that they eat after completing the training. The data are given in Table 8.1.

In this design the independent variable is time, with the data collected before and after the mindfulness training. The dependent variable is the number of bars eaten. This is a relatively new area of research, so a two-tailed hypothesis may be deemed appropriate: The amount of chocolate eaten will vary from before to after participating in mindfulness training.

Steps for calculating the repeated *t* test:

1. The first stage is to calculate the difference score (d) by taking the score in condition B, the after mindfulness training score, and subtracting from it the score in condition A, the before mindfulness training score. Consequently, *d* = B−A, and you can see this in the fourth column in the table. For example, participant 1 initially ate 10 bars per week and this reduced to 9 bars per week after the mindfulness training. Therefore, for this person *d* = 9−10, and you can see that their consumption reduced by one bar (*d* = −1) per week.

HOW CAN I TELL IF SCORES DIFFER BETWEEN CONDITIONS?

Table 8.1: Raw data and the first steps of the calculation for the repeated t test.

Participant number	Before mindfulness training (A)	After mindfulness training (B)	d (B-A)	d^2
1	10	9	-1	1
2	15	8	-7	49
3	12	10	-2	4
4	8	5	-3	9
5	6	2	-4	16
6	11	10	-1	1
7	4	5	1	1
8	9	6	-3	9
Sum (Σ)	75	55	$\Sigma d = -20$	$\Sigma d^2 = 90$
Mean ($\bar{x}$)	9.375	6.875		

2. Next square each of the difference scores to give you d^2. Taking the example of participant 1, their d score was -1, so for them $d^2 = -1^2$, giving a d^2 score of 1.
3. You now need to add up, or sum (Σ), d and d^2. This will give you $\Sigma d = -20$ and $\Sigma d^2 = 90$.
4. Now you want to calculate $(\Sigma d)^2$, so $-20^2 = 400$. Make sure you are really clear about the difference between $(\Sigma d)2$, which is the sum of all the difference scores which is then squared (to give 400 in this example), and $\Sigma d2$, which is the squared difference scores which are then summed (90 in this example).
5. Finally, you should calculate the mean ($\bar{x}$) for each condition, which you will need to interpret the finding. The standard deviation is also useful for when you need to interpret the direction of any significant differences you find (i.e. which condition has higher scores) and consider whether the variability is similar in both conditions, and you can revise how to calculate both of these descriptive statistics in Chapter 5.
6. You should also make a note of the number of participants in the study (N), which in this example is 8.

Now that you have all of these values, you simply need to enter them all into the equation and complete it. Luckily the equation is somewhat simpler for the repeated t test than for the independent t test! You can see the repeated measures t test in Equation 8.1.

$$t = \frac{\Sigma d}{\sqrt{\frac{(N * \Sigma d^2) - (\Sigma d^2)}{N - 1}}}$$

Equation 8.1: Equation for the repeated t test.

7. First, take all of the values you calculated above and insert them into the equation.

$$t = \frac{-20}{\sqrt{\frac{(8 * 90) - 400}{8 - 1}}}$$

8. Now complete the multiplication within the brackets.

$$t = \frac{-20}{\sqrt{\frac{(720) - 400}{8 - 1}}}$$

9. Next complete the two subtractions on the bottom part of the equation.

$$t = \frac{-20}{\sqrt{\frac{320}{7}}}$$

10. Then complete the division on the lower part of the equation.

$$t = \frac{-20}{\sqrt{45.7142857}}$$

11. Next complete the square root.

$$t = \frac{-20}{6.761234}$$

12. Finally complete the division to calculate the t statistic.

$$t = -2.958$$

Remember that the t statistic is calculated from the difference between the conditions, represented in the top part of the equation, and the difference within the conditions, which is represented within the lower part of the equation. Therefore, if you look at the penultimate step of the calculation in step 11, you can see that there is far more between group variability (−20) than within group variability (6.761234). This means that the variability in the dataset is best explained by our experimental manipulation, but is this effect great enough to produce a significant result?

Is the repeated t test significant?

To find out whether our result is significant, we need to look at the critical values table in Appendix 3. For the repeated t test, the degrees of freedom are simply calculated by taking the total number of participants (N), and subtracting 1 from this. We then need four pieces of information to establish whether our result is significant, or not:

1. Is the hypothesis one-tailed or two-tailed? We came up with a two-tailed hypothesis.
2. What is our alpha level? We will use the psychology standard of $\alpha = .050$.
3. What are our calculated degrees of freedom (df)? For a repeated t test, they are:
    - df = N−1
    - df = 8−1
    - df = 7
4. What is our calculated t value? We just worked this out as $t = -2.958$

With all of this information we can now look at the section of the critical values table for the t statistic, shown in Figure 8.3. We first find the correct column for a two-tailed test and an alpha of .050, and then look for the row for a df of 7. We can then see that the critical t value for our analysis is 2.365, whereas our calculated value is −2.958 (you can just ignore the sign for this, positive and negative values should be treated the same). Given that we need our

	Level of significance of a one-tailed test						
	α = .100	α = .050	α = .025	α = .010	α = .005	α = .001	α = .0005
	Level of significance of a two-tailed test						
df	α = .200	α = .100	α = .050	α = .020	α = .010	α = .002	α = .001
1	3.078	6.314	12.71	31.82	63.66	318.31	636.62
2	1.886	2.920	4.303	6.965	9.925	22.327	31.599
3	1.638	2.353	3.182	4.541	5.841	10.215	12.924
4	1.476	2.015	2.776	3.747	4.604	7.173	8.610
5	1.476	2.015	2.571	3.365	4.032	5.893	6.869
6	1.440	1.943	2.447	3.143	3.707	5.208	5.959
7	1.415	1.895	2.365	2.998	3.499	4.785	5.408
8	1.397	1.860	2.306	2.896	3.355	4.501	5.041
9	1.383	1.833	2.262	2.821	3.250	4.297	4.781
10	1.372	1.812	2.228	2.764	3.169	4.144	4.587

Figure 8.3: Section of the critical values table for the *t* statistic.

calculated value to be equal to or greater than the critical value, we can conclude that our *t* test is significant.

When reporting your findings, it is always good to check whether your analysis is also significant at smaller alpha levels. Remember that the alpha level gives your chance of having committed a Type I Error, or claiming that you found something that does not really exist beyond your small sample of participants. The smaller the alpha level, the more confident we can be of our findings. If we continue to look along the row for df = 7, the next alpha level is .020 and the critical value is 2.998. This is slightly larger than our calculated value of −2.958. We must therefore stick to reporting our *t* test being significant with a *p* value of $p < .050$.

Also remember that, if your calculated value is negative, you can imagine that the critical value is also negative, and that you want your calculated value to be more extreme than the critical value. If you take a look back at Figure 7.5 in Chapter 7, you can see this clearly illustrated.

Interpreting and writing up a repeated *t* test

The way in which we report a repeated measures *t* test is the same way as we would report an independent *t* test. We need to report two different sets of information: the inferential statistics (the *t* test) and the descriptive statistics (means and standard deviations from each condition). A repeated *t* test needs to be reported using the APA conventions, and these are the same as for the independent *t* test, shown in Figure 8.4. Remember to integrate the inferential and descriptive statistics so that you use the descriptives to illustrate the direction of any significant feeling.

A significant repeated measures *t* test might be reported in the following way: Mindfulness training was found to significantly reduce the number of chocolate bars consumed

ARE p VALUES ENOUGH?

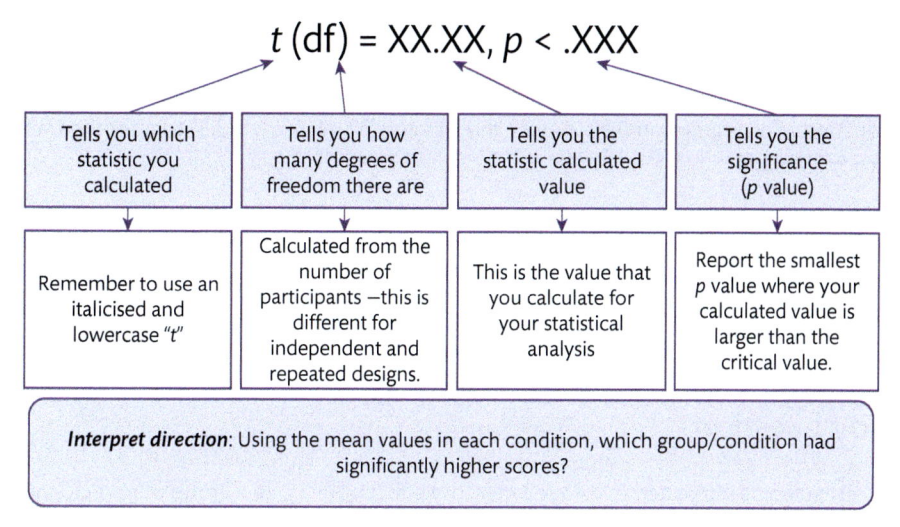

$$t\ (df) = XX.XX, p < .XXX$$

- **Tells you which statistic you calculated** → Remember to use an italicised and lowercase "t"
- **Tells you how many degrees of freedom there are** → Calculated from the number of participants — this is different for independent and repeated designs.
- **Tells you the statistic calculated value** → This is the value that you calculate for your statistical analysis
- **Tells you the significance (p value)** → Report the smallest p value where your calculated value is larger than the critical value.

Interpret direction: Using the mean values in each condition, which group/condition had significantly higher scores?

Figure 8.4: APA convention for reporting a repeated t test.

($t\ (7) = -2.96, p < .050$) with a reduction in consumption from before the training (M = 9.4, SD = 3.5) to after the training (M = 6.9, SD = 2.9).

Are p values enough? Effect sizes for the repeated t test

As with the independent t test, **effect sizes** are often presented in conjunction with the significance statistics. The effect size for the repeated t test is the same as for the independent t test, **Cohen's d**. It is calculated and interpreted in the same way as for the independent t test, which you can see in Figure 8.5. On the left of the figure you can see the conventions for interpreting the size of the effect, and the equation is top right. The values from this example, with before training being condition 1 and after training being condition 2, are in the middle right of Figure 8.5, and the calculated d value is bottom right of the Figure. You can see the fully worked calculations in the online resources.

As the APA recommend, effect sizes should be presented and interpreted in addition to the p value, and the formatting is that the d value should be given immediately after the

Effect size	Interpretation
≥ 0.2	Small effect
≥ 0.5	Medium effect
≥ 0.8	Large effect

$$d = \frac{\bar{x}_1 - \bar{x}_2}{\sqrt{\frac{SD_1^2 + SD_2^2}{2}}}$$

$$d = \frac{9.4 - 6.9}{\sqrt{\frac{3.5^2 + 2.9^2}{2}}}$$

$$d = 0.78$$

Figure 8.5: Calculating and interpreting Cohen's d effect size for the independent t test.

p value. You should also interpret the magnitude of the effect size, so your write up might look something like this: Mindfulness training was found to significantly reduce the number of chocolate bars consumed ($t(7) = -2.96, p < .050, d = 0.78$) showing a medium effect size and a reduction in consumption from before the training ($M = 9.4, SD = 3.5$) to after the training ($M = 6.9, SD = 2.9$).

The dataset created for this chapter was inspired by

Jenkins, K. T., & Tapper, K. (2014). Resisting chocolate temptation using a brief mindfulness strategy. *British Journal of Health Psychology, 19*, 509–522.

Study questions

1. A researcher is interested in delayed memory effects. They give a group of participants a list of fifty words to learn and test their memory one hour later. They then invite the participants to return to the lab a week later to repeat the memory test. When looking at the descriptive statistics they notice that the standard deviation is far larger for the second phase of testing. Given that this is a repeated measures design, why might this be the case?

2. Below are the results of three different *t* test analyses. For each one there is an error in APA format. Identify the error and report the statistic in the correct way.

   2.1. $t = 2.4 (31), p < .050$

   2.2. $t (df = 12) = 3.2, p < .010$

   2.3. $t (24) = 3.3, p > .005$

3. For each of the experimental scenarios below, what would the critical *t* value be to report a significant effect with an alpha level of .050?

   3.1. A researcher thinks there will be a difference in creativity between the morning and afternoon. They test twenty participants.

   3.2. A researcher suspects that participants will have faster reaction time to famous faces than to unfamiliar faces. They test fifteen participants.

   3.3. A researcher believes that eating chocolate every day for a week will increase happiness. They test 25 participants.

Additional dataset

We are generally very good at looking at people's emotional expressions and identifying the emotion that they are currently feeling and expressing. For this dataset participants are asked to look at two photographs of a person smiling. In one of the photographs the person is genuinely smiling in response to listening to a joke. In the other photograph the person in simply posing the smile. Participants are asked to rate how happy the person looks, on a scale of 1–7, where higher scores indicate that the person looks happier (see Table 8.2).

Table 8.2: Raw data for the additional dataset.

Participant number	Genuine smile	Posed smile
1	7	4
2	5	5
3	6	3
4	4	5
5	7	6
6	5	5
7	6	3
8	7	4
9	7	5
10	5	3

1. What method of analysis will you use to analyse this dataset?
2. Suggest a suitable hypothesis for this analysis.
3. Calculate the t statistic and determine whether it is significant.
4. Interpret and write up your findings using APA standards.
5. Think of two confounding variables that might explain some of the random variance within this dataset. For each one, suggest exactly how this variable might explain some of the variability (i.e., could you specify that a particular kind of person would be better or worse at the task). If you were to write about these within a discussion, you would want to find references to support your ideas, so try to find a reference for each of the three variables.

Are p values enough? An additional exercise

Calculate Cohen's d effect size and integrate this analysis into your write up and interpretation from question 4 in the additional dataset above.

This dataset was inspired by

Gunnery, S. D., Hall, J. A., & Ruben, M. A. (2013). The deliberate Duchenne smile: Individual differences in expressive control. *Journal of Nonverbal Behavior, 37,* 29–41.

Example paper using this statistic

Wheatley, T., & Haidt, J. (2005). Hypnotic disgust makes moral judgments more severe. *Psychological Science, 16,* 780–784.
   In this paper, participants were hypnotised and made to feel a disgust response to a word that would not normally be associated with disgust (often or take, depending on which group participants were in). They

were then asked to rate some short stories for how disgusting and immoral they were. These stories either contained the newly associated disgust word, or it didn't. Repeated *t* tests were them used to compare ratings between the 'hypnotic disgust present' and 'hypnotic disgust absent' conditions. Below you can see how they clearly present their findings in APA format, and they use the means (M) in each condition to interpret the direction of the significant differences they find. Unfortunately they did not present the standard deviations in each condition, which would have been helpful for the reader to get a good understanding of the data they were presenting.

> **How to run this analysis in SPSS . . .**
>
> If you would like to see how to run this analysis in SPSS, and to find other materials including full answers to study questions, please go to the online resources:
> www.oup.com/uk/bourne/

9 How can I tell if scores differ between three or more groups? One-way independent measures ANOVA

In this chapter you will learn...

- Why you cannot run multiple *t* tests if you have three or more conditions
- The logic behind the ANOVA and the *F* ratio
- Calculating the *F* ratio
- Interpreting and reporting an ANOVA
- How to calculate and interpret an effect size for an ANOVA

Introduction

In the previous two chapters we learned how to calculate and interpret **t tests** in designs where there are only two groups or conditions. However, research is not always this simple, and you are likely to encounter more complex designs in your studies. As with the *t* test, you will need to define your **independent variable** (IV) and **dependent variable** (DV), remembering that the DV must be a continuous score. However, where there are more than two conditions in an experimental design you need a different method of analysis, an **Analysis of Variance**, more commonly known as an **ANOVA**. With this method of analysis you can compare as many conditions as you wish!

Why not just run lots of *t* tests? Understanding familywise error

We've just got to grips with *t* tests, and although the equations are a little daunting, we now know how to calculate and interpret them. So why can't we just run a few *t* tests if we have a more complex design? Take, for example, an experimental scenario where we want to

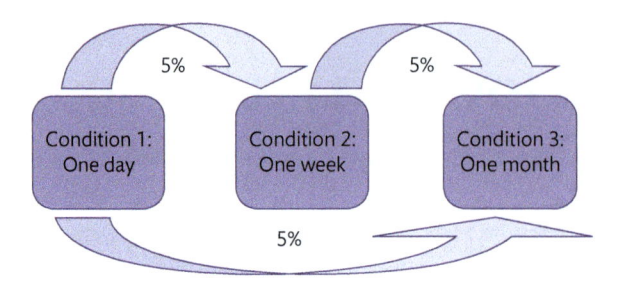

Figure 9.1: Representation of the multiple comparisons that would need to be conducted in a design with three conditions.

compare grumpiness levels after three different enforced periods of abstinence. In one condition participants are not allowed chocolate for one day, in another they cannot have chocolate for a week, and in the third condition they are made to avoid chocolate for a month. We could analyse this dataset with three different *t* tests (one day vs. one week, one day vs. one month and one week vs. one month). You can see these graphically in Figure 9.1. Although this would involve a few calculations, it would be a relatively straightforward solution.

Unfortunately, the approach of calculating multiple *t* tests might be straightforward, but statistically it would be a disaster! Remember our standardised alpha level of .050? This means that for each statistical test we run, we are willing to accept up to a 5% chance of making a **Type I Error**, which means there is a 5% chance of claiming to have found an effect that does not really exist (or a false positive). If you are running multiple statistical tests, there is a 5% chance for each analysis. Therefore if you have three *t* test comparisons, we are inflating our chances of having committed a Type I Error by roughly three times as much. This is really bad, because we want to be confident that any significant differences that we claim to find actually do exist!

This increase in Type I Error is called **familywise error rate**. The more conditions you have, the more *t* tests you would have to run to compare all of the possible pairs of conditions, and therefore the familywise error rate increases more and more with each extra condition added. To avoid inflating the Type I Error in this way it is preferable to analyse all of the conditions within one single analysis, which is why the ANOVA is such an important method of analysis when moving towards more complex experimental designs.

The logic behind the ANOVA

Although the ANOVA is slightly more complex than the *t* test, both in terms of the experimental design and the way in which the statistic is calculated, the logic behind the ANOVA is exactly the same as the logic behind the *t* test. Again, we simply want to understand where the variability in the dataset comes from. We need to calculate how much of the variability can be explained by the differences between our conditions, our **between groups variance** (also called **experimental variance** or **model variance**), and how much is **within groups**

THE LOGIC BEHIND THE ANOVA

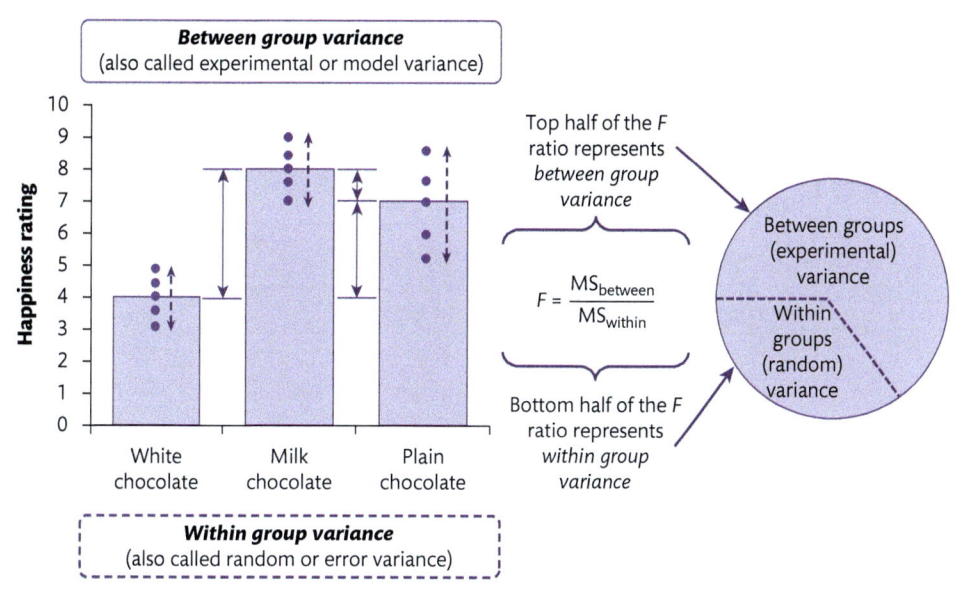

Figure 9.2: Understanding variability in an ANOVA. On the left, you can see the within variance (dashed arrows) and between variance (solid arrows) in a three condition ANOVA. In the centre is the final calculation for the F ratio, showing how the two parts of the equation represent the amount of between groups variance and the amount of within groups variance, as shown in the variance cake on the right of the figure.

variance (also called **random variance** or **error variance**) that exists within the groups. A significant result arises when the variability is better explained by the experimental variance than the random variance. We can look back at the variance cake analogy in Chapter 7, and this holds true for the ANOVA and the ***F* ratio**, the statistic that you calculate when you conduct an ANOVA. You can see this in Figure 9.2.

With the *t* test, we ended up with a division calculation where the top half represented the amount of experimental variance and the bottom half represented the amount of random variance. In an ANOVA, the same thing is true. The calculation gives us an *F* ratio, and therefore an *F* ratio of 1 means that there is exactly the same amount of between and within groups variance. A larger *F* ratio tells us that there is more experimental variability than random variability in the dataset.

Calculating an ANOVA is quite different to the two previous *t* tests that we worked on. For the independent and repeated *t* tests we had one big equation that allowed us to calculate the final *t* statistic. For an ANOVA we will be calculating an *F* statistic, but this is calculated in a number of smaller stages, rather than in one big equation. You can see these four stages summarised in Figure 9.3, and each of these will be explained in more detail next. In Figure 9.4 you can see an ANOVA summary table. These tables are really helpful for summarizing the various stages of the ANOVA calculation, and will be explained as we work out way through the calculations. You can see how each of the four stages of the ANOVA calculations are shown in different columns of the ANOVA summary table.

HOW CAN I TELL IF SCORES DIFFER BETWEEN THREE OR MORE GROUPS?

Stage One: Calculate Sums of Square (SS)
SS provides a measure of variation within our dataset. SS is calculated for total, between and within variation separately.

Stage Two: Calculate degrees of freedom (df)
df adjust the calculation according to our design. Adjustment is for the number of participants (N) and conditions (k)

Stage Three: Calculate Mean Squares (MS)
MS is calculated with SS divided by df. This adjusts the measure of variation according to our design (N and k).

Stage Four: Calculate F ratio
F ratio is calculated by dividing the $MS_{between}$ (experimental variation) by the MS_{within} (random variation)

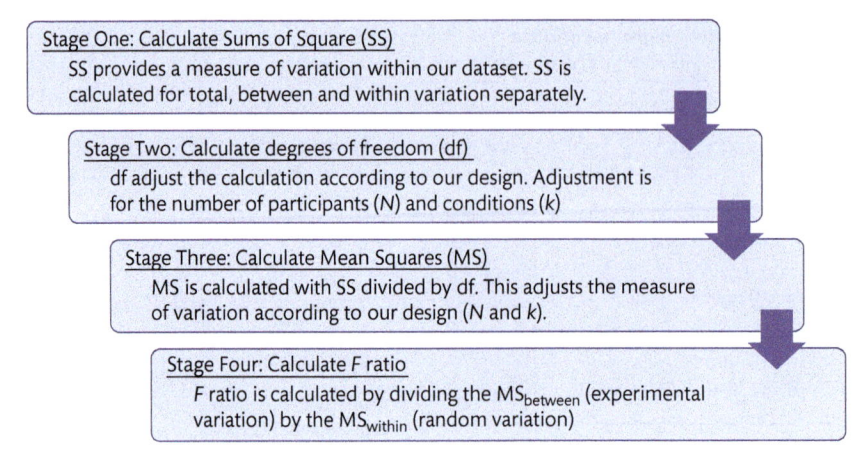

Figure 9.3: The stages of ANOVA calculations required to compute an F ratio.

	Stage One: Sums of Squares (SS)	Stage Two: Degrees of Freedom (df)	Stage Three: Mean Squares (MS)	Stage Four: F ratio
Between groups variance (experimental)	$SS_{between}$	$df_{between} = k - 1$	$MS_{between} = SS_{between} / df_{between}$	F ratio = $MS_{between} / MS_{within}$
Within groups error variance (random)	SS_{within}	$df_{within} = df_{total} - df_{between}$	$MS_{within} = SS_{within} / df_{within}$	
Total variance in the dataset	SS_{total}	$df_{total} = N - 1$		

Figure 9.4: An ANOVA summary table to help you collate and understand the different parts of the calculations.

Stage one: calculate the Sums of Squares (SS)

The **Sums of Squares (SS)** is, effectively, a measure of how much variation there is in the dataset. By now you should be quite comfortable with the idea that a dataset contains lots of variability (SS_{total}) which represents the whole 'variance cake'. This cake can then be divided into two slices, one that represents the between groups, or experimental, variance ($SS_{between}$) and another that represents the within groups, or random variance (SS_{within}). Once these three values have been calculated, they can be put into the first data column of the ANOVA summary table, the column with the 'Stage One' arrow in Figure 9.4.

Stage two: calculate the degrees of freedom (df)

Next we have to calculate our **degrees of freedom (df)**. In the *t* test analyses we didn't look at the df until quite late in the analysis, when we were looking up the significance of our calculated *t* value. For the ANOVA, the df are an integral part of the equation, so they need to be calculated far earlier in the computations. As with the SS, there are three different df values to calculate. The $df_{between}$ is calculated with $k-1$, where k represents the number of conditions in your design. Therefore, if you have three conditions, the $df_{between}$ will be 2 (3−1 = 2). If you have ten conditions, the $df_{between}$ will be 9 (10−1 = 9).

The df_{total} is $N-1$, where N is the total number of participants across all of the conditions. So if you have 100 participants in total, the df_{total} will be 99 (100−1 = 99). If you have 72 participants, the df_{total} will be 71 (72−1 = 71). The df_{within} is then simply $df_{total}-df_{between}$. Therefore, if you have three conditions and one hundred participants, your df_{within} would be 97 (99−2 = 97). If you have 10 conditions and 72 participants, the df_{within} will be 62 (71−9 = 62).

The point of all these calculations is that we are going to want to adjust the SS, our measure of variance, according to the experimental design that we have. Imagine that we are running our chocolate and happiness study, and we have a very small sample with just five participants in each condition. Now imagine that just one of those participants has a really high happiness score, far higher than any other participant. You might say that their score is an outlier. In a very small sample, this one extreme score will make a big difference to the amount of variance that there is in the dataset. If you now imagine exactly the same scenario, but with fifty participants in each condition, the one outlying score now has less of an impact on the overall measure of variance.

Consequently, the degrees of freedom are calculated so that we can adjust the measurement of variation in our data according to our design, specifically, according to the number of participants (*N*) and the number of conditions (*k*). If you look again at the ANOVA summary table in Figure 9.4, you can see the 'Stage Two' column that contains these three df values.

Stage three: calculate the Mean Squares (MS)

The **Mean Squares (MS)** is where we use the df to adjust the amount of variation calculated with the SS. We will calculate an $MS_{between}$ that represents the amount of between groups variance in the data, adjusted by the number of groups that there are. This is calculated by taking the $SS_{between}$ and dividing this by the $df_{between}$. We will also need to calculate an MS_{within}, which will represent the random, or within groups variance in the data, adjusted by the total number of participants in the study. This is calculated by taking the SS_{within} and dividing this by the df_{within}. We now have two values, the $MS_{between}$ and the MS_{within}. If you look back at the simplified equation in Figure 9.2, you can see that we now have all the values that we need to calculate the *F* ratio. These MS values can be entered into the 'Stage Three' column of Figure 9.4.

Stage four: calculate the *F* ratio

The final *F* statistic calculation is actually very simple now that we have just two MS values, in the far right column of the ANOVA summary table in Figure 9.4. Remember that the $MS_{between}$ represents the amount of variance explained by the differences between the conditions and the MS_{within} represents the random error variance (i.e. that within conditions). The *F* ratio is simply calculated by taking the $MS_{between}$ and dividing it by the MS_{within}. As such the F statistic is actually an F ratio, and it calculates the ratio between the explained (good) variance and the error (bad) variance. If the F ratio equals 1 there is exactly the same amount of explained and random variance. An F ratio greater than 1 means that there is more explained variance and an F ratio less than 1 means there is more error variance.

Calculating and interpreting an ANOVA: a worked example

For this worked example we will be looking at how mobile phone use might influence driving safety. Three separate groups of student participants spend 20 minutes in a driving simulator and during this time they have to say each time they spot a potential hazard. The first group is a control group, and they are not having a phone conversation at all. The second group is having a neutral (phone) conversation (discussing what needs to be bought from the shop for dinner) and the third group is having an emotive conversation (discussing revision for an upcoming exam).

This is an independent measures design as each participant takes part in only one condition. The IV is the type of conversation and there are three conditions: no conversation, neutral conversation, and emotive conversation. The DV is the number of hazards spotted. For this experiment, a two-tailed hypothesis is devised: the number of hazard spotted will vary across the three different conversation conditions. You can see the raw data in Table 9.1.

When you have your table of raw data, there are a few stages of calculations for us to complete before we can move on to the main calculations of the SS, df, MS and F ratio.

Table 9.1: Data and initial calculations for the ANOVA.

	None		Neutral		Emotive	
	Score (x)	Squared (x^2)	Score (x)	Squared (x^2)	Score (x)	Squared (x^2)
	12	144	11	121	4	16
	10	100	6	36	6	36
	15	225	8	64	3	9
	9	81	10	100	7	49
	11	121	9	81	5	25
	8	64	7	49	8	64
Totals (T)	65	735	51	451	33	199
Square of totals (T^2)	4225		2601		1089	
Mean ($\bar{x}$)	10.83		8.5		5.5	
Standard deviation (SD)	2.50		1.87		1.87	

1. The first thing is nice and simple. You need to identify how many participants are in each condition (n) and the total number of participants (N). Note the difference between the lowercase n and the uppercase N as we will be using both later, and confusing these is an easy way to make an error in the calculations!

CALCULATING AND INTERPRETING AN ANOVA

2. Next, calculate the mean and standard deviation for each condition. You can revise how to calculate these by going back to Chapter 5. We will need these values when we come to interpreting and writing up our findings.

3. Now we need to start calculating some values to work towards the final ANOVA calculation. First, take each raw score and square it (x^2). A raw score, an individual data point, is denoted as x. You can see the x values in columns 2, 4 and 6 and the x^2 values in columns 3, 5, and 7 of Table 9.1. So for the first participant in the emotive condition x^2 is $4^2 = 16$.

4. You now need to calculate the totals (T) for the raw scores and squared scores. This simply involves adding up the values and you can see these in the row labelled 'Totals (T)'.

5. Now square the Totals for the raw data, giving you the T^2 values. You only need to do this for the raw scores, not the squared scores.

Using the data in Table 9.1, we can now calculate some values that are needed for calculating the F ratio statistic.

6. $\sum T^2$ is calculated by summing all of the T^2 totals calculated in Stage 5.
   - $\sum T^2 = 4225 + 2601 + 1089$
   - $\sum T^2 = 7915$

7. $(\sum x)^2$ is calculated by adding up the three T scores (so all of the x scores across the three conditions) calculated in Stage 4 (giving you $\sum x$) and then squaring it.
   - $(\sum x)^2 = (65 + 51 + 33)^2$
   - $(\sum x)^2 = 149^2$
   - $(\sum x)^2 = 22201$

8. $\sum x^2$ is the squared totals (T^2) all added together. Just be very careful not to confuse $\sum x^2$ and $(\sum x)^2$! $\sum x^2$ is summing the squared totals, whereas $(\sum x)^2$ is summing the totals and then squaring them.
   - $\sum x^2 = 735 + 451 + 199$
   - $\sum x^2 = 1385$

Stage one revisited: calculate the Sums of Squares (SS)

We are now ready to calculate the Sums of Squares (SS) values, and we will end up with three different SS values. Remember that the $SS_{between}$ represents the experimental variance between the conditions, the SS_{within} represents the error variance, and the SS_{total} represents all of the variance in the dataset. Actually, $SS_{between} + SS_{within} = SS_{total}$, so you can think about this like calculating the size of the two slices of variance cake, and together these make a complete cake! At this stage you can start entering your calculated values into an ANOVA summary table.

9. $SS_{between} = \dfrac{\sum T^2}{n} - \dfrac{(\sum x)^2}{N}$ We have all of these values calculated above, so we simply need to enter them into the equation. We then calculate the two division sums within the equation and then calculate the subtraction.
   - $SS_{between} = \dfrac{7915}{6} - \dfrac{22201}{18}$

- $SS_{between}$ = 1319.16667 − 1233.38889
- $SS_{between}$ = 85.77778

10. $SS_{total} = \sum x^2 - \dfrac{(\sum x)^2}{N}$ Again, we have already calculated these values, so enter them into the equation, calculate the division and then the subtraction.
    - $SS_{total} = 1385 - \dfrac{22201}{18}$
    - SS_{total} = 1385 − 1233.38889
    - SS_{total} = 151.611

11. $SS_{error} = SS_{total} - SS_{between}$. Given that the between and error variance make up the total amount of variance, it is pretty easy to now calculate the error variance!
    - SS_{error} = 151.611−85.77778
    - SS_{error} = 65.8332

Stage two revisited: calculate the degrees of freedom (df)

With the SS values completed, we now need to calculate three different degrees of freedom (df). One for the between, one for the error and one for the total. The df_{total} is calculated from our total sample, the $df_{between}$ is calculated from the number of conditions that we have, and the df_{error} is again simply the difference between them. Don't forget to add these values to your ANOVA summary table.

12. $df_{between}$ = k−1 Note that k represents the number of conditions in the design, so we have three conditions (control, neutral, and emotive).
    - $df_{between}$ = 3−1
    - $df_{between}$ = 2

13. df_{total} = N−1 Remember that N represents the total number of participants in the whole sample.
    - df_{total} = 18−1
    - df_{total} = 17

14. $df_{error} = df_{total} - df_{between}$ This is now a nice and simple calculation.
    - df_{error} = 17−2
    - df_{error} = 15

Stage three revisited: calculate the Mean Squares (MS)

We will now use the SS values and the df values together to calculate the mean square, or MS values, and these get us almost to the point of calculating the F ratio. From this point onwards, all of the calculations can also be done directly in the ANOVA summary table.

15. $MS_{between} = SS_{between}/df_{between}$
    - $MS_{between}$ = 85.77778/2
    - $MS_{between}$ = 42.88889

16. $MS_{error} = SS_{error}/df_{error}$
    - $MS_{error} = 65.8332/15$
    - $MS_{error} = 4.38888$

Stage four revisited: calculate the *F* ratio

Now we are onto the final stage of the analysis, calculating the *F* ratio! Remember what the two MS values represent. The $MS_{between}$ represents the differences between our conditions, whereas the MS_{error} represents the random variance in the dataset. As such, we can already see that there is far more explained variance than random variance within our dataset.

17. $F = MS_{between}/MS_{error}$
    - $F = 42.88889/4.38888$
    - $F = 9.772$

We now have our calculated *F* ratio, with a value of 9.77. Remembering that the larger the *F* ratio, that greater the amount of explained variance between the groups than error variance, we can guess that we probably have an interesting finding. However, we still want to know whether our *F* ratio is significant, and if so, how significant it is.

The ANOVA summary table

In Table 9.2 you can see the completed ANOVA summary table for the worked example that we have just completed. This can be a really helpful way of guiding you through the calculations, and it is also a very visual way to look at your data and try to think through where the variability in your data are coming from. Looking at the two MS values, it is pretty clear that there is far more experimental (between) variance in the dataset than random (within) variance. One final thing to note with the ANOVA summary table is that it should not typically be included in a research report (unless you have been told to do so by your course tutor that is). You very rarely see these tables in published research; they are more a convenient tool that helps the researcher to better understand their data.

Table 9.2: The completed ANOVA table for the worked example.

	Sums of Squares (SS)	Degrees of freedom (df)	Mean Squares (MS)	*F* ratio
Between groups variance (experimental)	85.7778	2	42.88889	9.772
Within groups error variance (random)	65.8332	15	4.38888	
Total variance in the dataset	151.611	17		

Is the ANOVA significant?

As with the *t* tests, we have a critical *F* values table (see Appendix 3). Actually, we have three tables, one for an α of .050, one for an α of .010 and the last one with an α of .001. The tables also all assume a two-tailed hypothesis. To look up the significance of our *F* ratio, we need the following four pieces of information:

1. What is our alpha level? We will stick with the psychology standard of α = .050.
2. What are our calculated $df_{between}$? We've already calculated this as $df_{between}$ = 2.
3. What are our calculated df_{error}? This is already calculated above as df_{error} = 15.
4. What is our calculated *F* ratio? We worked this out to be *F* = 9.77.

Looking at the section of the table shown in Figure 9.5, which is for an alpha of .050, you simply need to look along the top to find the appropriate column for the between degrees of freedom, which is 2 in this example, and down the first column to find the appropriate row for the error degrees of freedom, which is 15 in our example. We can then see the critical *F* ratio where the column and row intersect, giving us a critical *F* ratio of 3.68. Our calculated *F* ratio must be equal to or greater than the critical value to say that our finding is significant with α = .050. Our calculated value is *F* = 9.77, which is larger than the critical value of 3.68, and therefore we have a significant result.

It is always good to present a finding with the smallest alpha level at which the finding is significant. Remember that the alpha represents the chance of having made a Type I Error, or having found an effect within our sample that does not really exist within the population. The

Critical *F* values for α = .050

	$df_{between}$									
	Level of significance of a two-tailed test									
df_{error}	1	2	3	4	5	6	7	8	9	10
3	10.13	9.55	9.28	9.12	9.01	8.94	8.89	8.85	8.81	8.79
4	7.71	6.94	6.59	6.39	6.26	6.16	6.09	6.04	6.00	5.96
5	6.61	5.79	5.41	5.19	5.05	4.95	4.88	4.82	4.77	4.74
6	5.99	5.14	4.76	4.53	4.39	4.28	4.21	4.15	4.10	4.06
7	5.59	4.74	4.35	4.12	3.97	3.87	3.79	3.73	3.68	3.64
8	5.32	4.46	4.07	3.84	3.69	3.58	3.50	3.44	3.39	3.35
9	5.12	4.26	3.86	3.63	3.48	3.37	3.29	3.23	3.18	3.14
10	4.96	4.10	3.71	3.48	3.33	3.22	3.14	3.07	3.02	2.98
11	4.84	3.98	3.59	3.36	3.20	3.09	3.01	2.95	2.90	2.85
12	4.75	3.89	3.49	3.26	3.11	3.00	2.91	2.85	2.80	2.75
13	4.67	3.81	3.41	3.18	3.03	2.92	2.83	2.77	2.71	2.67
14	4.60	3.74	3.34	3.11	2.96	2.85	2.76	2.70	2.65	2.60
15	4.54	3.68	3.29	3.06	2.90	2.79	2.71	2.64	2.59	2.54
16	4.49	3.63	3.24	3.01	2.85	2.74	2.66	2.59	2.54	2.49

Figure 9.5: Critical values table for the *F* ratio.

$$F(df_{between}, df_{error}) = XX.XX, p < .XXX$$

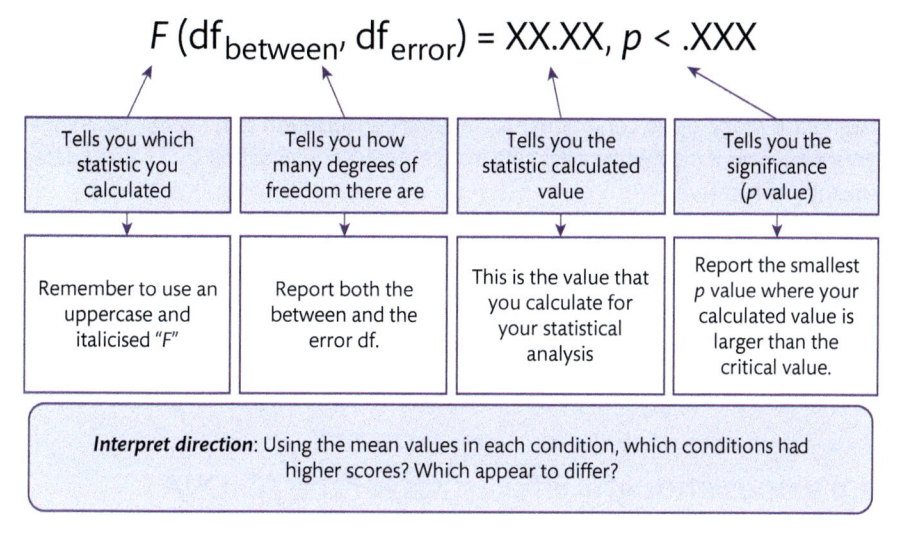

- Tells you which statistic you calculated
  - Remember to use an uppercase and italicised "F"
- Tells you how many degrees of freedom there are
  - Report both the between and the error df.
- Tells you the statistic calculated value
  - This is the value that you calculate for your statistical analysis
- Tells you the significance (p value)
  - Report the smallest p value where your calculated value is larger than the critical value.

Interpret direction: Using the mean values in each condition, which conditions had higher scores? Which appear to differ?

Figure 9.6: APA convention for reporting an ANOVA.

smaller the alpha value, the smaller our chance of having made this mistake, which is clearly a good thing!

There are additional tables for the alpha levels of .010 and .001, and you can look up the critical F ratios in exactly the same way. Doing this, we can see that the critical value when $\alpha = .010$ is 6.36 and when $\alpha = .001$ it is 11.34. As such, we can see that our calculated F ratio of 9.77 is greater than the critical value when $\alpha = .010$, but it is not greater than the critical value when $\alpha = .001$. Therefore, when we report our finding we can say that it is significant at $p < .010$.

Interpreting and writing up an ANOVA

As with all statistics, the APA has a standardised way of presenting this information that allows us to easily and succinctly present our statistical analysis, and you can see this in Figure 9.6. In addition to this information about whether our findings are statistically significant or not, we also need to present the mean and standard deviation within each condition, and we can use this information to help interpret a significant finding.

An ANOVA might be written up in the following way: There was a significant difference in the number of hazards detected across the three conditions ($F(2, 15) = 9.77, p < .010$). In the control condition, where no conversation took place, the most hazards were detected (M = 10.8, SD = 2.5), fewer hazards were detected when participants were engaged in a neutral conversation (M = 8.5, SD = 1.9) and the fewest hazards were detected by participants who were having an emotive conversation (M = 5.5, SD = 1.9).

A problem with interpreting ANOVAs

So far, other than a very long winded set of calculations, the ANOVA has been relatively straightforward. However, you may be a little unsatisfied with our conclusions when interpreting the ANOVA. We know that overall there is a significant difference in the number of hazards detected across three different conditions, and we know that the most hazards are detected when not engaging in a conversation at all and that the fewest hazards are detected when engaging in an emotive conversation. However, is there is significant difference between each of the three conditions? Is a neutral conversation significantly worse than no conversation, or is it only when engaging in an emotive conversation that hazard detection significantly reduces?

For now, we will just stick to interpreting the descriptive statistics to understand any significant findings that we have, but it is possible to conduct further analyses that allow us to ask more specific questions about our dataset, such as which specific conditions may significantly differ. There are two types of analysis that can be done to compare conditions: planned and post hoc contrasts. These are discussed in more detail in Chapter 18, if you are interested in finding out more!

Are *p* values enough? Effect sizes for the ANOVA

At the end of each of the *t* test chapters we discussed **effect sizes**, which are often used alongside tests of statistical significance to provide a measure of the size of any effects found within a dataset. For an ANOVA the most frequently used effect size is partial eta squared, which is written as η_p^2. You can find the eta symbol (η) in the Word symbols menu under the Greek subset, the *p* for partial should be subscript, and the 2 for squared should be superscript.

The equation to calculate η_p^2 is actually very simple as it just uses the Sums of Squares (SS) that we calculated in Stage One (steps 9–11) of our ANOVA calculations, and Cohen suggested the criteria for small, medium and large effect sizes that you can see on the left of Figure 9.7. You can see the equation and the calculations in the middle of Figure 9.7. The values from the example we calculated in this chapter are entered into the equation in the middle of the figure, and the calculated value is shown at the bottom. If you would like to see the fully worked calculations, then these are in the online resources.

The η_p^2 effect size should be presented immediately after the *p* value, so if we were writing up the results of the ANOVA from this chapter in APA format, it would be: There was a

Effect size	Interpretation
≥ 0.01	Small effect
≥ 0.06	Medium effect
≥ 0.13	Large effect

$$\eta_p^2 = \frac{SS_{between}}{SS_{between} + SS_{error}}$$

$$\eta_p^2 = \frac{85.778}{85.778 + 65.833}$$

$$\eta_p^2 = 0.566$$

Within groups (random) variance 43%

Between groups (experimental) variance 57%

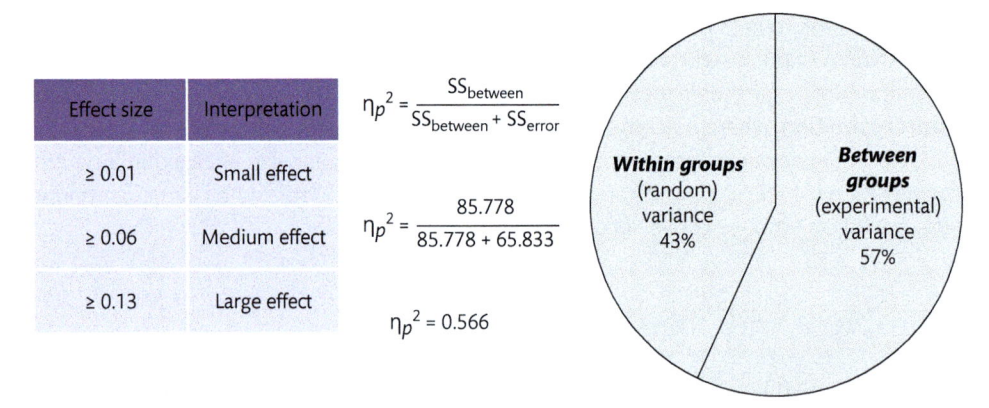

Figure 9.7: Calculating and interpreting η_p^2 effect size for an ANOVA.

significant difference in the number of hazards detected across the three conditions ($F(2, 15) = 9.77$, $p < .010$, $\eta_p^2 = 0.57$) with a large effect size.

It is worth taking a moment to understand what η_p^2 actually tells us though, as it goes back to our variability cake that we saw in Figure 9.2. The value is easiest to understand if converted to a percentage, so multiply it by 100. For this example it would be 0.57*100 = 57%. What η_p^2 tells us is how much of the variability in the DV can be explained by the IV, so how big is the slice of the variability cake that can be explained by the between groups, or experimental variance. For our dataset, we now know that 57% of the variability in hazard detection can be explained by the condition that participants were placed within (no, neutral or emotive conversation). You can see what the variability cake would look like for this ANOVA on the right of Figure 9.7.

Thinking more widely about ANOVAs

In this chapter we have gone through the process of calculating and interpreting a simple independent measures ANOVA with just one IV. Just as there are both independent measures *t* tests and repeated measures *t* tests, there is also a repeated measure ANOVA. Actually, there is quite a large family of ANOVA tests, each of which is suited to a slightly different experimental design. To find out more about these other types of ANOVA, please take a look at Chapter 18.

The dataset created for this chapter was inspired by

Briggs, G. F., Hole, G. J., & Land, M. F. (2011). Emotionally involving telephone conversations lead to driver error and visual tunnelling. *Transportation Research Part F: Traffic Psychology and Behaviour, 14*, 313–323.

Study questions

1. An ANOVA is preferable to multiple *t* tests. For each of the following designs, state how many different conditions there are, how many pairs of *t* tests would be needed to analyse the dataset, and list all of the pairs of variables that would need to be compared.
    1.1. A researcher wishes to compare IQ between participants with blonde hair, brown hair, black hair and auburn hair.
    1.2. A researcher is interested in how extraversion differs across the lifespan and therefore compares participant's extraversion scores within each decade of life, including participants from age 20 years through to age 89 years.
    1.3. A researcher is interested in reaction times to different versions of a visual illusion that vary according to the background pattern in the stimuli: plain, horizontal stripes, vertical stripes, diagonal strips or a chequered background.
2. Calculate the total, error and between degrees of freedom for the following experimental designs:
    2.1. Four conditions, with 12 participants in each condition.
    2.2. Three conditions, with 25 participants in each condition.
    2.3. Five conditions, with 9 participants in each condition.

3. For each of the following results, look up whether the finding is significant or not, and report the finding in APA format, reporting the smallest alpha level at which the analysis is significant.
    3.1. $F(2, 36) = 8.6$
    3.2. $F(3, 11) = 4.2$
    3.3. $F(4, 24) = 4.9$

Additional dataset

This dataset is inspired by research showing that people are nicer, or more prosocial, after eating sweet foods. In this example three different sets of participants were recruited. At the beginning of the experiment one group ate chocolate, another ate chili crisps and there was also a control group who ate nothing. They all then completed an agreeableness questionnaire, which gives scores from 1–12, where higher scores indicate a more agreeable personality. The data are presented in Table 9.3.

Table 9.3: Raw data for the additional dataset.

Nothing	Chocolate	Chili crisps
6	12	2
7	10	8
8	8	6
5	11	4
4	12	12
7	7	8
9	9	5
5	10	10

1. What method of analysis will you use to analyse this dataset?
2. Suggest a suitable hypothesis for this analysis.
3. Calculate the F ratio and determine whether it is significant.
4. Interpret and write up your findings using APA standards.
5. There is far more variability in one of the conditions than in the other two. Which condition has the greatest amount of error variance and suggest reasons why this might be? Suggest three measureable variables that might account for some of this error variance.

Are p values enough? An additional exercise

Calculate the η_p^2 effect size and integrate this analysis into your write up and interpretation from question 4 in the additional dataset section above.

This dataset was inspired by:

Meier, B. P., Moeller, S. K., Riemer-Peltz, M., & Robinson, M. D. (2012). Sweet taste preferences and experiences predict prosocial inferences, personalities, and behaviors. *Journal of Personality and Social Psychology, 102*, 163.

Example paper using this statistic

Flatt, N., & King, N. (2010). Brief psycho-social interventions in the treatment of specific childhood phobias: A controlled trial and a 1-year follow-up. *Behaviour Change, 27*, 130–153.

In this paper the researchers are examining the efficacy of a one-off, three hour exposure therapy to treat specific childhood phobias. The IV has three separate groups: the new exposure therapy, the existing treatment through psycho-education, and a waiting list control group. On page 138 they report the findings of a one-way independent ANOVAs, with treatment type as the IV, and pre-treatment fear levels as the DV. They did find significant pre-treatment differences across the groups, with significantly higher scores in the psycho-education group than in the waiting list group. One thing to notice with their reporting is that they only report the *p* value to two decimal places, but according to the APA standards, it should be reported to three decimal places.

How to run this analysis in SPSS . . .

If you would like to see how to run this analysis in SPSS, and to find other materials including full answers to study questions, please go to the online resources:
www.oup.com/uk/bourne/

Part 3
Correlational design

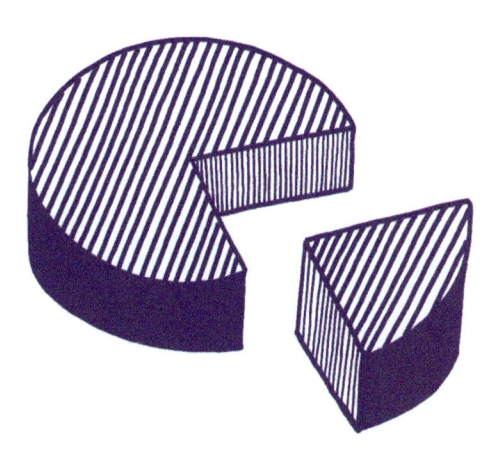

10 How to design a correlational study

In this chapter you will learn . . .

- The different types of relationships that we can look for when running a correlation analysis, and also which types we cannot
- Which types of variables can be included in correlational studies, and also which types cannot
- How to handle confounding variables in correlational designs
- The difference between correlation and predictive models

Introduction

Correlational designs are very, very different to the experimental designs that we discussed in Part 2. The beauty of experimental designs is that we can manipulate independent variables and compare different groups or conditions. In a **correlational design** we do not manipulate any variables. Instead, we measure naturally occurring variables, ones that cannot be manipulated.

For example, personality traits, intelligence, memory score, age, and height are all variables that we could include in a correlational study. In such a study we would be aiming to see if there is a significant **relationship** between two of these variables, and to identify the strength of this relationship.

What kinds of relationships can we find with a correlation?

When we are looking for a **correlation**, we are looking to see if there is a relationship between two variables. That is, as scores on one variable increase, do the scores on the other variable change systematically?

In Figure 10.1. you can see three examples of the relationships we might find. These relationships are 'perfect' and you wouldn't see this in real data that you collect in a psychology study. However they do clearly show the kinds of relationships that you can see through correlational designs. Each point on a scatterplot represents one participant and the straight line that runs through the graph, known as the line of best fit, illustrates the overall relationship between the two variables across all of the participants.

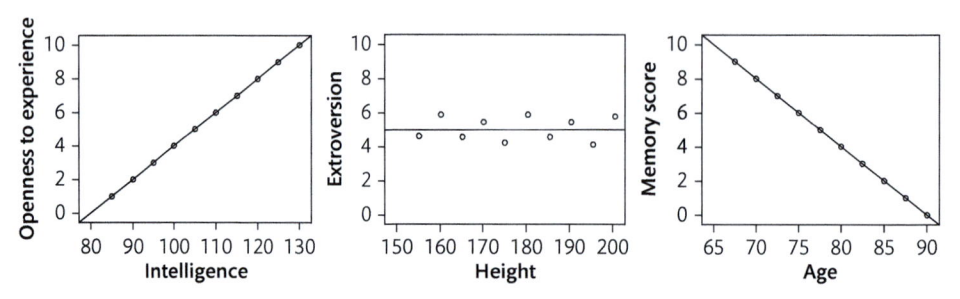

Figure 10.1: Examples of positive (left), no (middle) and negative relationships (right) between variables.

Positive relationships

If we were to look at the relationship between intelligence and the personality trait openness to experience, we might find a **positive relationship** (see Figure 10.1 left). So the more intelligent a person is the more open they are to new experiences, whereas the less intelligent a person is, the less open to new experiences they are. A positive relationship means that as scores on one variable increase, scores on the other variable also increase.

Negative relationships

We would get a very different relationship if we were to look at the correlation between memory and age in older participants. Here we might expect a **negative relationship** (see Figure 10.1 right). A younger person would be expected to have a higher memory score, whereas an older person is likely to have a lower memory score. A negative relationship means that as scores on one variable increase, scores on the other variable decrease.

No relationship

A third possibility may emerge if we were to look at the relationship between the personality trait of extroversion and a person's height. It is unlikely that there is any kind on systematic relationship between these two variables. This might look like the middle example in Figure 10.1. Therefore, an extroverted person may be taller, but they also may be shorter. No relationship means that as scores on one variable increase, scores on the other variable change in a random way.

Relationships and hypotheses

When you design a correlational study, you will need to develop a **hypothesis** (you can revise these in Chapter 1). For these kinds of studies a **one-tailed hypothesis** would be one where you specify whether you are expecting to find a positive or a negative relationship. You may predict a positive relationship between intelligence and openness, or a negative relationship between age and memory in older adults. If you were to develop a **two-tailed hypothesis** you would predict that there will be a relationship between the two variables, but you would not specify whether the relationship would be positive or negative.

What kinds of variables can we use in a correlational study?

It is really, really important to think carefully about the variables that you want to measure when designing a correlational study. First, you can only look at a correlation between two variables. This means that a correlational study is very simple, and just looks at whether there is a relationship between these two variables.

Continuous variables and the correlation motto

Second, and more importantly, both of the variables must give you continuous scores, and therefore be **continuous variables**. If you have measured a variable that does not exist on a continuum, such as whether a person is found guilty or innocent following a criminal trial, or the degree that they are studying, you cannot use it in a correlation analysis. I've lost count of the number of times that I've seen this done incorrectly in published pieces of research, and every time I see it I feel ridiculously frustrated!

Remember that when we are looking for a correlation we want to be able to say the sentence ... *As the scores on one variable increase, scores on the other variable increase/decrease*. Therefore, the scores that you measure need to vary in an increasing and decreasing manner. The examples that we mentioned earlier, personality traits, intelligence, memory score, age, shoe size and height, are all continuous variables. For each of these variables there are a wide range of possible scores, ranging from low scores through to high scores.

Categorical variables: a common pitfall

You cannot calculate a correlation for variables that are categorical. For example, you could not correlate intelligence with the variable of sex, as this variable simply represents one of a limited number of categories a person belongs to. This is the example I most often see in published research that I find particularly frustrating.

Categorical variables and the correlation motto

Remember the sentence that we are trying to complete when we look for a correlation ... *As the scores on one variable increase, scores on the other variable increase/decrease*. Now try to complete that sentence if you were trying to look at the correlation between intelligence and sex. As intelligence increases, a person's sex ... It cannot increase or decrease! It makes no sense to try to correlate a continuous variable with a categorical variable such as sex.

Let's take another example. We want to look at the correlation between intelligence and degree subject choice, so we ask 100 students to complete an intelligence test and ask them what subject they will be studying. There are likely to be many different degree subjects reported, so there are lots of categories within the variable, but there is absolutely no logical order to the categories. Again, our standard correlation sentence would be nonsense. As intelligence increases, degree subject choice ... ?!

HOW TO DESIGN A CORRELATIONAL STUDY

Figure 10.2: Artificial relationships with variables unsuitable for correlation analysis.

Anytime you are thinking about a correlations design, whether it is for your own research or when reading about the research of others, always try to complete the 'correlation sentence'. It is only likely to make sense if both of the variables are continuous.

Distorting the picture with categorical variables

Another reason why it is important never to use a categorical variable in a correlation analysis is that it is very easy to manipulate the analysis to show anything you want (this is not a good thing). Imagine we want to look at the relationship between happiness and the type of chocolate that a person chooses to eat; white chocolate, milk chocolate or plain chocolate. We ask 50 participants to complete a happiness questionnaire and to report which type of chocolate is their favourite. Depending on how you decide to order the categories, and what number you allocate to each one in the analysis, you can create any type of relationship that you want.

If you look at Figure 10.2, you can see exactly the same data producing a positive relationship, a negative relationship and no relationship. In the example on the left white chocolate is given a value of 1, milk chocolate is given a value of 2 and plain chocolate is given a value of 3. This may seem like an intuitive way of ordering the categories, but they are just categories and we have had to allocate numbers to each one. This is possibly the biggest clue that the variable it categorical and not continuous! When we order the categories in this way, there is a significant positive correlation between the two variables (although please note that there is actually little difference in the happiness ratings between milk and plain chocolate).

The example in the middle has the categories ordered in a different way, and with this methods we no longer have a significant correlation of any kind. The example on the right has the categories ordered in yet another way, and now we have a significant negative relationship.

Depending on how we order the different types of chocolate, we can create any type of correlation that we want. That's not good science! It does not mean that we cannot look at the relationship between happiness and chocolate consumption, it just means that we need to think more about how we measure chocolate consumption. It must be a continuous variable, with scores ranging from low to high that exist in a predetermined order. We may decide to measure how many times a week a person eats chocolate, or we could ask them for the percentage of cocoa they prefer in their chocolate, or we could ask them to complete a chocolate addiction questionnaire. These three variables all exist on a continuum and could be beautifully correlated with how happy a person is.

Correlation does not imply causation

There is a second design issue that comes up quite frequently with correlational studies that often leads to findings being misinterpreted or misreported. When we are looking at a correlation we are looking for how one variable changes in relation to another variable. In absolutely no way, shape or form does a significant correlation between two variables suggest that a change in one variable causes a change in the other variable.

Far too often good science is badly reported in the media, and often this comes from a reporter suggesting that a correlational piece of work had shown a causal relationship. For example, the headlines are always telling us to consume less chocolate, wine or meat for some health benefit, and the next day we are told we should actually consume more of exactly the same thing. In the Wider Reading of this chapter there is a link to a website that shows a large number of significant correlations between variables that seem totally randomly picked, and where claims of causality would seem bizarre.

It does not matter how strongly correlated two variables are, we can never conclude a **causal relationship** from a correlational design. There are a number of alternative possible explanations and issues. Let's take the example again of a possible relationship between happiness and the amount of chocolate that one consumes.

The first issue is that the relationship between chocolate consumption and happiness may not be a direct one. The relationship may in fact work via another variable that we did not measure, or maybe more than one additional variable. For example, people who eat more chocolate may have lower levels of stress, due to the stress relieving properties of chocolate. There then may be a separate negative relationship between lower levels of stress and higher levels of happiness. If this were the case there is actually no direct relationship between chocolate consumption and happiness, but they are spuriously correlated.

A second problem is that, even if there were some causal relationship, it is impossible to determine the direction of a causal relationship from a simple correlation. Is it that eating more chocolate makes people happier, or is it that happier people eat more chocolate?

If your research question requires you to look at causal relationships between variables, you actually need to be looking at an experimental design. You could take two groups of participants, randomly allocate half to a no chocolate condition and half to a daily chocolate condition and then measure their happiness a month later. With this type of design you can get closer to understanding the possible causal relationship between chocolate consumption and happiness.

Confounding variables in correlational designs

In any correlational design it is important to seriously consider possible **confounding variables** in your study (you can look back at Chapter 2 to revise the basics of what confounding variables are). Confounding variables are *unmeasured* variables that may explain some of the variability in your dataset. It is probably impossible that any relationship between two human behaviours can be simply explained with two variables. We are complex things and there may be many other variables that could contribute to the relationship we are looking at.

HOW TO DESIGN A CORRELATIONAL STUDY

We have already briefly touched upon confounding variables in this chapter in our chocolate and happiness example when we considered the role of stress. This variable could explain some of the relationship that we are looking at. Other possible confounds in this design might be how much a person likes chocolate, their age, their level of self-control, and probably many, many others.

Confounding variables can explain some highly significant correlations between variables that seem to be entirely unrelated. You'll remember my favourite example that there is a strong correlation between ice cream sales and the number of shark attacks that occur each year in Australia. It seems unlikely that there is a direct relationship between these two variables, but it can probably be quite easily explained by the confounding variable of temperature. The warmer it is, the more people will want to eat ice cream. The warmer it is, the more likely people are to swim in the sea, and more people in the water increases the chances of a shark attack.

What to do with confounding variables

It is possible to design a correlational study in such a way that you decide to measure a small number of potential confounding variables. Once these variables are measured, they become **control variables**. It is impossible to design a study that takes into account all of the possible confounding or control variables. With a more complex design than we are able to cover in this book, some control variables can be measured and controlled for statistically. However, even with the simplest correlational design you can consider what the possible unmeasured confounds are within your design in your discussion.

Try to think about how a particular confound might influence your findings. Would it influence all of your participants, or just a small subset of them? A possible confound in our chocolate and happiness study is people being on a diet, which you can see in Figure 10.3.

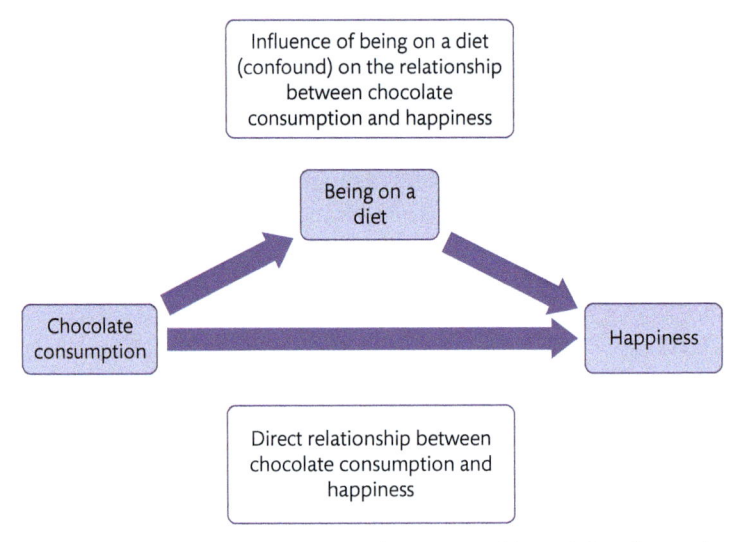

Figure 10.3: Illustration of possible direct relationships between variables, and the influence that confounding variables can have on a relationship.

However not all of our participants will have been on a diet, therefore the confound will only have influenced a small amount of our data and it is likely that the relationship we find will still exist, even if we were to remove all of the dieters from our study.

You should also try to think about the way that a confound might influence a correlation. Imagine we found a positive correlation between chocolate consumption and happiness. A possible confound is the level of stress that someone is experiencing. If it were possible to take away the influence of stress on this relationship, do you think it would become stronger, become weaker, or not change at all?

These are really fundamental questions to ask about your design, and such issues deserve at least a small amount of attention in the discussion of any study using a correlational design. Ensure that you include some research to support your ideas though. So for our example, you would need to search for papers looking at the relationships between stress and chocolate consumption, and separately the relationship between stress and happiness.

Using correlational designs to form predictive models

A correlation looks at the possible relationship between two continuous variables, but this is really the simplest type of correlational study design. For any design that is slightly more complex a different type of analysis is needed: a **regression analysis**. Regressions can be incredibly complex (and these are discussed a little more in Chapter 18), but for the purposes of this book we will just be looking at the simplest type, a simple linear regression.

Linear regression

Similar to a correlation, a simple linear regression looks at the relationship between two continuous variables, but it gives us far more information about that relationship. Importantly, it adds the ability to use the scores on one variable to predict the scores on another variable.

Imagine we are trying to predict the chances of a person crashing their car on the basis of their age. This is a very simple version of what car insurance companies try to do when they give you a quote. They will have a large database of information about road traffic accidents and they can look up, for example, the correlation between age and risk of crashing. When you give them your age, they use the data they have to try to predict how likely you are to have a crash. The more likely you are, the more they will charge you for your insurance premium.

When we run a simple linear regression analysis we have to decide which of our variables will be the predictor variable, and which will be the outcome variable. In the car insurance example, age would be the predictor and risk of crashing would be the outcome. It is important to think about the previous research and theories when deciding which variable should be a predictor and which should be an outcome, as these decisions should be theoretically motivated.

Going back to our chocolate and happiness example, if the theoretical background suggested that the chemicals in chocolate can cause improvements to mood, then we might decide that chocolate consumption could be the predictor variable and happiness could be the outcome variable. Alternatively, the previous research that we have reviewed might look at how mood influences eating patterns, and to examine this we would treat happiness as the predictor variable and chocolate consumption as the outcome variable.

Describing variables in a regression analysis

Very importantly, the terminology that you use when describing variables in a regression analysis differs greatly from the terminology that you use when describing variables in an experimental design. Throughout Part 2 of this book, which concentrated on experimental designs and analyses, we talked about independent variables (what you manipulate) and dependent variables (what you measure). In a regression analysis this is not appropriate as nothing is being manipulated. Therefore you should be talking about your **predictor variable** and your **outcome variable**.

With a regression it is very, very easy to fall into the trap of assuming that some form of causation is being shown. This is absolutely not the case. You are the one deciding which variable is the predictor and which is the outcome. So although there may intuitively be a causal direction (eating chocolate causes you to be happier), this is just your own assumption. There is nothing in the design or the data collected that provides evidence for a causal relationship.

The magic behind how regression can be used as a predictive tool is explained fully in Chapter 12, but it is pretty cool, which is why regression is absolutely my favourite method of statistical analysis.

Study questions

1. A researcher has run a study looking at memory in older adults over the age of 65 years old. They want to see whether memory scores are correlated with age and IQ.
    1.1. For each of these variable pairs (memory and age, memory and IQ), what kind of relationship would you predict?
    1.2. Suggest three additional variables that might be interesting to measure and analyse when looking at memory function. Remember that the variables must be continuous scores. For each of your suggested variables, what kind of relationship do you predict there will be with memory?
2. It is often suggested that taking nutritional supplements improves cognitive function.
    2.1. What possible problem is there in the logic of this statement if the study uses a correlational design?
    2.2. What kind of relationship would you predict for the correlation between the number of nutritional supplements taken per week and cognitive ability?
    2.3. Suggest three possible confounding variables that might influence this relationship.
3. Imagine you are designing a study to look at intelligence.
    3.1. Think of three variables that you could include in your study. Remember that all three variables must be *continuous scores*. One variable should be expected to be positively correlated with intelligence, one should be negatively correlated with intelligence and the other should not be correlated with intelligence at all.

4. You have been asked to run a study looking at the relationships between the number of friends a child has and some four additional variables that they are particularly interested in: 1. Age of the child. 2. Whether they are male or female. 3. Whether they are an only child or have siblings. 4. Whether they attend chess club, dance club or football club.

   4.1. For each of these four variables decide whether it is suitable for use within a correlation design or not. If it is not suitable, suggest an alternative similar variable that would be suitable for including in a study with a correlational design.

Wider reading

Bleske-Rechek, A., Morrison, K. M., & Heidtke, L. D. (2015). Causal Inference from Descriptions of Experimental and Non-Experimental Research: Public Understanding of Correlation-Versus-Causation. *The Journal of General Psychology*, *142*, 48–70.
This is a really interesting paper where they run a series of studies looking at how people tend to attribute causal explanations to correlational findings.

www.tylervigen.com/spurious-correlations
There are some totally bonkers and random correlations between variables, and this website shows how there can be highly significant correlations between the most unlikely pairs of variables. I think my favourite correlation has to be the almost perfect positive correlation between the amount of cheese consumed by Americans and the number of people in the US who died by becoming entangled in their bedsheets. Could this be explained by cheese giving people nightmares, which causes them to thrash about whilst sleeping?!

For full answers to study questions, and to explore a range of other materials, visit the online resources at: **www.oup.com/uk/bourne/**

11 How can I tell if two variables are correlated? Pearson's correlation

In this chapter you will learn . . .

- How variability in data allow you to look at relationships between variables
- How to calculate a Pearson's *r* value
- How to understand what an *r* value tells you about the data you have collected and the relationship between the two variables
- How to find out of the *r* value indicates a significant correlation
- How to interpret and write about *r* values and correlational analyses
- How to interpret *r* values as effect sizes

Introduction

As we saw in Chapter 10, when we are looking at relationships between variables we are looking at two continuous variables, and we are asking whether variability in the scores on one variable changes systematically in relation to the other variable. Remember the sentence we want to complete when we are looking at correlations ... *As the scores on one variable increase, scores on the other variable increase/decrease.*

Correlations between variables can show either positive or negative relationships. When we calculate the **Pearson's correlation** statistic we end up with an **_r_ value**. This *r* value maps directly onto the type of relationship that exists within the data: a positive *r* values shows that there is a **positive relationship** between the two variables, whereas a negative *r* value shows that there is a **negative relationship** between two variables. The *r* value varies from −1 through to +1, so if you ever calculate an *r* value outside of these values something has gone horribly wrong!

A *r* value of −1 means that there is a perfect negative relationship between two variables, an *r* value of +1 means that there is a perfect positive relationship between two variables, whereas an *r* value of 0 indicates that there is absolutely no relationship at all between two variables. In Figure 11.1 you can see examples of these three *r* values in **scatterplots** where the line running through the graph, the line of best fit, shows the relationship between the two variables.

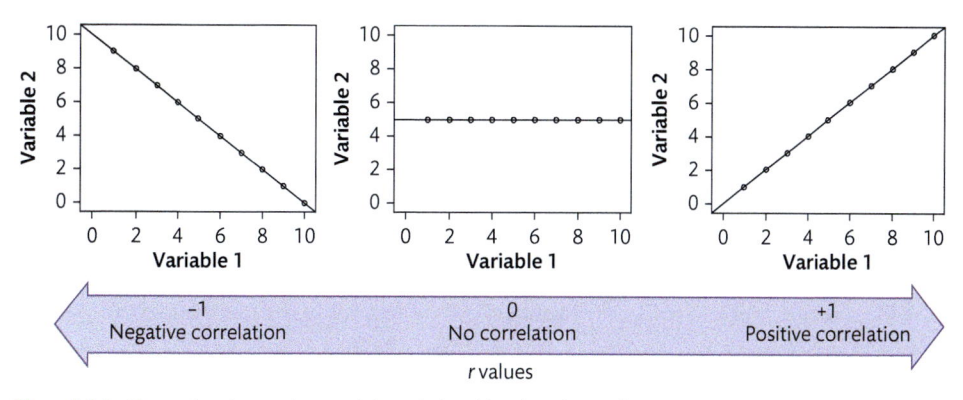

Figure 11.1. Figure showing *r* values and the relationships that they indicate.

In reality we very rarely see perfect positive or perfect negative correlations. If we did, it would probably mean that we have two different measures of the same thing—for instance, if we were to measure a person's height in centimetres and in metres they would be perfectly correlated. So, given the rarity of a −1 or +1 *r* value, when we are looking for correlations between two variables, we hope for a value away from 0, but how far away from 0 suggests that we have found a meaningful relationship?

There are some conventions that allow us to define how strong a correlation is. Different ways of categorizing correlations exist (and statisticians can really argue about where the boundaries should fall!), but Figure 11.2 shows one way that correlations can be classified along with graphs showing you roughly how strong the relationship is.

While it is great to be able to roughly describe a correlation between two variables, we ideally want to know whether a relationship is significant or not. Luckily it is quite easy to do this, and in this chapter we will learn how to calculate the *r* statistic and work out how significant a relationship is.

The logic behind a Pearson's correlation: understanding the role of variability

In Part 2 of this book, in the chapters on experimental designs and methods of analyses, we talked a great deal about how vital it is to understand the variability in a dataset. The *t* tests and ANOVA are based on calculating the amount of experimental (between groups) variance and random (within groups) variance in a dataset, and then seeing whether there is more variability between groups (which is good) or within groups (which is bad). You can take a look back at the beginning of Chapter 7 if you want to revise this.

Although the correlation is a very different kind of analysis to a *t* test, it actually works in a very similar way in terms of looking at different types of variability within a dataset. When you look at a scatterplot that shows a relationship between two variables, such as those in Figure 11.2, you often see a **line of best fit**, which is the straight line drawn through the raw data points. You will read far more about this in Chapter 12, but for the

HOW CAN I TELL IF TWO VARIABLES ARE CORRELATED?

	Positive relationships	Negative relationships
0 to +/- .09 No relationship		
+/- .10 to +/- .29 Weak relationship		
+/- .30 to +/- .59 Moderate relationship		
+/- .60 to +/- .99 Strong relationship		
+/- 1.00 Perfect relationship		

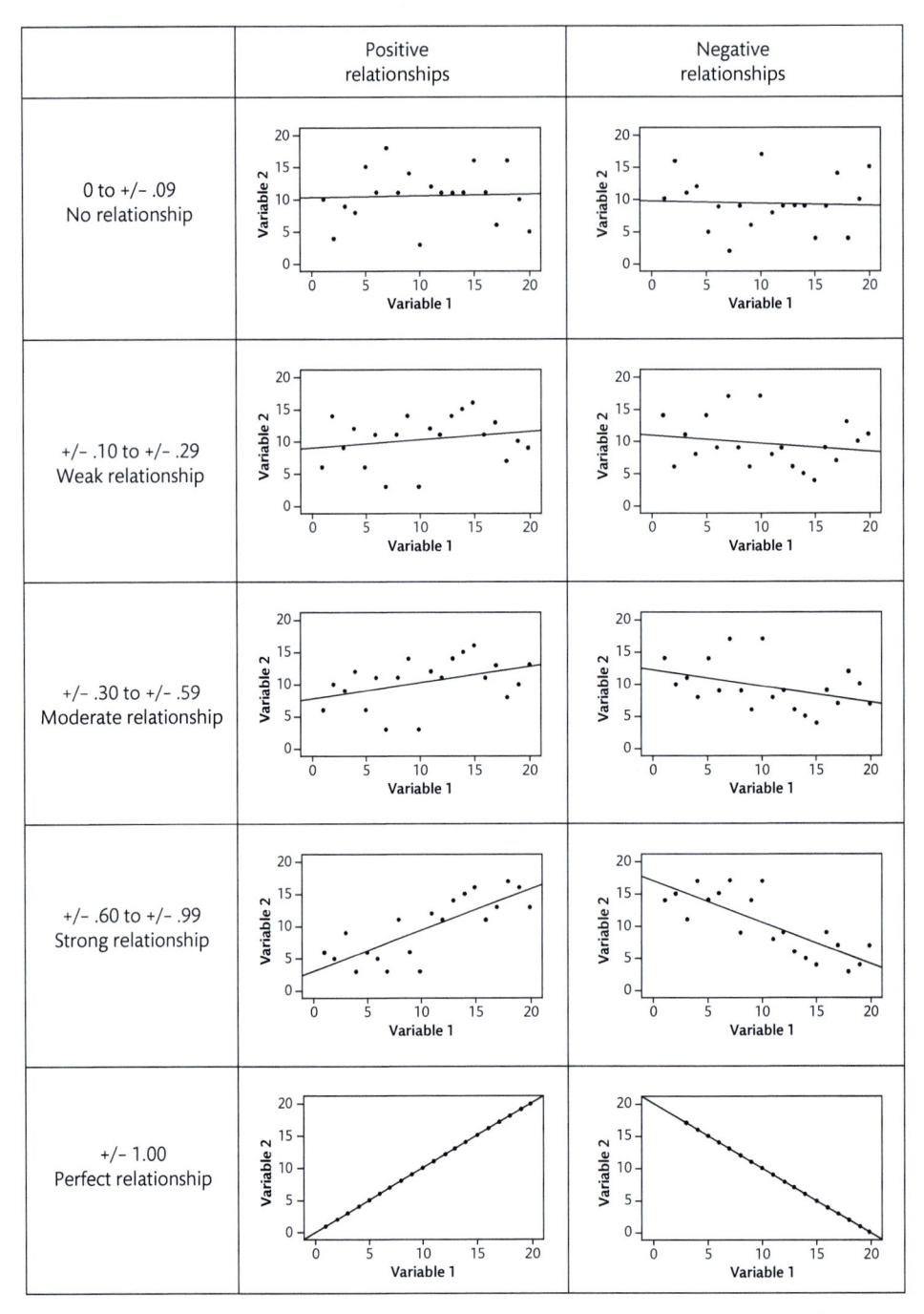

Figure 11.2: Conventions for describing the strength of a correlation between two variables and illustrative scatterplots.

What does the Pearson's correlation do?

If all of the raw data points sit very close to this line, then the relationship is very consistent, whereas if they fall far from the line there is more variability in the relationship. Consequently, the Pearson's correlation looks at how much the data points change together, which is known as **covariance**. For a positive relationship, this would mean that as scores on one variable increase, scores on the other variable also increase in a similar way. For a negative relationship, this would mean that as scores on one variable increase, the scores on the other variable decrease in a similar way.

The more two variables covary and change in a similar way, the more covariance there will be. This is the number that is calculated on the top part of the r equation that you can see at the top of Figure 11.3. The bottom part of the equation looks at the variance within each variable that exists in isolation when you look at it on its own. In a very similar way to the final calculation of the t and F statistics, you end up dividing one number by another. For the correlation you divide the covariance (the amount that the two variables change together) by the random variance around this relationship. The more similar these numbers are, the stronger the calculated correlation will be.

The two graphs in Figure 11.3 show you the relationship between chocolate consumption and happiness in data collected from two different labs. If you look at the example in the left panel of Figure 11.3, then you can see that all of the raw data points sit quite close to the line of best fit, and therefore covary together quite closely. This means that as the amount

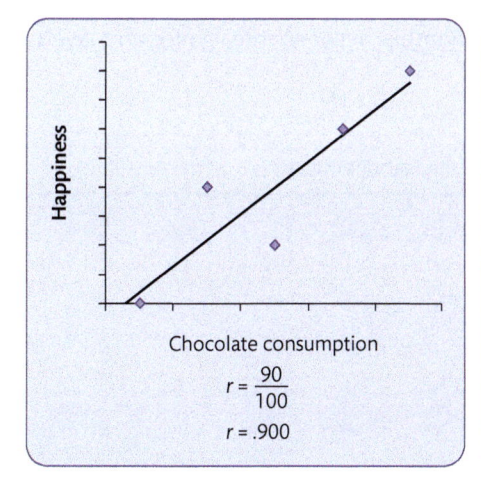

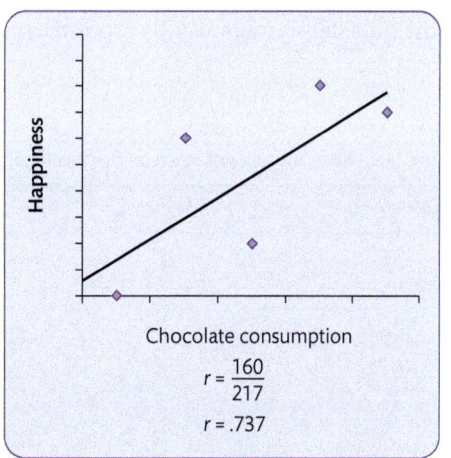

$$r = \frac{\text{covariance between variables}}{\text{variance within variables}}$$

$$r = \frac{90}{100}$$
$$r = .900$$

$$r = \frac{160}{217}$$
$$r = .737$$

Figure 11.3: Understanding the variance in the calculation of Pearson's r correlation.

of chocolate consumed increases, happiness also increases in a very similar way. When the r value is calculated, you can see that the correlation is a very strong one, with an r value of .900. Looking at the panel on the right of Figure 11.3, you can see that whilst the slope of the best fit line may not look too different to the one on the left, the data points sit further from it. This means that as chocolate consumption increases, so does happiness, but not in such a consistent way. Whilst there is still a good amount of covariance in the way the numbers change together to show the correlation, there is also a fair amount of variance in where the data points fall around that line (the distance between the raw data points and the line of best fit). Looking at the final calculation for this r value, although the numbers are larger, the division gives a smaller r value, meaning that the relationship is weaker. For correlations, it is not necessarily just about the *strength* of the relationship, but also how *consistent* it is.

Calculating and interpreting a Pearson's correlation: a worked example

It has been suggested that more intelligent people are likely to be greater worriers. In this worked example we will analyse some imaginary data from six participants who completed a task to measure their intelligence and a worrying questionnaire. The intelligence task provides scores ranging from 5 through to 20 where higher scores represent higher levels of intelligence. The worrying questionnaires gives scores from 1 through to 10, with higher scores representing higher levels of worrying. The raw data are given in the first two columns of Table 11.1.

Before running the analysis, we need to think about our hypothesis. Remembering that your hypothesis should be based on previous research (in this case, that more intelligent people are likely to be greater worries, as above), would you devise a one-tailed or two-tailed hypothesis? If you have a two-tailed hypothesis you would predict that there will be a relationship, but you would not specify whether it will be positive or negative. If you had a one-tailed hypothesis, you would further specify whether you thought the relationship would be positive or negative. For this analysis I think a one-tailed hypothesis would be most suitable, so there will be a positive relationship between intelligence and levels of worry.

Table 11.1. Raw data and first steps of the calculation of the Pearson's r value.

Intelligence (a)	Worry (b)	$a*b$	a^2	b^2
16	10	160	256	100
12	7	84	144	49
18	9	162	324	81
9	6	54	81	36
15	8	120	225	64
11	7	77	121	49
$\Sigma = 81$	$\Sigma = 47$	$\Sigma = 657$	$\Sigma = 1151$	$\Sigma = 379$

CALCULATING AND INTERPRETING A PEARSON'S CORRELATION

Steps for calculating Pearson's r value:

1. Before you complete any calculations at all you should note that one variable has been given the label of 'a' and the other the label of 'b'. This annotation is used when describing the calculations. So intelligence is variable 'a' and worry is variable 'b'. Make a careful note of this!

2. First, for each participant multiply the values of a and b (see column 3). So for the first participant 16 * 10 = 160.

3. Next square each of the a values (a^2 in column four) and each of the b values (b^2 in column five). So for the first participant 16^2 = 256 and 10^2 = 100.

4. With all of these values, sum ($\sum$) the values within each of the columns (the final row in the table).

5. You now need to calculate $(\sum a)^2$ and $(\sum b)^2$. Note that $(\sum a)^2$ is different from $\sum a^2$. For the first you sum all of the a values and then square this single value. For the second you add each of the squared values of a. So for this part of the calculation take the summed intelligence scores and square them, 81^2 = 6561, and take the summed worry scores and square them, 47^2 = 2209.

Table 11.2. Summary of the values needed to enter into the correlation equation.

Values from variable a	Values from variable b	Other values needed
$\sum a = 81$	$\sum b = 47$	$\sum a*b = 657$
$\sum a^2 = 1151$	$\sum b^2 = 379$	$N = 6$
$(\sum a)^2 = 6561$	$(\sum b)^2 = 2209$	

With all of these values calculated, you now have everything you need to start working on the equation to calculate the r value. It can be useful to put the values that you have calculated so far in a summary table. The Pearson's r correlation equation initially looks a bit complex and scary, but we've already done most of the calculations, and putting them into a summary table, like Table 11.2, can help when transferring the values into the equation. We also need to note the number of participants (N), which in this example is 6.

The Pearson's correlation equation is given below, in Equation 11.1. As with most statistics, there are a few different versions of the equation, but they all give the same answer. So if you do see different equations to calculate r, please don't worry as they will all give the same r value. Although it looks a little big and cumbersome, we already have loads of the calculations completed in Table 11.2. We can now continue with the steps of the Pearson's r calculation.

$$r = \frac{(N*\sum a*b)-(\sum a * \sum b)}{\sqrt{\left((N*\sum a^2)-(\sum a)^2\right)*\left((N*\sum b^2)-(\sum b)^2\right)}}$$

Equation 11.1: Pearson's correlation coefficient equation.

6. Now input the values from Table 11.2 into the equation. Hopefully it already looks more manageable!

$$r = \frac{(6*657)-(81*47)}{\sqrt{((6*1151)-6561)*((6*379)-2209)}}$$

7. Complete the multiplication sums within the brackets on the lower part of the equation.

$$r = \frac{(6*657)-(81*47)}{\sqrt{(6906-6561)*(2274-2209)}}$$

8. Now complete the remaining sums within the brackets, the multiplications on the top of the equation and the subtractions on the lower part.

$$r = \frac{3942-3807}{\sqrt{345*65}}$$

9. Next calculate the subtraction on the top of the equation and the multiplication on the lower part.

$$r = \frac{135}{\sqrt{22425}}$$

10. Almost there! Now calculate the square root sum.

$$r = \frac{135}{149.75}$$

11. Finally, calculate the division to calculate the Pearson's r value.

$$r = .902$$

Looking at the Pearson's r value, we can already work out a couple of things about the relationship between intelligence and worry. First, the value is positive. This means that there is a positive relationship between intelligence and worry. Thinking back to our correlation sentence, this means we can say that as intelligence scores increase, levels of worrying also increase. Second, the value is +.902. Remember that Pearson's r values run from −1 through to +1, with +1 being a perfect positive correlation. Looking at the conventions for describing correlations, we could describe this relationship as a strong correlation between intelligence and worry.

Is the Pearson's correlation significant?

Of course, we really want to know whether an r value of +.902 is significant! To find this out we need the critical values table (see Appendix 3) and four pieces of information:

1. Is the hypothesis one-tailed or two-tailed? For this example, it was one-tailed.
2. What is our alpha level? We will be using the psychology standard of $\alpha = .050$.

CALCULATING AND INTERPRETING A PEARSON'S CORRELATION

	Level of significance of a one-tailed test					
	$\alpha = .100$	$\alpha = .050$	$\alpha = .025$	$\alpha = .010$	$\alpha = .005$	$\alpha = .0005$
	Level of significance of a two-tailed test					
df	$\alpha = .200$	$\alpha = .100$	$\alpha = .050$	$\alpha = .020$	$\alpha = .010$	$\alpha = .001$
1	.9511	.9877	.9969	.9995	.9999	.9999
2	.8000	.9000	.9500	.9800	.9900	.9990
3	.6870	.8054	.8783	.9343	.9587	.9911
4	.6084	.7293	.8114	.8822	.9172	.9741
5	.5509	.6694	.7545	.8329	.8745	.9590
6	.5067	.6215	.7067	.7887	.8343	.9249
7	.4716	.5822	.6664	.7498	.7977	.8983
8	.4428	.5494	.6319	.7155	.7646	.8721

Figure 11.4. Section of the critical values table for Pearson's correlation.

3. What are our calculated degrees of freedom? For a correlation it is N-2.
   - df = 6 - 2
   - df = 4
4. What is our calculated *r* value? It is +.902.

You will notice that to calculate the degrees of freedom we calculate the N minus 2 (N–2), whereas for the previous analyses we have done, the degrees of freedom have used some form of N–1. So why is it N–2 instead? Well, imagine you want to draw a line of best fit in a scatterplot, a bit like we did in Figure 11.2. The fewest number of data points you could have to draw this line is two, one at each end. So with two data points, you have no degrees of freedom. Therefore, any additional data points, or participants, give you some degrees of freedom. Consequently, N–2 gives you the number of degrees of freedom that are needed.

In Figure 11.4 you can see a section of the correlation critical values table. Using the information above we can look for the correct column for a one-tailed hypothesis with an alpha level of .050 and the correct row for 4 df. We can then find the critical value for a correlation within this design. In this case the critical value is .7293, which is the smallest *r* value that would be deemed significant. This means that our calculated *r* value needs to be equal to, or larger than, the critical value to be significant. Our calculated value of .902 is larger than the critical value, so we have a significant result with an alpha level of .050.

While it is great to know that we have a significant finding, it is important to report the smallest *p* value at which the result is significant, so you should always check to see if your analysis is significant at a lower alpha level. To do this, follow the row along and check which is the smallest alpha level at which your calculated *r* value is greater than the critical *r* value. For this example, it is an alpha level of .010 (the alpha level of .005 shows a critical *r* value greater than your calculated *r* value) This means that there is less than a 1% chance of having made a Type I Error and of us claiming to have found a significant correlation which does not, in fact, exist.

HOW CAN I TELL IF TWO VARIABLES ARE CORRELATED?

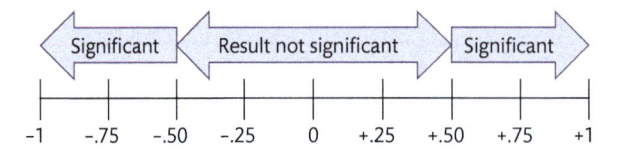

Figure 11.5: Interpreting the significance of negative calculated *r* values. In this example the critical value is .49, so calculated *r* value of .50 would be significant, but a calculated *r* value of .48 would not.

What should you do with a negative *r* value?

You may have noticed that the critical values are all positive, but we can also get negative *r* values. How should you use the critical values table when you have a negative correlation? Essentially, just imagine that the critical values all have negative signs in front of them. You still want your negative calculated *r* value to be more extreme than the negative critical *r* value. So if you calculated an *r* value of −.50 and the critical value were −.49, you would have a significant result as −.50 is more extreme than −.49. However, if the critical value were −.51 your result would not be significant as the calculated value of −.50 is no longer more extreme than the critical value. You can see this graphically in Figure 11.5.

Interpreting and writing up a Pearson's correlation

When writing up a results section for a correlation analysis it is important to remember that there are two parts to include: whether the result is significant or not, and if it is significant whether the relationship is positive or negative. If the relationship is negative, don't forget to include the negative sign before the *r* value, however there is no need to include a plus sign before a positive *r* value. If your result is not significant, then remember that there is no relationship between the two variables, so therefore you should not interpret whether there is a positive or a negative relationship. There is no relationship between the two variables!

Using the APA standards shown in Figure 11.6, we could report our correlation in the following way: There is a significant positive correlation between the two variables ($r(4) = .90$, $p < .010$), this shows that individuals with higher levels of intelligence tend to report higher levels of worrying.

Are *p* values enough? Effect sizes for Pearson's correlation

Pearson's *r* can be treated as an effect size in itself, without the need for additional calculation, because it exists on a continuous, standardised scale that runs from −1.0 (a perfect negative correlation) through to +1.0 (a perfect positive correlation). This means that a particular *r* value can be interpreted in the same way as an effect size (small, medium, or large), regardless of the sample size that it has come from. Cohen did propose some interpretative criteria for the *r* statistic, to help with interpreting the effect size: a small effect size would be *r* equal to or greater than .10, a medium effect size equal to or greater than .30 and a large effect size equal to or greater than .50. For the dataset analysed in this chapter, the *r* value was .90, indicating a large effect size.

$$r(df) = .XX, p < .XXX$$

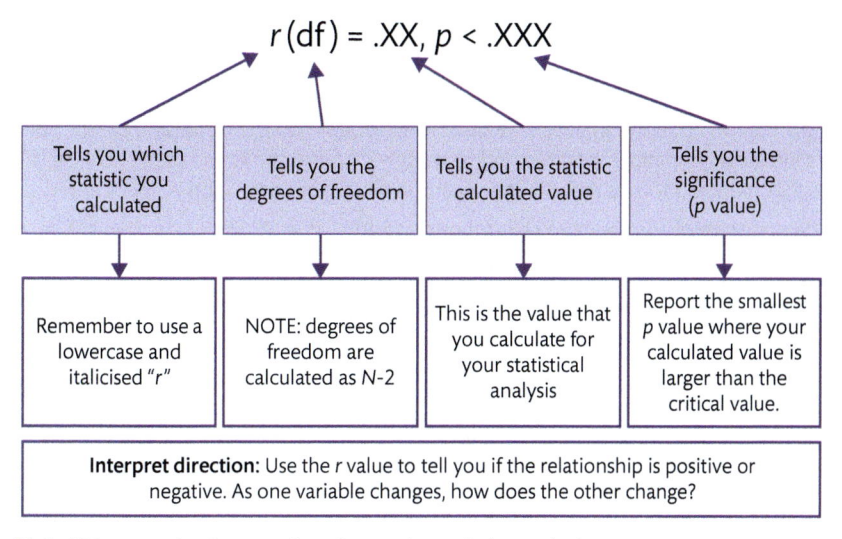

- **Tells you which statistic you calculated** → Remember to use a lowercase and italicised "r"
- **Tells you the degrees of freedom** → NOTE: degrees of freedom are calculated as N-2
- **Tells you the statistic calculated value** → This is the value that you calculate for your statistical analysis
- **Tells you the significance (p value)** → Report the smallest p value where your calculated value is larger than the critical value.

Interpret direction: Use the r value to tell you if the relationship is positive or negative. As one variable changes, how does the other change?

Figure 11.6: APA convention for reporting a Pearson's correlation analysis.

Which variables can't you use for a Pearson's correlation?

Whilst the variables that can and cannot be used in a correlation analysis were discussed at great length in the previous chapter, it is a really important point to remember, and therefore it is worth reiterating here. Correlations can only be used to analyse the relationship between two continuous variables, so either interval or ratio data. If you remember back to Chapter 2, interval and ratio data are **parametric variables**, and Pearson's correlation is a parametric analysis. If you have a nominal (categorical) variable, then a correlation analysis is not suitable at all. Hopefully I will have convinced you of that in the last chapter. However, what would you do if one or both of your variables measure ordinal data? Ordinal data are **non-parametric** in nature, and therefore not suitable for analysis with a parametric Pearson's correlation. Instead, you should use a non-parametric method of analysis. These are covered later in this book, with the logic behind non-parametric statistics being discussed in Chapter 13, and the non-parametric correlation covered in Chapter 16.

The dataset created for this chapter was inspired by

Penney, A., Miedema, V., & Mazmanian, D. (2015). Intelligence and emotional disorders: Is the worrying and ruminating mind a more intelligent mind? *Personality and Individual Differences*, 74, 90–93.

Study questions

1. Below are four different r values. For each r value, what type of relationship is indicated by these r values? Comment on the strength and also the direction of the relationship.
    1.1 $r = +.75$
    1.2 $r = -.16$

1.3 $r = +1.23$

1.4 $r = -.45$

2. Although a significant finding is any finding where the *p* value is equal to or less than .050, it is important to report the smallest *p* value at which your finding is significant. For the following three imaginary findings, report the finding using APA conventions and use the critical values table in Appendix 3 to give the smallest *p* value at which the correlation is significant.

    2.1 Sample size of 15, one-tailed hypothesis and an *r* value of .613.

    2.2 Sample size of 10, one-tailed hypothesis and an *r* value of .426.

    2.3 Sample size of 24, two-tailed hypothesis and an *r* value of .426.

    2.4 Sample size of 20, two-tailed hypothesis and an *r* value of .741.

3. Sample size is a really important factor when considering whether a correlation is statistically significant or not. Using the critical values table, and assuming a two-tailed test with an alpha level of .050, answer the following questions:

    3.1 If you had a correlation *r* value of .50, what is the minimum number of participants that you would need to find a significant correlation?

    3.2 If you had a correlation value of .45, what is the minimum number of participants that you would need to find a significant correlation?

    3.3 If you have a sample size of 20 participants, what is the smallest *r* value that would be deemed to be significant?

    3.4 If you have a sample size of 35 participants, what is the smallest *r* value that would be deemed to be significant?

Additional dataset

Many people talk about going for 'retail therapy' when they are feeling a little down. To examine this, ten participants are asked to report how many times they have gone shopping in the past month and to complete a happiness questionnaire, which gives scores ranging from 0 (very unhappy) through to 10 (very happy) (see Table 11.3).

Table 11.3. Data for analysis.

Number of shopping trips in the past month	Happiness rating (0-10, high scores = happy)
4	5
1	2
6	5
2	4
7	8
9	5
3	1
12	8
6	2
4	3

1. What method of analysis will you use to analyse this dataset?
2. Suggest a suitable hypothesis for this analysis.
3. Calculate the *r* statistic and determine whether it is significant.
4. Interpret and write up your findings using APA standards.
5. Suggest three possible confounding variables within this study. For each confound, how would you measure it, and how do you think it would change the relationship between shopping and happiness?

Are *p* values enough? An additional exercise

Interpret the *r* value as an effect size and integrate this into your write up and interpretation from question 4 in the addition dataset section above.

This dataset was inspired by

Atalay, A., and Meloy, M. (2011). Retail therapy: A strategic effort to improve mood. *Psychology and Marketing*, 28, 638–659.

Example paper using this statistic

Willmot, P., & McMurran, M. (2015). Development of a self-report measure of social functioning for forensic inpatients. *International Journal of Law and Psychiatry*, 39, 72–76.
In this paper the authors are aiming to develop and validate a new questionnaire, and as part of this they use Pearson's correlations. In section 3.3.1, page 74, they examine the correlations between the questionnaire that they have developed and some different questionnaires that already exist and have been frequently used in research. The logic here is to look at the validity of their questionnaire. If it really measures social functioning, then it should correlate with other measures that are relevant to social functioning, such as an anti-social measure.

How to run this analysis in SPSS . . .

If you would like to see how to run this analysis in SPSS, and to find other materials including full answers to study questions, please go to the online resources:
www.oup.com/uk/bourne/

12 How can I tell if one variable can predict another? Simple linear regression

In this chapter you will learn...

- How the line of best fit can be described with the intercept and slope values
- The logic behind the predictive equation in a linear regression analysis
- That the R^2 value represents the amount of variability explained in the regression model
- How to calculate and interpret the intercept and slope values
- How to calculate a predicted outcome value from an existing dataset
- How to calculate and interpret an effect size for regression

Introduction

At the end of Chapter 10 I introduced you to the idea of regression as a predictive model. That is, with a regression analysis you can move beyond just looking at whether there is a relationship between two variables, to actually looking at whether the scores for one variable can predict the scores on another variable.

In the last chapter (Chapter 11) we discovered that there is a significant positive **correlation** between a person's intelligence and the amount that they worry. Imagine that there was another participant in that study, they successfully completed the intelligence task, but due to a computer error their score on the worrying questionnaire is missing. On the basis of what we know about the relationship between intelligence and worry from the complete sets of data that we have from six participants, could we predict what the worry score might have been for the seventh participant?

This is exactly what a regression analysis does. First, we will use a simple **linear regression analysis** to provide a more detailed examination of the relationship between two variables than a correlation can give. Second, we will use this information to build a predictive model that will allow us to calculate a possible outcome score for any individual.

Regression models: a note about terminology

Terminology is very important when we are working with regression models. In an experimental design we talk about independent and dependent variables. This terminology is not valid for correlational designs as nothing is being experimentally manipulated (even though you do sometimes see this terminology used in published research!). Instead, we will talk about **predictor variables** and **outcome variables**. These are not experimentally manipulated in any way, we are simply measuring existing variables, such as worry or intelligence.

Your predictor variable is the variable that you think is able to predict the scores on another variable, which is the outcome variable. In our correlation example we might treat intelligence as the predictor variable and worry as the outcome variable. We can then ask whether a person's intelligence might be able to successfully predict their level of worrying. If the previous research allows, it might be possible to add a directional prediction to form a one-tailed hypothesis. For example, that higher levels of intelligence can predict higher levels of worry, so predicting a positive relationship between the two variables. Alternatively, a two-tailed hypothesis might be more suitable where you would simply hypothesise that intelligence can predict levels of worry, but you do not suggest whether the relationship might be positive or negative.

For this chapter we will be looking at a very simple linear regression, where we look at the relationship between two continuous variables and consider whether scores on one can successfully predict scores on the other. In practice, published research rarely uses such a simplistic predictive model. More often multiple regression analyses are used, and these are discussed in more detail in Chapter 18. However, to illustrate the basic concepts behind this slightly complex method of analysis we are going to keep things really simple and stick to looking at whether scores on one continuous variable can predict scores on another continuous variable: simple linear regression.

Linear regression and the line of best fit

As the name suggests, linear regression looks at a relationship between two variables that can be best described using a straight line. In Figure 12.1 you can see three example datasets with a **line of best fit** plotted that represents the relationship between the two variables. This line is absolutely fundamental in any form of linear regression analysis. One really important thing to remember in regression analyses is that the predictor variable is always plotted on the **x-axis** (the horizontal axis) and the outcome variable is always plotted on the **y-axis** (the vertical axis). So, for our example, intelligence would be plotted on the x-axis, and worry would be plotted on the y-axis.

Drawing the line of best fit: slope and intercept

Imagine that you are speaking to someone on the phone and you need to describe how they should draw the line of best fit shown in the middle graph in Figure 12.1. What two pieces of information would you need to give that person so that they could draw the line onto another graph, without seeing the original?

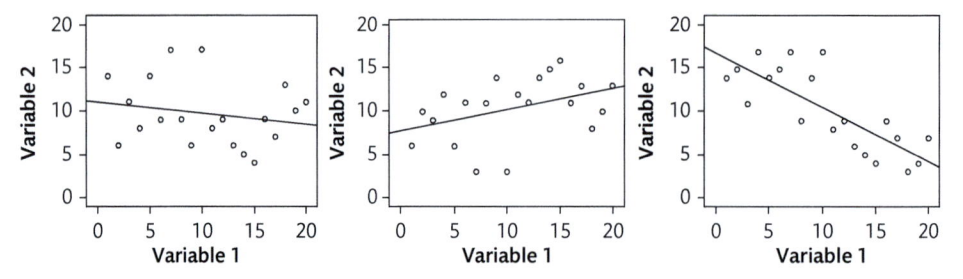

Figure 12.1: Examples of best fit lines shown on scatterplots.

You would need to tell them where the line starts on the y axis (the vertical axis) and also the angle at which the line sits. Where the line starts on the y axis is the **intercept** and the angle is the **slope**. If you know the intercept and the slope, you can draw any line of best fit. If you take a look at Figure 12.2, the graph on the left shows three different lines of best fit that have exactly the same slope, but intercept with the y axis at different points. The graph on the right shows three different lines of best fit where the intercept is exactly the same, but the slope of each of the lines varies.

Building a predictive model

Knowing the slope and the intercept of the line of best fit from an existing set of data means that we can build a regression equation that allows us to predict the outcome score of any person not included within the original dataset for whom we know the predictor variable score. If we know someone's intelligence score, can we predict their level of worry? Using some imaginary data, we will now work through an example to show how this works.

The intercept value tells us where the line of best fit intercepts with the y-axis when the x-axis is at the value of 0. If you look at Figure 12.3 you can see that the line of best fit starts, or intercepts, at 1.5. This means that when the predictor variable, the intelligence measure, has a value of 0, the outcome variable, the worry measure, has a value of 1.5. This works like a baseline value. When our predictor variable (shown on the x-axis) is 0, the intercept value tells us what we predict the score would be on the outcome variable (shown on the y-axis). So if we were to measure someone's intelligence and they got a score of 0, we would predict that they would have a worry score of 1.5.

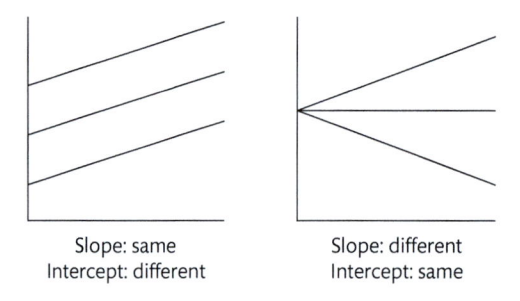

Figure 12.2: Illustrations of lines of best fit where the slopes and intercepts are either the same or different.

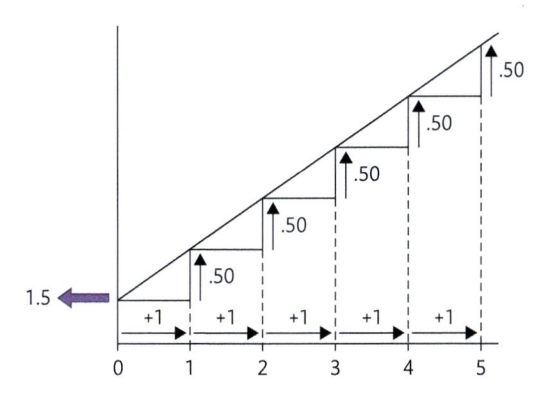

Figure 12.3: Graph with a line of best fit showing the intercept, with a value of 1.5, and the slope, with a value of 0.50.

Now we have a baseline score, we want to know how much levels of worry would increase if the intelligence score were to increase by just one point. This is our slope value, and we can see in Figure 12.3 that for this example the slope value is 0.50. This means that, for our dataset, if intelligence increases by one point, we predict that the level of worry increases by 0.50 points. Because the line of best fit is a straight line, the slope is the same right the way through the graph. So for every one point increase in intelligence, level of worry increases by 0.50 points.

Slope values: positive and negative

When looking at the slope value it is important to note whether the value is positive or negative, as this tells you something really important about the relationship between the two variables, similar to the positive and negative values for a Pearson's *r* value. A positive slope value tells you how much the outcome variable increases with a one unit increase in the predictor variable, whereas a negative slope value tells you how much the outcome variable decreases with a one unit increase in the predictor variable.

With this information, we can now build a predictive model to predict the level of worry for any individual for whom we have an intelligence score. *Our intercept, or baseline, score is 1.5, and we know that for each one point increase in the predictor (intelligence) there will be a 0.5 increase in the outcome (worry).*

If someone has an intelligence score of 1, we therefore take our baseline value of 1.5 and add one lot of 0.50 to it, giving that person a predicted worry score of 2.0. If someone has an intelligence score of 2 we take our baseline score of 1.5 and add two lots of 0.50 to it, giving a predicted worry score of 2.5. We can keep going with this through all of the possible itelligence scores, but the idea is the same, and is illustrated in Figure 12.4.

The regression equation

What we have just worked through is essentially the predictive equation for the regression model. If you take a look at Figure 12.5. you can see the equation. It shows that to predict an outcome score (Y), we need to take the intercept value ($β_0$) and then add to that increases in

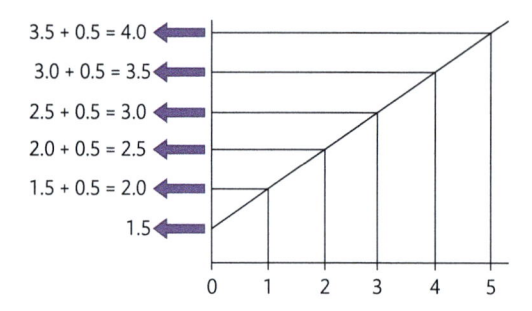

HOW CAN I TELL IF ONE VARIABLE CAN PREDICT ANOTHER?

Figure 12.4: Graph showing how the intercept and slope values can be used to build a predictive model.

$$Y = \beta_0 + (\beta_1 * X)$$

- The value to be predicted outcome variable
- Intercept value
- Slope value
- The value you know: predictor variable

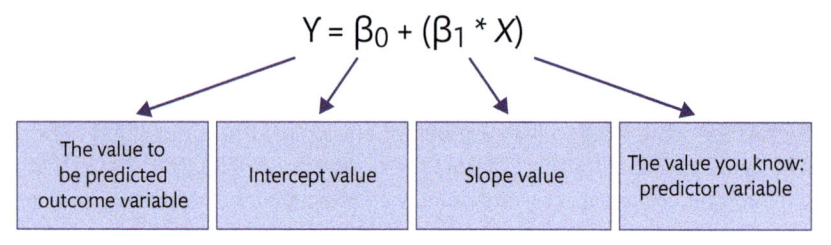

Figure 12.5: The predictive regression equation explained.

the slope (β_1) for however many times is needed according to the value of the predictor variable (X) that we know. β is pronounced as **beta**.

So, if you know the intercept and slope values for any dataset, you can just enter these into the regression equation. Using our fictional intelligence and worry data, this is mapped out for you in Table 12.1. The predictive equation is shown in the top row and the calculations for the first few predictor values are shown in the lower part of the table. If you now take a look back Figure 12.4. you can see how the values are the same.

That is the logic behind using simple linear regression as a predictive model. When you actually run a regression analysis there are two stages to the analysis. First, we can look at the strength of the relationship between a predictor and outcome variable, and second, we can then use that information to build a predictive model using the predictive equation we just looked at.

Table 12.1: An example of the calculations for the predictive equation.

	Y = 1.5 + (0.5 * x)	
Predictor value	Completed equation	Predicted outcome score
1	Y = 1.5 + (0.5 * 1)	2.0
2	Y = 1.5 + (0.5 * 2)	2.5
3	Y = 1.5 + (0.5 * 3)	3.0
4	Y = 1.5 + (0.5 * 4)	3.5
5	Y = 1.5 + (0.5 * 5)	4.0

Working through a regression analysis: looking at delayed gratification

A regression analysis is slightly different from the statistics that we have already encountered that usually have a single test statistic, such as the t, F, or r statistic. Once the statistic has been calculated you can look up whether it is significant or not, and then interpret and write up your findings. A regression analysis is slightly different in that there are a few different statistics to calculate, and for the type of simple regression analysis that we will be looking at in this chapter, there is no need to look up statistical significance! We do, however, start a regression analysis by looking at whether there is a significant correlation between two variables. We learned how to do this in Chapter 11.

In this chapter we will be looking at a fictional dataset that is inspired by the delayed gratification task. This task is frequently used in developmental research where children are sat in front of a treat, usually sweets. They are told that they need to wait a little while, and if they wait they can have a bigger treat than what is in front of them, but if they eat the smaller treat in front of them, they cannot have anything else. Older children are good at waiting for the bigger treat, which is delayed gratification, whereas younger children can't help but quickly eat the smaller treat in front of them.

The example dataset for this chapter uses a child's age (in years) as the predictor variable, and the length of time (in minutes) it takes them to eat the piece of yummy looking chocolate in front of them as the outcome variable. These data are given in Table 12.2. We will now work through the various parts of the regression calculations to understand whether a child's age can successfully predict how long they can delay gratification before eating the chocolate treat in front of them.

How much variance is explained? The R^2 statistic

Regression analyses often start by looking at the Pearson's correlation between the two variables. We learned how to do this in Chapter 11, so I won't go through all the calculations, but if you were to do so you would find that there is a significant positive correlation between a

Table 12.2: Example dataset for regression analysis.

Age (years)	Time to eating chocolate (minutes)
7	5
5	3
8	6
4	2
7	4
5	4
9	6
5	5

child's age and the time it takes them to eat the chocolate ($r(6) = .83$, $p < .010$). This shows that the older a child is, the longer it takes them to give in and eat the yummy chocolate.

An important statistic for regression is the **R^2 value**. This represents the amount of variability in the outcome variable that can be explained by the predictor variable. For our example we could ask, how much of the variability in the time taken to eat the chocolate can be explained by the child's age? Some children ate the chocolate very quickly, whereas some waited for a few minutes. This variability is likely to come from a few different sources, but we have only measured one; the child's age. Whilst younger children tended to eat the chocolate more quickly than the older children, other unmeasured variables may also explain why some children waited longer than others. For example, some children may like chocolate more than others, some children may be more obedient than others, and some children may be hungrier than others. All of these confounding variables can explain some of the variability in the outcome variable.

In a regression analysis, we want to ask how much of the variability in the outcome variable can be explained exclusively by the predictor variable. This comes from the R^2 statistic, which is incredibly easy to calculate. It is simply the Pearson's r value squared. For our example the r value is .825, which we would need to square so $.825^2 = .681$. So for this example $R^2 = .681$. Typically, the R^2 statistic is presented as a percentage of the total variance explained. To calculate this, simply multiple the R^2 value by 100. So for our example we can say that 68.1% (.681*100 = 68.1) of the variability in the time taken for a child to eat some chocolate can be explained by their age.

Given that there is potentially 100% of the variability in the outcome variable to be explained, if we know the amount of explained variance we can easily calculate the amount of unexplained variance in the model. This is shown in a variance 'cake' in Figure 12.6. Thinking about how to take your research forward, it is always really important to think about how we can explain this unexplained variance. It may be explained by some measurement error, or by some confounds (such as the ones suggested above).

A final point to bear in mind is that this is a fictional dataset, designed for educational purposes; 68.1% of variability is a huge amount, and you will very rarely see such a high amount of variability explained exclusively by the predictor variable in real data. In practice, the variability explained in a regression model is likely to be far less. How do you know whether the

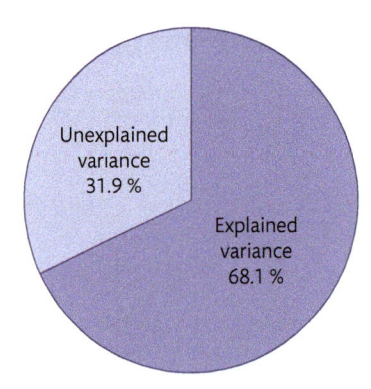

Figure 12.6: Chart showing the explained and unexplained variance within the regression model.

amount of explained variability is 'good'? There is no easy way to answer this within a simple linear regression analysis, but as a guide, if the correlation is significant then the amount of variability explained is likely to be of interest to you as a researcher.

Calculating the slope and intercept

Next we want to calculate the intercept value, referred to as β_0, and the slope value, referred to as β_1. The equations for the intercept and slope values are given in Figure 12.7. As you can see, we actually need to calculate the slope first as that value then forms part of the intercept calculation.

Stage 1: Calculate the slope: β_1

$$\beta_1 = \frac{SP}{SSx}$$

where SP is the Sum of products and SSx is the Sum of squares for x (predictor).

Stage 2: Calculate the intercept: β_0

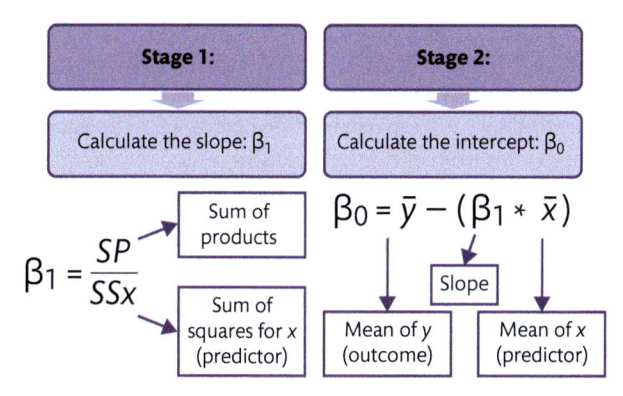

$$\beta_0 = \bar{y} - (\beta_1 * \bar{x})$$

where β_1 is the Slope, $\bar{y}$ is the Mean of y (outcome), and $\bar{x}$ is the Mean of x (predictor).

Figure 12.7: Equations to calculate the slope and the intercept values for a regression analysis.

The raw data are given again in Table 12.3 where you can see that the age variable is denoted as x and the time variable is denoted as y. Remember that x is the predictor variable and y is the outcome variable, and also that $\bar{x}$ means the mean of x value and therefore that $\bar{y}$ means the mean of y values.

Table 12.3: Raw data and calculated values for the computation of the intercept and slope values.

	Age (x)	$x - \bar{x}$	Time (y)	$y - \bar{y}$	$(x - \bar{x}) * (y - \bar{y})$	$(x - \bar{x})^2$
	7	0.75	5	0.625	0.46875	0.5625
	5	−1.25	3	−1.375	1.71875	1.5625
	8	1.75	6	1.625	2.84375	3.0625
	4	−2.25	2	−2.375	5.34375	5.0625
	7	0.75	4	−0.375	−0.28125	0.5625
	5	−1.25	4	−0.375	0.46875	1.5625
	9	2.75	6	1.625	4.46875	7.5625
	5	−1.25	5	0.625	−0.78125	1.5625
Sum (∑)	50		35		14.25	21.50
Mean	6.250		4.375			

Steps for calculating the slope (β_1):

1. First, we need to calculate the Sum of Products, or SP, which forms the top half of the calculation. What the SP does is look at the difference between each raw score and the mean within each variable, so it is looking at deviation from the mean (step 1.2). You then multiply the deviation scores calculated for each participant by each other (step 1.3). The more the scores on each variable differ from the mean, the larger this number will be. These values are then all added up (step 1.4) to give you an overall measure of how much the values differ from the mean within the dataset.

    1.1. For the age (x) and time (y) variables, sum ($\sum$) the values and then use these values to calculate the mean for each of the variables. You can see this in the bottom two rows of the table.

    1.2. Next, for each of the variables, you want to take the mean value away from each raw data point. For the age variable this is $x - \bar{x}$, shown in the third column, and for the time variable this is $y - \bar{y}$, shown in the fifth column. For the age variable the mean is 6.25, so subtract this from each participant's age, and for the time variable the mean is 4.375, so subtract this from each participant's time score.

    1.3. Now, for each person multiply the two values that you just calculated in step 1.2, giving you the $(x - \bar{x}) * (y - \bar{y})$ value in the sixth column of the table. For example, for the first participant you would calculate 0.75 * 0.625, which equals 0.46875.

    1.4. Finally, sum ($\sum$) these values, shown in the second row from the bottom in column six. This gives you the Sum of Products, or SP, which is 14.25.

2. Second, we will calculate the Sums of Squares for the x variable, referred to as SSx. This is quite simple as you just take the $x - \bar{x}$ values from column three, and square them, as shown in the final column in the table. Sum ($\sum$) these values and you will have the SSx, which is 21.5.

3. Finally we can calculate β_1, which is SP/SSx. Therefore β_1 = 14.25/21.5, giving us a slope value of 0.663. Remember that this means the change in the outcome variable for a one point increase in the predictor variable. So for a one year increase in age, the time delay before eating the chocolate increases by 0.663 minutes.

Steps for calculating the intercept (β_0):

1. The intercept is simply calculated from three values, and we have already calculated all of these. We will need the mean of the outcome variable y ($\bar{y}$), the mean of the predictor variable x ($\bar{x}$) and the slope value.

2. Enter the values into the equation shown on the right of Figure 12.7 and you will get:
    - β_0 = 4.375 - (0.663 * 6.25)
    - β_0 = 4.375 - 4.14375
    - β_0 = 0.231

3. We therefore know that the intercept value is 0.231. Remember that this works a bit like our baseline score. So if a participant were to have a score of 0 for the predictor variable of age, we would predict that the time it takes them to eat the chocolate would be 0.231 minutes.

Table 12.4: Predicted values for the delayed gratification chocolate experiment.

Age: predictor value	$Y = 0.231 + (0.663 * x)$	
	Completed equation	Predicted time to eat chocolate
4	Y = 0.231 + (0.663 * 4)	2.883
5	Y = 0.231 + (0.663 * 5)	3.546
6	Y = 0.231 + (0.663 * 6)	4.209
7	Y = 0.231 + (0.663 * 7)	4.872
8	Y = 0.231 + (0.663 * 8)	5.535

Now that we have calculated both the intercept and the slope values we can use these to build a predictive model to predict how long it will take a child to eat the chocolate treat, simply on the basis of knowing their age. The predictive equation is shown in the top row of Table 12.4, and a few example calculations are shown in the lower part of the table. For example, on the basis of the data we have collected we could predict that a child of five years old would be able to wait around three and a half minutes before devouring the delicious chocolate!

Writing up a regression analysis

When a regression analysis is written up the Pearson's correlation and R^2 square value are both presented, with the R^2 often expressed as the percentage of variance explained. The slope value is usually also presented and used to interpret how the outcome changes with a one unit increase in the predictor variable. Although the intercept is vital for using the regression as a predictive model, is it typically not reported within a write-up. It is very important to include the direction of the relationship in your write up and to explicitly describe whether the outcome variable increases or decreases with increases in the predictor variable. The writing up of the example analysis from this chapter may, therefore, read something like this ...

There is a significant positive correlation between a child's age and the time it takes them to eat the chocolate ($r(6) = .83$, $p < .010$), with age accounting for 68.1% of the variability in time taken to eat the chocolate. For each year older a child is, they are likely to wait an additional 0.663 minutes longer before eating the chocolate.

Are *p* values enough? Effect sizes for linear regression

Often, in a regression analysis, the R^2 is treated like an effect size. In fact, if you look back at the ANOVA effect size in Chapter 9, partial eta squared is the same as R^2 and gives you exactly the same value. However, in published research you may sometimes see Cohen's f^2, which is an effect size for regression calculated from the R^2. On the top right of Figure 12.8, you can see this simple equation. Middle right in figure you can see the data from the worked example of this chapter entered into the equation, and bottom right you can see the calculated f^2

HOW CAN I TELL IF ONE VARIABLE CAN PREDICT ANOTHER?

Effect size	Interpretation
≥ 0.2	Small effect
≥ 0.5	Medium effect
≥ 0.8	Large effect

$$f^2 = \frac{R^2}{1 - R^2}$$

$$f^2 = \frac{.681}{1 - .681}$$

$$f^2 = 2.135$$

Figure 12.8: Calculating and interpreting Cohen's f^2 effect size for linear regression.

value. If you'd like to see the full workings for this calculation, please visit the online resources.

As with Cohen's d, there are set criteria for deciding whether the Cohen's f^2 effect size is small, medium or large, and you can see these on the left of Figure 12.8. If you were to include the effect size in the interpretation write up of the analysis from this chapter, it might look something like this: There is a significant positive correlation between a child's age and the time it takes them to eat the chocolate (r (6) = .83, p < .010), with age accounting for 68.1% of the variability in time taken to eat the chocolate with a large effect size (f^2 = 2.14). For each extra year in age, delay before eating the chocolate increases by 0.663 minutes.

The dataset created for this chapter was inspired by

Steelandt, S., Thierry, B., Broihanne, M. H., & Dufour, V. (2012). The ability of children to delay gratification in an exchange task. *Cognition*, 122, 416-425.

Study questions

1. For the following three pairs of variables, decide which you think should be the predictor variable and which you think should be the outcome variable. Why do you think they should be this way around?
   1.1. Parent's IQ and their child's IQ
   1.2. Extraversion and the number of siblings someone has
   1.3. Performance on language task and number of months since acquiring brain injury

2. Using the following r values, calculate the R^2, present this as a percentage and also present the percentage of unexplained variance in the model.
   2.1. r = .169
   2.2. r = -.538
   2.3. r = .743

3. The following data are from an imaginary study looking at whether a person's confidence (questionnaire measure with scores from 10 indicating low confidence through to 50

ARE p VALUES ENOUGH?

indicating high confidence) can predict how positively they rate the expression on a neutral face stimuli (1-5, higher scores indicate more positive ratings). The intercept value of β_0 is -1.6 and the β_1 slope value is 0.23.

- **3.1.** Explain what the intercept value shows and comment on anything that seems a little strange about this.
- **3.2.** Interpret the slope value.
- **3.3.** Predict the positivity ratings of the following participants and then comment on the predicted outcome scores.
    - **3.3.1.** Predict the positivity rating of someone who gets the lowest possible score on the confidence questionnaire.
    - **3.3.2.** Predict the positivity rating of someone who gets the highest possible score on the confidence questionnaire.

Additional dataset

The data for this example looks at whether you can use the number of Twitter posts that someone has made in the past week to predict how narcissistic they are. Narcissism involves thinking very highly of yourself and therefore thinking in a very self-centred way, and it is measured using a questionnaire with scores ranging from 1 (low narcissism) through to 15 (high narcissism) (see Table 12.5)

1. Explain how you will analyse this dataset and why this method of analysis is appropriate?
2. Suggest a suitable hypothesis for this analysis.
3. Calculate the R^2 (you may need to first look back at Chapter 11 to calculate Pearson's r).
4. Calculate the β_0 and β_1 values.
5. Interpret and write up your findings using APA standards.

Table 12.5: Data for additional example.

Number of Twitter posts in past week	Narcissism (1-15, high scores = narcissistic)
15	10
2	3
24	12
8	6
10	7
16	9
3	5
7	6
5	4
11	8

6. Calculate the predicted narcissism scores for the following imaginary participants:
    6.1. Participant 1: 6 Twitter posts per week.
    6.2. Participant 2: 0 Twitter posts per week.
    6.3. Participant 3: 14 Twitter posts per week.

Are *p* values enough? An additional exercise

Calculate Cohen's f^2 effect size and integrate this analysis into your write up and interpretation from question 5 in the additional dataset section above.

This dataset was inspired by

Davenport, S. W., Bergman, S. M., Bergman, J. Z., & Fearrington, M. E. (2014). Twitter versus Facebook: Exploring the role of narcissism in the motives and usage of different social media platforms. *Computers in Human Behavior, 32,* 212-220.

Example paper using this statistic

Ramos, V. F. M. L., Esquenazi, A., Villegas, M. A. F., Wu, T., & Hallett, M. (2016). Temporal discrimination threshold with healthy aging. *Neurobiology of Aging, 43,* 174-179.

This paper looks at temporal discrimination threshold in older adults. Temporal discrimination threshold is simply the shortest time between exposures to two separate stimuli where you can actually tell that there are two separate stimuli. In this study they gave older participants two quick and painless electric shocks to their hands, and asked them if there were two shocks or one. The interval at which they no longer perceive the two separate stimuli, but instead report only one shock is their individual temporal discrimination threshold. They used simple linear regression with age as a predictor variable, and threshold as the outcome variable. They actually had three separate outcome variables (left hand, right hand and both hands), so they ran three separate linear regression analyses. In Table 1 in the paper you can see the R^2 for each of these, and the regression coefficient is the beta value. You may notice that they also report a *p* value for each of the analyses, showing that all three regression analyses were significant. If you look at the first paragraph of the results section, you will also see that they have noted the regression equation for this analysis, with the intercept being 47.28 and the slope being 0.66.

How to run this analysis in SPSS ...

If you would like to see how to run this analysis in SPSS, and to find other materials including full answers to study questions, please go to the online resources:
www.oup.com/uk/bourne/

Part 4

Non-parametric statistics

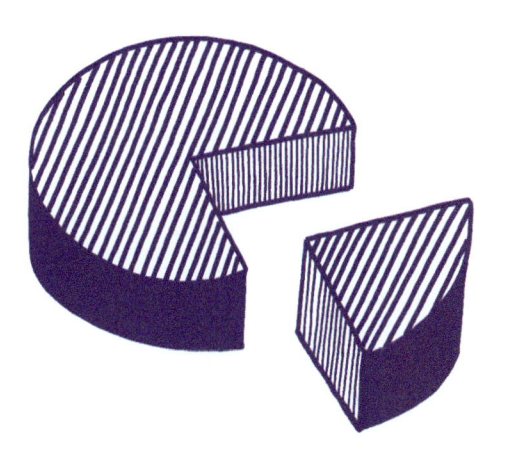

13 When and why might I need to use non-parametric statistics?

> **In this chapter you will learn...**
>
> - What the assumptions are for running parametric statistics
> - How to decide whether to use parametric or non-parametric statistics
> - How non-parametric statistics work
> - Some of the debates around the use of non-parametric statistics

Introduction

All of the analyses that we have discussed in previous chapters are **parametric statistics**. Parametric methods are typically viewed as the 'gold standard' approaches to analysing data, and you have to satisfy certain **parametric assumptions** in order to use them. In this chapter we will discuss what the parametric assumptions are, how you know whether you have satisfied them or not, what the non-parametric equivalents are of the methods of analyses we have covered, and how those non-parametric methods work.

What are the assumptions of parametric analyses?

There are four different assumptions that you need to satisfy in order to safely run a parametric test. In this book we have covered a few different parametric tests: **t tests**, **ANOVA**, **correlation**, and **regression**. Before running any of these methods of analysis you should ensure that you have met the four parametric assumptions. The four assumptions are summarised in Box 13.1, but each will be explained in detail in this chapter. The first two of the assumptions are to do with how you design your study. As such, you have control over these design elements and you should strive to design studies that meet these two assumptions. Unfortunately the other two assumptions cannot be checked until after you have completed data collection as they relate to properties of the dataset.

> **Box 13.1: Assumptions of parametric analyses.**
>
> Assumptions met through good design if
> - All observations are independent
> - Data collected are at interval or ratio level
>
> Assumptions tested after data have been collected
> - Data are (roughly) normally distributed
> - Homogeneity of variance

Assumption 1: Independence of observations

Independence of observations is actually a very simple assumption, and it means that the data you collect from one person or one condition should not influence the data collected from other participants or conditions. This is really important as every participant should have a fair opportunity to gain the same scores as everyone else. If the data collected from some participants is somewhat restricted or influenced by the data collected from other participants, then this isn't really fair. All participants should be treated and able to provide data in a comparable and fair way. An example might be useful here . . .

Imagine that I am interested in running a study on how lucky people are, and I have 100 participants. In my 'lucky hat' I have 100 tokens, labelled from 1 through to 100. The higher the number, the luckier you are. I give the hat to my first participant and ask them to select out their 'luckiness' value. They get a nice high score, keep their token, and hand the hat onto the next participant. The experiment continues in the same way, but now the second participant only has 99 options left for how lucky they are. So their score, or the data they provide, is influenced by the previous participant's performance.

Now think about what happens with the very last participant in the study. They only have one possible 'luckiness' value left, which seems really unfair! Actually, the only participant that had a fair chance in this study was the very first participant. They were the only participant who was able to gain every luckiness value available in this study. Every other participant's data would have been influenced by previous participants, and as such the 'observations' that we gained from them were not independent from one another.

Another example could be a study on learning that involves participants being either the learner or the teacher. Now, you could save yourself lots of time by testing two participants at a time, one in each role. However, the data collected from these two participants is no longer independent as how one of them behaves will influence how the other behaves. Consequently the assumption of independence of observations will have been violated. Instead, it might be better to test one participant at a time, with someone from the research team pretending to be a participant in the other role.

A note about repeated designs

Obviously this assumption is violated to some extent in a repeated design as the participant provides data for multiple conditions. As one person will provide two data points to the dataset, one in each of the conditions, then these two data points are not independent. If you are doing an experiment where you measure IQ at two different times of day, whilst the IQ measurement may change a little, a participant with a very high IQ will have a high IQ at both times of day, or a participant with a very low IQ will have a low IQ at both time points. Consequently, not every single data point can be entirely independent. However, it is still necessary to ensure that there is independence of observations between participants.

As I said, this assumption is really to do with good methodological design, and as such it is under your control. For example, in the luckiness study, all I have to do is ask each participant to put their luckiness token back into the hat before handing it onto the next participant. With this small tweak to the design every participant is able to gain every score from 1 through to 100 in the study, meaning that the parametric assumption of independence of observations has been met.

Assumption 2: Variables are measured at interval or ratio level

This assumption is to do with the way in which your data are scored. As we saw in Chapter 2, there are four different 'levels' of data that can be collected, and these are summarised again in Figure 13.1. As you can see, the first two levels would require a non-parametric test, whereas the second two can be used with parametric tests.

Choosing the right variables

Because you decide how to measure the variables that you are interested in, where possible, you should aim to collect data that can be analysed using parametric methods. This might not be possible, and if the best way to measure your variable requires a non-parametric approach, then this is fine. The important thing is that you consider whether a level of measurement that would allow for a parametric analysis is possible. If it is, then you should go for that. But if nominal or ordinal data are the best way to measure the variable, then stick with that and use a non-parametric analysis.

Non-parametric

Nominal (categorical) data
- Frequency of belonging to a "category"
- Example: Handedness, classed as left, right, or mixed handed?

Ordinal data
- Clear order to data, but distance between points may vary
- Example: Place in a race, 1st, 2nd, 3rd place, etc. ...

Parametric

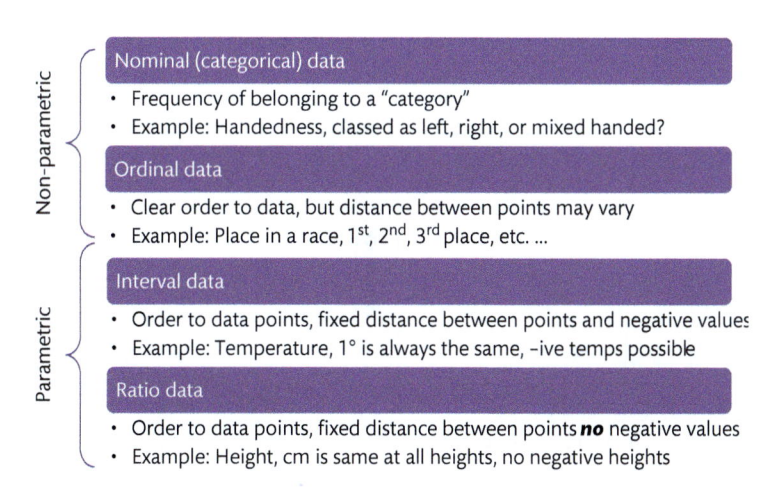

Interval data
- Order to data points, fixed distance between points and negative values
- Example: Temperature, 1° is always the same, –ive temps possible

Ratio data
- Order to data points, fixed distance between points **no** negative values
- Example: Height, cm is same at all heights, no negative heights

Figure 13.1: Levels of measurement, divided into non-parametric and parametric levels.

Assumption 3: Data are (roughly) normally distributed

In Chapter 5 we spent some time discussing the different distributions that data can have. I'll briefly recap on this here, but you can look back at Chapter 5 if it has been a while since you read that chapter. In Figure 13.2 you can see three different **histograms** that show the distribution of three different datasets. For each graph, along the bottom of the graph are scores from low scores through to high scores, and the height of each bar represents the frequency with which that score occurs.

Imagine that the data plotted in Figure 13.2 shows extraversion personality scores. The top example shows a perfect normal distribution where most people have about 'average' extraversion scores, there are a few very extroverted people and a few very introverted people, but there are similar numbers of extroverts and introverts. The bottom left example shows positively skewed data, where the tail is on the positive, or high, end of the distribution scores. Here we have many introverts and a small number of extroverts. The bottom right example shows negatively skewed data, where the tail is on the negative, or low, end of the distribution scores. Here we have many extroverts and a small number of introverts. There are some other types of non-normal distributions that can occur in datasets, and if you look back at Chapter 5 you can see some more examples.

In order to use parametric methods of analysis the data that you have collected should be roughly normally distributed. Now, what does 'roughly' normally distributed actually mean? The data don't have to be perfectly normal, but they should roughly fit within the traditional bell curve shape of the normal distribution.

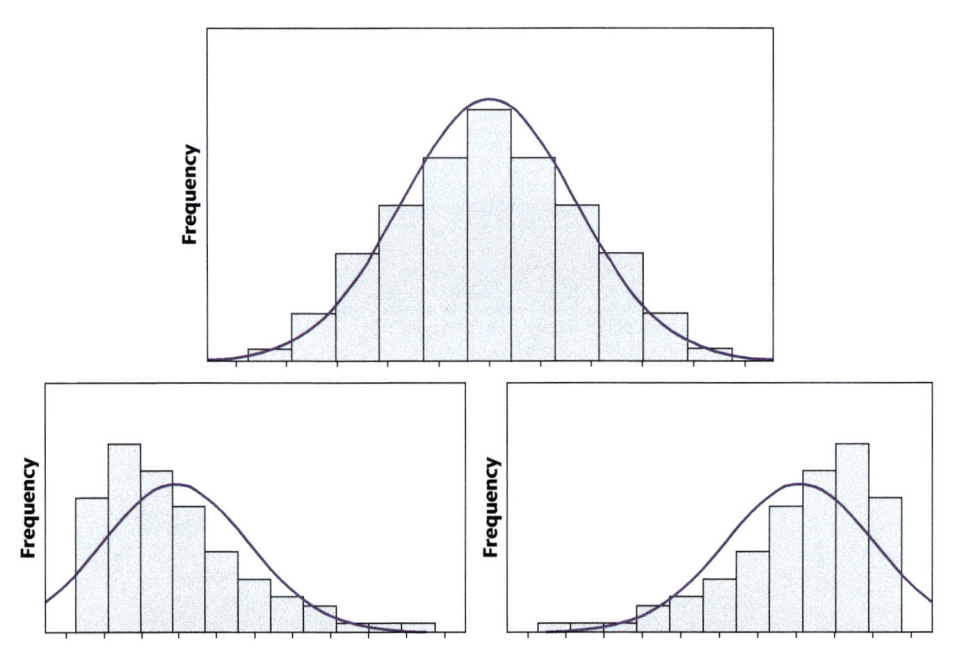

Figure 13.2: The top figure shows a perfect normal distribution, bottom left shows a positively skewed distribution and bottom right shows a negatively skewed distribution.

Assumption 4: Homogeneity of variance

This assumption relates to the extent of the variability that exists in your data, and it is particularly relevant to independent experimental designs. If you think back to the independent *t* test, we have two separate groups of participants, and we want to see if their scores differ between the two independent groups (look back at Chapters 6 and 7 if you want a more detailed recap). **Homogeneity of variance** means that we want the variance within each group to be similar. What we don't want to find in our data is **heterogeneity of variance**, which means that the variances are different. To remember the difference between these two, remember that the prefix 'hetero' means different, whereas the prefix 'homo' means the same. Ok, what does this all really mean, and why should you care?

In Chapter 5 we discussed a study that looked at how caffeine might influence memory, and we compared a no caffeine (decaffeinated coffee) condition to a caffeine (fully caffeinated coffee) condition. This study was run in two different labs, and you can see the results in Figure 13.3. Although the mean memory scores were identical in both of the labs, there was very little variance *within* the two conditions in Lab One but lots of variance *within* the two conditions in Lab Two. However, within each lab, the amount of variability in each condition is comparable. This is homogeneity of variance, and this is how the variability across conditions should look. Whether there is lots of variance or very little variance, you want similar amounts.

The reason for the importance of homogeneity of variance becomes quite evident when you look at the data collected by a third lab and shown in Figure13.3. In Lab Three, the means are identical to those in the previous two studies, but now the variability is quite different in each of the conditions. For participants in the 'no caffeine' condition the scores are quite consistent, whereas in the 'caffeine' condition there is a wide spread of variability in the data. This is very problematic as it becomes quite difficult to be confident of any comparisons we might make between the two conditions. Something very different is clearly happening in the 'caffeine' condition that is causing some participants to have very high memory scores, whereas others have memory scores that look relatively indistinguishable from scores in the 'no caffeine' condition.

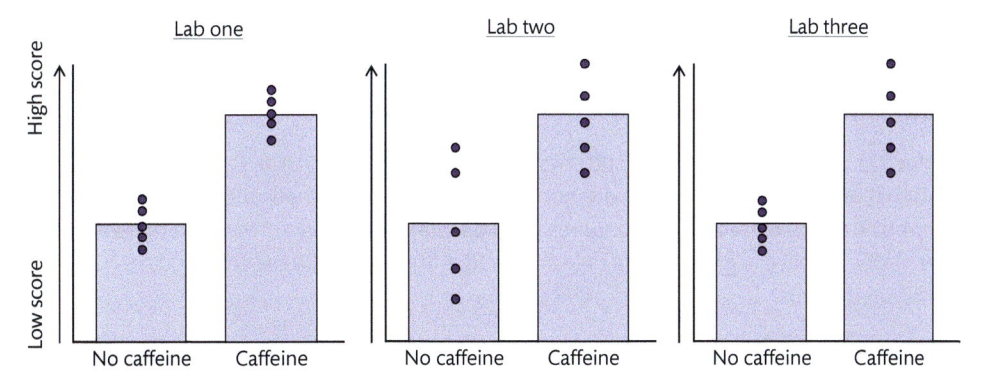

Figure 13.3: Three different outcomes of studies with identical mean scores, but differing patterns of variability. In Labs One and Two, there is homogeneity of variance (similar variances in each condition), whereas in Lab Three there is heterogeneity of variance (different variances in each condition).

Is it really fair to statistically compare the two conditions from Lab Three, and to possibly conclude that caffeine increases memory performance? There is clearly heterogeneity of variance in this dataset, as the amount of variability in the two conditions is far greater in one condition than in the other. For a parametric analysis to be robust, there should be homogeneity of variance between conditions, and if there is evidence for heterogeneity of variance, then non-parametric analyses may be more appropriate.

What assumptions about variance are there for repeated measures and correlations?

Homogeneity of variance is a key assumption for independent experimental designs, but for repeated experimental designs the assumption is slightly different, and it is called **sphericity**. Importantly, sphericity cannot be calculated for repeated *t* tests as the computation requires there to be more than two conditions in the design. As such, you don't need to worry about this assumption for the repeated *t* test that we have covered in this book. The assumption also does not directly apply to correlations and regressions, but instead the equivalent assumption is **homoscedasticity**. Again, this assumption is beyond the scope of what we will be covering in this book, but there is some suggested wider reading at the end of this chapter.

How do I know if I have violated the parametric assumptions?

For the assumptions of independence of observations and level of measurement, this should be clear when you are designing your study. You should always aim to devise the best methodology to address your research question. Ideally you would do this by selecting variables that can be measured in such a way that parametric analysis is possible. However, if aspects of your design, such as your choice of variable, require a non-parametric analysis, then that is what you should use. In addition, regardless of how well you designed your study, you cannot check for the assumptions of normal distribution and homogeneity of variance until after you have collected your data. Therefore you should always check on these two assumptions before analysing your data.

How do I know if my data are normally distributed?

There are some quite complex statistics (the Kolmogorov–Smirnov test or Shapiro-Wilks test) that will tell you if your data are normally distributed, or whether they are significantly skewed. Running these analyses requires specialist statistical programmes, but there are simpler methods that can give you a fair idea of whether the data you have collected are normally distributed or not.

Using histograms

The simplest method is to create a histogram of the data you have collected, and produce a graph similar to those shown in Figure 13.2. This can easily be done by hand or in Excel.

However you are still reliant on simply looking at the distribution and deciding whether the data are 'roughly' distributed or not. There may be a little bit of skew in your data, but is it enough to say that the data are not normally distributed? This can be a difficult call to make, especially if you don't have much experience in working with lots of datasets.

Using descriptive statistics

Another method is slightly more numeric, and relies on the relationship between the normal distribution, mean, standard deviation and the percentage of your sample that you expect to find within particular boundaries. This is discussed in detail in Chapter 5, but to recap you can see in Figure 13.4 that you would normally expect 68% of your sample to have scores that fall between one standard deviation below and above the mean and 95% would be expected to fall between two standard deviations above and below the mean.

You can therefore look at your descriptive statistics, which you learned to calculate in Chapter 5, to help you decide whether your data points are normally distributed. Imagine that you have collected IQ scores from 100 people, and the mean IQ score is 100 with a standard deviation of 15. If your data are normally distributed, you would expect about 68 people to have IQ scores falling between 85 and 115 (mean ±1 standard deviation), and about 95 people to have IQ scores falling between 70 and 130 (mean ±2 standard deviations). If, for example, your dataset had 83 participants with IQ scores between 85 and 115 and 92 people with IQ scores between 70 and 130, then you might suspect that your data are not normally distributed.

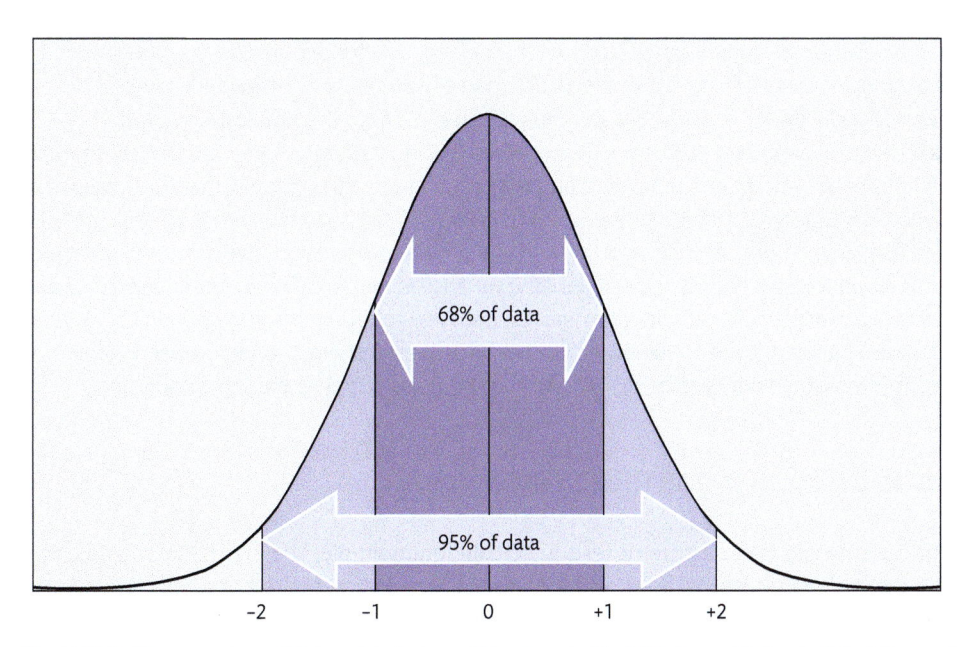

Figure 13.4: The percentage of data points that would be expected to fall between ±1 standard deviation and ±2 standard deviations in a normal distribution.

One thing to note is that it is difficult to evaluate if data are normally distributed when you have small sample sizes. There isn't really a clear and definitive answer to how large a sample size needs to be to robustly evaluate normality, but the magic number of 30 seems to be mentioned quite often when reading about this topic.

Thinking about normality across different designs

It is also important to think about how you would evaluate normality across the different designs covered in this book:

- Independent *t* tests and ANOVA: Normality should be examined in each condition, and if any condition appears to not be normally distributed, then a non-parametric test should be used.
- Repeated *t* tests: This works slightly differently, as you should look at the normality of the *difference scores* which you compute in the first step of the calculations for the repeated *t* test (see Chapter 8).
- Correlations: Look at the distribution for each variable, and if either or both are not normally distributed, then a non-parametric test should be used.
- Regression: The assumptions get rather complicated for regression analyses, and are somewhat beyond the scope of this book. However, I've suggested some further reading at the end of this chapter if you are really interested in finding out more!

How do I know if I've violated the homogeneity of variance assumption?

If you have run an experimental study with an independent measures design, you should be evaluating whether you have met the assumption of homogeneity of variance or not. This can be statistically determined using a Levene's test, but perhaps the simplest way to do this is to calculate the variance in each group (we covered this in Chapter 5), and then compare the size of the variability between the smallest and largest variance values that you have just calculated. Convention suggests that if the largest variance is no more than four times greater than the smallest variance, then everything is fine and you can assume that you have met the homogeneity of variance assumption. For example, if the variance in the 'no caffeine' condition was 1.2 and the variance in the 'caffeine' condition was 4.5, then you could assume homogeneity of variance and use a parametric *t* test. However, if the variance in the 'caffeine' condition was 5.0, then the assumption would not have been met and you should use a non-parametric equivalent.

How do non-parametric tests work?

The logic behind non-parametric tests is, actually, quite simple. The idea is that the data violate the parametric assumptions, and therefore a non-parametric test attempts to make the data more appropriate for analysis. To do this, the data are transformed by turning them into **ranked scores**. This means that the smallest number gets a rank score of 1, the next largest number gets a rank score of 2, and so on.

HOW DO NON-PARAMETRIC TESTS WORK?

Raw score	Ranked scores
27	1
28	2.5
28	2.5
30	4
31	6
31	6
31	6
35	8
39	9
45	10

Ranked scores for these two values should be 2 and 3, so calculate the mean of these values:
Rank score = (2+3)/2
Rank score = 2.5

Ranked scores for these three values should be 5, 6, and 7, so calculate the mean of these values:
Rank score = (5+6+7)/3
Rank score = 6

Figure 13.5: An example of how to rank data, and how to calculate tied rank scores.

In Figure 13.5 you can see an example of how to rank data. In this example, the raw data look like they may not be normally distributed as there are lots of scores on the lower end of the distribution and a 'tail' of higher scores, suggesting that the data may be positively skewed. In the second column you can see the ranked scores, and also, very importantly, how to deal with tied scores. For example, there are two scores of 28. These should have been given ranked scores of 2 and 3; however it doesn't seem fair to give two identical raw scores different ranked scores. To get around this problem, we simply calculate the mean ranked score across the tied raw scores, which in this case means that the two raw scores of 28 become two ranked scores of 2.5 (the mean of the rank scores 2 and 3).

It is quite easy to see how ranking data resolves lots of the issues around 'dodgy' data by looking at an example of skewed data in both raw and ranked form. In Figure 13.6, on the left you can see a histogram of some positively skewed data where there are lots of smaller scores, but there is a long 'tail' of higher scores. On the right you can see a histogram of these data after they have been ranked so that each rank score occurs only once (there were no tied ranks).

If you find that you need to run a non-parametric equivalent of a *t* test or a correlation, you will see that the first stage of the calculations is to rank the data, in the same way that has

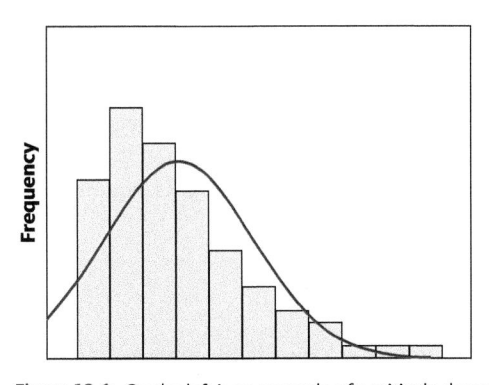

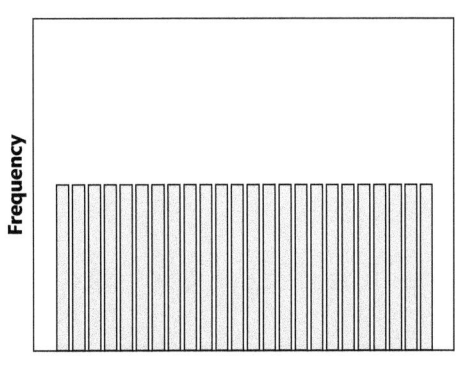

Figure 13.6: On the left is an example of positively skewed data, with lots of lower scores and a 'tail' of larger scores. On the right is the data after being transformed into rank scores, where each rank score occurs only once.

been shown above. The test statistic is then calculated on the basis of the rank scores, rather than the raw scores.

What are the non-parametric equivalents of the parametric tests we have learned?

All of the statistical tests covered in Parts 2 and 3 of this book are parametric tests, however, they (mainly) have non-parametric equivalents and some of these will be covered in the rest of the chapters in this section. You can see this summarised in Figure 13.7. In Chapter 14 we cover a non-parametric test that does not have a parametric equivalent, the chi square test. This method of analysis is used when you have collected only nominal (categorical) data. In Chapter 15 we will be looking at the non-parametric equivalents of the *t* tests, and in Chapter 16 the non-parametric correlation.

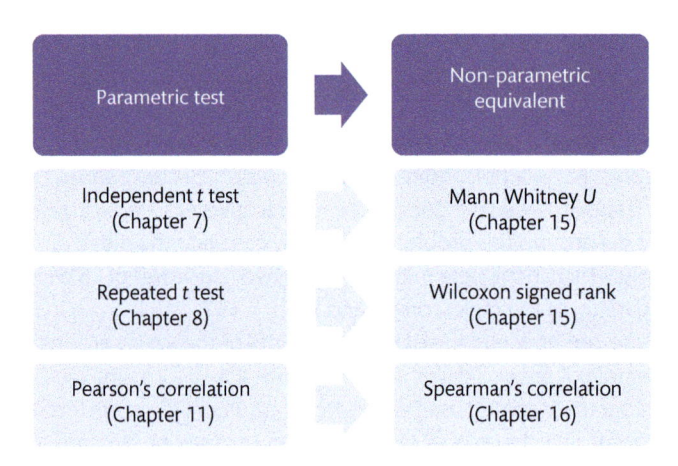

Parametric test	Non-parametric equivalent
Independent *t* test (Chapter 7)	Mann Whitney *U* (Chapter 15)
Repeated *t* test (Chapter 8)	Wilcoxon signed rank (Chapter 15)
Pearson's correlation (Chapter 11)	Spearman's correlation (Chapter 16)

Figure 13.7: Parametric tests and their non-parametric equivalents.

Interpreting non-parametric statistics with descriptive statistics

In each of the parametric tests we have covered in previous chapters, we have used descriptive statistics to help us interpret our findings, mainly relying on the mean to decide which condition has the higher scores. However, if our data are non-parametric then the mean is not suitable. Instead you should use the median to interpret and present your findings. You can look back at Chapter 5 to revise how to calculate this.

Are non-parametric statistics really needed?

Having spent this whole chapter explaining to you why you might need to use non-parametric statistics, I want to finish this chapter on a slightly controversial point! The need for and use of non-parametric statistics is a topic that is frequently argued about by statisticians. Some people claim they are rarely actually needed. The further reading for this chapter goes into these debates in more detail, and they make for some very interesting reading, but I just want to briefly discuss one aspect of the argument, and a point that I am often asked by students . . . Should **Likert scales** be analysed using parametric or non-parametric statistics?

Likert scales are used very frequently in psychological research, and particularly in questionnaires. These are the scales where you are asked to make a response from a number of categories ranging from, for example, "strongly agree" through to "strongly disagree", or from "never" through to "always". These scales are then scored, depending on the number of categories they contain. For example, "strongly agree" may be scored as 5 and "strongly disagree" scored as 1, where there are five options on the Likert scale.

Many people claim that Likert scales are ordinal as you don't know that the difference between 'strongly agree' and 'somewhat agree' is the same as the distance between 'somewhat agree' and 'neither agree nor disagree'. For this reason many people argue that Likert scales can only be analysed using non-parametric methods. However, there is now considerable evidence that parametric methods are still robust when analysing Likert scale data (see the further reading for more detail).

There is also a difference between analysing a single Likert scale item and analysing the summed score from across many Likert scale items within a questionnaire. If you are analysing a single Likert item there may be a stronger argument for needing non-parametric statistics. However, if you are adding up score across a large number of Likert scale items, then parametric methods are usually fine.

People tend to have quite strong views on whether Likert scales should analysed with parametric or non-parametric tests. I fall into the parametric camp. However, it is best to check with the person teaching you statistics what they think as they will be marking your work!

Study questions

1. Imagine that you want to run a study look at political attitudes. Devise four separate variables that could be interesting to measure, with one of each type of:
    1.1. Nominal data
    1.2. Ordinal data
    1.3. Interval data
    1.4. Ratio data
2. Imagine you have run a study where you have collected scores that reflect levels of aggression in children. There were 200 participants, and the data have been analysed to show that the mean is 27 and the standard deviation is 5. Answer the two questions below, and then consider whether you think the data are normally distributed or not.
    2.1. Calculate the scores that are the boundaries of ±1 SD around the mean. What are these scores? 155 participants had scores within this range. What percentage of the total sample is this, and is this value similar to what you would expect if the data were normally distributed?

2.2. Calculate the scores that are the boundaries of ±2 SD around the mean. What are these scores? 162 participants had scores within this range. What percentage of the total sample is this, and is this value similar to what you would expect if the data were normally distributed?

3. For this example, you are looking at the aggression scores for a subset of children in the previous example, and you can see these data in Table 13.1.

   3.1. Calculate the mean and variance for each group. You can look back at Chapter 5 if you need a reminder of how to do this.

   3.2. Comparing the variance in each group, is there evidence of homogeneity of variance or heterogeneity of variance in this dataset?

   3.3. Would you recommend a parametric or non-parametric statistical test?

Table 13.1: Example data of aggression scores for boys and girls.

Boys	Girls
37	26
25	21
21	19
24	28
16	29
38	24
29	30
18	25

Wider reading

Norman, G. (2010). Likert scales, levels of measurement and the 'laws' of statistics. *Advances in Health Sciences Education, 15,* 625–632.
   This is a great and very easy to read paper that considers whether some of the 'laws' around using non-parametric statistics are really necessary.

Carifio, J., & Perla, R. (2008). Resolving the 50-year debate around using and misusing Likert scales. *Medical Education, 42,* 1150–1152.
   This paper talks specifically about the Likert scale debate, and is quite short and simple to read.

For full answers to study questions, and to explore a range of other materials, visit the online resources at: **www.oup.com/uk/bourne/**

14 Do my data fit the expected frequencies? Chi squared

> **In this chapter you will learn ...**
> - The difference between a chi square goodness of fit and a chi squared test of association, and when to use each type of test
> - The difference between observed and expected frequencies
> - How to calculate each type of chi squared test
> - How to write up and interpret each type of chi squared test

Introduction

The first non-parametric test we will learn about is the chi-squared test. This is one of the simplest, elegant and most 'cake'-like analyses we will cover in this book (to revise why statistics are like a cake, take a look back at Chapter 5). Often it is one of the first tests of statistical significance taught in statistics courses due to its intuitive beauty. It is used to analyse frequency data, so how many people 'belong' to each category that you are interested in. Remember that frequency data, also known as categorical or nominal data, are non-parametric and therefore we need a special kind of statistic to analyse a dataset that is only comprised of categorical data: a chi squared.

This analysis works on the idea of comparing the **frequency data** that you observe to the random chance of that frequency occurring in order to determine whether your observed frequencies are occurring as you would expect by random chance, or whether they are larger (or smaller) than would be expected in certain groups. Imagine that we are looking at how frequently we get a 'heads' or a 'tails' when tossing a coin. By random chance you would expect each outcome to occur 50% of the time. Therefore, if you tossed a coin ten times, by random chance you would expect each outcome to occur five times. However, you got 'heads' eight times and 'tails' just twice, and these are your observed frequencies. The important question is, are these observed frequencies of 8 and 2 significantly different from your expected frequencies of 5 and 5? This is what the chi squared test will tell us.

Chi squared and the goodness of fit

Let's take a very simple example. I'm interested in handedness. Is being right handed more frequent than being left handed? If being left or right handed happened totally at random what percentage of people would you expect in each category? Given that there are two categories, left or right, we would predict that 50% of our sample is left handed and that 50% of our sample is right handed. This is our **expected frequency**: the frequency we would predict if belonging to each category were totally random.

The next question to ask is: Are the frequencies that occur in our dataset, the **observed frequencies**, significantly different from the random expected frequencies? I ask 100 people to tell me whether they are left handed or right handed. This is my observed data and I find out that there are 18 left handers and 82 right handers in my sample. This leads us to a really interesting question: Is the frequency of the two types of handedness in our observed data significantly different from the frequencies that we would expect randomly?

We would answer this kind of a research question with a **chi squared goodness of fit test** as we are just looking at frequencies in categories across one variable, handedness, with two separate categories, being left or right handed. Later in this chapter we will work through an example of this method of analysis, but for now I just want to consider how this type of analysis works and when you would want to use it.

Technically it is possible to look at frequencies in any number of categories within a single variable using a chi squared goodness of fit test; however, it is not often used with more than five or six categories. Another study you could run and analyse using a chi squared goodness of fit test might be the type of chocolate a person would choose to eat: white chocolate (evil chocolate), milk chocolate (beautiful chocolate) or plain chocolate (OK chocolate). This study would analyse frequencies across three categories. Alternatively, you might be interested in the kind of pet a person would prefer to have: dog, fish or tortoise.

As with any analysis, it is important to think about your hypothesis, and this should be clearly justified by the previous research that you consider in your introduction when writing up. However, for a chi square analysis, the experimental hypothesis must be two-tailed. A one-tailed hypothesis is not possible as we are simply asking whether the observed frequencies 'fit' a random distribution or not.

Different designs and the chi squared test of association

As I said, the chi squared goodness of fit test is beautifully simple and elegant. However, research is rarely as simple as just having one categorical variable. What happens if you have two different variables that we want to look at? For example, we think that there may also be an age difference in handedness due to changes in educational policy around teaching left handers how to write and we want to analyse this. We now have two different variables: handedness with two categories (left or right) and age with two categories (25 years old or younger, 55 years old or older). This would give us a 2 x 2 design (see Table 14.1). We need a slightly different kind of analysis for this type of design, a **chi squared test of association**

Table 14.1: Example dataset suitable for analysis using a 2 x 2 chi squared test of association.

	Left handed	Right handed
25 years old or younger	13	37
55 years old or older	5	45

CALCULATING AND INTERPRETING A CHI SQUARED GOODNESS OF FIT

Table 14.2: Example dataset using a 3 x 2 chi squared test of association (left) and a 3 x 3 chi squared test of association (right).

	Not a psychopath	Psychopath		Extrovert	Depends	Introvert
White chocolate	17	62	Dog	38	31	29
Milk chocolate	84	32	Fish	25	41	63
Plain chocolate	48	57	Tortoise	42	46	48

(also sometimes known as a chi squared test of independence), and we will work through an example of this method of analysis later in this chapter.

Looking at our other two examples, we might also want to look at a second variable. When we describe chi square analyses that include two variables, it is important to note how many categories there are within each variable. For the chocolate example, we wanted to know whether people would choose to eat white, milk or plain chocolate (three categories). We might also want use a standardised questionnaire to classify people as either a psychopath or not (two categories). We would now have a 3 x 2 design (see Table 14.2 left). With our pet of choice example (dog, fish or tortoise: 3 categories) example, we might also ask each participant how they would describe their personality: extrovert, depends on the situation, or introvert (3 categories)? This would then give us a 3 x 3 design (see Table 14.2, right).

We now have two different ways of analysing frequency data:

1. *Chi squared goodness of fit* test analyses frequencies across different categories within one variable

2. *Chi squared test of association* analyses frequencies across categories for two variables.

One really important thing to always remember when running any kind of chi squared is that we are comparing the observed frequencies that we have actually recorded in our sample of participants to the random frequencies that we would expect by chance and asking the question: are our observed frequencies significantly different to what we would expect by chance?

Calculating and interpreting a chi squared goodness of fit: a worked example

In this first analysis, we will look at the simple handedness data frequencies, where we have 18 left handed participants and 82 right handed participants. We want to see whether this distribution of handedness differs from what we would randomly expect, i.e. having half left handed and half right handed participants. To do this, we need to calculate the expected frequencies, which we would expect to have occurred by random chance. We then compare these values to the actual observed frequencies. The greater the difference between the observed and expected frequencies, the larger the calculated chi square value will be, and the more likely it is that we will have a significant result.

First we need to develop a hypothesis. For this study my hypothesis is that the observed frequencies of left and right handedness will occur significantly differently from chance expectations (remember that the hypothesis has to be two-tailed). Next we will calculate the

DO MY DATA FIT THE EXPECTED FREQUENCIES?

chi squared statistic. We can do most of the calculations by organizing a simple table (see Table 14.3).

Steps for calculating the chi squared goodness of fit:

1. First, note down the observed (O) frequencies in each category.
2. Next, calculate the expected (E) frequencies in each category. To do this, take the total number of participants and divide it by the number of categories that you have. So 100 participants divided by two categories gives us an expected (E) frequency of 50 in each cell (100/2 = 50). In a chi squared goodness of fit analysis, the expected frequency will always be the same in each cell and should be the same number in each cell.
3. You now want to calculate the difference between the observed and the expected frequencies for each category (O−E). Here we can see that we have 32 *fewer* left handers than we would expect by random chance, but 32 *more* right handers than we would expect by random chance. These difference values are sometimes called the **residual values** and they are important for interpreting the direction of any significant effects we might find. So, are there more or less people within that category than you would expect by random chance?
4. The problem with our residual values is that we will have both positive and negative values, so if we just add these up to see the overall difference between the observed and expected frequencies they will just cancel each other out to give a value of 0. To deal with this we next square the residual value for each category, giving us $(O-E)^2$.
5. We now have another problem as the squaring of the residual values has given us huge numbers, so looking at these would lead to us overestimating the difference between the observed and the expected frequencies. To return these values to our original scale, you divide them by the expected frequency, giving us $\frac{(O-E)^2}{E}$.
6. Now we are on the final stage of the calculations. For each category of the variable, we have a value that represents the difference between the observed and the expected frequencies: 20.48 in each case. We now just have to add up ($\sum$) these values to give us the final χ^2 value: 20.48 + 20.48 = 40.96.

Table 14.3: Steps of the basic calculations for the chi squared goodness of fit test.

		Left handed	Right handed
Step 1:	Observed data: O	18	82
Step 2:	Expected data: E	50	50
Step 3:	Residual value: O − E	18 − 50 = **−32**	82 − 50 = **32**
Step 4:	$(O-E)^2$	−32² = **1024**	32² = **1024**
Step 5:	$\frac{(O-E)^2}{E}$	1024/50 = **20.48**	1024/50 = **20.48**

Having now calculated our first chi squared value, we can take a look at the equation that represents this calculation (see Equation 14.1). This simply describes the six stages of calculations we went through in our table. For each cell we calculated the difference between the observed and expected frequencies (step 3), squared this (step 4), divided it by the expected frequencies (step 5) and then summed ($\sum$) all of these values (step 6).

$$\chi^2 = \sum \frac{(O-E)^2}{E}$$

Equation 14.1: Chi squared equation.

Is the chi squared goodness of fit analysis significant?

For our handedness analysis, we ended up with a χ^2 value of 40.96, but what does this actually mean? The first thing to note is the bigger the χ^2 value the greater the difference between our observed and our expected frequencies. Therefore, a small χ^2 value means that there is little difference between our observed and our expected frequencies, and our residual values will have been small. Conversely, if we find a huge χ^2 value, then this shows that the frequency of our observed data is much different to the frequencies that we would expect by random chance.

But is a χ^2 value of 40.96 big enough to be interesting? Does it show a significant finding? To find this out, we need to look up the significance on the critical values table (see Appendix 3). In order to find out whether our finding is statistically significant, we need to know three things:

1. What is our alpha level? In other words, what is our criterion for saying a statistical test is significant? We will be using the psychology standard of $\alpha = .050$.

2. What are our calculated degrees of freedom? The calculation for the degrees of freedom in a chi squared goodness of fit is the number of categories minus 1. So we need to look at the row where the degrees of freedom equals 1.
   - df = number of categories −1
   - df = 2 − 1
   - df = 1

3. What is our calculated χ^2 value? We just calculated this to be $\chi^2 = 40.96$.

In Figure 14.1 you can see a small section of the critical values table for the chi squared statistic. Looking at the row for one degree of freedom and the column for a p value of .050 you can see the critical χ^2 value is 3.841. If our calculated χ^2 value is equal to or larger than the critical χ^2 value, then our analysis is significant at $p < .050$. We can see here that our calculated χ^2 value of 40.96 is much larger than the critical χ^2 value of 3.841, so therefore our analysis is significant with a p value of .050. This means that our observed frequencies are distributed significantly differently from our expected frequencies, and there is less than a 5% chance that we have committed a Type I Error.

Although this is good, it is useful to see if our finding is significant at smaller p values as this will show even less chance of us having committed a Type I Error. To do this, look along the row to find the smallest alpha level (p value) where our calculated χ^2 value of 40.96 is larger than the critical value. This shows us that our finding is significant even at a p value of .001,

df	p = .050	p = .025	p = .010	p = .005	p = .001
1	3.841	5.024	6.635	7.879	10.828
2	5.991	7.378	9.210	10.597	13.816
3	7.815	9.348	11.345	12.838	16.266
4	9.488	11.143	13.277	14.860	18.467
5	11.070	12.833	15.086	16.750	20.515

Figure 14.1: Section of the critical values table for the chi squared test.

the smallest p value that is conventionally used in psychological research. This means that there is less than a 0.1% chance of us having committed a Type I Error.

Interpreting and writing up a chi squared goodness of fit

We now know that we have a statistically significant finding, but we must report this according to the APA standards (see Figure 14.2). We can therefore say that our chi squared goodness of fit analysis is significant (χ^2 (1, N = 100) = 40.96, $p < .001$). You can find the chi symbol, χ, in Word by going to the Insert > Symbol menu and looking under the Greek alphabet.

Although we have now determined that we have a significant finding, what does this actually mean? Remember that knowing we have a significant finding isn't really that interesting unless we know what that significant finding is actually telling us about our data.

We must always remember to interpret the direction of our findings. To do this, we need to look back at our residual values (O–E). A *positive* residual shows that there are *more* participants than you would expect by chance in that category. A *negative* residual shows that there are *fewer* participants than you would expect by chance in that category. Using these residual values, we can say that being left handed occurs less often than you would expect by random chance, as the residual value is negative. In contrast, being right handed occurs more often than you would expect by random chance, as the residual value is positive.

$$\chi^2 \text{ (df, } N = \text{XX)} = \text{XX.XX, } p < .\text{XXX}$$

- Tells you which statistic you calculated
  - χ^2 means chi square (Get the chi symbol from Insert > Symbol in Word)
- Tells you the degrees of freedom and number of participants
  - df = degrees of freedom
  - N = number of participants
- Tells you the statistic calculated value
  - This is the value that you calculate for your statistical analysis
- Tells you the significance (p value)
  - Report the smallest p value where your calculated value is larger than the critical value.

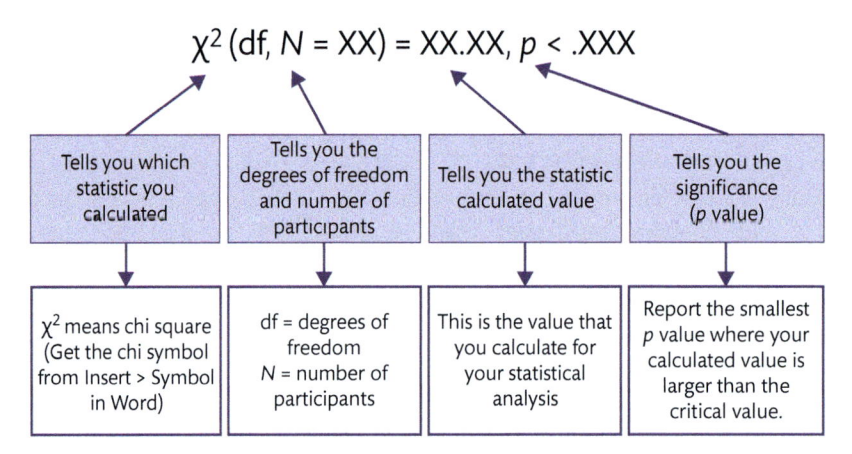

Figure 14.2: APA standard for the reporting of a chi squared goodness of fit test.

After all this analysis, we can conclude that the frequency of occurrence for being left or right handed differs significantly from what you would expect by random chance (χ^2 (1, N = 100) = 40.96, p < .001) with left handedness occurring less often than you would expect and right handedness occurring more often than you would expect.

Calculating and interpreting a chi squared test of association: analysing more than one variable

We now know how to calculate a chi squared goodness of fit for one categorical variable, but what if we have more than one variable that we would like to analyse? Previous research has suggested that a person's sense of smell becomes more sensitive after drinking wine, therefore we could run a study where we give half of the participants wine and the other half a non-alcoholic wine drink. We then get them to smell a sample with a subtle lemon smell and ask them if they can identify the scent or not. What if we would like to know is if the detection of the scent differs significantly from chance when also taking into account whether the person drank wine or grape juice. We might hypothesise that, for those who drank wine, successful scent detection will occur more often than expected. In this analysis we now have two variables: drink consumed (wine or grape juice) and whether the lemon scent was detected or not. Each variable has two possible categories, giving us a dataset suitable for analysis with a 2 x 2 chi squared test of association. This is sometimes also called the test of independence.

Calculating the expected frequencies is slightly more complex in this type of chi square, so it is helpful to complete an additional table before we start the main analysis (see Table 14.4). Your observed data will give you four values. So we have 13 participants drinking grape juice who did not detect the lemon scent, 5 participants drinking wine who did not detect the scent, 37 grape juice drinking participants who did detect the scent and 45 wine drinking participants who did detect the lemon scent.

We then need to calculate the total number of grape juice drinking participants (13 + 37 = 50) and the total number of wine drinking participants (5 + 45 = 50). These are the row total values. Then we calculate the total number of people who did not detect the scent (13 + 5 = 18) and the total number who did (37 + 45 = 82). These are the column totals.

Finally we will calculate the grand total, which is the total number of participants in the study (13 + 37 + 5 + 45 = 100). We will use these values to calculate the expected frequencies in the next stage of the chi squared calculations.

Table 14.4: Calculating the row, column and grand totals for a chi squared test of association.

		Scent detected?		
		Not detected	Detected	Row total
Drink	Grape juice	13	37	50
	Wine	5	45	50
	Column total	18	82	Grand total = **100**

DO MY DATA FIT THE EXPECTED FREQUENCIES?

Table 14.5: Stages of calculation for the chi square test of association.

	Grape juice	Not detected	Detected
Step 1:	Observed data (O)	13	37
Step 2:	Expected data (E)	(50 * 18)/100 = **9**	(50 * 82)/100 = **41**
Step 3:	O − E	13 − 9 = **4**	37 − 41 = **−4**
Step 4:	$(O − E)^2$	$4^2 = 16$	$−4^2 = 16$
Step 5:	$\frac{(O − E)^2}{E}$	16/9 = **1.7778**	16/41 = **0.3902**
	Wine	Not detected	Detected
Step 1:	Observed data (O)	5	45
Step 2:	Expected data (E)	(50 * 18)/100 = **9**	(50 * 82)/100 = **41**
Step 3:	O − E	5 − 9 = **−4**	45 − 41 = **4**
Step 4:	$(O − E)^2$	$−4^2 = 16$	$4^2 = 16$
Step 5:	$\frac{(O − E)^2}{E}$	16/9 = **1.7778**	16/41 = **0.3902**

We are now ready to calculate the chi squared statistic. The equation is the same as we used previously: $\chi^2 = \sum \frac{(O−E)^2}{E}$. You can see the observed data in step one of Table 14.5. Note that we have two parts to this calculations table. The top half will be used for our calculations for grape juice drinking participants and the lower half will be used for our calculations for wine drinking participants.

Steps for calculating the chi squared test of association:

1. Enter the observed data into each of the four cells that we have: grape juice, not detected; grape juice, detected; wine, not detected; and wine, detected. These values tell us the number of people in our sample that 'belong' to each category.

2. Next, calculate the expected frequencies for each of the four cells. This will be different for each category, or cell, and is calculated by multiplying the row total by the column total and dividing this by the grand total: expected = (row total * column total)/grand total. These are the values that we previously calculated in Table 14.4.

3. Now calculate the difference between the observed and expected frequencies: O−E. Remember that this gives us the residual values that will be important later when we want to interpret the direction of any significant findings.

4. You now square this residual value: $(O−E)^2$.

5. In step 5 you divide this value by the expected value within that cell $\frac{(O−E)^2}{E}$.

6. Finally we complete the final stage of the chi square test of association where we calculate the χ^2 value by adding up (Σ) the $\frac{(O−E)^2}{E}$ value from each cell. Take a look again at Equation 14.1 and you will see that this is the equation for calculating the chi square

statistic. Therefore χ^2 = 1.7778 + 0.3902 + 1.7778 + 0.3902. Our final calculated statistic is χ^2 = 4.34.

Again, we now need to look up whether our calculated χ^2 value is significant. Is the distribution of scent detection for grape juice and wine drinkers significantly different from the expected frequencies? We need to look up the significance on the critical values table (see Appendix 3). In order to find out whether our finding is statistic, we need to know three things:

1. What is our alpha level? Again, we will be using the psychology standard of α = .050.

2. What are our calculated degrees of freedom? The calculation the degrees of freedom for the chi squared test of association is different from the goodness of fit analysis. This is so that that both of the variables can be taken into account.
   - df = (number of categories in rows −1) * (number of categories in columns −1)
   - df = (2 − 1) * (2 − 1)
   - df = 1 * 1
   - df = 1

3. What is our calculated χ^2 value? We just calculated this to be χ^2 = 4.34.

Is the chi squared test of association analysis significant?

We now need to look up whether our calculated χ^2 value is significant, and we do this in exactly the same way as we did for the chi squared goodness of fit. Looking at the critical values table (Appendix 3, Table A3.4), we can see that the critical χ^2 value for a p value of .050 is 3.841. Our calculated χ^2 value of 4.34 is larger than the critical χ^2 value of 3.841. Therefore our chi squared analysis is significant with a p value of .050, meaning that there is less than a 5% chance of having committed a Type I Error.

Ideally we will report the smallest p value at which our calculated χ^2 value is greater than the critical χ^2 value, because the smaller the p value, the more confident we can be of our findings. However, the critical χ^2 value for p = .025 is 5.024. Our calculated χ^2 value is less than this, so therefore we will have to report that our findings are significant at p = .050.

Interpreting and writing up a chi squared test of association

Again, we need to report our statistical analysis using the APA reporting standards shown in Figure 14.2 and then interpret the direction of our significant findings using the residual values (the difference between the observed and the expected frequencies). We can therefore say that our chi square test of association was significant (χ^2 (1, N = 100) = 4.34, p < .050). For grape juice drinking participants, there were more people who did not detect the scent than would be expected by random chance (as can be seen by the positive residual value of 4) and fewer people who did detect the scent than would be expected by random chance (as can be seen by the negative residual value of −4). For wine drinking participants, there were fewer people who missed the scent than would be expected by random chance (as can be seen by the negative residual value of −4) and more people who did detect the scent than would be expected by random chance (as can be seen by the positive residual value of 4).

In published research you sometimes see the chi squared test of association followed up by further chi square goodness of fits tests to help further understand the dataset. For example, we might split our dataset into two, depending of the type of drink, and then conduct two separate goodness of fit tests. One would look at the frequencies of detecting or not detecting the scent for grape juice drinkers, and the other would look at the frequencies of detecting or not detecting the scent for wine drinkers.

Are there any assumptions for using the chi squared test?

There are two key considerations that you should bear in mind when you run a chi square test. First, each participant should only provide one frequency score to the dataset. So what should you do if the participants in your design contribute more than one frequency score to the dataset? For example, what if you look at voting preferences (left, centre, right) both before and after taking part in a political science course? Here each participant contributes two frequency scores, one before and one after the course. In this situation, there is a different method of analysis that you would need to use, the McNemar test. This is, essentially, a chi square test for repeated measures designs.

The second assumption is regarding adequate sample size, as it has been suggested that the chi square test is not accurate with smaller samples. As such, it is generally recommended that you have a minimum of 20 participants to conduct a chi square test. With a chi squared test of association, things get a little more complicated, and here we look at the expected frequencies. In a 2x2 design, if any of the expected frequencies are less than five, then the test may not be stable. If this is the case in your dataset, then you can apply Yate's correction, in which you simply subtract 0.5 from the residual value ($O - E$).

If your design is more complex than 2x2, such as a 2x3 or 4x6 design, then it is ok to have a small number of cells where the expected frequency is less than five. The chi square is robust with up to 20% of the cells having an expected frequency less than five. Imagine you have a 2x3 chi square, with psychopath or not being one variable and choice of white, milk or plain chocolate being the other variable. In this design you have six cells in total. If you have one cell with an expected frequency of 3, then this is fine as that one cell represents 16.67% of the cells and you can continue with the analysis. However, if you had two cells with expected frequencies of 3, then this would be problematic as they represent 33.33% of the cells. One solution in this situation is to combine categories and then recalculate the expected frequencies. For example, you might combine the milk and plain chocolate categories, and then compare this combined 'chocolate' category to the white chocolate 'not really chocolate' category.

How is the chi squared analysis typically used in psychological research?

There are two slightly different ways that you might see the chi squared test used in psychological research. It can be used as a statistic in its own right, such as how we have used it in this chapter. For example, the chi squared statistic is often used in research on visual perception, where participants can either see an illusion, or not.

However, you might sometimes see the chi square statistic in the methods section of a paper. If you remember back to Chapter 6, where we talked about experimental design, one key methodological issue in an independent measures design is to try to make the two separate groups of participants as similar as possible. For example, you might want the number of males and females, the number of people educated to degree level, or maybe the number of people in relationships, to be similar in each group. The chi square test can be used to help evaluate the similarity of the two groups. So, for example, is the number of males and females in each group comparable? If the groups are similar, then you would expect the chi square analysis to not be significant, showing that the observed frequency of males and females within each group does not differ from the expected, random frequency.

The dataset created for this chapter was inspired by

Endevelt-Shapira, Y., Shushan, S., Roth, Y., & Sobel, N. (2014). Disinhibition of olfaction: Human olfactory performance improves following low levels of alcohol. *Behavioural Brain Research*, 272, 66–74

Study questions

Each of these study questions describes a research study. For each study you should identify how many variables there are and, for each variable, how many categories there are. You then need to decide how the data should be analysed and describe your suggested method of analysis (e.g., a 2 x 4 chi square test of association). Finally, devise a hypothesis for the study.

1. A researcher is completing a study on the popularity of different types of television programmes. They ask 1,000 people which type of TV show they would prefer to watch: documentary, drama, or reality TV.
2. The researcher suspects that there might be a sex difference in choice of TV program watched. How could you take this into account with the design and analysis?
3. You are asked by a sweet making company to design a study in which you will find out whether consumers prefer their original recipe sweets or their new and improved recipe sweets. They have allowed you to add one variable of your choice to the study, however they have asked that the data be suitable for analysis with a chi square. How would you develop this study and how would you analyse the dataset?

Additional dataset

Do you still have your childhood teddy, and do you feel nicer when holding it? Researchers have shown that people engage in more prosocial behaviours when holding a teddy bear (Tai, Zheng, & Narayanan, 2011).

We have run a follow up study where participants were asked to either hold a teddy bear or not whilst waiting to participate in a psychology study. What they didn't know is that the study was already taking place. When the researcher entered the room they dropped the large pile of papers that they were carrying. We then recorded whether the participant offered help immediately, offered help after a delay, or whether they didn't offer to help. The data collected are shown in Table 14.6 below.

1. What method of analysis will you use to analyse this dataset?

Table 14.6: Data for the additional dataset example.

	Not holding teddy	Holding teddy
No help offered	N = 10	N = 3
Delayed help offered	N = 17	N = 14
Immediate help offered	N = 3	N = 13

2. Suggest a suitable hypothesis for this analysis.
3. Calculate the χ^2 statistic and determine whether it is significant.
4. Interpret and write up your findings using APA standards.
5. Suggest how you could redesign the 'teddy' variable so that the study would have a 3x3 categorical design.

This dataset was inspired by

Tai, K., Zheng, X., and Narayanan, J. (2011). Touching a teddy bear mitigates negative effects of social exclusion to increase prosocial behavior. *Social Psychological and Personality Science*, 2, 618–626.

Example paper using this statistic

Joseph, A. J., Tandon, N., Yang, L. H., Duckworth, K., Torous, J., Seidman, L. J., & Keshavan, M. S. (2015). Schizophrenia: Use and misuse on Twitter. *Schizophrenia Research*, *165*, 111–115.

In this paper the researchers categorised tweets that referred to schizophrenia on the basis of how medically appropriate the information was and whether sarcasm was used. Tweets about diabetes were used as a comparison medical condition. They conducted a large number of chi square analyses and these are quite nicely summarised in Tables 2 and 3. However, if you were just reporting one or two chi square analyses you would most likely do this just within the text of your results.

How to run this analysis in SPSS ...

If you would like to see how to run this analysis in SPSS, and to find other materials including full answers to study questions, please go to the online resources:
www.oup.com/uk/bourne/

15 Are there differences between groups or conditions? Mann-Whitney *U* and Wilcoxon signed rank tests

> **In this chapter you will learn...**
> - How to calculate a Mann-Whitney *U* test and the logic behind analysing rank scores
> - How to find out if your result is significant or not, and how to interpret and write up a Mann-Whitney *U* test
> - How to calculate a Wilcoxon signed rank test and the logic behind examining ranked difference scores
> - How to find out if your result is significant or not, and how to interpret and write up a Wilcoxon signed rank test
> - How to use *z* scores to analyse large datasets

Introduction

In this chapter we will be covering two different **non-parametric statistics**: Mann-Whitney *U* and Wilcoxon signed rank tests. Both are tests that would be used when you have used an **experimental design** (or a quasi-experimental design), but, for some reason, you require a non-parametric test. The content of this chapter really builds on a number of previous chapters in this book, so I'll start by briefly highlighting the important points, and where in the book you need to go to if you wish to revise any key issues.

An experiment is a design that involves manipulating a variable, your **independent variable** (IV), and seeing whether that manipulation has any impact on another measurable variable, your **dependent variable** (DV). For example, your IV manipulation could be whether you give your participants white chocolate or milk chocolate, and your DV measurement could be happiness. With this experimental design we could examine whether eating white chocolate or milk chocolate makes people happier. In a nutshell, that is experimental design, but if you feel the need for a quick refresher then take a quick look back at Chapter 6.

Within any experimental design there is one key design feature that has a big impact on the type of analysis that you would choose to run: whether the design is **independent measures**, so with different groups of participants in each condition, or whether the design is **repeated measures**, so with one set of participants repeating the experiment under different conditions. Again, you can look back at Chapter 6 if you would like to recap on this. If you have an experimental design with two conditions and different participants in each condition you need to run an independent measures *t* test (covered in Chapter 7), but if you have the same participants repeating the same experiment under two different conditions, then you would want to run a repeated measures *t* test (covered in Chapter 8).

Great, so we are happy with the idea of independent and repeated *t* tests, but let's just throw a spanner in the works. These are both **parametric tests**, which means that your design and data need to meet certain assumptions for you to be able to run them. In Chapter 14 we spent a long time discussing these assumptions and how to decide whether you have met or violated them. If I wanted to run an independent measures *t* test, but I've violated one of the parametric assumptions, then instead I would run the non-parametric **Mann-Whitney *U* test**. If I was needing a repeated *t* test, but had violated one of the assumptions, then I would need to run the non-parametric **Wilcoxon signed rank test**. We will be covering how to calculate and interpret both of these tests in this chapter.

Before moving on to look at the two tests, it is important to bear in mind that although both the Mann-Whitney *U* and the Wilcoxon signed rank tests are non-parametric approaches to be used when parametric assumptions have been violated, this doesn't mean that they are totally free of any assumptions. For both of these tests, it is still important to ensure that the **independence of observations** assumption has been met, even though they are robust if the assumptions of **levels of measurement**, **distribution** or **homogeneity of variance** have been violated.

Mann-Whitney *U* test (two independent groups)

To illustrate how to calculate the Mann-Whitney *U* test we are going to analyse some data from a (fictional) study that looked at levels of self-esteem in patients who had either a left hemisphere or right hemisphere brain lesion. This is because some previous research has suggested that self-esteem is differently processed by the two hemispheres of the brain. Self-esteem is measured using a questionnaire, with high scores indicating high levels of self-esteem and a maximum score of 50. The data are shown in Table 15.1, with the mean and variance for each group calculated for you.

Looking at the descriptive statistics, it is very clear that there is a possible issue of heterogeneity of variance as the variance is far larger in the left hemisphere lesion group than in the right hemisphere lesion group. The convention is usually that the larger variance should be no more than four times the size of the smaller one. For this dataset, this means that the larger value should be no greater than 45.2 (11.3*4 = 45.2), but the variance for the left hemisphere lesion group is much greater than this at 182.7. As the parametric assumption of homogeneity of variance has been violated in this dataset, we will need to run a Mann-Whitney *U* test, rather than a parametric independent *t* test.

MANN-WHITNEY *U* TEST

Table 15.1: Raw data and descriptive statistics for the self-esteem study.

	Left hemisphere lesion	Right hemisphere lesion
	46	22
	31	27
	49	19
	24	23
	41	18
	49	27
	12	25
	27	24
Mean	34.875	23.125
Variance	182.70	11.30

The logic behind the Mann-Whitney *U* test

When you calculate a Mann-Whitney *U* test, the first stage is to rank the data, so you might find it helpful to quickly look back at Chapter 13 to revise how this is done. This ranking is done across all of the participants, *ignoring which group they belong to*. The participant with the lowest score in the entire dataset gets a rank of 1, the participant with the next score up gets a rank of 2, and so on. Consequently, participants with lower scores get lower rankings. Once we have ranked the data we will add up the rank scores within each group. This gives us three possible outcomes, which you can see illustrated graphically (with five participants in each group) in Figure 15.1.

1. Participants in the left hemisphere lesion group have lower ranked scores, whereas participants in the right hemisphere lesion group have higher ranked scores. This analysis is likely to be significant. You can see this in the graph on the left of Figure 15.1.

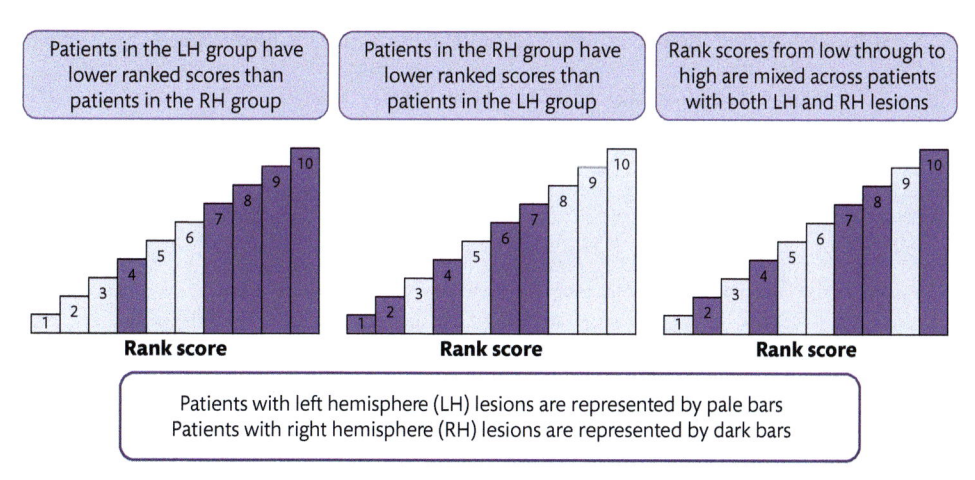

Figure 15.1: Imagining rank scores across two different conditions (left or right hemisphere lesions), in three possible outcome scenarios for a Mann-Whitney *U* test.

ARE THERE DIFFERENCES BETWEEN GROUPS OR CONDITIONS?

2. Participants in the right hemisphere lesion group have lower ranked scores, whereas participants in the left hemisphere lesion group have higher ranked scores. This analysis is likely to be significant. You can see this in the graph in the centre of Figure 15.1.

3. Participants from both groups have a mix of high and low ranked scores. This analysis is not likely to be significant. You can see this in the graph on the right of Figure 15.1.

The Mann Whitney U test takes the smallest summed rank score, and uses this to determine significance. The smaller the summed rank score, the more significant the difference between the two groups will be. This is because, if the two groups are similar, then the summed rank scores for each group will also be similar. If the two groups are different, one will have a small summed rank score and the other will have a large summed ranked score. The larger the difference, the more extreme the summed rank scores will be in each condition. Consequently, we look at the U statistic for the smaller rank scored group. When we look up the critical values, unusually we want our calculated U to be *smaller* than the critical U. This is because a smaller U represents a greater difference between the two conditions.

Calculating and interpreting a Mann-Whitney U test: a worked example

We will now work through the calculations for a Mann-Whitney U test, using the self-esteem study data. But before starting on the calculations, you should always devise your hypothesis, and decide whether to have a one-tailed (directional) or two-tailed (non-directional) prediction. For this analysis I think a two-tailed prediction is most appropriate as there is very little research in this area, and particularly not with a patient group. Therefore, I will simply predict that there will be a difference in self-esteem between the two groups of patients.

Steps for calculating the Mann-Whitney U test:

1. The first thing that needs to be done is to rank the data, and very importantly you must rank all of the data in one go, regardless of which condition the data come from. You can see this done in Table 15.2. As we have a total of 16 participants (eight in each condition), this means that the ranked scores should go from 1 for the lowest self-esteem score,

Table 15.2: Raw and ranked values for calculating the Mann-Whitney U test.

	Left hemisphere lesion (Group 1)		Right hemisphere lesion (Group 2)	
	Raw score	Rank	Raw score	Rank
	46	14.0	22	4.0
	31	12.0	27	10.0
	49	15.5	19	3.0
	24	6.5	23	5.0
	41	13.0	18	2.0
	49	15.5	27	10.0
	12	1.0	25	8.0
	27	10.0	24	6.5
Rank total		$T^1 = 87.5$		$T^2 = 48.5$

through to 16 for the highest self-esteem score. Remember that if you have values that occur more than once, then you need to calculate the mean rank for the tied values (go back to Chapter 13 to revise this). For example, two participants gained the highest score of 49, and these should have been given the ranks of 15 and 16, so they were given a rank of 15.5, which is the mean of 15 and 16.

2. Next, you need to add up the ranked scores separately for the two groups, giving you T^1 (for the first condition, the left hemisphere lesion group) and T^2 (for the second condition, the right hemisphere lesion group).

   - $T^1 = 14 + 12 + 15.5 + 6.5 + 13 + 15.5 + 1 + 10$
   - $T^1 = 87.5$
   - $T^2 = 4 + 10 + 3 + 5 + 2 + 10 + 8 + 6.5$
   - $T^2 = 48.5$

3. We can now look at the equation for the Mann-Whitney U. We actually need to calculate the U statistic twice, once for each group. The equation is quite simple, and only uses the N (number of participants) in each condition and the T (rank totals) for each condition. There are some slightly different versions of the U equation, but they will all give you the same calculated U value.

4. Calculating U_1 for group 1: Left hemisphere lesion group.

$$U_1 = (N_1 * N_2) + \left(N_1 * \frac{(N_1 + 1)}{2} \right) - T_1$$

- Insert the correct values into the equation.

$$U_1 = (8 * 8) + \left(8 * \frac{(8 + 1)}{2} \right) - 87.5$$

- Calculate the addition sum within the brackets.

$$U_1 = (8 * 8) + \left(8 * \frac{(9)}{2} \right) - 87.5$$

- Calculate the division sum within the brackets.

$$U_1 = (8 * 8) + (8 * 4.5) - 87.5$$

- Calculate the each of the multiplications within the brackets.

$$U_1 = (64) + (36) - 87.5$$

- Finish the calculations by completing the addition and then the subtraction.

$$U_1 = 12.5$$

5. Calculating U_2 for group 2: Right hemisphere lesion group.

$$U_2 = (N_1 * N_2) + \left(N_2 * \frac{(N_2 + 1)}{2}\right) - T_2$$

- Insert the correct values into the equation.

$$U_2 = (8 * 8) + \left(8 * \frac{(8 + 1)}{2}\right) - 48.5$$

- Calculate the addition sum within the brackets.

$$U_2 = (8 * 8) + \left(8 * \frac{(9)}{2}\right) - 48.5$$

- Calculate the division sum within the brackets.

$$U_2 = (8 * 8) + (8 * 4.5) - 48.5$$

- Calculate the each of the multiplications within the brackets.

$$U_2 = (64) + (36) - 48.5$$

- Finish the calculations by completing the addition and then the subtraction.

$$U_2 = 51.5$$

6. You now have two U values calculated, $U_1 = 12.5$ for the left hemisphere lesion group, and $U_2 = 51.5$ for the right hemisphere lesion group. You need to pick the smaller of the two values to be your final calculated U value. So for this analysis $U = 12.5$.

As a brief aside, there is a quick and easy way that you can use to double check that your calculations are correct, which can be reassuring to do. For this statistic if you add U_1 and U_2 together (12.5 + 51.5 = 64), this should give you the same value as multiplying n_1 by n_2 (8 * 8 = 64). If both sums give you the same value, 64 in this case, you can be confident that your calculations are correct.

Is the Mann-Whitney U test significant?

We now want to see whether our calculated U value is significant. To do this we need the critical values table (see Appendix 3), and the following four pieces of information:

1. Is the hypothesis one-tailed or two-tailed? We came up with a two-tailed hypothesis.
2. What is our alpha level? We will stick with the psychology standard of $\alpha = .050$.
3. How many participants were there in each condition?
   - For the left hemisphere lesion condition: $N_1 = 8$
   - For the right hemisphere lesion condition: $N_2 = 8$
4. What is our calculated U value? We just worked this out as $U = 12.5$

		n_2 (number of participants in larger group)							
		2	3	4	5	6	7	8	9
n_1 (number of participants in smaller group)	2	-	-	-	-	-	-	0	0
	3	-	-	-	0	1	1	2	2
	4	-	-	0	1	2	3	4	4
	5	-	0	1	2	3	5	6	7
	6	-	1	2	3	5	6	7	10
	7	-	1	3	5	6	8	10	12
	8	0	2	4	6	7	10	13	15
	9	0	2	4	7	10	12	15	17
	10	0	3	5	8	11	14	17	20
	11	0	3	6	9	13	16	19	23
	12	1	4	7	11	14	18	22	26
	13	1	4	8	12	16	20	24	28

Figure 15.2: Looking up the critical value for the Mann-Whitney *U* test.

When you look at the critical values tables in the Appendices you will see there are two different tables. One gives the critical values for an α = .050 when you have a two-tailed test, and the other gives the critical values for an α = .050 when you have a one-tailed test. We had a two-tailed hypothesis, so we will use the appropriate table. You can see a section of this table in Figure 15.2. We had eight participants in each condition, so using the look up column for 8 and the look up row for 8, we can see that the critical *U* value for this design is 13.

Very importantly, for this analysis you want your calculated *U* value to be equal to or *smaller* than the critical *U* value. This is totally opposite to all of the other critical values tables! So for our example, the critical *U* is 13, and our calculated *U* is slightly smaller than this at 12.5, meaning that our analysis is significant at an α = .050 with a two-tailed prediction. As with all the statistics we have discussed, it is good to check that our analysis is significant at a smaller alpha level, as that means we can be more confident of our findings. However, $p < .050$ is the smallest *p* value at which this finding is significant.

Interpreting and writing up a Mann-Whitney *U* test

In Figure 15.3 you can see the APA convention for presenting the results of a Mann-Whitney *U* test. Unusually there is no need to report the number of participants or degrees of freedom for the analysis, although you do sometimes see people reporting the N anyway! There are also a few different ways of presenting the descriptive statistics to interpret the direction of any significant finding you may have. The analysis is non-parametric, and therefore many people will use the median values to interpret which group has significantly higher scores. This is probably a good way to interpret a significant Mann-Whitney *U* test as the median is quite robust if there are any outliers or if the distribution is skewed (look back at Chapter 5 for revise how to calculate the median). Other people still present the mean values of the raw data, but these could be skewed and not accurately reflect the data. Occasionally you will see

$$U = XX.XX, p < .XXX$$

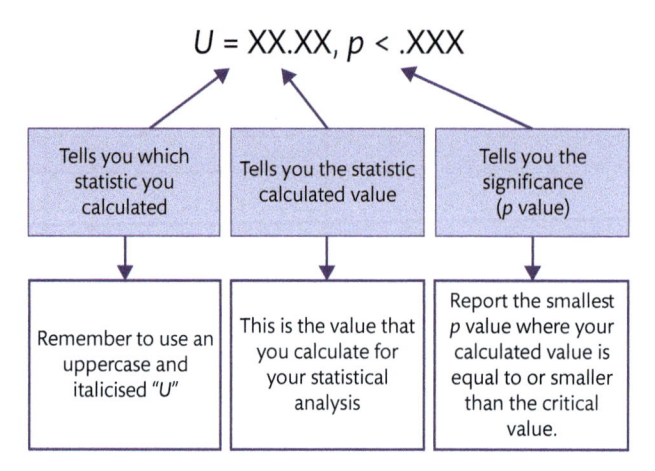

- Tells you which statistic you calculated → Remember to use an uppercase and italicised "U"
- Tells you the statistic calculated value → This is the value that you calculate for your statistical analysis
- Tells you the significance (p value) → Report the smallest p value where your calculated value is equal to or smaller than the critical value.

Figure 15.3: APA convention for reporting a Mann-Whitney *U* test.

the mean of the ranked scores in each condition used to interpret findings. I would recommend using the median though.

For our example analysis, we might report our findings in the following way ... There was a significant difference in self-esteem for the two groups (U = 12.5, p < .050). Patients with left hemisphere lesions had significantly greater self-esteem (median = 36) than patients with right hemisphere lesions (median = 23.5).

The dataset created for this analysis was inspired by:

McKay, R., Arciuli, J., Atkinson, A., Bennett, E., & Pheils, E. (2010). Lateralisation of self-esteem: An investigation using a dichotically presented auditory adaptation of the Implicit Association Test. *Cortex, 46*, 367–373.

Wilcoxon signed rank test (two repeated conditions)

The Wilcoxon signed rank test is the non-parametric equivalent of the repeated *t* test, so you would have one set of participants who repeat the same experiment under different conditions, and for some reason only a non-parametric analysis would be suitable.

For this example we will be looking at some data inspired by a developmental psychology study that looked at how well adults can interpret the emotional expressions of babies, and whether this is influenced by the baby using a dummy. The original study found that adults rated the infant's emotional expressions as less intense if they had a dummy. In this dataset ten adults are shown two images of babies who are crying, one with a dummy and one without a dummy. They are asked to rate how upset they think each of the babies are, using a seven point Likert scale ranging from 1 (not at all upset) through to 7 (very upset). As the data are ordinal, and the previous research using this measure has tended to use non-parametric tests, we will also analyse our dataset using a non-parametric test.

The logic behind the Wilcoxon signed rank test

As with the Mann-Whitney U test, the Wilcoxon signed rank test is based on the analysis of the ranked data. However, remember that this is a repeated measures design, and therefore we first want to see how the scores have changed, for each participant, between the two conditions. To do this, the first stage of the calculation is to simply look at the difference scores for each participant. If their scores have increased, they will have a positive value for their change score. If their scores have decreased, they will have a negative value for their change score. If there is little change in their scores, then the change score will be very small and close to 0.

With these change, or difference, scores calculated, we now need to rank the data to resolve whichever issues are present in the data that mean they are not suitable for a parametric analysis. They are first ranked whilst ignoring the sign of the change scores (whether they are negative or positive), and then the signs are added back in. When you sum the ranks of the positive ranks, which show increasing scores, and sum the ranks of the negative ranks, which show decreasing scores, we get a measure of how the participant's scores changed. There are three possible outcomes (with ten participants in total), which you can see illustrated graphically in Figure 15.4.

1. Most of the participants had increasing ranks. Therefore the summed positive (increasing) ranks will be a large number, and the summed negative (decreasing) ranks will be small. This analysis is likely to be significant, showing that the participants' scores increased. You can see this in the graph on the left of Figure 15.4.

2. Most of the participants had decreasing ranks. Therefore the summed negative (decreasing) ranks will be a large number, and the summed positive (increasing) ranks will be small. This analysis is likely to be significant, showing that participants' scores decreased. You can see this in the graph in the centre of Figure 15.4.

3. There was a roughly equal mix of increasing and decreasing ranks, and therefore the two summed rank scores for increasing and decreasing scores will be similar. This analysis is not likely to be significant. You can see this in the graph on the right of Figure 15.4.

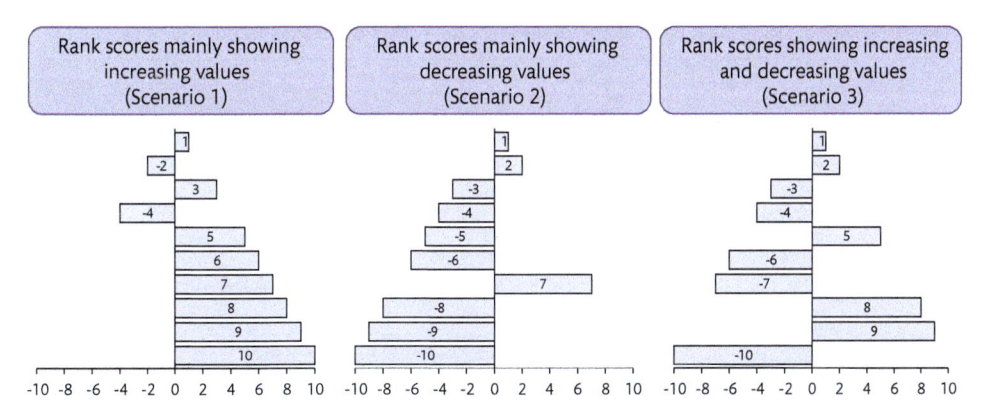

Figure 15.4: Imagining ranked difference scores, in three possible outcome scenarios for a Wilcoxon signed rank test.

Calculating and interpreting a Wilcoxon signed rank test: a worked example

Before actually calculating the Wilcoxon signed rank test (which you may be relieved to hear is actually quite simple!), we need to develop our hypothesis. Given the previous research in this area a one-tailed hypothesis seems justified, so I have the directional hypothesis that participants will rate the faces as more upset when the baby does not have a dummy. The raw data are shown in the first two columns of Table 15.3.

Steps for calculating the Wilcoxon signed rank test:

1. First thing to calculate is the difference scores, and this is done using $Y - X$, so the rating in the no dummy condition (condition Y) minus the rating in the dummy condition (condition X). You can see these difference scores in column three of the data table.

2. Next, you need to rank these scores, and you can see these in column four of the data table. However, bear in mind the following two really important points:
   - If there are any 0 difference scores, where an identical rating was given in both conditions, ignore this value in the rankings. You can see this happened for the final participant in this dataset.
   - Ignore the sign of the difference for this stage. It doesn't matter whether the values are positive or negative, simply the actual number. Within this dataset there were two difference scores of −1 and one difference score of +1. These were all ranked together, and should have taken ranks 1, 2, and 3, but because they were tied ranks, they were given the mean rank score of 2.

3. You now need to give the sign back to the ranked values. So if the original difference score was negative, make the ranked value negative, but if the original difference score was positive, then keep it positive. You can see these values in the fifth column of the data table.

4. Now you need to sum all of the positive ranked scores and all of the negatively ranked scores separately, which you can see done in the final two columns of the table.
   - $W+ = 8 + 5 + 2 + 6.5 + 9 + 6.5 + 4$

Table 15.3: Raw data and initial calculations for the Wilcoxon signed rank test of the dummy study.

Dummy (Condition X)	No dummy (Condition Y)	Difference (Y − X)	Rank	Signed rank	Sum of positive ranks	Sum of negative ranks
2	7	5	8	8	8	
4	3	−1	2	−2		−2
3	6	3	5	5	5	
6	7	1	2	2	2	
1	5	4	6.5	6.5	6.5	
1	7	6	9	9	9	
2	6	4	6.5	6.5	6.5	
3	5	2	4	4	4	
4	3	−1	2	−2		−2
3	3	0	−	−		
					W+ = 41	W− = −4

- W+ = 41
- W− = −2 + −2
- W− = −4

5. The smaller of the two W values is our calculated value, so for this analysis W = −4.
6. Finally, you need to calculate the number of participants, minus the number of participants that had tied scores (so difference scores of 0). We had ten participants, but one had a tied score, and therefore we have an N of 9 (N = 10 − 1).

Is the Wilcoxon signed rank test significant?

We now want to see whether our calculated W value is significant. To do this we need the critical values table (see Appendix 3), and the following four pieces of information:

1. Is the hypothesis one-tailed or two-tailed? For this analysis we had a one-tailed hypothesis.
2. What is our alpha level? We will stick with the psychology standard of $\alpha = .050$.
3. How many participants without tied scores were there?
   - N = 10−1
   - N = 9
4. What is our calculated W value? We just worked this out as W = −4

A section of the critical values table is shown in Figure 15.5. If you have a one-tailed prediction then read the alpha levels from the upper row, whereas you have a two-tailed prediction then read the alpha levels from the lower row. You should start by looking at the column for an alpha level of .050, but remember that it is always best to report the lowest alpha value at which your analysis is significant, so look across to the right to the smaller alpha values and check those too. As with the Mann-Whitney U test, you need your calculated value to be equal to or *smaller* than the critical value in the table. If your calculated value is negative, you can ignore the sign. It is just the magnitude of the number that counts. So you can imagine our calculated W to be 4, and just ignore the minus for the purposes of looking up the critical values.

	Level of significance of a one-tailed test				
	$\alpha = .050$	$\alpha = .025$	$\alpha = .010$	$\alpha = .005$	$\alpha = .001$
	Level of significance of a two-tailed test				
N	$\alpha = .100$	$\alpha = .050$	$\alpha = .020$	$\alpha = .010$	$\alpha = .002$
4	−	−	−	−	−
5	0	−	−	−	−
6	2	0	−	−	−
7	3	2	0	−	−
8	5	3	1	0	−
9	8	5	3	1	−
10	10	8	5	3	0

Figure 15.5: Looking up the critical values for a Wilcoxon signed rank test.

$$W = XX.XX, p < .XXX$$

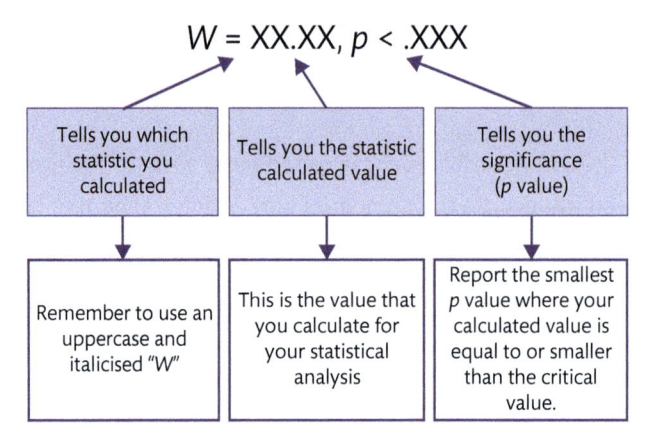

- **Tells you which statistic you calculated** → Remember to use an uppercase and italicised "W"
- **Tells you the statistic calculated value** → This is the value that you calculate for your statistical analysis
- **Tells you the significance (p value)** → Report the smallest p value where your calculated value is equal to or smaller than the critical value.

Figure 15.6: APA convention for reporting a Wilcoxon signed rank test.

Looking at the critical values table, for an alpha of .050 for a one-tailed prediction with an N of 9, the critical value is 8. Our calculated W is smaller than that, so we know that our finding is significant with $p < .050$. Looking across to the other alpha levels, we can also see that our calculated value is smaller than the critical value of 5 for an alpha of .025, but it is greater than the critical value of 3 for an alpha of .010. Therefore we can conclude that we have a significant difference at $p < .025$.

Interpreting and writing up a Wilcoxon signed rank test

As with writing up any analysis, you should use APA conventions, and these are shown in Figure 15.6. Again, there is no need to report the number of participants or the degrees of freedom. You may also sometimes see different descriptive statistics used in the interpretation of a significant Wilcoxon signed rank test in published research, but I'd always suggest that you stick with the median when working with non-parametric dataset.

The write up of this analysis would look something like this . . . Adults rated babies' emotional expressions as less upset when the baby had a dummy (median = 3.0) than when they did not (median = 5.5), and this difference was significant ($W = 4, p < .025$).

The dataset created for this analysis was inspired by:

Rychlowska, M., Korb, S., Brauer, M., Droit-Volet, S., Augustinova, M., Zinner, L., & Niedenthal, P. (2014). Pacifiers disrupt adults' responses to infants' emotions. *Basic and Applied Social Psychology, 36*, 299–308.

Non-parametric tests of difference with large samples: z scores

One limitation of these two non-parametric tests is that they are not robust with larger sample sizes. For a Mann-Whitney *U* test, this means more than 20 participants in each condition, and for the Wilcoxon signed rank test, this means more than 30 participants in total.

NON-PARAMETRIC TESTS OF DIFFERENCE WITH LARGE SAMPLES

z score for Mann Whitney U test	z score for Wilcoxon signed rank test
$$z = \dfrac{U - \dfrac{N_1 * N_2}{2}}{\sqrt{\dfrac{N_1 * N_2 * (N_1 + N_2 + 1)}{12}}}$$	$$z = \dfrac{W - \dfrac{n(n+1)}{4}}{\sqrt{\dfrac{n*(n+1)*(2n+1)}{24}}}$$

Figure 15.7: Equations to calculate z for non-parametric tests of differences.

Occasionally you will see a z score presented alongside these statistics. We talked about z scores a great deal in Chapter 5, so it might be helpful to take a quick look back at this.

In Figure 15.7 you can see the equations for these, and they are both relatively straightforward to compute as we have already calculated all of the component parts in our earlier calculations. For the Mann-Whitney U z score, you simply need to know the calculated U statistic, and the number of participants in each condition (N_1 and N_2). For the Wilcoxon signed rank test, the n is the total sample size, after any tied ranks have been removed (so what was calculated in step 6). The '$2n$' in the equation just means $2*n$. If you present the z statistic, you would add this after the U or W statistic, but before the p value. You can see an example of this in the Wider Reading for this chapter.

Study questions

1. Imagine that you have conducted a Mann-Whitney U test and have a two-tailed hypothesis with an alpha of .050. For each of the following sets of N_1 and N_2, what is the critical value?
   1.1. $N_1 = 12$, $N_2 = 4$
   1.2. $N_1 = 9$, $N_2 = 5$
   1.3. $N_1 = 8$, $N_2 = 6$
2. If you were calculating a Wilcoxon signed rank statistic, assuming a two-tailed hypothesis, what is the smallest alpha at which the following analyses would be significant?
   2.1. $W = 17$, $N = 15$
   2.2. $W = 85$, $N = 24$
   2.3. $W = 12$, $N = 30$
3. A research group ran two studies looking at chocolate addiction and scores on an addictive personality questionnaire. In the first study they compare the addictive personality scores of self-confessed chocolate addicts ($n = 15$) and people who do not consider themselves to be chocolate addicts ($n = 18$). In the second study they look at a group of 20 chocolate addicts and want to compare their addictive personality scores before and after they participate in a six-week treatment programme to address their addiction. The addictive personality questionnaire they use is well known for providing data that are not normally distributed, so they decide to use non-parametric analyses. They have two-tailed predictions for both studies. The calculated statistics for each study are below. Interpret the findings and write them up as if they were a results section in a lab report

3.1. $U = 9$

3.2. $W = 16$

Additional dataset for Mann-Whitney U

Some published research has suggested that people behave differently in shops when there is a scent of chocolate in the air. In this study participants were asked to do their weekly shop in a supermarket. For some of the participants there was no scent introduced to the shop, whereas for others the scent of chocolate was given throughout the supermarket. Note that there were different numbers of participants in each condition: 10 in the no scent condition and 8 in the chocolate scent condition. The researchers recorded how much participants spent (rounded up to the nearest pound), however there appeared to be an extremely high outlying score in the chocolate condition (one participant bought all of the chocolate in the shop!) and therefore they decide to calculate a non-parametric Mann-Whitney U test. You can see the raw data in Table 15.4.

Table 15.4: Raw data for the chocolate shopping study.

No scent condition (Group 1)	Chocolate scent condition (Group 2)
45	67
36	45
27	152
56	59
29	74
36	56
32	39
41	63
38	
25	

1. What method of analysis will you use to analyse this dataset?
2. Suggest a suitable hypothesis for this analysis.
3. Calculate the appropriate statistic and determine whether it is significant.
4. Interpret and write up your findings using APA standards.
5. Suggest three possible confounding variable for this study, and how you might measure each of these.

This dataset was inspired by

Doucé, L., Poels, K., Janssens, W., & De Backer, C. (2013). Smelling the books: The effect of chocolate scent on purchase-related behavior in a bookstore. *Journal of Environmental Psychology*, 36, 65–69.

Additional dataset for Wilcoxon signed rank

This dataset looks at memory in patients with Multiple Sclerosis, measured before and after participating in a neurorehabilitation programme. The scores are the total number of correct responses on a memory test, with a maximum of 25. As there are some extremely low scores, or outliers, in the 'before' condition, it is best to use a non-parametric test. The raw data are given in Table 15.5.

Table 15.5: Raw data for the Multiple Sclerosis rehabilitation study.

Before (Condition X)	After (Condition Y)
18	24
12	12
4	13
15	14
20	22
2	9
15	18
13	22
10	16
21	24
19	17
17	18

1. What method of analysis will you use to analyse this dataset?
2. Suggest a suitable hypothesis for this analysis.
3. Calculate the appropriate statistic and determine whether it is significant.
4. Interpret and write up your findings using APA standards.
5. The researchers used the same version of the memory test at both time points. Do you think this could be a methodological weakness? If so, why and how could you improve their design?

This dataset was inspired by

Leavitt, V. M., Wylie, G. R., Girgis, P. A., DeLuca, J., & Chiaravalloti, N. D. (2014). Increased functional connectivity within memory networks following memory rehabilitation in multiple sclerosis. *Brain Imaging and Behavior*, 8, 394–402.

Example papers using these statistics

Kennedy-Behr, A., Rodger, S., & Mickan, S. (2013). Aggressive interactions during free-play at preschool of children with and without developmental coordination disorder. *Research in Developmental Disabilities*, 34, 2831–2837.

In this paper the authors use a Mann-Whitney U test to compare aggressive behaviour in children with a developmental coordination disorder and typically developing children. You will notice that they use the mean and standard deviation to interpret their findings, however many researchers would actually use the median when interpreting non-parametric statistics. They also report the z statistic that we discussed at the end of this chapter.

Wheatley, T., & Haidt, J. (2005). Hypnotic disgust makes moral judgments more severe. *Psychological Science*, *16*, 780–784.

The majority of the analyses in this paper were conducted using a repeated t test, but on page 782 you will see that they also use a Wilcoxon signed rank test. This is because of outliers in their sample, which tends to skew the distribution of a dataset.

How to run these analyses in SPSS...

If you would like to see how to run these analyses in SPSS, and to find other materials including full answers to study questions, please go to the online resources:
www.oup.com/uk/bourne/

16 Is there a relationship between two variables? Spearman's correlation

In this chapter you will learn ...

- The importance of looking for tied ranks when calculating a non-parametric correlation and how to deal with them effectively.
- How to calculate a Spearman's correlation.
- How to interpret and write up a Spearman's correlation

Introduction

Spearman's correlation is the **non-parametric** equivalent of the **Pearson's correlation** that we covered in Chapter 11. A Spearman's correlation looks for a **relationship** between two continuous variables; however one or both of these will have violated the parametric assumptions we discussed in Chapter 13. So one of the variables might not have been measured at the **interval** or **ratio level**, or may not be **normally distributed** (remember that homogeneity of variance doesn't apply to correlations).

The values that you calculate with a Spearman's correlation and the way that you interpret these values are exactly the same as for a Pearson's correlation. Values run from −1, indicating a perfect **negative correlation**, through to +1, indicating a perfect **positive correlation**. You can see a summary of this in Figure 16.1, or take a look back at Chapters 10 and 11 to revise correlations.

The problem of Spearman's correlation and tied ranks

One of the great things about the Spearman's correlation is that it is pretty simple to calculate, especially in comparison with some of the statistics that you have already encountered! However, it does have one quite major stumbling block, which is that is cannot be used when you have tied **rank scores**. We talked about these in Chapter 13, and used them in our calculations in Chapter 15 when we ran non-parametric tests of differences. If there are no tied ranks in your dataset, then it is fine to calculate a Spearman's correlation. But if you have tied ranks, then you should treat the ranked scores as your raw data and calculate a Pearson's correlation on these values. So instead of using the Pearson's correlation to analyse the original data

IS THERE A RELATIONSHIP BETWEEN TWO VARIABLES?

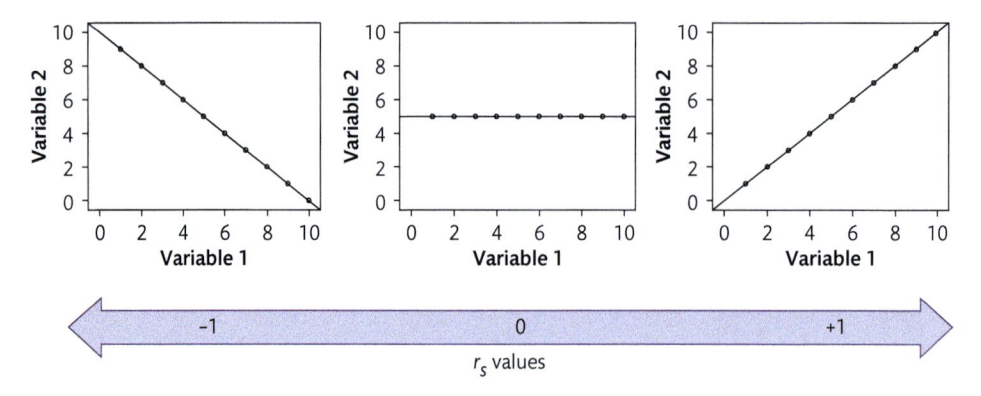

Figure 16.1: Correlations and the *r* values that reflect different strengths of relationships.

values that you collected, you should use the Pearson's correlation to analyse the ranked scores. You can see this summarised in Figure 16.2.

For this chapter, we will be looking at some fictional data that were inspired by research showing that there is a negative correlation between social media use and academic performance: so the more people use social media the worse their academic performance. In our example, we asked students aged 14 years old to report how many hours per week they spend on Facebook, and how they were placed within their class when the students were placed in order according to performance from best performing (1) to worst performing (15). Not all of the students agree to take part in the study, and some reported not having a Facebook account, and therefore not all places from the class performance ordering are included. As the

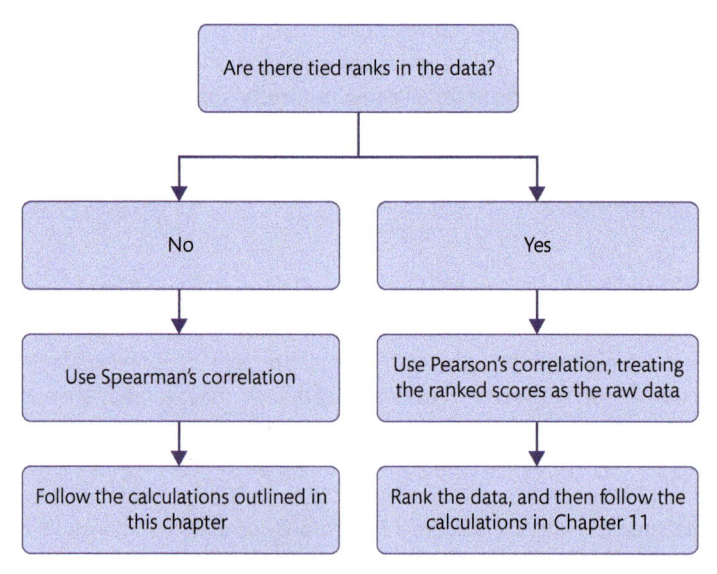

Figure 16.2: How to deal with tied ranks when you want to calculate a non-parametric correlation.

THE PROBLEM OF SPEARMAN'S CORRELATION AND TIED RANKS

second variable of placement within the class is ranked scores these data are not parametric and therefore a non-parametric correlational analysis will be needed.

We asked two separate labs to run this study. Given the strength of the previous research addressing this question, we have a one-tailed hypothesis, so a directional prediction: students who spend longer on Facebook will perform worse at school. Remember that poorer performing students will be placed lower in the class and consequently they will have larger rank numbers as the 15th placed student would have a rank score of 15. So poor performing, high ranked students, are predicted to spend longer on Facebook. Remember also that the 1st placed and best performing student would have a low rank score of 1, and we expect that they will spend less time on Facebook. Therefore, we expect to find a positive correlation: more hours on Facebook correlates with larger rank (poorer performing) score. You can see how this relationship might look in Figure 16.3. Each lab provides the data they collected for ten participants, which you can see in Table 16.1.

Looking at the data from Lab One, there are some tied ranks for the Facebook data (variable X). Two participants reported spending eight hours a week on Facebook, these participants share the ranks of 2 and 3, giving them a tied rank of 2.5. Two participants reported spending twelve hours a week on Facebook and these participants share the ranks of 5 and 6, resulting in tied rank scores of 5.5. Finally, another pair of participants spent 19 hours a week on Facebook. These participants should have had the ranks of 8 and 9, so their tied rank scores are 8.5.

As there are tied ranks in the data collected from Lab One, we cannot use the traditional Spearman's correlation equation. Instead, we need to use the Pearson's correlation that we covered in Chapter 11, and to complete these calculations using the ranked scores rather than the raw scores. If you were to do this, you would end up with an *r* value of –.899, indicating a negative correlation.

The data collected by Lab Two have no tied ranks, so it is okay to use the Spearman's correlation. You can see the equation in Equation 16.1. The *d* in the equation represents the difference between the two ranked scores for each participant. There are two more important things to

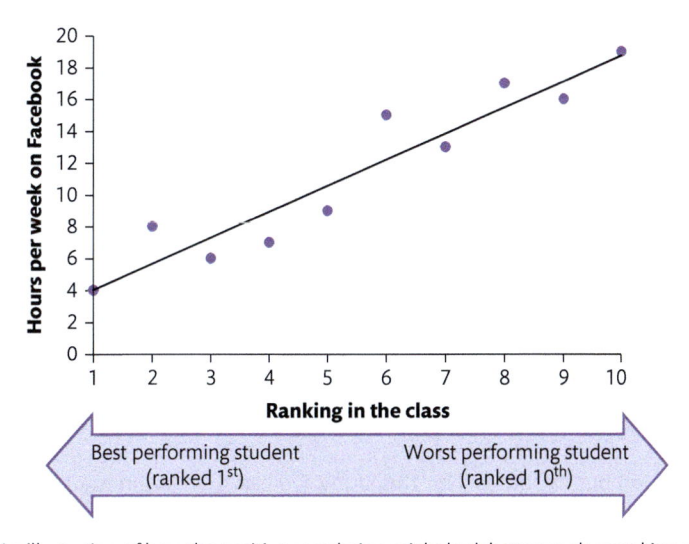

Figure 16.3: An illustration of how the positive correlation might look between class ranking and time spent on Facebook.

IS THERE A RELATIONSHIP BETWEEN TWO VARIABLES?

Table 16.1: Raw data and ranked scores from two separate labs collecting data for the Facebook and academic performance study.

Lab One data				Lab Two data			
Hours spent on Facebook (X)	X ranked	Ranking within the class (Y)	Y ranked	Hours spent on Facebook (X)	X ranked	Ranking within the class (Y)	Y ranked
10	4.0	22	7.0	7	1	3	1
5	1.0	31	10.0	12	3	10	5
19	8.5	18	6.0	32	10	23	9
12	5.5	16	5.0	16	4	8	4
8	2.5	24	8.0	25	8	20	8
15	7.0	12	3.0	19	5	28	10
12	5.5	15	4.0	28	9	16	7
22	10.0	9	1.0	9	2	7	3
8	2.5	25	9.0	22	7	15	6
19	8.5	10	2.0	21	6	5	2

note about the equation. First, the Spearman's statistic is known in full as Spearman's rho. Rho is a Greek letter, and this is sometimes used as the letter when you calculate Spearman's correlation, in that same way that you calculate a t for a t test or an r for a Pearson's correlation. The symbol for rho is ρ, and you will sometimes see this reported as the statistic. More commonly people just use r or r_s, with the subscript 's' signifying that the type of correlation calculated is Spearman's.

$$r_s = 1 - \frac{6 \sum d^2}{n^3 - n}$$

Equation 16.1: The equation for Spearman's correlation.

The other thing to note is that you will sometimes see the lower half of the equation written slightly differently, making the equation $r_s = 1 - \frac{6 \sum d^2}{n(n^2 - 1)}$. This will give you exactly the same result though, so it doesn't really matter too much which version of the equation you use. Let's now move on to calculate the Spearman's correlation for the data collected by the researchers in Lab Two.

Calculating and interpreting a Spearman's correlation: a worked example

Having established out hypothesis for this study, we can then begin to calculate the Spearman's correlation. Remember that this is a non-parametric test, and therefore we first need to rank the scores for each variable. With that done, we can begin to calculate the Spearman's correlation statistic.

CALCULATING AND INTERPRETING A SPEARMAN'S CORRELATION

If you imagine that we will find a strong positive correlation, we would find that low ranks on one variable are associated with low ranks on the other variable, and similarly that high ranks on one variable are associated with high ranks on the other variable. This means that the more similar the rank scores are, the more likely it is that the two variables are positively correlated. Remember the sentence that describes a positive relationship ... *As scores on variable X increase, scores on variable Y increase*. Consequently, one of the first stages of the calculations is to look at the difference scores between the ranks for each variable. If they are all very small, then we would be seeing a positive correlation between the two variables.

Hours spent on Facebook (X)	X ranked (Xr)	Ranking within the class (Y)	Y ranked (Yr)	d (Xr-Yr)	d^2
7	1	3	1	0	0
12	3	10	5	-2	4
32	10	23	9	1	1
16	4	8	4	0	0
25	8	20	8	0	0
19	5	28	10	-5	25
28	9	16	7	2	4
9	2	7	3	-1	1
22	7	15	6	1	1
21	6	5	2	4	16

Steps for calculating Spearman's correlation:

1. First, you need to rank the data for each variable separately. There are ten participants, so each variable should have rank scores from 1 (the lowest raw score) through to 10 (the highest raw score). You can see these values in columns two and four.

2. Next we need to calculate *d*, which is the difference score for each participant. This is calculated by subtracting the rank score for variable Y from the rank score for variable X (Xr-Yr). For the first participant, this is 1−1 = 0. For the last participant it is 6−2 = 4.

3. You then need to square the difference scores (d^2). For the first participant this is $0^2 = 0$, and for the last participant it is $4^2 = 16$.

4. Now add up the squared difference scores (Σd^2).

   - $\Sigma d^2 = 0 + 4 + 1 + 0 + 0 + 25 + 4 + 1 + 1 + 16$
   - $\Sigma d^2 = 52$

5. We can now insert these values into the equation. Remember that there were ten participants in our study, therefore *n* = 10.

   - $r_s = 1 - \dfrac{6 \Sigma d^2}{n^3 - n}$
   - $r_s = 1 - \dfrac{6 * 52}{10^3 - 10}$

6. Next, complete the multiplication on the top part of the equation and the n^3 on the lower part.

- $r_s = 1 - \dfrac{312}{1000 - 10}$

7. Then, calculate the subtraction on the lower part of the equation.

- $r_s = 1 - \dfrac{312}{990}$

8. Now complete the division sum.

- $r_s = 1 - 0.315$

9. Finally, calculate the subtraction to find out the Spearman's rho value.

- $r_s = .685$

Now that we have calculated the Spearman's correlation, it is worth stopping for a moment to think about what this value actually means. Remember that correlation values run from −1, meaning a perfect negative correlation, through 0, meaning no relationship at all, through to +1, meaning a perfect positive correlation. The r_s value is .685. First, this is a positive value, showing that the more time a student spends on Facebook, the greater their ranking within the class, meaning that they perform less well (the top student is ranked 1 remember). Second, the value is relatively large, however we do not yet know whether it is significant or not.

Is the Spearman's correlation significant?

To find out if our Spearman's correlation is significant we need the critical values table (see Appendix 3), and the following four pieces of information:
1. Is the hypothesis one-tailed or two-tailed? We came up with a one-tailed hypothesis.
2. What is our alpha level? We will stick with the psychology standard of $\alpha = .050$.
3. What are our degrees of freedom?

- df = n − 2
- df = 10 − 2
- df = 8

4. What is our calculated r_s value? We just worked this out as r_s value = .685

When you look at the critical values table in Figure 16.4, you want to look at the alpha values under the 'one-tailed' section. Doing so with the alpha = .050 column and the df = 8 row, you can see that the critical value is .564. The Spearman's rho is significant if your calculated value is equal to or more extreme than the critical value. Consequently we know that our result is significant with $p < .050$.

As ever, it is always good to report your calculation at the smallest alpha value for which the calculated value is more extreme than the critical value. The smaller the alpha, the more significant the finding and the less likely it is that you have committed a Type I Error. Looking at the alpha level of .025, the critical value is .648, which is less extreme than our calculated

CALCULATING AND INTERPRETING A SPEARMAN'S CORRELATION

df	Level of significance of a one-tailed or directional test					
	α = .100	α = .050	α = .025	α = .010	α = .005	α = .0005
	Level of significance of a two-tailed test					
	α = .200	α = .100	α = .050	α = .020	α = .010	α = .001
2	1.000	1.000	–	–	–	–
3	.800	.900	1.000	1.000	–	–
4	.657	.829	.886	.943	1.000	–
5	.571	.714	.786	.893	.929	1.000
6	.524	.643	.738	.833	.881	.976
7	.483	.600	.700	.783	.883	.933
8	.455	.564	.648	.745	.794	.903
9	.427	.536	.618	.709	.755	.873
10	.406	.503	.587	.678	.727	.846

Figure 16.4: Section of the Spearman's critical values table.

value, meaning that the correlation is significant at $p < .025$. For an alpha of .010, the critical value is .745, which is more extreme than our calculated value of .685. Therefore we cannot say it is significant at $p < .010$. The smallest alpha at which our calculated value is equal to or greater than our critical value is .025.

Interpreting and writing up a Spearman's correlation

When writing up a Spearman's correlation, there are two important pieces of information that you need to present: whether the relationship is significant or not and, if it is, the direction of the correlation (i.e. positive or negative). If the analysis is not significant then there is no relationship between the two variables, and therefore you cannot interpret the direction of that non-existing relationship. As usual, you would report the findings using APA conventions, which you can see in Figure 16.5.

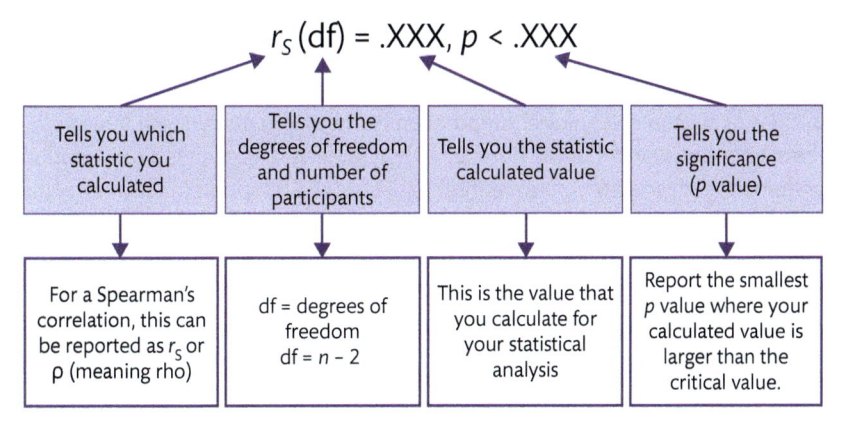

$$r_S(df) = .XXX, p < .XXX$$

- Tells you which statistic you calculated
  - For a Spearman's correlation, this can be reported as r_S or ρ (meaning rho)
- Tells you the degrees of freedom and number of participants
  - df = degrees of freedom
  - df = n − 2
- Tells you the statistic calculated value
  - This is the value that you calculate for your statistical analysis
- Tells you the significance (p value)
  - Report the smallest p value where your calculated value is larger than the critical value.

Figure 16.5: APA convention for reporting a Spearman's correlation.

If we were writing up our analysis for this chapter, we might say something like ... There was a significant positive correlation ($r_s(8) = .685$, $p < .025$). This shows that the more time a student spends on Facebook, the worse they are ranked in their class (large rank), indicating poorer academic performance.

The dataset created for this chapter was inspired by:

Junco, R. (2012). Too much face and not enough books: The relationship between multiple indices of Facebook use and academic performance. *Computers in Human Behavior*, 28, 187–198.

Study questions

1. Find the critical values for the following study designs when using a Spearman's correlation.

    1.1. One-tailed hypothesis, $n = 25$, $\alpha = .010$
    1.2. Two-tailed hypothesis, $n = 15$, $\alpha = .050$
    1.3. Two-tailed hypothesis, $n = 30$, $\alpha = .020$

2. For each of the following results, find the smallest alpha at which the result is significant when using a Spearman's correlation.

    2.1. $r_s = .572$, $n = 18$, two-tailed hypothesis
    2.2. $r_s = -.303$, $n = 21$, one-tailed hypothesis
    2.3. $r_s = .757$, $n = 12$, two-tailed hypothesis

3. Below are three results of Spearman's correlations, all of which come from studies with two-tailed hypotheses. Interpret each of the findings as if you were writing up the result for a results section of a lab report.

    3.1. $r_s(15) = .523$, $p < .050$
    3.2. $r_s(22) = -.644$, $p < .001$
    3.3. $r_s(28) = -.359$, $p > .050$

Additional dataset

Previous studies have shown that individuals with higher levels of social support are less likely to develop illnesses such as colds. Social support can be measured using questionnaires, however researchers have also found that the number of hugs a person receives is also a good measure of social support. In this dataset there are three variables: social support (measured by questionnaire, high scores indicate high levels of social support), number of hugs received over the past week, and the participants' rating of how likely they are to develop a cold after being close to someone sneezing and clearly ill with a cold. This rating is measured on a 10 point Likert scale, and therefore should be treated as non-parametric data. You can see the data in Table 16.2.

Calculate two separate non-parametric correlations. The first should look at the relationship between the social support measure and the self-rated likeliness to develop a cold. The other should look at the relationship between hugs and cold likelihood.

Table 16.2: Raw data for the hugs and colds study.

Participant number	Social support	Hugs per week	Cold likelihood
1	20	32	2
2	6	6	9
3	13	43	4
4	6	12	5
5	8	10	7
6	20	29	3
7	12	36	1

1. What method of analysis will you use to analyse each of the relationships?
2. Suggest a suitable hypothesis for each of these analyses.
3. Calculate the test statistics for each of the analyses and determine whether they are significant.
4. Interpret and write up your findings using APA standards.
5. Design a follow up study using an experimental design.

This dataset was inspired by

Cohen, S., Janicki-Deverts, D., Turner, R. B., & Doyle, W. J. (2015). Does hugging provide stress-buffering social support? A study of susceptibility to upper respiratory infection and illness. *Psychological Science, 26*, 135–147.

Example paper using this statistic

Hou, F., Xu, S., Zhao, Y., Lu, Q., Zhang, S., Zu, P., ... & Tao, F. (2013). Effects of emotional symptoms and life stress on eating behaviors among adolescents. *Appetite, 68*, 63–68.

If you look at Table 2 in this paper they summarise the Spearman's correlations between the variables they are interested in. If you look closely though, you will notice that some of the correlations are really very small, but apparently significant. This is a great example of how having a huge sample makes it very easy to get statistically significant findings, even when the magnitude of the findings are actually quite small. They had a sample of 5473 participants!

How to run this analysis in SPSS ...

If you would like to see how to run this analysis in SPSS, and to find other materials including full answers to study questions, please go to the online resources:
www.oup.com/uk/bourne/

Part 5

Beyond the basics

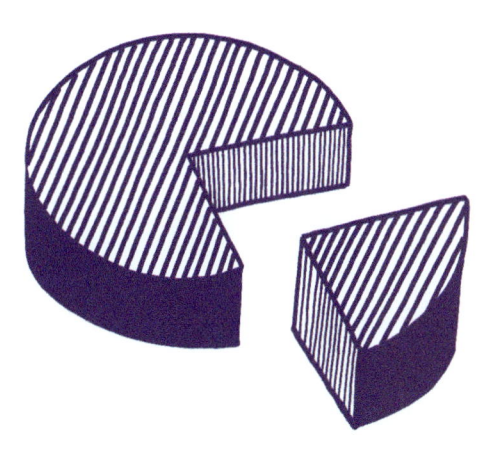

17 Which statistical test should I use?

> **In this chapter you will learn ...**
> - How to decide which type of design a psychological study has used
> - If you have a categorical design, how to decide whether to run a chi squared goodness of fit, or a chi squared test of association
> - If you have an experimental design, how to define your independent and dependent variables, and how to decide whether your design is independent or repeated
> - If you have a correlational design, to ensure that both variables are continuous, and if you wish to build a predictive model using linear regression, to decide which variable is the predictor and which is the outcome

Introduction

One of the most important things about becoming an independent researcher is being able to make the right decisions about your research project, right through from picking your initial design through to deciding how to analyse your data. To some extent, calculating a **test statistic** is not the most challenging part of analysing the dataset.

If I tell you that you need to run an independent *t* test on a dataset and I tell you which variable is the independent variable and which is the dependent variable, you simply need to find the right chapter in this book and diligently follow the step-by-step guide. Easy!

What is far more challenging is to look at a research design and to work out for yourself how the data should be analysed. It is perfectly possible to calculate entirely the wrong statistic on a dataset, and any findings would therefore be totally useless. Choosing the right statistical test can be a little daunting, but as long as you have a good understanding of your research design it really is just a case of asking yourself a series of questions about your study. The answers to these questions will magically lead you to the right statistical test.

What type of research design did you use?

The first big factor to consider is which research design you used. If you have designed the study yourself, hopefully you will already know this! In fact, if you have designed the study yourself you should know which method of analysis is suitable at the design stage. Whether

WHICH STATISTICAL TEST SHOULD I USE?

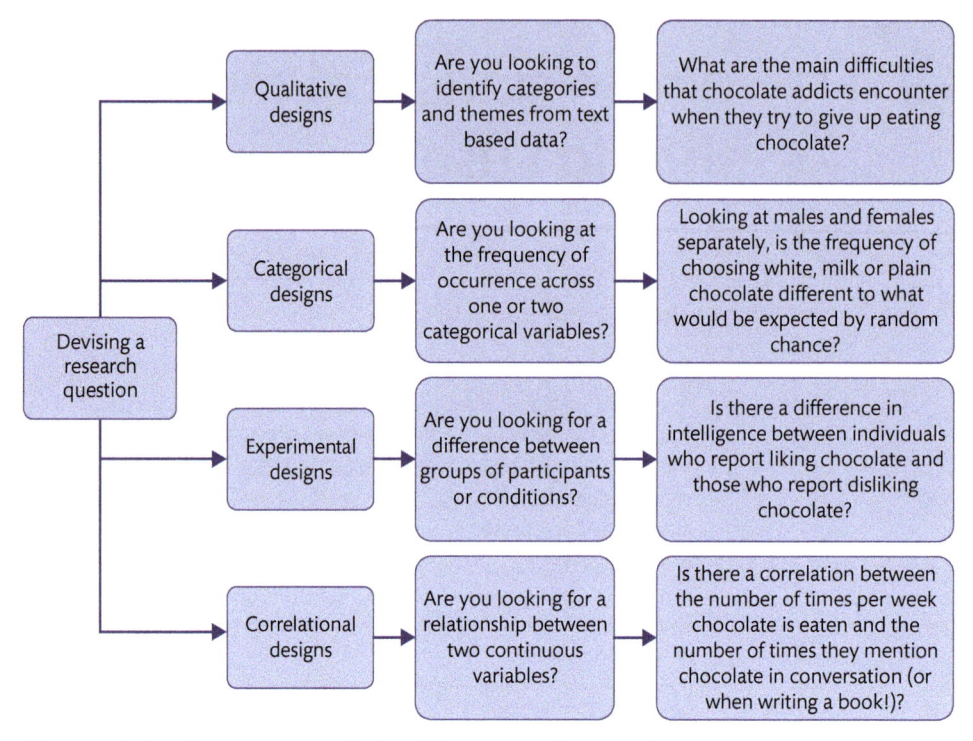

Figure 17.1: Flow chart summarizing the four different types of research design that can be used.

you take a **quantitative approach**, a **qualitative approach**, or even a **mixed methods approach**, always make sure that you think about design and analysis together at the very beginning of the research process.

You won't always be analysing a dataset from a piece of quantitative research that you have designed though, and in this situation you will need to establish which of the three basic quantitative research designs was used: **categorical (or frequency)**, **experimental** or **correlational**? Each of these designs is explained in great detail in Chapter 3, but the key questions to ask are summarised in Figure 17.1.

Once you are clear which design has been used, you can then think in more detail about the specifics of the design, and that will lead you to the appropriate statistical test for the dataset. A flow chart covering all of the statistical tests covered in this book is shown in Figure 17.2, but each branch is explained in more detail below.

Questions to ask yourself if you used a categorical design

If you used a categorical design you will be looking at **frequency data**, so how many participants fall within particular categories. This means that you will be using a **chi squared analysis** of some form. These are summarised on the left of Figure 17.2.

QUESTIONS TO ASK YOURSELF IF YOU USED A CATEGORICAL DESIGN

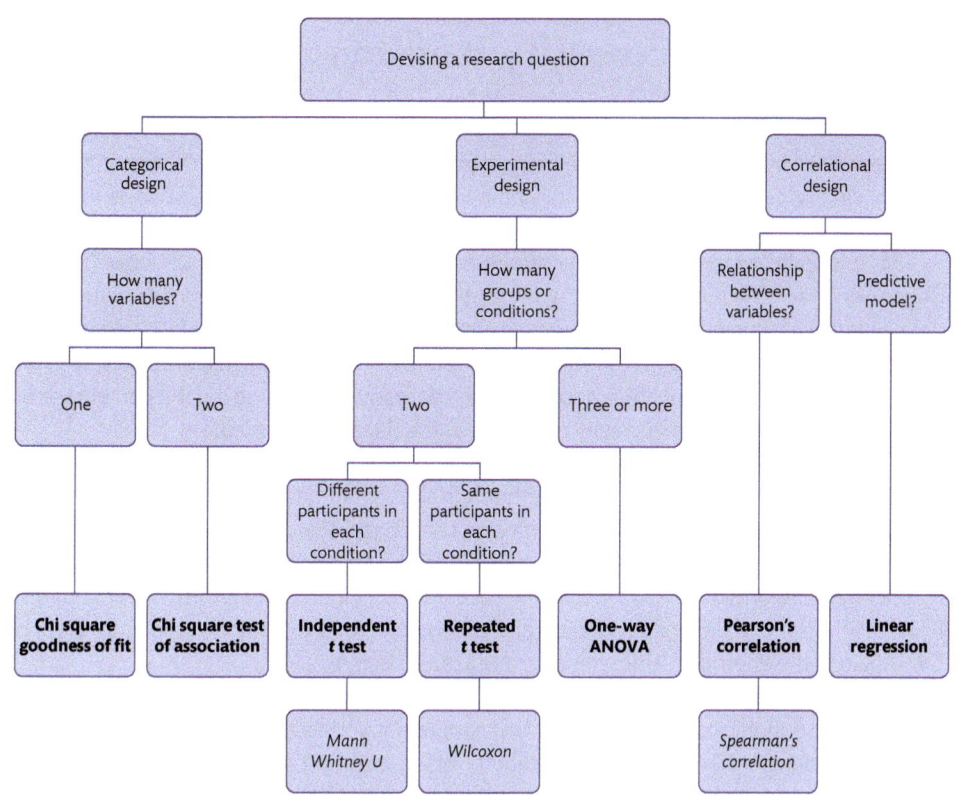

Figure 17.2: Flow chart showing the decision-making processes to follow when choosing any of the statistical tests covered in this book. Non-parametric equivalents are shown below the parametric test and presented in italics.

There is really only one question to ask yourself to determine what type of chi square analysis you need to use; how many categorical variables do you have? If you just looked at one variable you would use a **chi squared goodness of fit**, whereas if you have two or more categorical variables you would use a **chi squared test of association**.

For example, you may be interested in whether people are able to see a particular visual illusion. This will give you one categorical variable with two categories: illusion seen or not seen. In this case you would use a chi squared goodness of fit.

If you were to look at whether participants could see an illusion or not, across three different versions of the illusion you would instead use a chi squared test of association. This is because you have two categorical variables, type of illusion and whether the illusion is seen or not. It is really important to specify the number of categories in each variable when describing your chi square test of association. The illusion type variable has three categories and the illusion seen variable has two categories, and therefore you will calculate a 3x2 chi squared test of association.

When writing this up in a methods section, I would write something like ... A 3 (version of illusion) x 2 (whether the illusion is seen or not) chi squared test of association was used to analyse the collected data.

Questions to ask yourself if you used an experimental design

The decisions that you need to make are slightly more complex with an **experimental design**, simply because the designs can be a little more complex. The questions that you need to ask are outlined in Box 17.1.

First, it is really important to clearly establish what your **independent variable** (IV) and **dependent variable** (DV) are. Your DV must be a **continuous variable**, so one with a continuous range of scores, from low scores through to high scores. For example, if I were interested in the ability to recognise emotional expressions I might give participants a test where I can measure the accuracy of their recognition across many trials, giving me the percentage of emotional expressions they correctly recognise as the dependent variable.

For the IV, you need to decide whether it is an independent design, so different groups of participants in each condition, or whether it is a repeated design, with just one group of participants repeating the study under different conditions. This answers your second question! If I were interested in age differences in emotion recognition, then this would be an independent design as I would be comparing accuracy across different groups of participants. If I were interested in time of day effects, and tested one group of people in the morning and then again in the afternoon, this would be a repeated design.

Finally you need to determine how many conditions you have within your design. If you just have two conditions you will use a *t* **test**, whereas if you have three or more conditions you will need an **ANOVA**. For the age differences in emotion recognition example, there could be two groups that would be analysed using a *t* test: 20 years old or younger and 61 years or older. If we had more than two groups, we would need to use an ANOVA, for example we might have four age groups: 20 years old or younger, 21–40 years old, 41–60 years old and 61 years or older.

Once you have answered all of these questions, it is simply a case of following through the flow chart in Figure 17.2. The only other thing to consider is whether your study and/or dataset met the parametric assumptions. If there are any issues, such as non-normal distribution, then it may be necessary to use the non-parametric equivalent of the test, and these are also included in Figure 17.2 and shown in italics.

Box 17.1. Questions to consider when selecting a statistical test for an experimental design.

What is the dependent variable?
- Is it a continuous variable?

What is the independent variable?
- Is the design repeated or independent?
- How many groups/conditions are there?

When writing about the analysis you have run, for example in your methods section, ensure that you explicitly specify your IV and DV, whether your design is an independent or repeated design, the number of conditions that you have and what they are.

For example, if I were to analyse a study on age differences in the ability to recognise emotional expressions, I would write something like ... This study used a quasi-experimental design where the DV was the percentage of emotional expressions correctly identified. The IV was the age of the participant, with two conditions (younger or older) and an independent design. Consequently, an independent *t* test was conducted.

Questions to ask yourself if you used a correlational design

In this book we have only covered two quite simple **correlational designs**, and therefore the decisions to be made are relatively simple. You can see the options available to you in Figure 17.2. What is more complex is ensuring that the variables you have measured are actually suitable for these methods of analysis! It is always helpful to remember the correlation mantra when thinking whether you need to run a **correlation analysis**. Does it make sense to say ... *As the scores on variable X increase, the scores on variable Y will increase/decrease?*

The types of analysis that we have covered simply look at the relationship between two continuous variables. As I've mentioned before, this is something that some researchers get wrong, and I've seen this even in published research. Both of the variables must be continuous scores, which is scores that exist on a continuum with a large range of scores from low through to high scores. For a more detailed rant on this topic, please flip back to Chapter 10!

If you simply wish to see whether there is a relationship between two continuous variables you need to calculate a **Pearson's correlation**. You should check whether the parametric assumptions have been met though, and if any are violated you can run a **Spearman's correlation** instead. For example, if you have used ordinal data (ranked data), then these data would need to be analysed using a non-parametric method, and a Spearman's correlation would be the appropriate method of analysis.

For example, imagine you run a study looking at whether confidence changes with age. Here we have two continuous variables: a person's age and their confidence, which could be measured using a questionnaire. We could easily look at a correlation between these two variables, and our 'correlation sentence' might read ... As age increase, confidence increases. If we were to write this up in a methods section, we could describe the analysis in the following way ... A Pearson's correlation was calculated to examine the relationship between the two continuous variables of age and confidence.

You may want to move slightly beyond a simple correlation and look at whether you can use scores on one continuous variable to predict scores on another continuous variable. In this case you want to analyse your dataset with a simple **linear regression**. Just be sure to think very carefully about which variable will be your predictor and which will be your outcome. For our correlation example, it might make most sense to use a person's age to predict their confidence. In the methods section of a paper, we could therefore write ... The data were analysed using simple linear regression whereby the participant's age was the predictor variable and their score on a confidence questionnaire was the outcome variable.

Which test next?

The aim of this book is to give you a really good grounding in the core methods of analysis used in psychological research. However, this means that the methods covered represent a relatively small selection of the statistical tests that are available to you, and these are really very simple. As you progress through your studies the designs will become more complex, and the statistics become more complex too.

Hopefully by this stage in the book you feel quite confident in designing basic psychological studies, selecting the appropriate statistical test, and calculating and interpreting the statistic. With this solid foundation you should be well prepared to move on to more complex designs and analyses. For example, what happens if you want to analyse a dataset using an ANOVA, but you would like to control for a potential confounding variable? Or what happens if you want to manipulate more than one IV? How could you analyse a dataset using a regression, but with multiple predictor variables? All of these questions will be answered in Chapter 18, to give you a sneaky preview of the more advanced analyses that will become available to you.

Study questions

A number of study designs are briefly described below. For each one, decide which test you would use to analyse the data collected. Suggest a hypothesis (be specific as to whether it is one- or two-tailed), fully explain how you will analyse the dataset (as if you were writing up the piece of research), and predict the findings of the study.

1. There is some concern as to the psychological consequences of children's exposure to violent TV programmes, films, and computer games. A researcher asks a group of 50 adolescents, ages 12–15 years old, to keep a record of how many hours exposure they have to violent media and they complete a sleep quality questionnaire.
2. A researcher has read that individuals with dyslexia have superior visuo-spatial skills. They recruit 20 participants who have dyslexia and 20 control participants and ask them all to complete a test of visuo-spatial processing that provides a score of percentage accuracy.
3. It has been suggested that a person is more likely to cheat if it is their last opportunity to do so. 300 participants are asked to read a scenario in which they imagine they are playing poker. There are three different versions of the passage, one describes a game played at the beginning of the poker tournament, one describes a game played mid-tournament and one describes the final game of the tournament. In all three versions the participant is losing. They are asked: if the opportunity were there, would you cheat at the game or not?
4. There is some evidence that people's happiness changes according to the number of children they have. 300 adults are asked to complete a happiness questionnaire and also to report whether they have no children, one child, two children or 3+ children.
5. A researcher is interested to discover if one's personality changes after drinking alcohol. They ask 100 participants to complete an agreeableness questionnaire before a night out and then again at the end of the night, after having consumed alcohol.
6. Having collected the data, the researcher from the previous example discovers that the data are not normally distributed. How would this change the method of analysis that you had previously selected in question 5?

Wider reading

Nieuwenhuis, S., Forstmann, B. U., & Wagenmakers, E. J. (2011). Erroneous analyses of interactions in neuroscience: a problem of significance. *Nature Neuroscience*, 14, 1105–1107.

Selecting the correct statistical test is actually quite a tricky thing to do, and the wrong tests are sometimes chosen, even in some published research. The types of analyses discussed in this paper are beyond the scope of what was covered in this chapter, but amazingly they showed that roughly half of the papers they reviewed had selected the wrong statistical test!

For full answers to study questions, and to explore a range of other materials, visit the online resources at: **www.oup.com/uk/bourne/**

18 Moving beyond the basics of research and analysis: how do I understand more complicated research designs?

> **In this chapter you will learn ...**
> - How to read about more advanced statistical techniques for both experimental and correlational research designs
> - How to understand the logic behind some of the more complex analyses that you might read about in published research, and how they relate to the statistics you have learned in this book
> - About the criticisms of p values, and the alternative approach of effect sizes

The methods and statistics included in this book are quite introductory, but as you move on through your studies you will be learning about more advanced statistics. Before you get to that stage, you may already be reading about these more advanced methods in published research papers. This final chapter of the book will help you to transition from learning the basic foundations of research methods and analysis to understanding more complex approaches. With a strong grounding in the basics of statistics and some insight into the more advanced techniques that can be used, hopefully you can move forward with your psychological studies with confidence.

Getting to grips with published research: the basics

As a student, it is often tempting to read published research and trust the findings as established facts. However, hopefully now that you are nearing the end of this book you will feel more comfortable with the idea that no research is perfect. It is vital that you acknowledge the limitations of your own research, and that you always read published research with a critical mind. This can be more challenging when the research that you are reading uses complex methodological designs and statistical analyses. The aim of this book has been to give you a solid foundation, and in the rest of this chapter we will be building on this foundation to help you read more complex published research papers.

Getting to grips with published research: advanced experimental designs

In Chapter 9 we discussed a very simple **Analysis of Variance (ANOVA),** where we compared scores across three independent groups of participants. However, most published research that uses experimental techniques has somewhat more complicated designs. This doesn't necessarily mean that a more complicated design is better. You should always pick the simplest design that allows you to examine your research question, but a more complex question will require a more complex design. Although they may be more complicated, all of the different techniques that are used to analyse complex experimental designs are really just bigger versions of the simple ANOVA that you have already learned. They all work on the same logic of dividing the variability into explained and random variance, and then looking at the size of the variance slices. In Figure 18.1 you can see a summary of the main advanced techniques that you might read about in published research.

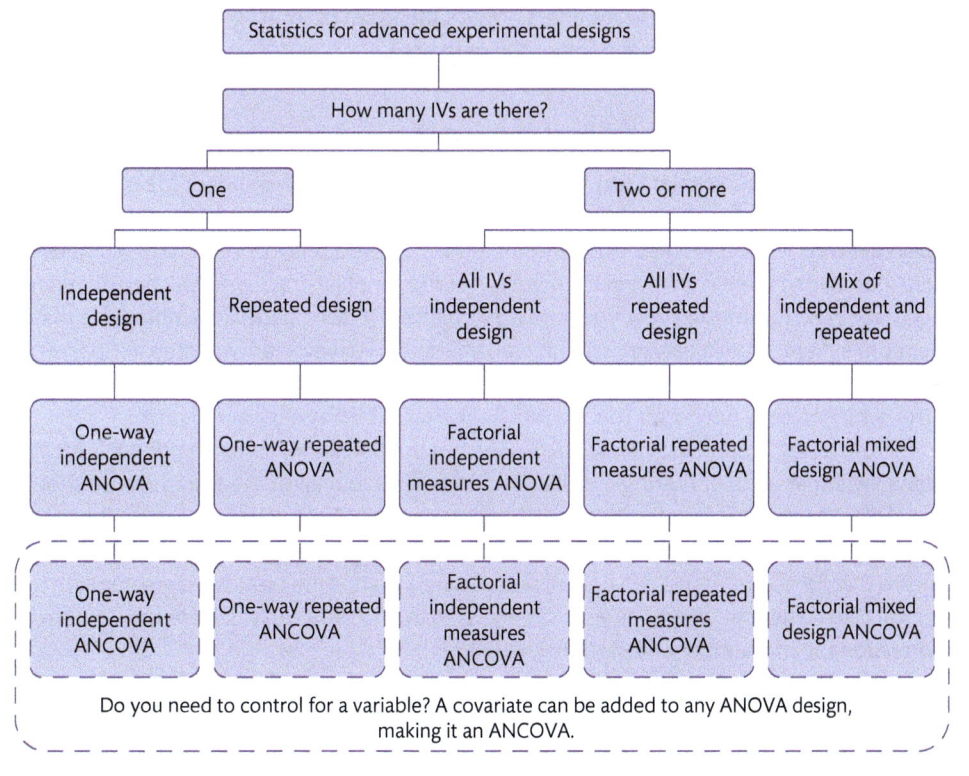

Figure 18.1: Statistical techniques used with advanced experimental designs with three or more conditions, or with two or more independent variables.

Breaking down a significant effect in an ANOVA

In Chapter 9 we learned all about the one-way independent measures ANOVA, and with the example dataset we found that the number of hazards detected differed significantly according to the type of conversation that the participant was having ($F (2, 15) = 9.8, p < .010$). We then looked at the descriptive statistics to see which group of participants detected the most hazards. This showed that the most hazards were detected by participants not engaged in a conversation (M = 10.8, SD = 2.5), detection rate dropped a little for those engaged in a neutral conversation (M = 8.5, SD = 1.9) and dropped more markedly for those engaged in an emotive conversation (M = 5.5, SD = 1.9).

Whilst this analysis allows us to draw some interesting conclusions about the influence of mobile phone conversations on hazard detection, you may have found the final conclusions a little frustrating. Great, we know that overall there is a significant difference, but do the separate conditions differ significantly from each other? Is the number of hazards detected when not engaged in a phone conversation significantly greater than the number detected within an emotive conversation? Most likely, but how about the difference between a neutral and an emotive conversation? It would be great to be able to know if each of the pairs of conditions differed significantly from each other. This is known as breaking down a significant effect in an ANOVA, and you will usually see an author explaining how they break down any significant effects when they describe their method of statistical analysis. Note, though, that you would only ever break down a significant effect. What's the point of looking for significant differences within an effect that is not significantly different?

Avoiding a familywise error: the Bonferroni correction

A simple way to do this might just be to run a whole load of independent measures *t* tests to compare each pair: none vs. neutral, none vs. emotive, neutral vs. emotive. Independent *t* tests are relatively easy to run, but, remember back to the alpha level and what a *p* value of .050 means: that there is a 5% chance of a Type I Error, or of having found an effect that does not really exist. Put another way, you have a 5% chance of having data with a difference that is no more extreme than a dataset with no real difference. However, as we noted in Chapter 9, if a researcher runs three *t* tests, they substantially increase the chance of committing a Type I Error, which is really not good. This inflation is known as **familywise error rate**.

There is a way around familywise error, which is the *Bonferroni correction* that adjusts the alpha level that is used. The logic is that the total risk across all of the tests you run should equal 5%. Therefore, if a researcher runs three *t* tests they would calculate a new alpha level by taking .050 and dividing it by 3: .050/3 = .017. This gives a new alpha level of .017, which means that for each *t* test we can only accept it as significant if the *t* statistic is greater than the critical value when the *p* value is equal to or less than .017. You can calculate the Bonferroni correction for any number of tests (N): $\alpha = .050/N$.

Planned and post hoc contrasts

Whilst the Bonferroni correction gets around the issue of familywise error, there are far more elegant solutions. You will see Bonferroni corrected tests in some publications, but it is these other solutions that you are likely to see more often in contemporary published research: **planned contrasts** and **post hoc contrasts.** Typically, when a researcher finds a significant effect in an ANOVA they will use one of these types of contrast to understand where the difference came from, to understand which conditions differ, and which do not. Whether a researcher uses planned or post hoc contrasts to break down depends entirely on their hypothesis, but the key issue is whether you plan specific comparisons to make in advance of running the analyses (planned contrasts), or whether you simply make all possible pairwise comparisons (post hoc contrasts). Remember back to the very beginning of the book where we talked about two types of hypotheses: **one-tailed hypotheses** were we specify the predicted direction of any differences, and **two-tailed hypotheses** where we predict that there will be a difference, but we make no prediction about the possible direction of any significant effects. If a researcher has a one-tailed hypothesis they would typically use a planned contrast to break down a significant ANOVA effect as they have specific contrasts in mind to test their very specific hypothesis. In contrast, if they have a two-tailed hypothesis then they do not have specific predictions to test, but instead are looking in a more open way for any differences that exist within the dataset, and therefore they would use a post hoc contrast to breakdown a significant ANOVA effect (see Figure 18.2). When these analyses are run using a statistics programme, such as SPSS, the alpha is automatically corrected, so there is no issue with familywise error, and Bonferroni corrections are not needed.

Comparing three or more conditions in a repeated design: one-way repeated measures ANOVA

Some of you may have noticed that we learned about two different types of *t* tests, one for an independent measures design and one for a repeated measures design. However, when

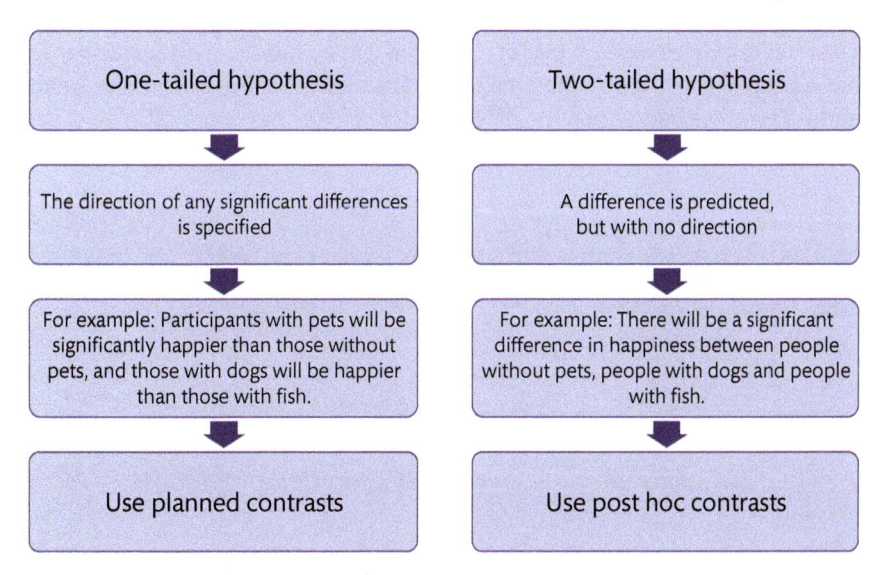

Figure 18.2: How to decide whether to use planned or post hoc contrasts.

we moved onto one-way ANOVAs, we only considered a one-way independent measures ANOVA. This does not mean that a one-way repeated ANOVA does not exist.

Repeated ANOVAs have exactly the same logic as independent ANOVAs: you are looking at the ratio of explained variability to random variance. The exact calculations are different though, as there are the same participants within each condition. A consequence of this is that the random variance is reduced. With different participants in each condition in an independent design there is always the risk that the groups vary due to individual differences between groups. What if, by random chance, one of the groups just happens to be more intelligent, faster, older, or whatever? This means that the assumptions around **homogeneity of variance** are slightly different (you can take a look back at Chapter 13 to revise what this means).

Sphericity and understanding where variability comes from in a repeated measures design

Sphericity is the equivalent assumption to homogeneity of variance for repeated designs. So if you see sphericity mentioned in a paper, they are talking about the assumption behind a repeated ANOVA that is equivalent to homogeneity of variance. Understanding sphericity is actually quite helpful when trying to understand where the variability comes from in a repeated measures design. Because the random variance is reduced as a result of the same participants being in all conditions, sphericity looks at the variability in a slightly different way. Rather than looking at the amount of variability in the scores within each condition, it instead looks at the difference scores.

Imagine a study with three repeated conditions, where participants are asked to report their happiness after eating one, two or three bars of chocolate. If you take a look at Tables 18.1 and 18.2, you can see the data collected by two separate imaginary labs. On the left of each table you can see the happiness ratings after eating different quantities of chocolate, with higher scores indicating greater levels of happiness. On the right of each table you can see the difference scores calculated for each pair of conditions. For example, the first participant in Lab One had a happiness rating of 2 after one bar of chocolate, and this increased to 4 after two bars and 7 after three bars. When the difference (or change) scores are calculated, you can see that their happiness increased by 2 going from one to two bars of chocolate (4 − 2 = 2),

Table 18.1: Data from Lab one: Evidence of *sphericity* as the changes across conditions are *consistent*

Happiness scores in each condition			Difference in happiness scores between conditions		
1 bar	2 bars	3 bars	2−1	3−2	3−1
2	4	7	2	3	5
3	5	7	2	2	4
5	8	9	3	1	4
4	6	8	2	2	4
2	3	5	1	2	3
		Variance in difference scores	0.5	0.5	0.5

Table 18.2: Data from Lab two: *No evidence of sphericity* as the changes across conditions *vary*

Happiness scores in each condition			Difference in happiness scores between conditions		
1 bar	2 bars	3 bars	2–1	3–2	3–1
2	2	8	0	6	6
9	5	1	–4	–4	–8
6	6	6	0	0	0
1	2	3	1	1	2
9	7	3	–2	–4	–6
Variance in difference scores			4	17.2	33.2

increased by 3 going from two to three bars of chocolate (7 – 4 = 3) and increased by 5 when going from one to three bars of chocolate (7 – 2 = 5).

If you just take a look at the difference scores in the data collected in Lab one, you can see that a similar pattern emerges across all of the participants. The more chocolate people have, the happier they are. In the bottom row of the table, you can see the variance calculated for the difference scores (you can take a look back at Chapter 5 if you need a reminder of how variance is calculated). Across all three of the difference scores the variance is very similar and small. This means that the IV manipulation of the amount of chocolate given to participants had a consistent effect on all of the participants within this study. This is exactly what you would be hoping for as a researcher as it shows sphericity in your dataset.

The data collected by Lab two look quite different, and the effect that chocolate is having on the participants' happiness is far more random. The first participant in Lab two is pretty miserable after one or two bars of chocolate, but after three bars they suddenly become happy (that participant may be me!). In contrast, the second participant is really happy after one bar of chocolate, and then becomes less and less happy as they eat more and more chocolate. The third participant's happiness does not change at all with the different amounts of chocolate eaten. If you look at the difference scores in the right of the table, you can clearly see how variable the change in happiness is across the different participants, and the variance statistics in the final row support this. The manipulation of giving participants increasing amounts of chocolate is having quite a random and variable effect on the participants. Consequently, even if there were mean differences across the three conditions, you may not trust them as much as the change in scores is not consistent. In this case the assumption of sphericity has been violated. There are some corrections that can be applied to the degrees of freedom to take into account any sphericity in the dataset, and if you are using SPSS, these will be automatically calculated and given to you. These corrections allow you to still use the repeated ANOVA, even when the assumption of sphericity has been violated.

The key thing here is that, when you have a repeated design, it is not just about wanting the scores in each condition to differ. You want them to differ in a consistent way across participants. Differences that arise in a random way are not very informative for a researcher, whereas differences that are consistent across all participants are easier to interpret and may be more robust.

You may have noticed that I've only mentioned sphericity for a repeated ANOVA, but not for the repeated *t* test. This is because sphericity cannot be calculated for a *t* test, where there only two conditions. With two conditions, you can only calculate one set of difference scores, and therefore there is nothing to compare these scores to. Consequently, you will only ever see sphericity when looking at an ANOVA with a repeated measures IV.

Going back to the actual analysis and reporting of a repeated ANOVA, if a researcher does find a significant result, they still need to break down this effect in the same way as they would for an independent design. So they would run Bonferroni corrected repeated *t* tests, planned contrasts or post hoc contrasts to see which conditions differ significantly.

Analysing multiple independent variables: factorial ANOVAs

Quite often an experimental design will require the manipulation of more than one **independent variable** (IV). You will find that much of the published experimental research uses this type of more complex design. It is technically possible to manipulate as many IVs as you wish, although studies very rarely manipulate more than three or four. An experimental design where two or more IVs are manipulated is called a factorial design, and therefore the data would be analysed using a **factorial ANOVA**.

Factorial ANOVAs: independent, repeated, and mixed designs

If you take a look at Figure 18.1 you will see that there are three types of factorial ANOVA: independent, repeated and mixed design. To decide which method of analysis is appropriate a researcher needs to look at each IV separately and decide whether it has an independent or a repeated measures design. If all of the IVs have an independent design, then they would analyse the data using a factorial independent measures ANOVA. If all of the IVs have a repeated design, then they would analyse the data using a factorial repeated measures ANOVA. If the IVs have a mix of independent and repeated designs, then they would analyse the data using a factorial mixed design ANOVA.

A few examples might be helpful here. Imagine that a researcher runs a series of studies looking at memory for unfamiliar faces. The following three studies would each use a different factorial design:

- Factorial independent design: IV1 is age, comparing two independent groups of adults age 50-69 years and those age 70 years or older. IV2 is diagnosis group, comparing two independent groups where one has been diagnosed with dementia and the other has not (they are a control group).
- Factorial repeated design: IV1 is the emotional expression on the face to be learned, with participants seeing faces with three different types of expressions: no emotional expression, a positive expression and a negative expression. IV2 is the length of time they see each face for during the learning phase of the experiment: 10 seconds, 20 seconds, 30 seconds or 40 seconds.
- Factorial mixed design: IV1 is training group, comparing two independent training strategies to improve face learning in police officers. IV2 is time, with the test repeated three times, before training, immediately after training and six months later.

When a researcher describes a factorial ANOVA they need to tell the reader about the type of design used, but also about the number of conditions in each of the IVs. The three designs outlined above would be described in the following way:

- A 2 (age: 50-69 years vs. 70 years plus) * 2 (diagnosis: dementia vs. control) independent measures ANOVA.
- A 3 (emotional expression: neutral, positive, negative) * 4 (time: 10, 20, 30, or 40 seconds) repeated measures ANOVA.
- A 2 (type of training, independent design) * 3 (time: before, immediately after, six months later, repeated design) mixed design ANOVA.

By describing factorial ANOVAs in this way researchers can give the reader lots of information about the analysis in a very succinct way. They know how many IVs there were, the design for each IV, the number of conditions for each IV and what those conditions are.

Manipulating more than two independent variables

Each of the above examples has two IVs, but more IVs could have been manipulated within any of the designs. The two-way (two IVs manipulated) repeated design, could easily be turned into a three-way design by manipulating another IV. Imagine that the researchers had also wanted to look at age differences within this study, which would give them another IV of independent design with two groups. The analysis would therefore be described as a 3 (emotional expression: neutral, positive, negative) * 4 (time: 10, 20, 30, or 40 seconds) * 2 (age: less than 20 years old vs. greater than 50 years old) mixed design ANOVA.

Factorial ANOVAs: main effects

In a factorial ANOVA you do not get just one *F* ratio and one significance result, it gets a bit more complicated than that. You will see a mixture of main effects and interactions. A **main effect** tells us whether there are differences across one IV which can be uniquely explained by that IV whilst totally disregarding any of the variance explained by any other variable in the design. You will get a main effect *p* value for each IV within the design, so if the study has a two-way design you will see two main effects and if it has a three-way design you will see three main effects. You can see this summarised in Figure 18.3.

Factorial ANOVAs: interaction effects

In addition to the main effects, you will also get some **interaction** effects. These are often the most interesting part of a factorial ANOVA. An interaction tells us if the differences across one of the IVs change depending on the different conditions of another IV. Interactions are quite complicated concepts, and it is easier to explain these with a figure. If you take a look at Figure 18.4 you can see the results of four different studies that are looking at differences between people diagnosed with clinical depression and a control group (IV1) and another IV (IV2) that has two levels, or conditions, that are imaginatively named *X* and *Y*.

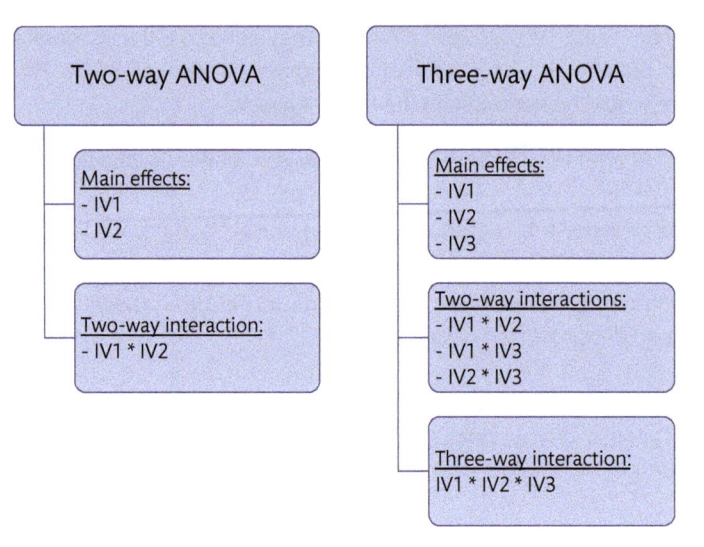

Figure 18.3: Main effects and interaction effects within a two-way and a three-way factorial ANOVA.

In the first example you can see that both groups get quite similar scores, with participants in the control group just scoring slightly higher. For both groups they score higher in condition Y than in condition X, and there is no interaction. The second example shows a crossover interaction, which is the example most often used when teaching about interactions. Here you can see that in condition X the participants diagnosed with depression scored higher than those with no diagnosis, whereas in condition Y the opposite was true and the control group scored higher than the depression diagnosis group. This is an interaction because the difference between the control and clinical groups is contingent upon whether you are looking at condition X or condition Y.

The other two examples also show interaction effects, as an interaction simply means that the differences in one IV, say the clinical group difference effect, is contingent upon the other IV. So in the third example there is no clinical group difference in condition X, and in condition Y scores increase for those in the control group and decrease for participants with a

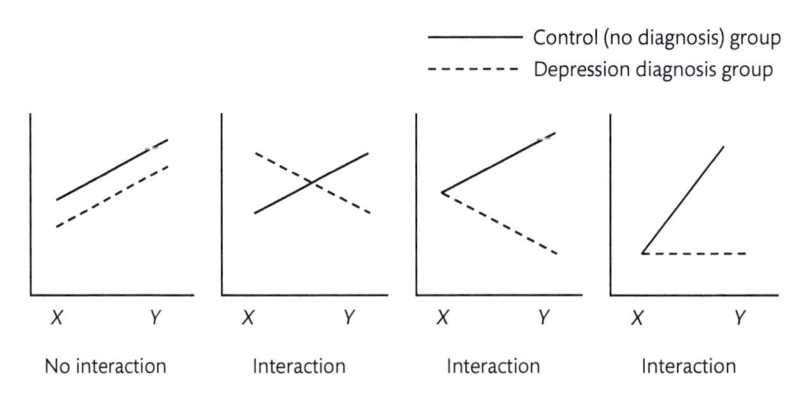

Figure 18.4: Examples of different interaction effects in a two-way 2 * 2 factorial ANOVA.

depression diagnosis. In the final example, scores between conditions *X* and *Y* do not differ for participants diagnosed with depression, but they do for those in the control group. Another way to think about this is whether the 'lines' are parallel. In the first example the lines in the graph are parallel and there is clearly no interaction, whereas the other three examples all show different types of interactions. We will be returning to this example again in the study questions at the end of this chapter.

Considering main effects and interactions

Let's look at another example, taking the first experimental scenario in the unfamiliar face memory studies from earlier. Remember that this was a 2 (age: 50-69 years vs. 70 years plus) * 2 (diagnosis: dementia vs. control) independent measures of ANOVA. You can see three possible outcomes from the analysis of this study in Figure 18.5. In the example on the left, first think about the main effect of age by imagining combining the data from the dementia and control patients. If you do this, you can clearly see that, overall, when ignoring any possible differences between dementia and control patients, there is a main effect of age, with reduced memory accuracy for older participants. Now think about the main effect of diagnosis group by combining the younger and older groups for each separate diagnosis group. There isn't much difference at all between the two groups, so it is likely that there wouldn't be a main effect of diagnosis. Finally, we want to think about the possible interaction between age and diagnosis. The two lines are parallel and quite close together, so the reduction in accuracy in the older age group seems to occur to the same extent in both groups, meaning that there is no interaction between the two variables.

In the middle example in Figure18.5, the effects are quite different. Overall, there is no main effect of age (imagine combining the scores for each age group across the two diagnosis groups, however, if you ignore age, scores are overall higher for the control group than for the dementia group, showing a main effect of diagnosis. Finally, there appears to be a significant

Main effect of age	**Main effect of age**	**Main effect of age**
Significant	Not significant	Significant
Main effect of diagnosis	**Main effect of diagnosis**	**Main effect of diagnosis**
Not significant	Significant	Significant
Interaction	**Interaction**	**Interaction**
Not significant	Significant	Significant

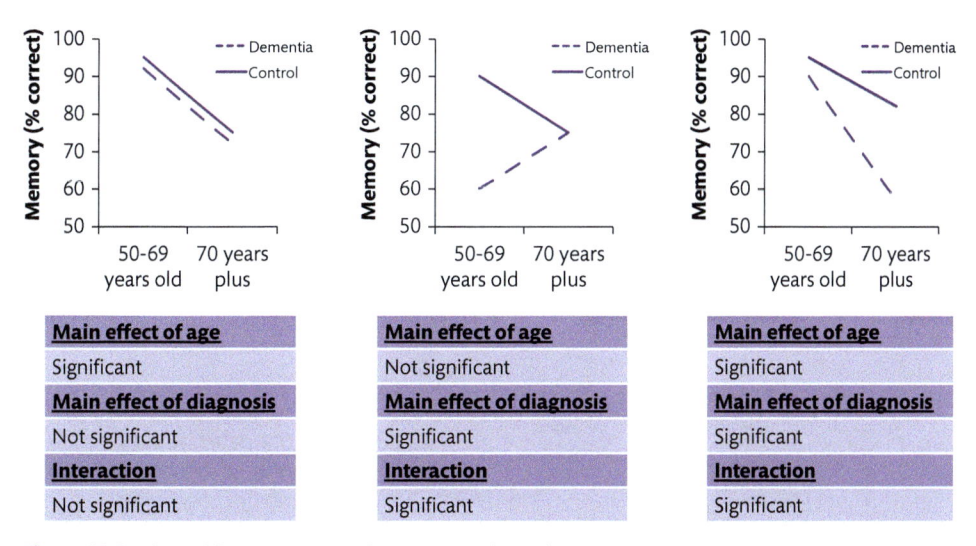

Figure 18.5: Three different outcomes from a 2 * 2 independent measures ANOVA.

interaction, with accuracy decreasing for the control group, but increasing for the dementia group, showing a marked difference in the changes according to age, depending on group.

Finally, the example of the right of Figure 18.5, there is yet another set of possible effects. There is, overall, a significant main effect of age, with accuracy decreasing in the older group. The main effect of diagnosis group is also significant. If you ignore the effects of age, those with dementia are less accurate than those in the control group. There is also a significant interaction, whilst both groups show a reduction in accuracy in the older group, this is far more extreme in the dementia group than in the control group.

The number of interaction effects that you see depends on the complexity of the design as determined by the number of IVs that you manipulate. Whether these interactions are significant or not is something you will find out in the analysis. If you look back at Figure 18.4 you can see that there is just one possible interaction in a two-way design, the interaction between IV1 and IV2. Therefore, in a two-way design researchers will end up with three different results to interpret and write up: the main effect of IV1, the main effect of IV2 and the interaction between IV1 and IV2. For each of these effects they will have an F ratio and a p value, and each effect that is significant will need to be interpreted to understand the direction of the differences.

Factorial ANOVAs and the variability cake

As with any type of analysis, this all comes back to the variability cake. In a one-way design we simply looked at the ratio between explained and random variance. With a two-way design we now have four slices of variance cake, and these can be seen in Figure 18.6. In this example there is relatively little variability that is uniquely explained by IV1, and this is probably not significant. However, a fair amount of variability is uniquely explained by IV2, and therefore this would probably be significant. The part of the analysis that explains the most unique variance is the interaction effect, which is likely to be significant.

Of course, designs can become far more complex even than a factorial two-way ANOVA. Technically you can manipulate as many variables as you want, but the ANOVAs become more unwieldy and brain melting the more IVs you add. If you look back at Figure 18.4 you can see all of the unique effects that you would get with a three-way ANOVA: three main

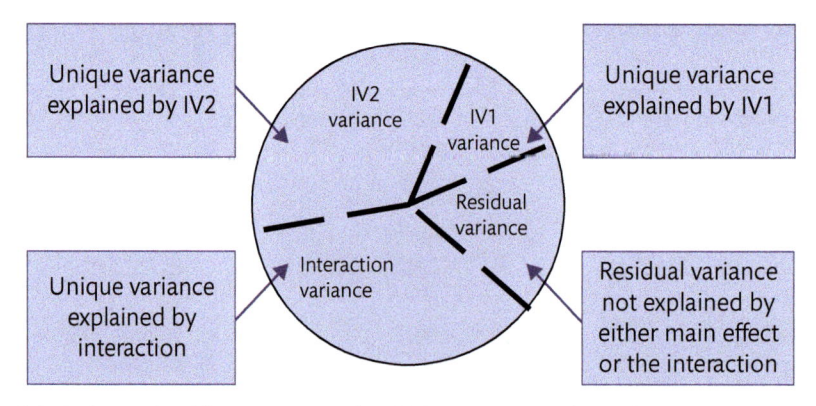

Figure 18.6: Explaining the difference sources of variability in a two-way factorial design.

effects, three two-way interactions and a three-way interaction. Just imagine the number of main effects and interactions you would have to interpret, break down and write up if you manipulated four or five IVs! There is no rule as to how many IVs you can manipulate, but I've rarely seen ANOVAs beyond a four-way design, even in published research.

Analysing confound variables in an experimental design: analysis of covariance (ANCOVA)

The final kind of analysis that can be used with advanced experimental designs is an **ANCOVA**, or **analysis of covariance**. Throughout this book we have talked about the issue of **confound variables** and **control variables**. These are variables that can systematically explain some of the variability in the data we collect. For example, imagine we run an experiment where we measure participants' IQ, give them chocolate, and then measure their IQ again. The aim of this experiment is to see if eating chocolate makes you smarter!

There are a number of possible unmeasured confounding variables in this design. For example, how often the participants normally eat chocolate, how much they like chocolate, their intelligence level, how used to completing psychometric tests they are, etc. The important thing is that these variables can *systematically* explain some of the variance that might normally be counted as **random variance**, or the variance that they explain might even overlap with some of the **experimental variance**. You might expect someone who really loves chocolate to show a greater increase in IQ, and someone who hates chocolate to show a smaller increase in IQ.

Confounds, control variables, and the variability cake

Wouldn't it be great if researchers could somehow deal with, and get rid of, this annoying covariance? If a confound is measured, it becomes a control variable, and luckily, there is a statistical method that allows us to analyse the effects of a control variable (or covariate): analysis of covariance, or ANCOVA. The logic behind the ANCOVA can be easily explained with our variability cake analogy. Remember that the cake represents 100% of the variability in our dataset and we are aiming to discover how best to explain where that variability comes from.

When a researcher runs an ANCOVA the analysis looks to see how much of the variability, or how big a slice of cake, can be explained by a measured control variable. If the control variable explains lots of the variability, then the covariate will be significant and the slice of cake will be big. We then want to look at the rest of the cake and calculate how much of the variance is explained by the experimental manipulation and how much is leftover random variance, just like we would with a normal ANOVA.

This means, in a simple one-way ANCOVA, we will end up with three slices of cake: a covariance slice, an experimental variance slice and a random variance slice. This means that, effectively, there are four possible outcomes from a one-way ANCOVA, and these are summarised in Figure 18.7. The outcomes depend on whether the experimental main effect is significant or not, and whether the covariate is significant or not. It is quite possible that the covariate could be hugely significant and soak up loads of the measured variability in the data, leaving the main experimental effect to be not significant (the top right cake in Figure 18.7). It is also possible that the covariate could explain a significant amount of variability, but that, from the

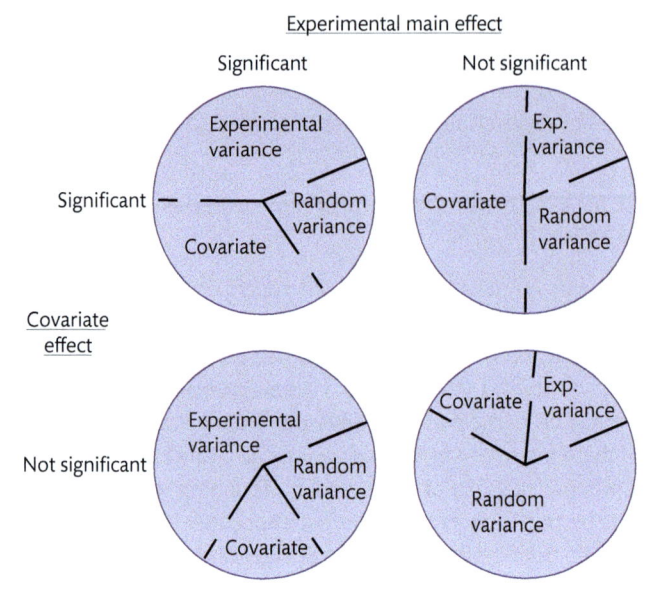

Figure 18.7: Possible outcomes from a one-way ANCOVA.

remaining variance in the cake, the main experimental manipulation could also be significant (the top left cake in Figure 18.7). Alternatively, it could be that the measured covariate does not actually significantly explain anything (both bottom cakes in the figure).

You can apply a covariate analysis to any type of ANOVA, with any type of design and any number of IVs. In Figure 18.7 the cake shows a one-way ANCOVA, but you can also add a covariate into any type of factorial ANOVA, making it a factorial ANCOVA. Of course, we would now have more slices of cake. Imagine the cake shown in Figure 18.7 and add another slice to represent the variance explained by a confounding variable. That would be a variance cake for a two-way ANCOVA.

Getting to grips with published research: advanced correlational designs

In Part 3 we learned how to look at **correlations** between two continuous variables, and then we stepped this up to **simple linear regression** where we could use a continuous **predictor variable** to predict the score on a continuous **outcome variable.** As with the ANOVA family, published correlational research tends to use more complex methods of correlational analyses, and these are summarised graphically in Figure 18.8.

Controlling for a control variable in a correlation analysis: partial correlation

Partial correlations are actually pretty simple. The last type of advanced experimental analysis that we discussed was an ANCOVA, where a researcher could analyse the amount of

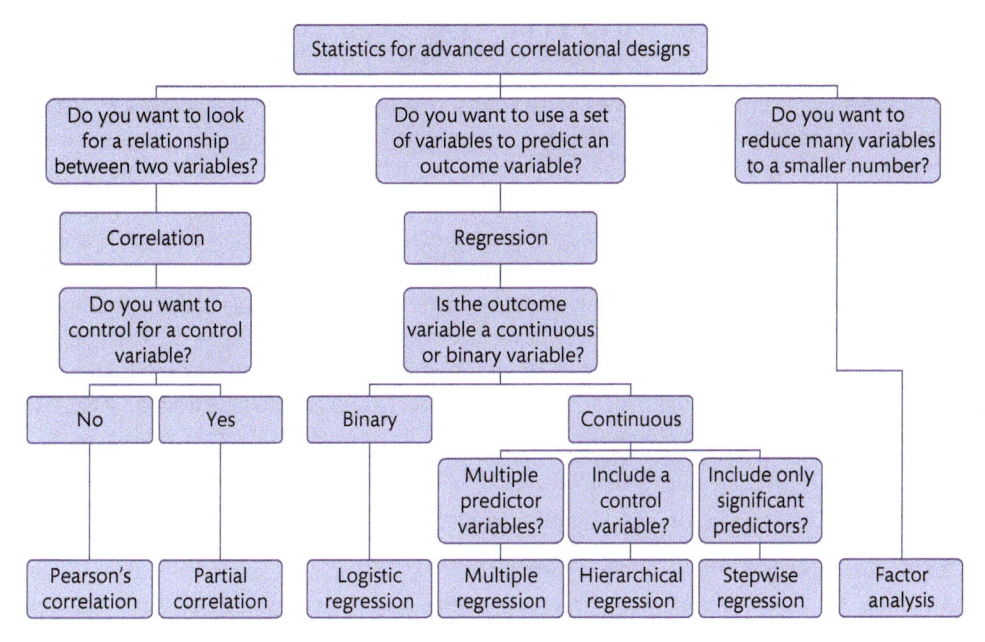

Figure 18.8: Statistical techniques used with advanced correlational designs.

covariance within a dataset, and having controlled for and explained away that variability, they could then look at the balance of experimental to random variability. The approach of explaining and getting rid of covariance is a really helpful one, and it can also be easily applied in correlational designs and analysis.

With a **Pearson's correlation** we simply looked at whether there was a relationship between two variables. It is also possible to run a partial correlation. With this method of analysis, any of the variability explained by the control variable is removed, and then the partial correlation tells you if there is then a correlation between the two variables. The logic here is exactly the same as for the ANCOVA. You divide the cake into three slices, remove the slice of control variable variance, and then consider whether the remaining variance is better explained by the strength of the relationship between the two variables, or the random variance in the dataset.

Analysing multiple predictor variables in a regression model: multiple regression

The real beauty of regression analyses comes when they are used to analyse more complex datasets that comprise multiple predictors and a single continuous outcome variable. When you read about regression analyses in published papers they will almost certainly be some form of **multiple regression**. This method allows the researcher to ask far more about their data. The key question, though, is likely to be: which of the predictor variables can significantly predict the outcome variable.

Do all of my predictors, looked at together, significantly predict the outcome variable?

A multiple regression analysis comes in two parts, which you can see in Figure 18.9. First, it tells you how good the overall model is; that is whether all of the predictors, lumped together, can significantly predict the outcome variable. Second, it looks at each of the separate predictor variables and tells you whether it is a significant predictor of the outcome variable. As a consequence, when you read about a multiple regression, there are lots of different components and a few different statistics that will have been reported.

When looking at the overall model, that is all of the predictor variables taken together in one big lump, you first look at the **R^2**. We talked about this statistic in Chapter 12. This statistic tells us how much of the variability in our dataset, or variance cake, can be explained by all of the predictor variables together. You will also see an F ratio and p value from an ANOVA, and this tells you whether the overall model can significantly predict the outcome variable.

Which individual predictors significantly predict the outcome variable?

For the second stage of the multiple regression the analysis looks at each individual predictor separately. Whilst the overall model might be highly significant, it is quite possible that not all of the individual predictor variables you included in the model are significant. For each predictor variable you will see a t statistic and a p value (similar to those discussed in Chapters 7 and 8) that tell you whether the individual predictor can significantly predict the outcome score. You will also see a **β value**, and these work in exactly the same way as in the simple linear regression that we discussed in Chapter 12. A β value tells you the change in the outcome variable that would be predicted from a one unit/point increase in the predictor variable. A positive β value means that you would expect scores on the outcome variable to increase as the predictor variable increases, whereas a negative β value means that you would expect scores on the outcome variable to decrease as the predictor variable increases.

As you can see, there is a lot you can find out about a dataset using multiple regression, but there are actually far more things that can be done with a multiple regression. We will move onto these next …

How good is the *overall model*?
Taking all of the predictor variables together, can they form a significant predictive model?
Statistics: R^2 and ANOVA

⬇

How good is each individual predictor?
Looking at each predictor variable separately, it is able to significantly predict the outcome variable?
Statistics: β, t and p

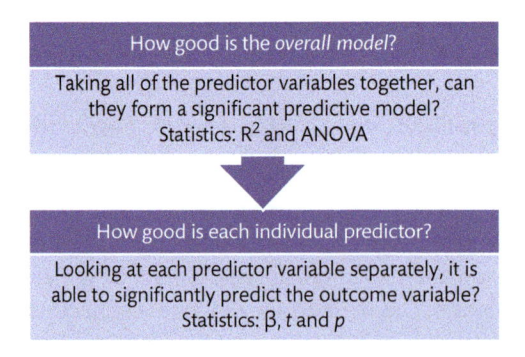

Figure 18.9: Stages of analysis and interpretation for a multiple regression analysis.

Using categorical predictors in a regression model: regression with categorical variables

You may remember back in Part 3 I had a bit of a rant about only being able to use correlations to look at relationships between continuous variables? Well, that is very strictly true for Pearson's and partial correlations. However, when using multiple regression it actually is quite possible to include categorical predictor variables, and you might read about this in published research. This does not mean that the researcher has necessarily made a mistake within their analysis. In a multiple regression you can include categorical predictors, but it can get quite complex. How complex it gets depends on the number of categories within the variable.

Binary categorical variables

A binary categorical variable is one that has two categories, and a simple example is the verdict in a criminal trial: innocent or guilty. It is actually quite simple and straightforward to include a binary variable like this in a multiple regression model. This is probably best explained with an example. Imagine that we are trying to predict how psychopathic people are, and one predictor we wish to include is the innocence or guilt of the participants as determined by the verdict in a trial. You can see the data in Figure 18.10, showing that guilty people tended to be more psychopathic, with a mean score of 11.8, whereas the innocent participants had slightly lower scores with a mean of 7.1.

Imagine that in our dataset we coded the predictor variable of trial verdict so that guilty people were coded with a value of 0, and innocent people were coded with a value of 1. This is represented in Figure18.10 left. Now remember what the β value tells us: the change in the outcome variable for a one unit increase in the predictor variable. We can see in the figure that innocent people tended to have a psychopathy score 4.7 lower than guilty people. Therefore, in the regression analysis, increasing the predictor variable score by one unit, from 0 (guilty) to 1 (innocent) would predict that scores decreased by 4.7, so a β value of −4.7.

But what would happen if we re-ordered the categories in the predictor variable, so this time innocent participants were coded as 0 and guilty participants were coded as 1, as shown in Figure 18.10 right. Now we would have a β value of +4.7. It is exactly the same difference,

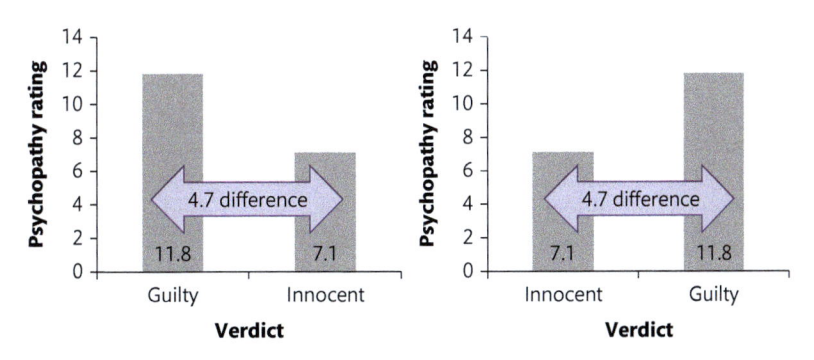

Figure 18.10: Understanding the logic behind including binary variables in multiple regression models.

whether we find that scores increase or decrease simply depends on how we order the two categories. But, fundamentally, because there are just two categories the *magnitude* of the difference will be exactly the same however we organise them. As long as we know which group was coded with 0 and which group was coded with 1 we can easily and accurately interpret a binary categorical predictor variable.

Categorical variables with three or more categories

Things become rather more complicated if you wish to include a categorical predictor variable that has three or more categories. This is because you could manipulate the order of the categories to create any kind of relationship you want! If you take a look back at Figure 10.2 from Chapter 10, you can see how I artificially created a negative relationship, a positive relationship and no relationship between happiness and chocolate type, simply by manipulating the order in which the different types of chocolate were coded. This does not mean that it is impossible to run a multiple regression analysis with a categorical predictor that has three or more categories. It is, however, relatively complex and requires something called dummy variable modelling. You can read more about this in the Wider Reading of this chapter.

How can regression models become more complex? Complex regression models

Multiple regressions get even more exciting when you move onto complex models, which actually refers to two separate techniques: **stepwise regression** and **hierarchical regression.** I must confess that hierarchical regression is my favourite method of analysis, so if I get slightly overexcited explaining it, that will be why!

Hierarchical regression

In a normal multiple regression, the researcher includes a few possible predictor variables to see whether they are significant or not. This is often referred to as the **enter method of regression.** Complex models allow us to build regression models that are a little more finessed, and that allow us to address different types of hypotheses. First, let's take hierarchical regression models. These models allow us to deal with confounding variables, in a similar way to the ANCOVA and partial correlations that we discussed earlier in this chapter.

Imagine that a researcher is trying to predict a child's reading age (the outcome variable) from the number of books that they have at home (the predictor variable). An obvious confound in this design would be the child's actual age (the older a child is, the better they are likely to be able to read), so it would be great if the researcher could enter this into the regression model first, see how much variance it can account for, then look at whether the number of books that a child has can predict their reading age, over and above the variance already explained with the confound. This is exactly what hierarchical regression does, and it is really the ANCOVA of the regression family. It is such an elegant and beautiful way to analyse a correlational dataset.

Stepwise regression

Stepwise regression is another form of complex regression modelling. However, it is quite a controversial method and the topic of the best ever titled journal article: *Why won't stepwise methods die?*[1]

Stepwise methods are relatively rare in current research as they are sometimes looked upon with a great deal of scepticism, but you still do see them occasionally. The logic behind stepwise methods is that you have a large set of predictor variables that you think may possibly predict an outcome variable. The analysis looks for the best, or most significant, predictor and enters this into block one of the regression model. It then looks at the remaining predictors and sees if any others are significant. If there are still significant predictors it takes the most significant of the remaining predictors and enters that into block two of the regression model. It keeps going like this, step by step, until all of the significant predictors have been entered into the regression model. Any predictors that are not significant are left out of the model entirely, and you have as many blocks as you have significant predictors.

To some extent this is a very exploratory technique, and this leads into the criticism of it. Often stepwise methods are adopted when people have a huge dataset with many variables and they do not have clear predictions for the relationships they might find. So you stick all the variables in and let the analysis tell you what is going on. This means that the model is not very hypothesis driven. This is in stark contrast to the far more refined hierarchical regression, where the hypotheses are clear and specific, with theoretically driven confound variables entered into block one and the predictor variables of interest entered into block two.

Using regression to predict binary outcome variables: logistic regression

All of the regression models discussed so far have had a continuous variable as the outcome, however it is possible to have a regression model with a binary categorical outcome variable. This is a **logistic regression**, and both continuous predictors and categorical predictors with any number of categories can be used within a logistic regression model. As the outcome variable is binary, and therefore not linear and on a continuum, the model no longer relies on assuming a linear relationship between the two variables, and you can stick in pretty much anything you want as a predictor (as long as it is numerical!).

This type of regression can be used to predict, for example, any kind of outcome variable that defines which of two groups a participant belongs to. This could be whether someone passes or fails their driving test, if someone has a diagnosis of Alzheimer's disease or not, or if someone continues into postgraduate education or employment after graduation.

Looking for groups of similar variables within a larger dataset: factor analysis

Factor analysis is most frequently used with questionnaire datasets, although it has also been used within individual differences and neuroscience research. The idea behind factor analysis is that you have a large number of variables, say questions on a questionnaire, and you want to see which questions are highly correlated. If a group of questions are very strongly correlated this shows that participants responded in a very similar way to these questions. It may

---

[1]Thompson, B. (1989). Why won't stepwise methods die? *Measurement and Evaluation in Counseling and Development*, 146–148.

therefore be assumed that this set of questions represents a single underlying 'thing' that all of these individual questions tap into.

It is important to note that factor analysis is very different from regression, because, although they are both based on looking at relationships between variables, the factor analysis has no specified predictor and outcome variables. Factor analysis simply looks at a set of variables, looks for relationships between them, and identifies sets of variables that seem to represent the same underlying variable.

A good example of this is a personality questionnaire. One of the most well-known and widely used inventories is the five factor model. This questionnaire comprises sixty separate questions, and in a factor analysis these are called manifest variables. If you were to run a factor analysis on these sixty questions you would find that they actually represent five underlying personality traits. These underlying variables are referred to as latent variables, and you can see these in Figure 18.11.

Factor analysis has two uses. First, it helps us to understand what is going on in a huge dataset by identifying underlying latent variables, which can then be interpreted and possibly researched further. Second, it can make a huge and unwieldy dataset far friendlier to approach and analyse. Can anyone seriously tell me that they would rather analyse all sixty

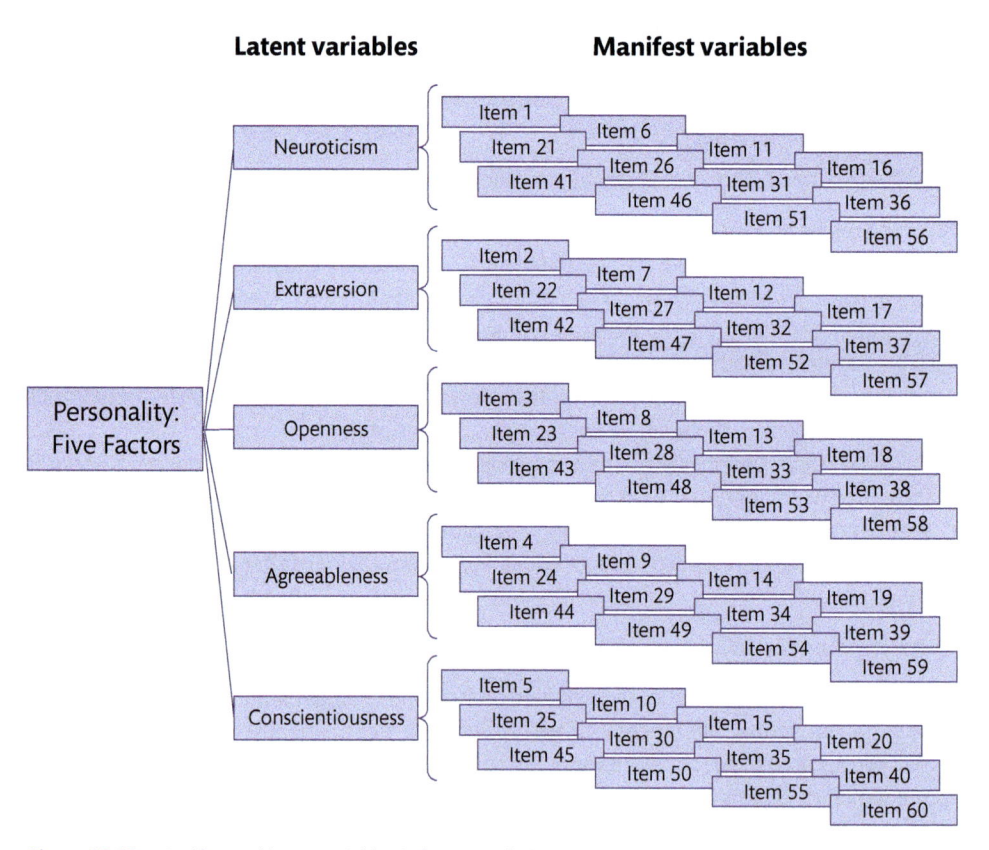

Figure 18.11: Manifest and latent variables in factor analysis.

manifest variables? Surely it would be preferable just to run the analysis on the five latent personality variables?

Presenting findings from complex analyses: graphing data

The statistics covered in the earlier chapters in this book are all quite simple, and therefore graphs are not really needed to help present the finding. When a design becomes more complex and involves multiple variables, graphs can be very helpful to summarise findings for the reader. For this reason, you will quite often see graphs presented in the results section of published research. There are some general rules that help to make complex findings more easily digestible in graphs:

- Graphs should be kept as simple as possible. The aim is not to present something pretty, but to present something that clearly and accurately represents the research findings.
- To help with simplicity, colour and 3D in graphs is generally best avoided. Unless they are meaningful for the findings that are being presented, it is better that graphs are kept simple and avoid unnecessary distractions. Adding a third dimension can also distort findings, making the presentation inaccurate.
- A figure caption is always included below the figure to give you a simple explanation of what is being presented. This can be very helpful in aiding the understanding and interpretation of complex graphs.
- Both of the axes on a graph are labelled to tell you what you are being shown, so whenever you look at graphs, check the axis labels to make sure you have a clear idea of what you are looking at.
- Look carefully at the scale of the axes in graphs: what are the minimum and maximum values shown, and how do these values relate to the possible minimum and maximum scores that can be achieved? Imagine you have two groups, one with 46% accuracy and one with 48% accuracy. If the axis starts at 45% and ends at 50% it will look like a really exciting finding! However, if the actual minimum and maximum values of 0% through to 100% are shown, it will be clear that there is very little difference between the two groups.
- If relevant, the unit of measurement will always be shown. For example, if the graph presents reaction times, were they measured in milliseconds, seconds, minutes or hours? The unit of measurement can make a huge difference to the interpretation of a result.

What type of graph should you use?

Generally, the type of graph that is used will be determined by the method of analysis that has been used. Experimental design analyses are typically presented using a bar or line graph. The graph should include a representation of not just the mean values within each condition but also some way of representing the dispersion within each condition. For correlational designs you would see a scatterplot that included a line of best fit. You can see good and bad examples of these types of graphs in Figure 18.12. The 'good' bar chart is simple in its format, the axes are clearly labelled and there are error bars to represent the variability in the dataset. In the 'good' scatterplot, the data points are simply presented, there is a line of best fit running though the raw data points, and the axes are clearly labelled.

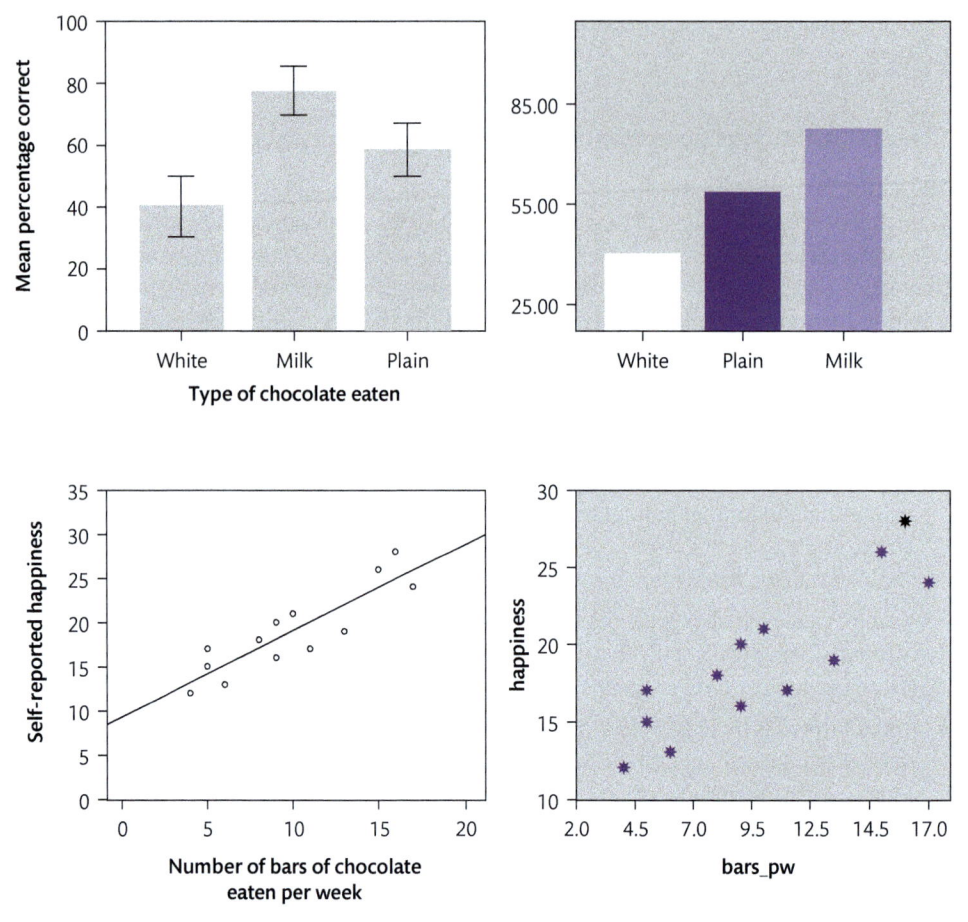

Figure 18.12: Examples of 'good' graphs (left) and 'bad' graphs (right) for experimental designs (top) and correlational designs (bottom).

Getting to grips with published research: issues and debates in statistical analysis

Whilst there are a number of general rules that you learn to follow when learning about statistical analyses, there are actually a few quite heated debates around the ways in which data are analysed and presented. When you read published research, you may encounter some of these arguments, so this section will highlight some of the key controversies that are currently being debated by psychological researchers.

Before moving onto the controversies around the **_p_ value**, I want to first discuss the way in which p values are presented in research papers. Throughout this book we have always reported that p is 'less than' a certain alpha level, for example $p < .050$ or $p < .001$. This is the appropriate way to report p values when you are calculating the statistics by hand and comparing them to a critical value in a lookup table. However, you may notice that you don't see this convention so often in published research papers. You are far more likely to see exact *p* values, such as $p = .049$ or $p = .002$.

If you use a computer programme, such as SPSS, to run your statistics, you will be given exact *p* values. According to the APA guidelines, you should always present exact *p* values where possible. Therefore, in published research, you almost always see exact *p* values, where *p* actually equals a particular alpha level. The only accepted exception to this is $p < .001$. It is widely accepted that once *p* values get smaller than .001, it is perfectly acceptable to report it as $p < .001$. But, if you have the exact *p* values and they are greater than .001, you should be presenting them.

Significance: are *p* values really any good?

For much of this book I have talked excitedly about *p* values and the excitement of finding significant results. However, there is a large and growing movement that is pretty scathing about **null hypothesis significance testing**. Although the critique of *p* values is not exactly new, it has become far more discussed and accepted in recent years, and as such you may come across some of these issues and ideas when reading published research.

What is the big problem with *p* values? Well, there are a few problems, and these are discussed in the Wider Reading for this chapter, but for now I just want to pick up on a couple of key issues.

The first thing is, why the magic α of .050? What is so inherently special about this value? At some point it was arbitrarily decided that this would be the criteria for significance, and we are still blindly following this decision. It might be argued that having a specific cut off point is silly in itself: what really is the difference between a not significant $p = .051$ and a significant $p = .050$?

A second issue is that *p* values are massively influenced by sample size. Take correlations, for example: if you have a two-tailed hypothesis and just ten participants the critical value for a correlation is .6319, but if you have more than 500 participants, the critical value drops massively to .0875! Remember that *r* values run from −1 through to +1, with 0 meaning no correlation. This means that, with a big enough sample, even a very tiny correlation can be statistically significant.

One consequence of these issues is that it can be very difficult to compare results across different studies or published research papers. There is a particular type of analysis that attempts to do this, a meta-analysis, and you might come across these when looking at published research. Imagine comparing two papers that run the same correlational study, one is significant but the other is not. It is quite possible that the significant paper actually found a far, far smaller correlation between the two variables, but because they tested a gazillion participants it is a significant finding.

Is there an alternative to the *p* value? Effect sizes

Whilst *p* values have been criticised, they are still one of the main sources of statistical evidence used to analyse the data collected within psychological research. However, the APA now recommends that *p* values are always presented alongside the **effect size**, and as such they are typically viewed as complementary. Nowadays most journals demand that both p values and effect sizes are reported. So, when reading papers, you will often see some additional values given after the p value, and these are most likely an effect size. We have seen effect sizes in each of the parametric statistics chapters within this book, so you should be aware that effect sizes are denoted by lots of different letters and symbols. For example, in the t test chapters (Chapters 7 and 8) we presented Cohen's d effect size statistic alongside the t test result: $t(8) = 2.98, p < .010, d = 1.89$. The effect size is typically presented after the p value in this way. There are many different effect size statistics, often with multiple possible effect sizes for the same statistical analysis. You can see a summary of some of the main effects sizes used by researchers in Table 18.3.

Advantages of effect sizes

There are two big advantages of effect sizes. The first is that they are unaffected by sample size, so the approach of just testing loads of participants to get a significant finding doesn't work! This also means that it is far easier to compare effect sizes across different studies. With p values, the same p value does not necessarily reflect the same thing across different samples. Imagine two studies that both have a significant difference where $p = .050$, but in one study there are ten participants, and in the other there are 1000 participants. Although the p value is exactly the same in both studies, because the **critical value** is looked up using the number of participants (degrees of freedom), the actual size of the statistical difference will not be the same in the two studies. In the study with just ten participants the difference will need to be far larger to achieve $p = .050$, and in the study with 1000 participants a p value of .050 can reflect actually quite a small difference. Effect sizes do not work in this way. The magnitude of an effect that is reflected by, for example, a Cohen's d of 1.89, would be the equivalent size regardless of the sample size. This is why effect sizes are used in meta-analysis studies, studies that statistically compare findings across a number of research findings on the same topic.

Table 18.3: Effect sizes for different statistical analyses, and conventions for defining small, medium and large effect sizes. Note that the calculated effect size should be equal to, or greater than, the defined value.

Statistical analysis	Effect size	Small effect	Medium effect	Large effect
t test	Cohen's d	0.2	0.5	0.8
ANOVA	partial η^2	0.01	0.06	0.13
Pearson's correlation	r	0.1	0.3	0.5
Regression	f^2	0.02	0.15	0.35
Chi square (2x2)	Phi Φ	0.1	0.3	0.5
Chi square (all others)	Cramer's V	Varies depending on the df within the design		
Mann Whitney U	r	0.1	0.3	0.5
Wilcoxon signed rank	r	0.1	0.3	0.5
Spearman's correlation	r_s	0.1	0.3	0.5

The second advantage is that they do not have a set cut-off point for what might be 'interesting/significant' or not. Instead, effect sizes are usually defined as showing a small, medium or large effect size. We have seen this throughout this book when we have discussed effect sizes, and you can see these again in Table 18.3. One really nice thing about effect sizes is that the effect size you might expect can vary depending on the research you are doing. If you are looking at something where the findings are likely to be quite subtle, it is perfectly fine to expect and to find a small effect size.

Effect sizes do get a little complex in that there are many different ways of calculating them, and the convention differs across the different methods of analysis. You might see them presented as a d, r, partial η^2 or w value, depending on the analysis that has been run, and there are many more types than that. To further complicate things, the conventions for defining what constitutes a small, medium or large effect size also vary depending on the type of effect size statistic used. So, you can see that effect sizes are far more complicated than the simple 'is it significant or not?' p value, but they also hold many advantages and are being used far more frequently.

Effect sizes and confidence intervals

In published research, you will sometimes see **confidence intervals** presented alongside effect sizes, which results from APA recommendations. Remember right back to the essentials of what we are trying to achieve with our research and statistical analysis; we want to understand something about a **population**, and to do this we study a smaller **sample** of participants in the hope that what we find in the sample reflects something that is true in the population. Confidence intervals (CIs) define a range of scores, around the mean that is calculated from our sample data, and we expect the true population statistic to fall within these two scores.

CIs are calculated with a particular confidence level in mind, typically either 90%, 95% or 99%. In psychological research, 95% is the most frequently used confidence level that is used. They give you two values which usually fall symmetrically either side of the mean. For example, if you have IQ scores where the mean is 120 and the CI is ±5, this means the interval ranges from 5 points below the mean to 5 points above the mean, making the CI 115 – 125. APA standards require you to present the confidence level and the upper and lower limits of the CI, separated by a comma and with brackets around the values, and these are usually presented alongside the mean and standard deviation. For example: M = 120, SD = 5, CI 95% (115, 125).

What does this all actually mean though? Remember that the CI tells you the range within which you would expect the population mean to fall. As such, it is a form of accuracy statistic; the smaller the CI around the mean the more likely it is that the population mean is close to the sample mean. If the CI is large, then your mean is likely to be less accurate as it might be quite different from the population mean. If you are studying a sample to understand a population, then you want your sample statistics to be as similar to the population statistics as possible. However, CIs are influenced by the sample size. The larger the sample is, the more likely it is that is reflects the population, and therefore CIs will be smaller with larger samples.

As I just mentioned, psychologists typically use a 95% CI, meaning that they can be 95% confident that the population mean falls within the specified upper and lower limit around the sample mean. If the confidence level changes, then the CI upper and lower limits will change. If you want to be more confident, and increase the confidence level to 99%, then the CI range will become larger so that you can be more confident that the population mean is captured within that range. Lowering the confidence level to 90% will make the CI smaller as you don't need to be so confident that the population mean falls within it.

Effect sizes and non-parametric statistics

Effect sizes for non-parametric statistics need to be calculated in a different way. Remember that effect sizes typically use means and standard deviations within their calculations, but these statistics are not appropriate for non-parametric analyses. The effect size for a chi squared depends on the design and number of cells. For a 2x2 chi squared, you would use Phi Φ, and for any other design you would used Cramer's V. The Mann Whitney U and Wilcoxon signed rank tests, the non-parametric equivalents of the t tests, have an effect size of r (not the same r as for Pearson's correlations!). This statistic is based on calculating a z score, which is then used as part of the r calculation. For Spearman's non-parametric correlation, the r_s value itself can be interpreted as an effect size. The conventions for defining small, medium and large effect sizes are shown in Table 18.3.

Detecting an effect: power analysis

A concept related to effect size is **power**. Going back to the issues with p values, is it really OK to just keep testing lots of participants until you find a significant result? How many participants are enough, and at what point should a researcher stop testing participants? This is what power analysis tells you, and researchers should usually do this when they are designing their study to help them decide how many participants they should test. This information is then typically presented in the methods section of a paper.

Power tells you the chance of detecting an effect, if it is there. Often the desired level of power in psychological research is 0.80, although it is not uncommon to use higher levels of power. What a power level of 0.80 means is that, by the time you have tested the specified number of participants you have an 80% chance of detecting something, if it indeed exists, so, if you've tested the right number of participants and not found anything, there's most likely nothing there to be found.

To calculate power researchers consider four things:

1. What effect size are you expecting? This will depend on the previous research in the area, but you should have a hypothesis that allows you to specify either a small, medium or large effect size.
2. What alpha level will you be using? This is likely to be the standard $\alpha = .050$.
3. What is your desired level of power? Typically a level of 0.80 is used.
4. What is your design? For example, how many conditions are there in an experimental design, or how many predictors in a correlational design?

There are some great online calculators that allow you to easily calculate power, and I've given links at the end of this chapter if you fancy playing with power analysis to see how the number of participants required varies depending on your design and criteria. The suggested numbers can be quite interesting. Just remember that you must run power analysis when you are designing a study, and once you have tested the appropriate number of participants, if the results are not significant, then I'm afraid there is nothing there to be found.

Statistics and the variability cake: a lesson to take away

Having a basic understanding of the statistics described in this chapter should enable you to tackle much of the published research that you will encounter through your studies. However, they all build on the same basic concepts that underlie the simple statistical analyses covered fully in this book. In the end, all statistics come down to cake! More specifically, the variability cake. All data contains variability, and as researchers we simply want to understand where that variability comes from.

With an experimental design we want to know whether more variability comes from our manipulated IV or from the random and unmeasured variables. In a more complex design we may have more slices in our cake depending on whether we are manipulating multiple variables or measuring possible confounds. But essentially, we are still just looking for the largest slice of cake.

In a correlational design we want to know whether the relationship between variables is best described by the slope of the best fit line, or the random variability that falls around it. But again, we just want to know which slice of the cake is largest. The slice that explains the covariance between the two variables, or the slice that explains the variance within the variables that does not change systematically with the relationship?

So there you go, research design and statistical analysis simply comes down to the size of slices of cake. I really hope you enjoy cake!

Study questions

1. Imagine that you were to run a one-way independent measures ANOVA where the DV is level of anxiety and the IV is five different intervention conditions: a no intervention control, a placebo medication, a prescribed medication, an alternative therapy medication, or cognitive behavioural therapy.
    1.1. If you were to break down this main effect using multiple t tests, how many would you need to run? Please list all of the pairwise t tests
    1.2. What would be the Bonferroni corrected alpha for these t tests?
    1.3. Suggest a hypothesis that would require the ANOVA to be broken down using post hoc contrasts.
    1.4. Suggest a hypothesis that would require the ANOVA to be broken down using planned contrasts.
2. Take a look back at Figure 18.4 and you will see the results of four different experiments where one IV is whether the participant has a clinical diagnosis of depression, or whether

they have no diagnosis and they are in the control group. The other IV has been imaginatively labelled X and Y. For each of the four studies, suggest what the second IV might be, what the two conditions are, and what the DV might be. Also specify whether each of the IVs are independent or repeated design and report the type of ANOVA that would be used to analyse the dataset. I've given an example of this for the first, no interaction example. Do something similar, but with different DVs and IV2s for the other three graphs.

- 2.1. No interaction example: The DV is level of self-rated anxiety. IV1 is the whether the participant reports that they have a fear of spiders, an independent design with two levels: not spider phobic or spider phobic. IV2 is whether the participant is in an empty room (condition X) or a room with a spider (condition Y). IV 2 is a repeated design. The data would be analysed using a 2*2 mixed design factorial ANOVA.
- 2.2. Interaction 1:
- 2.3. Interaction 2:
- 2.4. Interaction 3:

3. A researcher is interested in looking at whether each of the 'Big 5' personality traits can predict a person's level of depression. They look at each personality trait in a separate study, but in each they feel it is important to control for relevant confounding variables. For each study, suggest one continuous variable and one binary categorical variable that may be confounding variables. Also suggest the direction of the predictive effect for each variable.

- 3.1. Openness:
- 3.2. Conscientiousness:
- 3.3. Extraversion:
- 3.4. Agreeableness:
- 3.5. Neuroticism:

Example paper using advanced statistical techniques

Watling, D., & Bourne, V. J. (2013). Sex differences in the relationship between children's emotional expression discrimination and their developing hemispheric lateralization. *Developmental Neuropsychology, 38*, 496–506.

I've spent this whole book avoiding citing my own research for fear of being accused of being an egomaniac! However, this is the final example paper of this book, and in this paper Dawn Watling and I used a range of advanced statistical techniques, drawing on both experimental and correlational approaches. On page 500 we use a 3 × 2 factorial independent measures ANOVA, where we break down significant effects using a planned Helmert contrast. We then go on, a page later, to run a slightly complex (but very cool) hierarchical regression model that includes interactive predictors. This method of analysis is absolutely my favourite ever, which seems like a good way to end this book!

Wider reading and additional resources

Cumming G. (2014). The new statistics: Why and how. *Psychological Science*, 25, 7–29.
This paper provides a clear and quite accessible summary of the issues surrounding the traditional methods of analysis typically used in psychological research, and suggests alternative and improved methods for future research.

http://www.gpower.hhu.de/en.html
G Power is a free piece of software that allows you to run power analysis for a very wide range of different designs and methods of analysis.

For full answers to study questions, and to explore a range of other materials, visit the online resources at: **www.oup.com/uk/bourne/**

Glossary

Abstract Short summary found at the beginning of a research paper.

Active deception Purposeful deception of participants within a research study where participants are actively told something that is untrue.

Alpha (α) level Criteria set for accepting the null or alternative hypothesis, which reflects the probability of committing a Type I Error.

Alternative hypothesis A hypothesis that predicts effects, such as differences or relationships, will be found.

Analysis of Covariance (ANCOVA) Method of analysis that looks for differences between groups/conditions whilst controlling for the variability explained by a measured control variable.

Analysis of Variance (ANOVA) Method of analysis that looks for differences between groups/conditions.

Analytical pluralism Use of multiple qualitative methods on a single dataset.

Anonymity Collecting and storing participant data with no identifying information, such as their name, attached to it.

Appendices Section of supplementary materials presented at the end of a research report.

Beta (β) value Used in regression analyses, and shows the change in the outcome variable for a one unit increase in the predictor variable.

Between groups variance Variability in a dataset that can be explained by the experimental manipulation, so the differences between groups or conditions.

Binary categorical variable Variable that comprises of two groups, where participants can belong either to one group or the other (e.g., guilty or innocent, clinical group or control group).

Bonferroni correction Correction applied to the alpha (α) level when multiple statistical tests are used together, such as multiple *t* tests.

Categorical data/variable Data that simply defines which category participants belong to, such as type of pet owned, or degree subject studied.

Categorical design Study that collects data only using categorical variables. Typically analysed using a chi squared analysis.

Causal relationship A relationship between two variables where there is evidence that one of the variables has a direct, causal effect on the other variable.

Causality See 'Causal relationship'.

Central tendency Descriptive statistics that summarise roughly where the middle, or centre, of the dataset is.

Chi square goodness of fit Method for analysing categorical data from one variable.

Chi square test of association Method for analysing categorical data from two variables.

Codes Key features identified within the text of a qualitative dataset.

Cohen's *d* Effect size for *t* tests.

Cohen's f^2 Effect size for regression analyses.

Confidence intervals Range of values within which there is a specified probability that the population parameter will fall between.

Confidentiality Ensuring that data with identifying information is stored securely and can only be accessed by the research team.

Confounding variable An unmeasured variable that may explain some of the variability within a dataset. See also, covariate or control variable.

Construct validity Whether a measure actually measures what it is intended to measure.

Content validity Whether a measure measures all aspects of what it is intended to measure.

Continuous score/variable Variable where a wide range of scores are possible, ranging from smaller through to larger numbers (e.g., age, IQ, reaction time).

Control group Condition within an experimental design who have no treatment or manipulation applied, and are consequently compared to another condition where a treatment or manipulation has been applied.

Control variable Variable that is measured as it may explain variability within the dataset. This variable can potentially be statistically controlled for.

Convergent validity Convergent validity is shown by correlating scores on a measure with a separate one that claims to measure the same thing.

Correlation Relationship between two continuous variables.

GLOSSARY

Correlational design Research design that looks for correlations between variables.

Counterbalancing Technique within experimental design where alternative forms of the measure or manipulation are used in alternate orders.

Co-variable Variable that is measured as it may explain variability within the dataset. This variable can potentially be statistically controlled for.

Covariance Variance within a dataset explained by a control variable or co-variable.

Critical value Value that determines whether a calculated test statistic is deemed statistically significant at various alpha levels.

Cronbach's alpha Statistic used to determine the internal consistency of a measure.

Cross-sectional designs Experimental designs that compare independent groups of people that differ on a particular characteristic, often age.

Crossover effects When a participants performance in one condition influences performance in a different condition. See also 'fatigue effects' and 'practice effects'.

Data Pieces of information collected, as numbers in quantitative research and often text in qualitative research.

Debriefing Process for informing participants about the aims of a research study, after the participant has completed the study.

Deception When a participant in not fully informed about either the purposes of the study or what will be asked of them during the study. See also 'active deception' and 'passive deception'.

Deductive Conducting research by developing a theory, and then testing this through a research study. See also 'inductive'.

Degrees of freedom (df) Values used when looking up the critical values, and therefore the significance, of a statistical analysis.

Demand characteristics Aspects of a research design that may reveal the expected behaviours of participants, and may therefore influence the way that a participant behaves.

Dependent variable Data collected that are expected to differ according to the independent variable.

Descriptive statistics Measures of central tendency and dispersion that describe a quantitative dataset.

Design Strategy for and development of a research project.

Discourse Analysis Qualitative method of analysis that considers both spoken words and other non-word discourse markers (e.g. pauses, intonation)

Discriminant (or divergent) validity Form of validity shown by a lack of correlation between scores on a measure and scores on a measure that claims to measure something different.

Discussion Section of a research report that considers the findings of a study, relates these findings to the existing research, critiques the study and suggests future research directions.

Dispersion Descriptive statistic that shows the spread of data within a variable.

Distribution Frequency of scores that occur within each value possible within a variable, typically plotted in a histogram.

Double blind design Experimental design where neither the participants nor the researchers know which condition the participant has been allocated to.

Ecological validity Whether a research design accurately reflects the real life scenario that it is attempting to understand (e.g., courtroom setting).

Effect sizes Size of an effect, either experimental or correlational, that signifies the strength or magnitude of a finding.

Error variance Variability in a dataset that cannot be explained by differences between conditions (in an experimental design) or by relationships between variables (in a correlational design).

Ethical approval When an independent body reviews an application to conduct a research study to determine whether the design is ethical or not.

Ethical considerations Various aspects of a research design that need to be considered when designing a psychological study to ensure that participants are treated ethically.

Ethical guidelines Recommendations for ethical practice in research, as proposed by the British Psychological Society and the American Psychological Association.

Expected frequency Frequency with which data would be expected to occur by random chance in a chi square analysis.

Experimental design Research design that involves the manipulation of independent variables to compare conditions or groups.

Experimental hypothesis A hypothesis that predicts effects will be found.

Experimental variance Variability in a dataset that can be explained by the differences between conditions or groups.

External validity Whether the findings of the study can be generalised beyond the sample that is being tested.

GLOSSARY

Extraneous variable See confounding variable.

F ratio Test statistic for ANOVA, measuring the ratio between explained variance and random variance.

Factor analysis Method of analysis used to reduce a large number of variables down to a smaller number of variables.

Factorial ANOVA ANOVA where two or more independent variables are manipulated.

Falsifiable The possibility that a theory, hypothesis or prediction could be shown to be false.

Familywise error rate The increase in Type I Error with increasing numbers of analyses conducted on the same dataset.

Fatigue effects When a participant's performance deteriorates over time or across conditions due to tiredness, boredom, etc.

Focus groups Method of data collection in a qualitative study through bringing together a group of people to discuss the research question.

Frequency The number of times a particular score occurs.

Frequency data Variable that records the frequency with which a particular score or category occurs.

Grounded Theory Qualitative method that develops a theory through multiple iterations of data collection.

Heterogeneity of variance When the variability in scores across independent conditions is markedly different.

Hierarchical regression Method of multiple regression where control variables are entered into the model before predictor variables.

Histograms Graph representing frequency data.

Homogeneity of variance When the variability in scores across independent conditions is comparable.

Homoscedasticity Assumption in multiple regression that is related to the homogeneity of variance assumption.

Hypothesis The predicted outcome of a research study.

Independence of observations Assumption that the data provided by each participant should not be influenced by other participants.

Independent measures design Experimental design where independent groups of participants are compared.

Independent measures t test Statistical analysis to look for differences between independent groups of people.

Independent variable A manipulated variable within an experimental design.

Inductive Conducting research by collecting data, and then analysing this to develop a theory. See also 'deducive'.

Inferential statistics Analyses that provide significance statistics.

Informed consent Participants should be made fully aware of the purposes of a study and what they will be asked to do before they participate, and on this basis they may consent to take part.

Interaction effects Effects in experimental designs where differences in one independent variable change across the conditions of another independent variable.

Intercept The point on where the line of best fit goes through (or intercepts) the y-axis.

Internal consistency A form of reliability that aims for all of the items within a measure gaining similar scores, and therefore they are consistent in measuring the same thing.

Internal validity That a study is designed in such a way that no other variables could explain the findings.

Interpretative Phenomenological Analysis A form of qualitative analysis that focuses on the particular experiences of a very specific group of participants.

Inter-rater reliability When multiple people code the same set of data, the scores should be consistent.

Interval data Values that exist on a continuum, with the same distance between each number, where negative values are possible.

Interview Method of data collection for a qualitative study where the researcher typically asks open ended questions for the participant to respond to.

Introduction Section of a research report that reviews the relevant literature, and provides the rationale and hypotheses for the present study.

Kurtosis A measure of distribution that describes how 'peaky' (leptokurtic) or 'flat' (platykurtic) the distribution is.

Leptokurtic distribution A distribution that is particularly 'peaky'.

Levels of measurement Different ways of measuring variables, including nominal, ordinal, interval and ratio data.

Likert scales A method used to measure people's attitudes or opinions on a scale, typically with labels attached to each response (e.g., strongly agree through to strongly disagree) and with a set number of responses, often a five-point scale.

Line of best fit The straight line that is fitted to a scatterplot in a regression analysis that best describes the relationship between the predictor and outcome variables.

GLOSSARY

Linear regression Method of analysis where a predictor variable is used to predict an outcome variable on the basis of the linear relationship between them.

Logistic regression A form of regression where the outcome variable is a binary, categorical variable.

Longitudinal designs A form of experimental design with repeated measures where the same participants are tested multiple times over a long period of time.

Main effect A part of a factorial ANOVA that looks at the effect of an independent variable in isolation.

Manipulation The manipulation of an independent variable in an experimental design involves changing aspects of the variable across different conditions.

Mann-Whitney *U* test A non-parametric analysis that compares scores from two independent groups. The non-parametric equivalent of an independent measures *t* test.

Matching participants A technique used in experimental designs with independent groups of participants to ensure that the two groups are as comparable as possible.

Materials Section of the methods of a research report where the materials and measures used in the study are described.

Mean A descriptive statistic measure of central tendency calculated from all of the raw data.

Mean Squares (MS) An estimate of the variability in a dataset used in an ANOVA.

Median A descriptive statistic measure of central tendency taken from the middle score.

Mediating variable A variable that can explain the relationship between two variables of interest, such as a predictor variable and an outcome variable.

Methods The section of a research report that describes how the study was conducted.

Mixed methods A study that combines both qualitative and quantitative methodologies.

Mode A descriptive statistic measure of central tendency taken from the most frequently occurring score.

Model variance The variability in a dataset that can be explained by the relationship between variables.

Multiple regression A form of regression with multiple predictor variables and one outcome variable.

Naturalistic The aim of qualitative research to understand psychological phenomena in a naturally occurring setting.

Negative correlation/relationship A relationship where scores on one variable increase, while scores on the other variable decrease.

Negative skew A distribution where high scores are overrepresented and there is a tail in the lower scores.

Nominal data Scores in a variable that defines belonging to a particular group or category.

Non-normal distributions Distributions that are not normal, such as where there is skewness or kurtosis.

Non-parametric statistics Statistics that can be used when the parametric assumptions have been violated.

Normal distribution A distribution where the majority of the data falls in the middle of the plot, with smaller numbers of extreme scores that are symmetrically distributed on both sides (i.e., small and large values).

Null hypothesis A prediction of no effect.

Null Hypothesis Significance Testing An approach to data analysis that is focused on testing hypotheses.

Observational studies A methodological approach where data are collected by observing participant's behaviours.

Observed frequencies The raw data collected, or observed, when conducting a categorical study that is analysed using a chi square analysis.

One-tailed hypothesis A prediction that states a specific direction in the findings.

Operationalising A clear definition of a variable that allows you to measure it.

Opportunity sampling A method of recruiting participants on the basis of people being available at the time and place that data collection is occurring.

Ordinal data Data collected where the numbers exist in a particular order, but the distance between each number is variable.

Outcome variable The variable in a regression analysis that you want to predict using the predictor variable.

***p* value** The probability of committing a Type I Error, based on the analysis of a dataset.

Parametric assumptions The four assumptions that must be met in order to run a parametric statistical analysis.

Parametric statistics/tests A method of analysis that can be run on a dataset that meets the parametric assumptions.

Partial correlation A measure of the correlation between two variables, after taking into account the variance explained by a third control variable.

Partial eta squared The effect size for an ANOVA.

Participants The people who take part in a research study.

GLOSSARY

Passive deception Deception of participants within a research study where participants are not fully informed about some aspect of the design.

Pearson's correlation A parametric analysis that measures the linear relationship between two variables.

Peer review When a paper is submitted for publication, it is first reviewed by academics who are experts in that area of research.

Pilot study A small scale version of a study, run to check that the methods are effective.

Placebo group A group of participants within an experimental design who are given a 'treatment' that contains no actual medication.

Planned contrasts Analyses to break down a significant ANOVA main effect when there is a one-tailed hypothesis.

Platykurtic distribution A flat distribution.

Population The entire group of people that your study is intended to reflect.

Positive correlation/relationship A relationship in which scores on one variable increase while scores on the other variable also increase.

Positive skew A distribution where low scores are overrepresented and there is a tail in the higher scores.

Possible/potential harm The ethical principle that all participants should be protected from possible or potential harm, both physical and psychological harm.

Post hoc contrasts Analyses to break down a significant ANOVA main effect when there is a two-tailed hypothesis.

Power analysis An analysis to determine the number of participants required for a particular design.

Practice effects When a participant's performance improves over time or across conditions due to repeatedly completing the measures and learning how to improve their performance.

Predictor variable The variable in a regression analysis that you use to predict the outcome variable.

Primary source A research paper that you have read.

Procedure Section of the methods of a research report where the way that the study is run is described.

Qualitative research/methods/approach A methodological approach that mainly uses words as data.

Quantitative research/methods/approach A methodological approach that uses numbers as data.

Quasi-experimental design A form of experimental design where participants cannot be randomly allocated to conditions.

r value The statistic calculated when calculating a correlation.

R^2 value Statistic that represents the amount of variance in the outcome variable that can be explained by a predictor variable.

Random (within) variance Variability in a dataset that cannot be explained by the manipulation/relationship, but instead reflects measurement error, individual differences, etc.

Random sampling A way of sampling participants using an unbiased and random method, such as selecting random numbers.

Randomisation Allocating participants to a particular condition within an experimental design in a random way.

Randomised control trial An experimental method, often used in clinical research, where participants are randomly allocated to different conditions, usually including one or more treatment conditions and one or more control conditions (e.g., placebo, waiting list).

Range A descriptive statistic measure of dispersion, based on the difference between the smallest and largest number in a dataset.

Ranked scores Ordering raw data from the smallest to the largest, and then allocating new scores to each one, giving 1 to the smallest number and increasing rank scores accordingly.

Ratio level data Values that exist on a continuum, with the same distance between each number, where negative values are not possible.

References Section of a research report where all of the cited sources from the paper are listed, in alphabetical order and in APA format.

Regression analysis Method of analysis where a predictor variable is used to predict an outcome variable on the basis of the linear relationship between them.

Relationship The correlation between two continuous variables.

Reliability That the methods used in a research study produce consistent and repeatable data.

Repeated measures design An experimental design where the same participants repeat the study under multiple conditions.

Repeated t test Statistical analysis to look for differences across different conditions.

Replications The exact repetition of a research study, typically with the aim of finding the same results.

Research question Used within qualitative research to set up the aims of the study.

Residual values Values calculated in a chi squared analysis, based on the difference between the observed and the expected frequencies.

Results Section of a research report that presents the analysis conducted on the data collected, either quantitative or qualitative.

Right to withdraw The ethical principle that participants should be able to withdraw from participating in a research study at any time, and without penalty.

Sample The participants in a study, typically selected to reflect the relevant population of interest.

Sample size The number of participants included in a research study.

Scatterplots Graph used to present correlational data.

Scientific method The method based on devising a theory, developing a hypothesis, collecting data and then analysing it to further develop the theory.

Secondary source A source that summarises the work presented in other sources, such as a text book.

Semi-structured interview A method for collecting qualitative data where some questions are prepared in advance, but there is flexibility to ask further questions to follow up on specific issues that a participant may raise.

Significance The outcome of a statistical analysis when the probability of committing a Type I Error is less than 5%.

Simple linear regression Method of analysis where a single predictor variable is used to predict an outcome variable on the basis of the linear relationship between them.

Skewness A measure of how symmetric a distribution of scores is.

Slope The incline/decline or slant of the line of best fit in a regression analysis.

Spearman's correlation A non-parametric correlation.

Sphericity An assumption of a repeated measures ANOVA that is related to homogeneity of variance.

Split-half reliability A measure of internal consistency that randomly divides the items in a measure into two groups and then compares the groups to see how consistent, or reliable, they are.

Standard deviation A descriptive statistic measure of dispersion, calculated from all of the raw data in a dataset.

Standard normal distribution A symmetric distribution of scores where there is a greater frequency of scores around the centre of a measure with a mean of 0 and SD of 1.

Statistical significance The outcome of a statistical analysis when the probability of committing a Type I Error is less than 5%.

Stepwise regression A method of complex multiple regression where predictor variables are entered into the model in order of significance, and only significant predictors are included.

Stratified sampling A method of sampling that aims to match particular characteristics in the sample that exist in the population.

Subjective That qualitative research is sensitive to the views and interpretation of both the participant and the researcher.

Sums of Squares (SS) An estimate of the variability in a dataset used in an ANOVA.

Systematic sampling Sampling by allocating numbers to each potential participant, and then systematically selecting every Nth person.

***t* statistic** The statistic calculated in a *t* test.

Test statistic The statistic calculated in any analysis, such as the *r* statistic for a correlation, or the *F* statistic for an ANOVA.

Testable An aspect of the scientific method, that any theory must be testable.

Test-retest reliability A measure of reliability where, if the same person completes a measure on two separate occasions, the scores gain will be comparable.

Thematic Analysis A qualitative method that identifies key themes within a dataset.

Themes Recurring issues that are identified in qualitative datasets.

Theory An explanation or model of a particular behaviour or phenomenon.

Two-tailed hypothesis A prediction where no direction is specified.

Type I Error The incorrect rejection of a correct null hypothesis (i.e., a false positive, or claiming to have found something within your sample that does not exist in the population).

Type II Error The failure to reject a false null hypothesis (i.e., a false negative, or claiming to have found nothing within your sample that does exist in the population).

Unstructured interview A method of collecting qualitative data through an interview that does not have prepared and structure questions.

Validity That the methods used in a research study measure the phenomena that they are intended to measure.

Variability The spread of raw data points.

Variable Something that can be defined and measured.

GLOSSARY

Variance A descriptive statistic measure of dispersion, calculated from all of the raw data in a dataset.

Volunteer sampling A method of recruiting participants on the basis of people volunteering to participate in a study, often responding to an advert.

Wilcoxon signed rank test A non-parametric analysis that compares scores from two conditions. The non-parametric equivalent of a repeated measures t test.

Within groups variance Variability in a dataset that cannot be explained by the manipulation/relationship, but instead reflects measurement error, individual differences, etc.

X-axis The horizontal axis on a graph.

Y-axis The vertical axis on a graph.

z scores Standardised scores with a mean of 0 and a standard deviation of 1.

APPENDIX 1
Statistical symbols and conventions

One of the things that can be a little intimidating about statistics is the freaky, apparently meaningless symbols that you see constantly in the descriptions of statistics and equations. Below is a brief list of some of the more frequently used symbols and an explanation of what they mean.

+	Addition
−	Subtraction
*	Multiplication
/	Division
=	Equals
%	Percentage
<	Less than
>	Greater than
≤	Less than or equal to
≥	Greater than or equal to
±	Plus or minus
$\sum$	Sum (or add up)
√	Square root
$\bar{x}$	Mean (see also M)
d	Cohen's d effect size for t test analysis
df	Degrees of freedom
F	F ratio for Analysis of Variance
f^2	Cohen's f^2 effect size for regression analysis
H_0	Null hypothesis (hypothesis of no effect)
H_1	Alternative or experimental hypothesis (hypothesis of effect)
M	Mean (see also $\bar{x}$)
MS	Mean Square
n	Number of participants within a condition
N	The total number of participants in a study
p	Probability or p value
r	Pearson's correlation coefficient
R^2	R squared
r_s	Spearman's correlation coefficient

APPENDIX 1

SD	Standard deviation
SS	Sums of Squares
t	t test value
U	Mann-Whitney U test value
W	Wilcoxon signed rank test value
z	z score
α	Alpha, the probability of making a Type I Error
β	Beta coefficient in regression
η_p^2	Partial eta squared effect size for Analysis of Variance
χ^2	Chi squared

If you go to the online resources, there is also a numeracy skills quiz, covering the various aspects of basic maths that you need to do these introductory psychological statistics. Try doing the quiz online and your scores on the different elements should help you to build a personalised profile of your skills. This will identify your strengths and the areas of maths that you might like to revise before working on the statistical calculations in this book.

APPENDIX 2

Area under the normal curve (z scores)

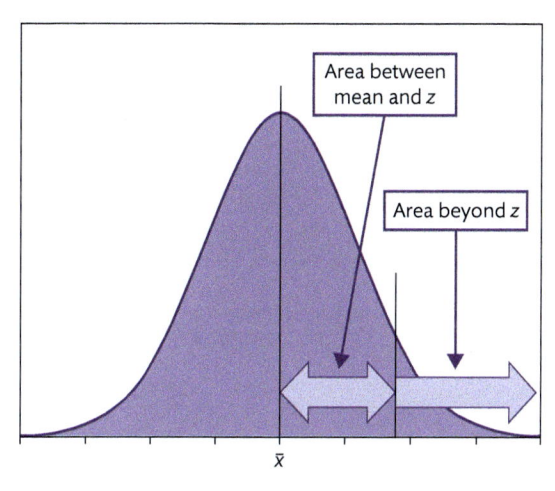

Fig AII.1: A normal distribution curve showing the area that represents scores that fall between the mean and the z score of interest, and the area that represents scores that are greater than the z score of interest.

Note: When looking up negative z scores, just treat them as a positive z score. As the curve is symmetric the values will be the same above and below the mean.

z	Area between $\bar{x}$ and z	Area beyond z	z	Area between $\bar{x}$ and z	Area beyond z
0.00	0.0000	0.5000	0.14	0.0557	0.4443
0.01	0.0040	0.4960	0.15	0.0596	0.4404
0.02	0.0080	0.4920	0.16	0.0636	0.4364
0.03	0.0120	0.4880	0.17	0.0675	0.4325
0.04	0.0160	0.4840	0.18	0.0714	0.4286
0.05	0.0199	0.4801	0.19	0.0753	0.4247
0.06	0.0239	0.4761	0.20	0.0793	0.4207
0.07	0.0279	0.4721	0.21	0.0832	0.4168
0.08	0.0319	0.4681	0.22	0.0871	0.4129
0.09	0.0359	0.4641	0.23	0.0910	0.4090
0.10	0.0398	0.4602	0.24	0.0948	0.4052
0.11	0.0438	0.4562	0.25	0.0987	0.4013
0.12	0.0478	0.4522	0.26	0.1026	0.3974
0.13	0.0517	0.4483	0.27	0.1064	0.3936

APPENDIX 2

z	Area between $\bar{x}$ and z	Area beyond z	z	Area between $\bar{x}$ and z	Area beyond z
0.28	0.1103	0.3897	0.66	0.2454	0.2546
0.29	0.1141	0.3859	0.67	0.2486	0.2514
0.30	0.1179	0.3821	0.68	0.2517	0.2483
0.31	0.1217	0.3783	0.69	0.2549	0.2451
0.32	0.1255	0.3745	0.70	0.2580	0.2420
0.33	0.1293	0.3707	0.71	0.2611	0.2389
0.34	0.1331	0.3669	0.72	0.2642	0.2358
0.35	0.1368	0.3632	0.73	0.2673	0.2327
0.36	0.1406	0.3594	0.74	0.2704	0.2296
0.37	0.1443	0.3557	0.75	0.2734	0.2266
0.38	0.1480	0.3520	0.76	0.2764	0.2236
0.39	0.1517	0.3483	0.77	0.2794	0.2206
0.40	0.1554	0.3446	0.78	0.2823	0.2177
0.41	0.1591	0.3409	0.79	0.2852	0.2148
0.42	0.1628	0.3372	0.80	0.2881	0.2119
0.43	0.1664	0.3336	0.81	0.2910	0.2090
0.44	0.1700	0.3300	0.82	0.2939	0.2061
0.45	0.1736	0.3264	0.83	0.2967	0.2033
0.46	0.1772	0.3228	0.84	0.2995	0.2005
0.47	0.1808	0.3192	0.85	0.3023	0.1977
0.48	0.1844	0.3156	0.86	0.3051	0.1949
0.49	0.1879	0.3121	0.87	0.3078	0.1922
0.50	0.1915	0.3085	0.88	0.3106	0.1894
0.51	0.1950	0.3050	0.89	0.3133	0.1867
0.52	0.1985	0.3015	0.90	0.3159	0.1841
0.53	0.2019	0.2981	0.91	0.3186	0.1814
0.54	0.2054	0.2946	0.92	0.3212	0.1788
0.55	0.2088	0.2912	0.93	0.3238	0.1762
0.56	0.2123	0.2877	0.94	0.3264	0.1736
0.57	0.2157	0.2843	0.95	0.3289	0.1711
0.58	0.2190	0.2810	0.96	0.3315	0.1685
0.59	0.2224	0.2776	0.97	0.3340	0.1660
0.60	0.2257	0.2743	0.98	0.3365	0.1635
0.61	0.2291	0.2709	0.99	0.3389	0.1611
0.62	0.2324	0.2676	1.00	0.3413	0.1587
0.63	0.2357	0.2643	1.01	0.3438	0.1562
0.64	0.2389	0.2611	1.02	0.3461	0.1539
0.65	0.2422	0.2578	1.03	0.3485	0.1515

z	Area between $\bar{x}$ and z	Area beyond z	z	Area between $\bar{x}$ and z	Area beyond z
1.04	0.3508	0.1492	1.42	0.4222	0.0778
1.05	0.3531	0.1469	1.43	0.4236	0.0764
1.06	0.3554	0.1446	1.44	0.4251	0.0749
1.07	0.3577	0.1423	1.45	0.4265	0.0735
1.08	0.3599	0.1401	1.46	0.4279	0.0721
1.09	0.3621	0.1379	1.47	0.4292	0.0708
1.10	0.3643	0.1357	1.48	0.4306	0.0694
1.11	0.3665	0.1335	1.49	0.4319	0.0681
1.12	0.3686	0.1314	1.50	0.4332	0.0668
1.13	0.3708	0.1292	1.51	0.4345	0.0655
1.14	0.3729	0.1271	1.52	0.4357	0.0643
1.15	0.3749	0.1251	1.53	0.4370	0.0630
1.16	0.3770	0.1230	1.54	0.4382	0.0618
1.17	0.3790	0.1210	1.55	0.4394	0.0606
1.18	0.3810	0.1190	1.56	0.4406	0.0594
1.19	0.3830	0.1170	1.57	0.4418	0.0582
1.20	0.3849	0.1151	1.58	0.4429	0.0571
1.21	0.3869	0.1131	1.59	0.4441	0.0559
1.22	0.3888	0.1112	1.60	0.4452	0.0548
1.23	0.3907	0.1093	1.61	0.4463	0.0537
1.24	0.3925	0.1075	1.62	0.4474	0.0526
1.25	0.3944	0.1056	1.63	0.4484	0.0516
1.26	0.3962	0.1038	1.64	0.4495	0.0505
1.27	0.3980	0.1020	1.65	0.4505	0.0495
1.28	0.3997	0.1003	1.66	0.4515	0.0485
1.29	0.4015	0.0985	1.67	0.4525	0.0475
1.30	0.4032	0.0968	1.68	0.4535	0.0465
1.31	0.4049	0.0951	1.69	0.4545	0.0455
1.32	0.4066	0.0934	1.70	0.4554	0.0446
1.33	0.4082	0.0918	1.71	0.4564	0.0436
1.34	0.4099	0.0901	1.72	0.4573	0.0427
1.35	0.4115	0.0885	1.73	0.4582	0.0418
1.36	0.4131	0.0869	1.74	0.4591	0.0409
1.37	0.4147	0.0853	1.75	0.4599	0.0401
1.38	0.4162	0.0838	1.76	0.4608	0.0392
1.39	0.4177	0.0823	1.77	0.4616	0.0384
1.40	0.4192	0.0808	1.78	0.4625	0.0375
1.41	0.4207	0.0793	1.79	0.4633	0.0367

z	Area between $\bar{x}$ and z	Area beyond z	z	Area between $\bar{x}$ and z	Area beyond z
1.80	0.4641	0.0359	2.18	0.4854	0.0146
1.81	0.4649	0.0351	2.19	0.4857	0.0143
1.82	0.4656	0.0344	2.20	0.4861	0.0139
1.83	0.4664	0.0336	2.21	0.4864	0.0136
1.84	0.4671	0.0329	2.22	0.4868	0.0132
1.85	0.4678	0.0322	2.23	0.4871	0.0129
1.86	0.4686	0.0314	2.24	0.4875	0.0125
1.87	0.4693	0.0307	2.25	0.4878	0.0122
1.88	0.4699	0.0301	2.26	0.4881	0.0119
1.89	0.4706	0.0294	2.27	0.4884	0.0116
1.90	0.4713	0.0287	2.28	0.4887	0.0113
1.91	0.4719	0.0281	2.29	0.4890	0.0110
1.92	0.4726	0.0274	2.30	0.4893	0.0107
1.93	0.4732	0.0268	2.31	0.4896	0.0104
1.94	0.4738	0.0262	2.32	0.4898	0.0102
1.95	0.4744	0.0256	2.33	0.4901	0.0099
1.96	0.4750	0.0250	2.34	0.4904	0.0096
1.97	0.4756	0.0244	2.35	0.4906	0.0094
1.98	0.4761	0.0239	2.36	0.4909	0.0091
1.99	0.4767	0.0233	2.37	0.4911	0.0089
2.00	0.4772	0.0228	2.38	0.4913	0.0087
2.01	0.4778	0.0222	2.39	0.4916	0.0084
2.02	0.4783	0.0217	2.40	0.4918	0.0082
2.03	0.4788	0.0212	2.41	0.4920	0.0080
2.04	0.4793	0.0207	2.42	0.4922	0.0078
2.05	0.4798	0.0202	2.43	0.4925	0.0075
2.06	0.4803	0.0197	2.44	0.4927	0.0073
2.07	0.4808	0.0192	2.45	0.4929	0.0071
2.08	0.4812	0.0188	2.46	0.4931	0.0069
2.09	0.4817	0.0183	2.47	0.4932	0.0068
2.10	0.4821	0.0179	2.48	0.4934	0.0066
2.11	0.4826	0.0174	2.49	0.4936	0.0064
2.12	0.4830	0.0170	2.50	0.4938	0.0062
2.13	0.4834	0.0166	2.51	0.4940	0.0060
2.14	0.4838	0.0162	2.52	0.4941	0.0059
2.15	0.4842	0.0158	2.53	0.4943	0.0057
2.16	0.4846	0.0154	2.54	0.4945	0.0055
2.17	0.4850	0.0150	2.55	0.4946	0.0054

z	Area between $\bar{x}$ and z	Area beyond z	z	Area between $\bar{x}$ and z	Area beyond z
2.56	0.4948	0.0052	2.94	0.4984	0.0016
2.57	0.4949	0.0051	2.95	0.4984	0.0016
2.58	0.4951	0.0049	2.96	0.4985	0.0015
2.59	0.4952	0.0048	2.97	0.4985	0.0015
2.60	0.4953	0.0047	2.98	0.4986	0.0014
2.61	0.4955	0.0045	2.99	0.4986	0.0014
2.62	0.4956	0.0044	3.00	0.4987	0.0013
2.63	0.4957	0.0043	3.01	0.4987	0.0013
2.64	0.4959	0.0041	3.02	0.4987	0.0013
2.65	0.4960	0.0040	3.03	0.4988	0.0012
2.66	0.4961	0.0039	3.04	0.4988	0.0012
2.67	0.4962	0.0038	3.05	0.4989	0.0011
2.68	0.4963	0.0037	3.06	0.4989	0.0011
2.69	0.4964	0.0036	3.07	0.4989	0.0011
2.70	0.4965	0.0035	3.08	0.4990	0.0010
2.71	0.4966	0.0034	3.09	0.4990	0.0010
2.72	0.4967	0.0033	3.10	0.4990	0.0010
2.73	0.4968	0.0032	3.11	0.4991	0.0009
2.74	0.4969	0.0031	3.12	0.4991	0.0009
2.75	0.4970	0.0030	3.13	0.4991	0.0009
2.76	0.4971	0.0029	3.14	0.4992	0.0008
2.77	0.4972	0.0028	3.15	0.4992	0.0008
2.78	0.4973	0.0027	3.16	0.4992	0.0008
2.79	0.4974	0.0026	3.17	0.4992	0.0008
2.80	0.4974	0.0026	3.18	0.4993	0.0007
2.81	0.4975	0.0025	3.19	0.4993	0.0007
2.82	0.4976	0.0024	3.20	0.4993	0.0007
2.83	0.4977	0.0023	3.21	0.4993	0.0007
2.84	0.4977	0.0023	3.22	0.4994	0.0006
2.85	0.4978	0.0022	3.23	0.4994	0.0006
2.86	0.4979	0.0021	3.24	0.4994	0.0006
2.87	0.4979	0.0021	3.25	0.4994	0.0006
2.88	0.4980	0.0020	3.26	0.4994	0.0006
2.89	0.4981	0.0019	3.27	0.4995	0.0005
2.90	0.4981	0.0019	3.28	0.4995	0.0005
2.91	0.4982	0.0018	3.29	0.4995	0.0005
2.92	0.4982	0.0018	3.30	0.4995	0.0005
2.93	0.4983	0.0017	3.31	0.4995	0.0005

APPENDIX 2

z	Area between $\bar{x}$ and z	Area beyond z	z	Area between $\bar{x}$ and z	Area beyond z
3.32	0.4995	0.0005	3.35	0.4996	0.0004
3.33	0.4996	0.0004	3.36	0.4996	0.0004
3.34	0.4996	0.0004	3.37	0.4996	0.0004
3.35	0.4996	0.0004	3.38	0.4996	0.0004
3.36	0.4996	0.0004	3.39	0.4997	0.0003
3.37	0.4996	0.0004	3.40	0.4997	0.0003
3.38	0.4996	0.0004	3.41	0.4997	0.0003
3.39	0.4997	0.0003	3.42	0.4997	0.0003
3.40	0.4997	0.0003	3.43	0.4997	0.0003
3.41	0.4997	0.0003	3.44	0.4997	0.0003
3.42	0.4997	0.0003	3.45	0.4997	0.0003
3.43	0.4997	0.0003	3.46	0.4997	0.0003
3.44	0.4997	0.0003	3.47	0.4997	0.0003
3.45	0.4997	0.0003	3.48	0.4997	0.0003
3.46	0.4997	0.0003	3.49	0.4998	0.0002
3.47	0.4997	0.0003	3.50	0.4998	0.0002
3.48	0.4997	0.0003	3.44	0.4997	0.0003
3.49	0.4998	0.0002	3.45	0.4997	0.0003
3.50	0.4998	0.0002	3.46	0.4997	0.0003
3.34	0.4996	0.0004			

APPENDIX 3
Critical values tables

Table A3.1 Critical values tables for the *t* statistic (independent and repeated designs)

df	Level of significance of a one-tailed test						
	α = .100	α = .050	α = .025	α = .010	α = .005	α = .001	α = .0005
	Level of significance of a two-tailed test						
	α = .200	α = .100	α = .050	α = .020	α = .010	α = .002	α = .001
1	3.078	6.314	12.71	31.82	63.66	318.31	636.62
2	1.886	2.920	4.303	6.965	9.925	22.327	31.599
3	1.638	2.353	3.182	4.541	5.841	10.215	12.924
4	1.533	2.132	2.776	3.747	4.604	7.173	8.610
5	1.476	2.015	2.571	3.365	4.032	5.893	6.869
6	1.440	1.943	2.447	3.143	3.707	5.208	5.959
7	1.415	1.895	2.365	2.998	3.499	4.785	5.408
8	1.397	1.860	2.306	2.896	3.355	4.501	5.041
9	1.383	1.833	2.262	2.821	3.250	4.297	4.781
10	1.372	1.812	2.228	2.764	3.169	4.144	4.587
11	1.363	1.796	2.201	2.718	3.106	4.025	4.437
12	1.356	1.782	2.179	2.681	3.055	3.930	4.318
13	1.350	1.771	2.160	2.650	3.012	3.852	4.221
14	1.345	1.761	2.145	2.624	2.977	3.787	4.140
15	1.341	1.753	2.131	2.602	2.947	3.733	4.073
16	1.337	1.746	2.120	2.583	2.921	3.686	4.015
17	1.333	1.740	2.110	2.567	2.898	3.646	3.965
18	1.330	1.734	2.101	2.552	2.878	3.610	3.922
19	1.328	1.729	2.093	2.539	2.861	3.579	3.883
20	1.325	1.725	2.086	2.528	2.845	3.552	3.850
21	1.323	1.721	2.080	2.518	2.831	3.527	3.819
22	1.321	1.717	2.074	2.508	2.819	3.505	3.792
23	1.319	1.714	2.069	2.500	2.807	3.485	3.768
24	1.318	1.711	2.064	2.492	2.797	3.467	3.745
25	1.316	1.708	2.060	2.485	2.787	3.450	3.725
26	1.315	1.706	2.056	2.479	2.779	3.435	3.707
27	1.314	1.703	2.052	2.473	2.771	3.421	3.690
28	1.313	1.701	2.048	2.467	2.763	3.408	3.674
29	1.311	1.699	2.045	2.462	2.756	3.396	3.659
30	1.310	1.697	2.042	2.457	2.750	3.385	3.646
40	1.303	1.684	2.021	2.423	2.704	3.307	3.551
60	1.296	1.671	2.000	2.390	2.660	3.232	3.460
80	1.292	1.664	1.990	2.374	2.639	3.195	3.416
100	1.290	1.660	1.984	2.364	2.626	3.174	3.390

Note: If the df for your design is not included in the table, use the next smaller df that is shown on the table e.g. if you have 72 df, you would use the df below that value on the table, so 60 df.

APPENDIX 3

Table A3.2a: Critical values for the F statistic Critical F values for $\alpha = .050$

df_{error}	$df_{between}$									
	1	2	3	4	5	6	7	8	9	10
3	10.13	9.55	9.28	9.12	9.01	8.94	8.89	8.85	8.81	8.79
4	7.71	6.94	6.59	6.39	6.26	6.16	6.09	6.04	6.00	5.96
5	6.61	5.79	5.41	5.19	5.05	4.95	4.88	4.82	4.77	4.74
6	5.99	5.14	4.76	4.53	4.39	4.28	4.21	4.15	4.10	4.06
7	5.59	4.74	4.35	4.12	3.97	3.87	3.79	3.73	3.68	3.64
8	5.32	4.46	4.07	3.84	3.69	3.58	3.50	3.44	3.39	3.35
9	5.12	4.26	3.86	3.63	3.48	3.37	3.29	3.23	3.18	3.14
10	4.96	4.10	3.71	3.48	3.33	3.22	3.14	3.07	3.02	2.98
11	4.84	3.98	3.59	3.36	3.20	3.09	3.01	2.95	2.90	2.85
12	4.75	3.89	3.49	3.26	3.11	3.00	2.91	2.85	2.80	2.75
13	4.67	3.81	3.41	3.18	3.03	2.92	2.83	2.77	2.71	2.67
14	4.60	3.74	3.34	3.11	2.96	2.85	2.76	2.70	2.65	2.60
15	4.54	3.68	3.29	3.06	2.90	2.79	2.71	2.64	2.59	2.54
16	4.49	3.63	3.24	3.01	2.85	2.74	2.66	2.59	2.54	2.49
17	4.45	3.59	3.20	2.96	2.81	2.70	2.61	2.55	2.49	2.45
18	4.41	3.55	3.16	2.93	2.77	2.66	2.58	2.51	2.46	2.41
19	4.38	3.52	3.13	2.90	2.74	2.63	2.54	2.48	2.42	2.38
20	4.35	3.49	3.10	2.87	2.71	2.60	2.51	2.45	2.39	2.35
22	4.30	3.44	3.05	2.82	2.66	2.55	2.46	2.40	2.34	2.30
24	4.26	3.40	3.01	2.78	2.62	2.51	2.42	2.36	2.30	2.25
26	4.23	3.37	2.98	2.74	2.59	2.47	2.39	2.32	2.27	2.22
28	4.20	3.34	2.95	2.71	2.56	2.45	2.36	2.29	2.24	2.19
30	4.17	3.32	2.92	2.69	2.53	2.42	2.33	2.27	2.21	2.16
35	4.12	3.27	2.87	2.64	2.49	2.37	2.29	2.22	2.16	2.11
40	4.08	3.23	2.84	2.61	2.45	2.34	2.25	2.18	2.12	2.08
45	4.06	3.20	2.81	2.58	2.42	2.31	2.22	2.15	2.10	2.05
50	4.03	3.18	2.79	2.56	2.40	2.29	2.20	2.13	2.07	2.03
60	4.00	3.15	2.76	2.53	2.37	2.25	2.17	2.10	2.04	1.99
70	3.98	3.13	2.74	2.50	2.35	2.23	2.14	2.07	2.02	1.97
80	3.96	3.11	2.72	2.49	2.33	2.21	2.13	2.06	2.00	1.95
100	3.94	3.09	2.70	2.46	2.31	2.19	2.10	2.03	1.97	1.93
200	3.89	3.04	2.65	2.42	2.26	2.14	2.06	1.98	1.93	1.88
500	3.86	3.01	2.62	2.39	2.23	2.12	2.03	1.96	1.90	1.85

Note: If the df for your design is not included in the table, use the next smaller df that is shown on the table e.g. if you have 72 df, you would use the df below that value on the table, so 70 df.

Table A3.2b: Critical values for the F statistic Critical F values for $\alpha = .010$

df_{error}	1	2	3	4	5	6	7	8	9	10
3	34.12	30.82	29.46	28.71	28.24	27.91	27.67	27.49	27.35	27.23
4	21.20	18.00	16.69	15.98	15.52	15.21	14.98	14.80	14.66	14.55
5	16.26	13.27	12.06	11.39	10.97	10.67	10.46	10.29	10.16	10.05
6	13.75	10.92	9.78	9.15	8.75	8.47	8.26	8.10	7.98	7.87
7	12.25	9.55	8.45	7.85	7.46	7.19	6.99	6.84	6.72	6.62
8	11.26	8.65	7.59	7.01	6.63	6.37	6.18	6.03	5.91	5.81
9	10.56	8.02	6.99	6.42	6.06	5.80	5.61	5.47	5.35	5.26
10	10.04	7.56	6.55	5.99	5.64	5.39	5.20	5.06	4.94	4.85
11	9.65	7.21	6.22	5.67	5.32	5.07	4.89	4.74	4.63	4.54
12	9.33	6.93	5.95	5.41	5.06	4.82	4.64	4.50	4.39	4.30
13	9.07	6.70	5.74	5.21	4.86	4.62	4.44	4.30	4.19	4.10
14	8.86	6.51	5.56	5.04	4.70	4.46	4.28	4.14	4.03	3.94
15	8.68	6.36	5.42	4.89	4.56	4.32	4.14	4.00	3.89	3.80
16	8.53	6.23	5.29	4.77	4.44	4.20	4.03	3.89	3.78	3.69
17	8.40	6.11	5.19	4.67	4.34	4.10	3.93	3.79	3.68	3.59
18	8.29	6.01	5.09	4.58	4.25	4.01	3.84	3.71	3.60	3.51
19	8.19	5.93	5.01	4.50	4.17	3.94	3.77	3.63	3.52	3.43
20	8.10	5.85	4.94	4.43	4.10	3.87	3.70	3.56	3.46	3.37
22	7.95	5.72	4.82	4.31	3.99	3.76	3.59	3.45	3.35	3.26
24	7.82	5.61	4.72	4.22	3.90	3.67	3.50	3.36	3.26	3.17
26	7.72	5.53	4.64	4.14	3.82	3.59	3.42	3.29	3.18	3.09
28	7.64	5.45	4.57	4.07	3.75	3.53	3.36	3.23	3.12	3.03
30	7.56	5.39	4.51	4.02	3.70	3.47	3.30	3.17	3.07	2.98
35	7.42	5.27	4.40	3.91	3.59	3.37	3.20	3.07	2.96	2.88
40	7.31	5.18	4.31	3.83	3.51	3.29	3.12	2.99	2.89	2.80
45	7.23	5.11	4.25	3.77	3.45	3.23	3.07	2.94	2.83	2.74
50	7.17	5.06	4.20	3.72	3.41	3.19	3.02	2.89	2.79	2.70
60	7.08	4.98	4.13	3.65	3.34	3.12	2.95	2.82	2.72	2.63
70	7.01	4.92	4.07	3.60	3.29	3.07	2.91	2.78	2.67	2.59
80	6.96	4.88	4.04	3.56	3.26	3.04	2.87	2.74	2.64	2.55
100	6.90	4.82	3.98	3.51	3.21	2.99	2.82	2.69	2.59	2.50
200	6.76	4.71	3.88	3.41	3.11	2.89	2.73	2.60	2.50	2.41
500	6.69	4.65	3.82	3.36	3.05	2.84	2.68	2.55	2.44	2.36

Column header: $df_{between}$

Note: If the df for your design is not included in the table, use the next smaller df that is shown on the table e.g. if you have 72 df, you would use the df below that value on the table, so 70 df.

APPENDIX 3

Table A3.2c: Critical values for the F statistic Critical F values for $\alpha = .001$

df_{error}	$df_{between}$									
	1	2	3	4	5	6	7	8	9	10
3	167.03	148.50	141.11	137.10	134.58	132.85	131.59	130.62	129.86	129.25
4	74.14	61.25	56.18	53.44	51.71	50.53	49.66	49.00	48.48	48.05
5	47.18	37.12	33.20	31.09	29.75	28.84	28.16	27.65	27.25	26.92
6	35.51	27.00	23.70	21.92	20.80	20.03	19.46	19.03	18.69	18.41
7	29.25	21.69	18.77	17.20	16.21	15.52	15.02	14.63	14.33	14.08
8	25.42	18.49	15.83	14.39	13.49	12.86	12.40	12.05	11.77	11.54
9	22.86	16.39	13.90	12.56	11.71	11.13	10.70	10.37	10.11	9.89
10	21.04	14.91	12.55	11.28	10.48	9.93	9.52	9.20	8.96	8.75
11	19.69	13.81	11.56	10.35	9.58	9.05	8.66	8.36	8.12	7.92
12	18.64	12.97	10.80	9.63	8.89	8.38	8.00	7.71	7.48	7.29
13	17.82	12.31	10.21	9.07	8.35	7.86	7.49	7.21	6.98	6.80
14	17.14	11.78	9.73	8.62	7.92	7.44	7.08	6.80	6.58	6.40
15	16.59	11.34	9.34	8.25	7.57	7.09	6.74	6.47	6.26	6.08
16	16.12	10.97	9.01	7.94	7.27	6.81	6.46	6.20	5.98	5.81
17	15.72	10.66	8.73	7.68	7.02	6.56	6.22	5.96	5.75	5.58
18	15.38	10.39	8.49	7.46	6.81	6.36	6.02	5.76	5.56	5.39
19	15.08	10.16	8.28	7.27	6.62	6.18	5.85	5.59	5.39	5.22
20	14.82	9.95	8.10	7.10	6.46	6.02	5.69	5.44	5.24	5.08
22	14.38	9.61	7.80	6.81	6.19	5.76	5.44	5.19	4.99	4.83
24	14.03	9.34	7.55	6.59	5.98	5.55	5.24	4.99	4.80	4.64
26	13.74	9.12	7.36	6.41	5.80	5.38	5.07	4.83	4.64	4.48
28	13.50	8.93	7.19	6.25	5.66	5.24	4.93	4.70	4.51	4.35
30	13.29	8.77	7.05	6.13	5.53	5.12	4.82	4.58	4.39	4.24
35	12.90	8.47	6.79	5.88	5.30	4.89	4.60	4.36	4.18	4.03
40	12.61	8.25	6.60	5.70	5.13	4.73	4.44	4.21	4.02	3.87
45	12.39	8.09	6.45	5.56	5.00	4.61	4.32	4.09	3.91	3.76
50	12.22	7.96	6.34	5.46	4.90	4.51	4.22	4.00	3.82	3.67
60	11.97	7.77	6.17	5.31	4.76	4.37	4.09	3.87	3.69	3.54
70	11.80	7.64	6.06	5.20	4.66	4.28	3.99	3.77	3.60	3.45
80	11.67	7.54	5.97	5.12	4.58	4.20	3.92	3.71	3.53	3.39
100	11.50	7.41	5.86	5.02	4.48	4.11	3.83	3.61	3.44	3.30
200	11.16	7.15	5.63	4.81	4.29	3.92	3.65	3.43	3.26	3.12
500	10.96	7.00	5.51	4.69	4.18	3.81	3.54	3.33	3.16	3.02

Note: If the df for your design is not included in the table, use the next smaller df that is shown on the table e.g. if you have 72 df, you would use the df below that value on the table, so 70 df.

Table A3.3: Critical values for the *r* statistic

	Level of significance of a one-tailed test					
	α = .100	α = .050	α = .025	α = .010	α = .005	α = .0005
	Level of significance of a two-tailed test					
df	α = .200	α = .100	α = .050	α = .020	α = .010	α = .001
1	.9511	.9877	.9969	.9995	.9999	.9999
2	.8000	.9000	.9500	.9800	.9900	.9990
3	.6870	.8054	.8783	.9343	.9587	.9911
4	.6084	.7293	.8114	.8822	.9172	.9741
5	.5509	.6694	.7545	.8329	.8745	.9509
6	.5067	.6215	.7067	.7887	.8343	.9249
7	.4716	.5822	.6664	.7498	.7977	.8983
8	.4428	.5494	.6319	.7155	.7646	.8721
9	.4187	.5214	.6021	.6851	.7348	.8470
10	.3981	.4973	.5760	.6581	.7079	.8233
11	.3802	.4762	.5529	.6339	.6835	.8010
12	.3646	.4575	.5324	.6120	.6614	.7800
13	.3507	.4409	.5140	.5923	.6411	.7604
14	.3383	.4259	.4973	.5742	.6226	.7419
15	.3271	.4124	.4821	.5577	.6055	.7247
16	.3170	.4000	.4683	.5425	.5897	.7084
17	.3077	.3887	.4555	.5285	.5751	.6932
18	.2992	.3783	.4438	.5155	.5614	.6788
19	.2914	.3687	.4329	.5034	.5487	.6652
20	.2841	.3598	.4227	.4921	.5368	.6524
21	.2774	.3515	.4132	.4815	.5256	.6402
22	.2711	.3438	.4044	.4716	.5151	.6287
23	.2653	.3365	.3961	.4622	.5052	.6178
24	.2598	.3297	.3882	.4534	.4958	.6074
25	.2546	.3233	.3809	.4451	.4869	.5974
30	.2327	.2960	.3494	.4093	.4487	.5541
35	.2156	.2746	.3246	.3810	.4182	.5189
40	.2018	.2573	.3044	.3578	.3932	.4896
50	.1806	.2306	.2732	.3218	.3542	.4432
60	.1650	.2108	.2500	.2948	.3248	.4079
70	.1528	.1954	.2319	.2737	.3017	.3798
80	.1430	.1829	.2172	.2565	.2830	.3568
90	.1348	.1726	.2050	.2422	.2673	.3375
100	.1279	.1638	.1946	.2301	.2540	.3211
150	.1045	.1339	.1593	.1886	.2084	.2643
300	.0740	.0948	.1129	.1338	.1480	.1884
500	.0573	.0735	.0875	.1038	.1149	.1464

Note: If the df for your design is not included in the table, use the next smaller df that is shown on the table e.g. if you have 72 df, you would use the df below that value on the table, so 70 df.

APPENDIX 3

Table A3.4: Critical values for the χ^2 statistic

df	$\alpha = .050$	$\alpha = .025$	$\alpha = .010$	$\alpha = .005$	$\alpha = .001$
1	3.841	5.024	6.635	7.879	10.828
2	5.991	7.378	9.210	10.597	13.816
3	7.815	9.348	11.345	12.838	16.266
4	9.488	11.143	13.277	14.860	18.467
5	11.070	12.833	15.086	16.750	20.515
6	12.592	14.449	16.812	18.548	22.458
7	14.067	16.013	18.475	20.278	24.322
8	15.507	17.535	20.090	21.955	26.124
9	16.919	19.023	21.666	23.589	27.877
10	18.307	20.483	23.209	25.188	29.588
11	19.675	21.920	24.725	26.757	31.264
12	21.026	23.337	26.217	28.300	32.909
13	22.362	24.736	27.688	29.819	34.528
14	23.685	26.119	29.141	31.319	36.123
15	24.996	27.488	30.578	32.801	37.697
16	26.296	28.845	32.000	34.267	39.252
17	27.587	30.191	33.409	35.718	40.790
18	28.869	31.526	34.805	37.156	42.312
19	30.144	32.852	36.191	38.582	43.820
20	31.410	34.170	37.566	39.997	45.315
30	43.773	46.979	50.892	53.672	59.703
40	55.758	59.342	63.691	66.766	73.402
50	67.505	71.420	76.154	79.490	86.661
100	124.342	129.561	135.807	140.169	149.449

Note: If the df for your design is not included in the table, use the next smaller df that is shown on the table e.g. if you have 72 df, you would use the df below that value on the table, so 50 df.

APPENDIX 3

Table A3.5a: Critical values for the U statistic critical values for U with $\alpha = .100$ with a two-tailed hypothesis, or $\alpha = .050$ with a one-tailed hypothesis.

									n_2 (number of participants in larger group)										
	2	3	4	5	6	7	8	9	10	11	12	13	14	15	16	17	18	19	20
2	–	–	–	–	–	–	–	–	–	–	–	–	–	–	–	–	–	–	–
3	–	0	0	1	2	2	3	4	4	5	5	6	7	7	8	9	9	10	11
4	–	0	1	2	3	4	5	6	7	8	9	10	11	12	14	15	16	17	18
5	–	1	2	4	5	6	8	9	11	12	13	15	16	18	19	20	22	23	25
6	–	2	3	5	7	8	10	12	14	16	17	19	21	23	25	26	28	30	32
7	–	2	4	6	8	11	13	15	17	19	21	24	26	28	30	33	35	37	39
8	–	3	5	8	10	13	15	18	20	23	26	28	31	33	36	39	41	44	47
9	–	4	6	9	12	15	18	21	24	27	30	33	36	39	42	45	48	51	54
10	–	4	7	11	14	17	20	24	27	31	34	37	41	44	48	51	55	58	62
11	–	5	8	12	16	19	23	27	31	34	38	42	46	50	54	57	61	65	69
12	–	5	9	13	17	21	26	30	34	38	42	47	51	55	60	64	68	72	77
13	–	6	10	15	19	24	28	33	37	42	47	51	56	61	65	70	75	80	84
14	–	7	11	16	21	26	31	36	41	46	51	56	61	66	71	77	82	87	92
15	–	7	12	18	23	28	33	39	44	50	55	61	66	72	77	83	88	94	100
16	–	8	14	19	25	30	36	42	48	54	60	65	71	77	83	89	95	101	107
17	–	9	15	20	26	33	39	45	51	57	64	70	77	83	89	96	102	109	115
18	–	9	16	22	28	35	41	48	55	61	68	75	82	88	95	102	109	116	123
19	–	10	17	23	30	37	44	51	58	65	72	80	87	94	101	109	116	123	130
20	–	11	18	25	32	39	47	54	62	69	77	84	92	100	107	115	123	130	138

n_1 (number of participants in smaller group)

APPENDIX 3

Table A3.5b: Critical values for the U statistic critical values for U with $\alpha = .050$ with a two-tailed hypothesis, or $\alpha = .025$ with a one-tailed hypothesis.

										n_2 (number of participants in larger group)									
	2	3	4	5	6	7	8	9	10	11	12	13	14	15	16	17	18	19	20
n_1 (number of participants in smaller group) 2	–	–	–	–	–	–	0	0	0	0	1	1	1	1	1	2	2	2	2
3	–	–	–	0	1	1	2	2	3	3	4	4	5	5	6	6	7	7	8
4	–	–	0	1	2	3	4	4	5	6	7	8	9	10	11	11	12	13	14
5	–	0	1	2	3	5	6	7	8	9	11	12	13	14	15	17	18	19	20
6	–	1	2	3	5	6	8	10	11	13	14	16	17	19	21	22	24	25	27
7	–	1	3	5	6	8	10	12	14	16	18	20	22	24	26	28	30	32	34
8	0	2	4	6	7	10	13	15	17	19	22	24	26	29	31	34	36	38	41
9	0	2	4	7	10	12	15	17	20	23	26	28	31	34	37	39	42	45	48
10	0	3	5	8	11	14	17	20	23	26	29	33	36	39	42	45	48	52	55
11	0	3	6	9	13	16	19	23	26	30	33	37	40	44	47	51	55	58	62
12	1	4	7	11	14	18	22	26	29	33	37	41	45	49	53	57	61	65	69
13	1	4	8	12	16	20	24	28	33	37	41	45	50	54	59	63	67	72	76
14	1	5	9	13	17	22	26	31	36	40	45	50	55	59	64	67	74	78	83
15	1	5	10	14	19	24	29	34	39	44	49	54	59	64	70	75	80	85	90
16	1	6	11	15	21	26	31	37	42	47	53	59	64	70	75	81	86	92	98
17	2	6	11	17	22	28	34	39	45	51	57	63	67	75	81	87	93	99	105
18	2	7	12	18	24	30	36	42	48	55	61	67	74	80	86	93	99	106	112
19	2	7	13	19	25	32	38	45	52	58	65	72	78	85	92	99	106	113	119
20	2	8	13	20	27	34	41	48	55	62	69	76	83	90	98	105	112	119	127

Table A3.6: Critical values for the W statistic

	Level of significance of a one-tailed test				
	$\alpha = .050$	$\alpha = .025$	$\alpha = .010$	$\alpha = .005$	$\alpha = .001$
	Level of significance of a two-tailed test				
N	$\alpha = .100$	$\alpha = .050$	$\alpha = .020$	$\alpha = .010$	$\alpha = .002$
4	-	-	-	-	-
5	0	-	-	-	-
6	2	0	-	-	-
7	3	2	0	-	-
8	5	3	1	0	-
9	8	5	3	1	-
10	10	8	5	3	0
11	13	10	7	5	1
12	17	14	10	7	2
13	21	17	12	9	4
14	25	21	15	12	6
15	30	25	19	16	8
16	35	29	23	19	11
17	41	35	28	23	14
18	47	40	32	27	18
19	53	46	37	32	21
20	60	52	43	37	23
21	67	58	50	44	32
22	75	65	55	47	34
23	83	73	62	54	40
24	91	81	69	61	46
25	101	89	76	68	51
26	110	98	84	75	58
27	119	107	93	83	63
28	130	116	101	91	71
29	141	126	111	101	80
30	152	136	119	106	85
31	163	147	129	118	95
32	175	159	140	127	102
33	187	170	151	137	111
34	200	183	163	149	123
35	213	195	175	159	130
36	227	208	185	171	139
37	241	221	198	182	153
38	256	234	211	194	163
39	271	249	224	209	176
40	286	264	238	219	186

APPENDIX 3

Table A3.7: Critical values for the r_s statistic

	Level of significance of a one-tailed test					
	$\alpha = .100$	$\alpha = .050$	$\alpha = .025$	$\alpha = .010$	$\alpha = .005$	$\alpha = .0005$
	Level of significance of a two-tailed test					
df	$\alpha = .200$	$\alpha = .100$	$\alpha = .050$	$\alpha = .020$	$\alpha = .010$	$\alpha = .001$
2	1.000	1.000	—	—	—	—
3	.800	.900	1.000	1.000	—	—
4	.657	.829	.886	.943	1.000	—
5	.571	.714	.786	.893	.929	1.000
6	.524	.643	.738	.833	.881	.976
7	.483	.600	.700	.783	.833	.933
8	.455	.564	.648	.745	.794	.903
9	.427	.536	.618	.709	.755	.873
10	.406	.503	.587	.678	.727	.846
11	.385	.484	.560	.648	.703	.824
12	.367	.464	.538	.626	.679	.802
13	.354	.446	.521	.604	.654	.779
14	.341	.429	.503	.582	.635	.762
15	.328	.414	.485	.566	.615	.748
16	.317	.401	.472	.550	.600	.728
17	.309	.391	.460	.535	.584	.712
18	.299	.380	.447	.520	.570	.696
19	.292	.370	.435	.508	.556	.681
20	.284	.361	.425	.496	.544	.667
21	.278	.353	.415	.486	.532	.654
22	.271	.344	.406	.476	.521	.642
23	.265	.337	.398	.466	.511	.630
24	.259	.331	.390	.457	.501	.619
25	.255	.324	.382	.448	.491	.608
26	.250	.317	.375	.440	.483	.598
27	.245	.312	.368	.433	.475	.589
28	.240	.306	.362	.425	.467	.580
29	.236	.301	.356	.418	.459	.571
30	.232	.296	.350	.412	.452	.563

APPENDIX 4
Short answers for study questions and additional datasets

In this appendix brief answers are given for all Study Questions and the final calculated statistics are given with a brief interpretation for each Additional Dataset. With this you can tell whether you have correctly calculated and interpreted the statistical test. Small differences in the calculations can lead to your calculated statistics being slightly different to the answers provided here. Generally these small differences are okay, but try to work to at least four decimal places in your calculations to ensure your answers are accurate. If you have come up with a very different answer, take a look at the fully worked answers in the online resources to see where you made a mistake in the calculations.

Chapter 1: An overview of how to do research

Brief answers to study questions

1. The exact wording of the hypotheses could be quite variable, so the suggestions below are indicative of the kind of thing you could have written. The most important thing is whether the hypothesis clearly maps onto the type specified.
    1.1. A two-tailed hypothesis should specify that a difference will be found, but with no direction given: People with and without pets will differ in their levels of satisfaction with life.
    1.2. A null hypothesis should specify no difference: There will be no difference in levels of general anxiety between participants with and without spider phobia.
    1.3. A one-tailed hypothesis should specify both that there will be a difference, and the predicted direction of that difference: Psychology students will have a significantly higher IQ than students studying a different degree subject.
2. When considering ethics application, different people may identify different concerns. Below are some of my thoughts on the ethics of the design, but you might have picked up on some additional issues. That is totally fine!
    2.1. Informed consent: It is good that the participants were asked to give informed consent, but as they are children the researcher should also ask for informed consent from an appropriate adult, such as a parent or the school's head teacher.
    2.2. Deception: There is no obvious deception, either implicit or explicit.
    2.3. Protecting participants from harm: There is the potential for harm in this design, in many ways (e.g., psychological harm due to a bullied child worrying about naming their bully, potentially exacerbating bullying occurring). If this study occurs, there needs to be some careful safeguards in place, such as a

detailed anti-bullying component added to classes during and after the study has occurred.

2.4. Right to withdraw: Children should not be compelled to answer questions that make them feel uncomfortable, especially when talking about bullying. This is also a potential source of harm to the children. This part of the research protocol would need to be changed before ethical approval could be granted.

2.5. Anonymity and confidentiality: Asking children to name their bully raises some potential issues. If names are to be stored then the researchers would need to include information about how the data will be stored securely (e.g., password protected) to maintain confidentiality. The researchers could alternatively be asked to redesign their study to avoid asking children to name their bully as this aspect of the design raises multiple ethical issues.

2.6. Debriefing: Given the sensitive nature of the research topic, I'd ask for a more detailed debriefing protocol. It would be better to debrief children individually, as the information given may need to be adapted depending on whether the child has been bullied or whether they have been identified as a bully. Class level debriefing is also necessary, particularly around anti-bullying content. I would also suggest that debriefing information is sent to parents, giving them advice in case their child discloses to them that they have either been bullied, or that they have bullied other children.

3. Within each of these ethics documents, you need to include every single piece of information specified in Figure 1.6. A full example of this is given in the long answers in the online resources (these provide example documents in full).

Chapter 2: How to design a psychological research study: the basics of methodology

Brief answers to study questions

1. For each of these designs there are many possibilities. These are just my suggestions. All assume that the data are collected when the participants are adults, but you could also have designed studies with children as participants.

    1.1. The first categorical variable is already specified as whether the child attended a nursery before the age of two years old? Yes or no. The second variable needs to measure the 'cognitive abilities' variable. A two category variable could be whether they completed a university degree: yes or no. A three category variable could be the highest level of education completed: A-levels, undergraduate degree or postgraduate degree.

    1.2. The IV needs to be two groups, so an obvious choice is whether the participant attended a nursery before the age of two years old? Yes or no. The DV then needs to be some measure or cognitive ability, so perhaps an IQ test could be used to give each participant an IQ score.

    1.3. For a correlational design you need two continuous variables. The variable to measure cognitive ability is relatively simple as we could measure IQ. The other variable

needs to be a continuous variable that addresses nursery attendance before the age of two, which is more difficult. Perhaps we could find out the length of time that the child attended a nursery before they turned two.
2. The answers to these next questions will depend a little on your correlational design.
    2.1. For the IQ variable, we will use a well-established IQ test, such as Raven's Progressive Matrices, and this will provide a standardised IQ score. Time spent at nursery before the age of two could be measured in months.
    2.2. One possible confound could be the child's parent's level of intelligence. This could influence both of the variables as cognitive ability is partly heritable (so a parent with high IQ is likely to have a child with high IQ) and it might be that a parent with a higher level of cognitive ability is more likely to return to work and therefore their child may be more likely to attend a nursery. This could be measured as a co-variable by also measuring the parent's IQ. Another possible issue could be the quality of the childcare, as higher quality childcare might be associated with greater cognitive benefits than lower quality childcare. There are various ways this could be measured, such as staff-child ratios or the level of training of staff.
3. These answers all relate to the IQ variable, measured using Raven's Progressive Matrices.
    3.1. Convergent validity: It would be good to use a very different form of intelligence test to validate the measure. Perhaps the National Adult Reading Test.
    3.2. Divergent validity: A number of variables could be expected to not correlate with IQ, such as height, or perhaps the amount of chocolate eaten per week?!
    3.3. Internal validity: To ensure internal validity, we might measure maternal IQ as a possible co-variable, and we would want to sample our participants to ensure that we get a wide range of IQ scores.
    3.4. Inter-rater reliability: Scoring on this measure is very objective, so this wouldn't really be an issue.
    3.5. Test-retest reliability: This has been looked at in a number previous research papers, and the measure has a high level of test-retest reliability.
    3.6. Internal consistency: Again, this is well established in previous research, with Cronbach's alpha usually being around 0.8 to 0.9, showing a good to excellent level of reliability.
4. For this study, I would avoid using an opportunity sample of university students as they are likely to all have high levels of intelligence, which may bias our findings and threaten the internal validity of the study. Instead I would use a volunteer sample, advertising in the local community to ensure a more representative sample with a wide range of IQ scores.

Chapter 3: How to find, read, write, and think about research papers

Brief answers to study questions

1. There are many different ways of combining search terms, but here are three I came up with.

1.1. (color OR colour) AND perception AND babies
1.2. 'colour perception' AND (perception OR processing) AND infants
1.3. color AND (perceiv * OR perception) AND development

2. You could put this paragraph together in many ways, but all four parts from Box 3.1 need to be addressed. An example is: 'Differing levels of education between the two groups could have been a confounding variable in this design. Educational achievement is correlated with intelligence (Deary, Strand, Smith, & Fernandes, 2007) and greater use of supplements (Radimer, Bindewald, Hughes, Ervin, Swanson, & Picciano, 2004). Given that level of education achievement may impact on both of the variables, it may be important to control for this variable in future studies. This may lead to a smaller correlation being found, however we could be more confident that the correlation reflected the actual relationship between intelligence and supplement use.'

3. Each of the references has various errors; the correctly formatted reference is also shown.
    3.1. The first names should not be shown, only the initials, and the journal name should be capitalised. Recent APA guidelines also say that it is not necessary to give the issue number: Cassady, J. C. (2004). The influence of cognitive test anxiety across the learning–testing cycle. *Learning and Instruction, 14*, 569–592.
    3.2. The month of publication is not needed, and the end page number should have been included. Again, the issue number was given, but this is no longer needed: Moneta, G. B., Spada, M. M., & Rost, F. M. (2007). Approaches to studying when preparing for final exams as a function of coping strategies. *Personality and Individual Differences, 43*, 191–202.
    3.3. The word 'and' should not be used, it should be an ampersand (&), and the journal title should be italicised, not underlined: Komarraju, M., Ramsey, A., & Rinella, V. (2013). Cognitive and non-cognitive predictors of college readiness and performance: Role of academic discipline. *Learning and Individual Differences, 24*, 103–109.

Chapter 4: Qualitative methods in psychological research

Brief answers to study questions

1. There are lots of different ways that you could develop the hypothesis and research question, but here are a couple of suggestions:
    1.1. Women athletes who take part in a cognitive behavioural training programme will feel more confident before taking part in a competitive race than women athletes who did not take part in the programme.
    1.2. What practices do women athletes feel best prepare them for the 100 metres race in the Paralympic Games?
2. Given the very specific participant group, Interpretative Phenomenological Analysis might be particularly suitable. You may have suggested a different method though.
3. In designing this study, you could take the following factors into consideration in a number of ways, but here are some of the key issues that I would pay particular attention to:

3.1. The representativeness of the sample: The sample is quite specified within the study outline, so you would need to sample from women who would be taking part in that particular event within that particular competition. You might want to particularly think about whether you could sample across different classification groups, athletes from different countries, with differing levels of experience, etc.

3.2. Reliability and validity: You could potentially examine the validity of the analysis by asking the participants to comment on the themes that are identified, and reliability could be considered by asking a second researcher to examine the transcripts and findings to verify their reliability.

3.3. Ethical considerations: Given that the participants are professional athletes, it would be important to ensure that the study design could not influence their performance in a negative way. For example, you would want to be careful in the way that questions are worded, and potentially sensitive questions should not be given at the end of the interview or focus group. It would also be important to take extra care over issues around anonymity and confidentiality as the athletes could be relatively easily identified as they will all be participants in a very specific public event.

Chapter 5: Basics of statistical analysis

Brief answers to study questions

1. Friendship example:

Lab	Boys Mean	SD	Girls Mean	SD	Significance p	Is the analysis significant? What is the chance of a Type I Error?	Which group has significantly more friends?	Comment on the variability in the dataset.
1	7.8	1.3	9.2	2.6	.049	Yes: 4.9%	Girls	More for girls
2	6.1	1.6	6.5	1.2	.500	No: 50%	Neither	Similar
3	6.8	3.5	5.2	2.9	.051	No: 5.1%	Neither	Slightly larger for boys
4	8.3	2.3	10.6	1.9	.005	Yes: 0.5%	Girls	More for boys

2. Generalised Anxiety Disorder example:
   2.1. Mean would be higher for the clinical group, giving a large amount of between group variability. There is likely to be variability within conditions, but this would be smaller than the variability between the conditions. The graph should look like the top example in Figure 5.16, with the clinical group having the higher scores, like the caffeine group.
   2.2. There probably would be a significant difference, so the between groups variance slice is likely to take up much of the cake with a far smaller slice of within groups variance (similar to the Lab One cake example in the chapter).

APPENDIX 4

3. Extraversion example:
   3.1. Area under the normal distribution curve:

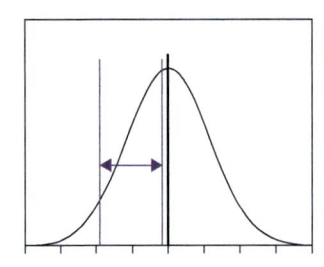

   3.2. I worked out three ways, but there could be more. Some are a bit convoluted!
      3.2.1. Area beyond (below) 45 minus the area beyond (below) 32.
      3.2.2. Total area beyond (below) the mean is 50%. Calculate the area between the mean and 45 and the area beyond (below) 32. Add these two together and subtract them from 0.50.
      3.2.3. Calculate the area between the mean and 32, then subtract from this the area between the mean and 45.

	All participants	Males	Females
Mode	10	10	12 and 14
Median	10	9	12
Mean	10.5	8.7	12.3
Range	16	13	12
Variance	16.58	14.68	13.12
Standard deviation	4.07	3.83	3.62

Brief answers for additional dataset

1. Females are more socially anxious, as can be seen by all three measures of central tendency.
2. Scores are dispersed more widely for males, as can be seen in all three measures of dispersion.
3. Females have bimodal social anxiety scores with both 12 and 14 occurring twice.
4. z score answers:
   4.1. 0.61 SD *below* the mean
   4.2. 0.6179 would be expected to score above 9.3
   4.3. 18.26% would be expected to score between 10.9 and 12.9.

Chapter 6: How to design an experiment

Brief answers to study questions

Experiment 1: A researcher is interested in whether there are differences in IQ between 12 year olds who are in state or private schools.
1. Describe the design: This would be quasi-experimental as you couldn't allocate children randomly to the two different types of school. The independent variable is type

of school, which is an independent measures design with two groups: private or state school. The dependent variable is IQ.
2. Devise a hypothesis: A two-tailed hypothesis could be that you would expect IQs to differ significantly between children educated in state and private schools.
3. Critique the experimental design: The biggest issue here is that the two groups of children are likely to come from quite different backgrounds, so how do you know if the IQs differ due to the school they are at, or some other confounds? You couldn't make this into a proper experiment as it would be unethical to randomly allocate children to different types of schools. Instead, I would try matching the children in the two different conditions on confounding variables that I thought might have a large impact on the children's IQs. Parents' level of education and income seem like two very obvious variables to match on, but there could be others. You may have identified some other points too.

Experiment 2: A neuropsychologist has developed a new app to aid memory in patients with dementia. They ask them to complete a memory test (giving a score out of 50), ask them to use the app for one month and then they repeat the memory test.
1. Describe the design: This is an experimental design with a repeated measures design. The independent variable is time, before or after using the app. The dependent variable is memory score.
2. Devise a hypothesis: A one-tailed hypothesis might state that you would predict memory scores will increase after using the app.
3. Critique the experimental design: There is an obvious flaw in this design in the lack of a control condition. How would you know whether memory scores increase due to the app or due to practice effects? I'd add a control condition where the participants just use their usual memory aids for the month between the two testing sessions. You could also have identified some additional weaknesses in the design.

Experiment 3: A researcher wants to see if mood improves after laughing. They randomly allocate each participant to one of two conditions: comedy video or snooker video. Participants watch the video for ten minutes and then complete a questionnaire that provides a score out of 100 that represents whether they are in a good mood (high score) or bad mood (low score).
1. Describe the design: This is an experimental design as participants were randomly allocated to conditions. It is an independent design with two conditions: comedy or snooker video. The dependent variable is the mood rating.
2. Devise a hypothesis: A one-tailed hypothesis might be that you would expect participants who were in the comedy condition to be in a significantly better mood than participants who were in the snooker condition.
3. Critique the experimental design: My main concern with this design is that we don't know what mood the participants were in before watching the videos. Even though they were randomly allocated to the conditions, by random chance it is possible that their moods could have differed before the experiment between the two groups. I would redesign this study to measure mood before and after watching the video. With this change, I might predict that mood will increase from before to after watching the comedy video, but that there will be no change in the snooker video condition. Again, you might also pick up on some other weaknesses.

Chapter 7: How can I tell if scores differ between two groups? Independent t test

Brief answers to study questions

1. Lab One is more likely to have found the significant difference. Although the mean difference is very slightly larger for Lab Two, the variability in the dataset (as seen in the SD) is much bigger. Therefore, there will be a greater amount of random variance in the study run in Lab Two, making a significant result far less likely.
2. Results in APA format are …
   2.1. $t(14) = 3.19, p < .010$
   2.2. $t(25) = 2.55, p < .020$
   2.3. $t(36) = 3.41, p < .002$
3. For each of the results …
   3.1. There is far more random variance, so the result will most likely be not significant.
   3.2. There is a similar amount of explained and random variance, so the result will most likely be not significant.
   3.3. There is far more explained variance, so the result will most likely be significant.

Brief answers for additional dataset

There is a significant difference in satisfaction with life ($t(14) = 2.9, p < .020$). Those with a more serious head injury report being more satisfied (M = 4.9, SD = 1.1) than those with a mild head injury (M = 3.0, SD = 1.4). (Go to the online resources for full answers, including the fully worked calculations.)

Are p values enough? An optional exercise

$d = 1.51$, reflecting a large effect size.

Chapter 8: How can I tell if scores differ between two conditions? Repeated t test

Brief answers to study questions

1. Given that the sample are the same people at both time points, the difference in variability cannot simply be explained by individual differences between two different groups of people! Therefore, it would be best to look for how the experimental paradigm might have changed between the two time points. Perhaps there was a different experimenter, or testing took place at a different time of day, or perhaps the instructions differed at time two? Any of these, plus many more reasons, might explain the increased random variance at time two.
2. Errors and correct statistics for each example …
   2.1. The degrees of freedom are in the wrong place: $t(31) = 2.4, p < .050$
   2.2. You do not need to write 'df = ': $t(12) = 3.2, p < .010$

2.3. The operator sign for the p value should be less than (<), not greater than (>): $t(24) = 3.3, p < .005$
3. To answer each of these questions you need to first work out two things: Is the hypothesis one-tailed or two-tailed? And how many degrees of freedom are there (N-1)? With this information you can look up the critical value for each scenario.
   3.1. Two-tailed. df = 19. Critical value = 2.093.
   3.2. One-tailed. df = 14. Critical value = 1.761.
   3.3. One-tailed. df = 24. Critical value = 1.711.

Brief answers for additional dataset

People rate a genuine smile (M = 5.9, SD = 1.1) as significantly happier than a posed smile (M = 4.3, SD = 1.1; $t(9) = 3.4, p < .005$). (Go to the online resources for full answers, including the fully worked calculations.)

Are p values enough? An optional exercise

d = 1.45, reflecting a large effect size.

Chapter 9: How can I tell if scores differ between three or more groups? One-way independent measures ANOVA

Brief answers to study questions

1. Familywise error as a result of conducting multiple t tests. The full list of pairwise comparisons are listed in the online resources.
   1.1. There are four categories, so six t tests would be needed.
   1.2. There would be seven decade categories: 20s, 30s, 40s, 50s, 60s, 70s and 80s. Therefore 21 t tests would be needed.
   1.3. There are five categories, so 10 t tests would be needed.
2. The df for between, total and error are shown below. Full calculations are in the online resources.
   2.1. $df_{between} = 3$, $df_{total} = 47$, $df_{error} = 44$
   2.2. $df_{between} = 2$, $df_{total} = 74$, $df_{error} = 72$
   2.3. $df_{between} = 4$, $df_{total} = 44$, $df_{error} = 40$
3. Results given in full and with interpretation of significance.
   3.1. $F(2, 36) = 8.6, p < .001$, a significant finding.
   3.2. $F(3, 11) = 4.2, p < .050$, a significant finding.
   3.3. $F(4, 24) = 4.9, p < .010$, a significant finding.

Brief answers for additional dataset

There was a significant main effect of type of food eaten ($F(2, 21) = 5.12, p < .050$). Agreeableness was highest in the chocolate condition (M = 9.88, SD = 1.81), lower in the chilli crisps condition (M = 6.88, SD = 3.27) and slightly lower in the control condition (M = 6.38, SD = 1.69). (Go to the online resources for full answers, including the fully worked calculations.)

Are *p* values enough? An optional exercise

$\eta_p^2 = 0.33$, indicating a large effect size.

Chapter 10: How to design a correlational study

Brief answers to study questions

1. Memory in older adults study:
    1.1. Memory and age: I would predict a negative relationship (as age increases, memory score decreases). Memory and IQ: Typically there is a positive correlation between IQ and memory, however both can change and reduce in later life, so this relationship might become weaker.
    1.2. Many, many variables could be suggested, the key thing is that they are continuous.
2. Supplements and cognitive function study:
    2.1. The statement assumes that correlation implies causation!
    2.2. There would most likely be a positive correlation (as the number of supplements taken increases, cognitive ability increases).
    2.3. There are many possible confounds that you could suggest!
3. Intelligence study:
    3.1. Again, there are many possible variables. Just make sure that they are continuous and that they show the three different kinds of relationship I specified.
4. Childhood friendships study:
    4.1. Age of child: a continuous variables that is suitable for a correlation analysis.
    4.2. Being male or female: this is a binary categorical variable and cannot be included in a correlation analysis. An alternative could be to measure level of masculinity or femininity.
    4.3. Whether they are an only child or have siblings: Again, this is a binary variable so not suitable, but you could instead as for the number of siblings that they have.
    4.4. Type of club attended: This categorical variable has three categories and is not suitable for a correlation analysis. There isn't really an obvious alternative, so it would be interesting to hear what you came up with!

Chapter 11: How can I tell if two variables are correlated? Pearson's Correlation

Brief answers to study questions

1. For these questions you should describe whether the correlation is positive or negative, and describe the strength of the relationship using the standard conventions.
    1.1. A strong positive relationship.
    1.2. A weak negative relationship.
    1.3. This was a bit of a trick question! This *r* value is not possible as it falls outside of the ±1 range.
    1.4. A moderate negative relationship.

2. For this question, remember that the degrees of freedom is N-2!
   2.1. $r(13) = .613, p < .010$
   2.2. $r(8) = .426, p > .050$
   2.3. $r(22) = .426, p < .050$ (Note that this finding is significant, whereas the previous finding was not, even though the r value was the same. This is because of the larger sample size in this example.)
   2.4. $r(18) = .741, p < .001$
3. This was quite a tricky question, so well done if you got the answers right! More guidance on how to complete these questions are in the online resources.
   3.1. 16 participants.
   3.2. 20 participants.
   3.3. $r = .4438$.
   3.4. $r = .3494$.

Brief answers for additional dataset

There is a significant positive correlation between the number of shopping trips per month and level of happiness ($r(8) = .716, p < .010$). Note that this reporting assumes a one-tailed hypothesis. (Go to the online resources for full answers, including the fully worked calculations.)

Are p values enough?

An r value of .716 indicates a large effect size.

Chapter 12: How can I tell if one variable can predict another? Simple linear regression

Brief answers to study questions

1. You could potentially argue that either variable should be the predictor or outcome, but these make the most sense to me:
   1.1. Parent's IQ is the predictor variable and child's IQ is the outcome.
   1.2. Number of siblings is the predictor variable and extraversion is the outcome.
   1.3. Months since acquiring brain injury is the predictor variable and performance on a language task is the outcome variable.
2. The unexplained variance is calculated as: $1-R^2$.
   2.1. $R^2 = .029$. There is 2.9% explained variance and 97.1% unexplained variance in the model.
   2.2. $R^2 = .289$. There is 28.9% explained variance and 71.1% unexplained variance in the model.
   2.3. $R^2 = .552$. There is 55.2% explained variance and 44.8% unexplained variance in the model.
3. The intercept value is negative, which makes interpretation a little trickier!
   3.1. The intercept value of −1.6 shows that if a participant gets a confidence score of 0 you would predict that their emotive rating would be −1.6. This is clearly impossible

as the scale runs from 1 to 5! This has happened because the lowest score on the confidence questionnaire is not 0.
- 3.2. For each one point increase on the confidence questionnaire, positivity ratings increase by 0.23.
- 3.3. Both of the predicted scores fall outside of the range of the scale for the positive emotion rating. This can sometimes happen in a regression analysis.
    - 3.3.1. Lowest possible score is 10: Predicted reaction time is 0.7
    - 3.3.2. Highest possible score is 50: Predicted reaction time is 9.9

Brief answers for additional dataset

There is a significant positive correlation between the two variables ($r(8) = .97$, $p < .005$) with the number of Twitter posts per week explaining about 93.9% of the variability in narcissism. The β_0 intercept value is 2.95 and the β_1 slope value is 0.40, showing that each extra Twitter post per week is associated with a 0.40 increase in narcissism.
- Participant 1: Predicted narcissism score of 5.35
- Participant 2: Predicted narcissism score of 2.95
- Participant 3: Predicted narcissism score of 8.55

(Go to the online resources for full answers, including the fully worked calculations.)

Are *p* values enough? An optional exercise

$f^2 = 15.38$, indicating a large effect size.

Chapter 13: When and why might I need to use non-parametric statistics?

Brief answers to study questions

1. You could have suggested a large number of variables for this task, but below are some of my ideas.
    - 1.1. A nominal variable would need to define categories that people can belong to, such as which political party the person voted for in the last general election: Conservative, Labour, Liberal Democrats, Other.
    - 1.2. An ordinal variable would require data that exist in a particular order, but with variable distances between the orders. I could list ten different aspects of political policy and ask participants to rank order them according to how important each one is when they decide which party to vote for. For each of the ten policies, I would then have ranked ordinal data.
    - 1.3. An interval variable needs to be continuous, with the same distance between each number, and where negative values are possible. I could devise a questionnaire where participants rate the extent to which they agree with different political statements on a seven point Likert scale. When the scores are summed across all of the items, they give a score from −70 indicating more leftwards political opinions, through to +70 indicating more rightwards political opinions.

1.4. A ratio variable needs to be continuous, with the same distance between each number, and where negative values are not possible. For this example I might look at people's social media accounts for the three months before a General Election, and count the number of times they post about political issues.
2. Full calculations are given in the online resources.
   2.1. Scores would range from 22 to 32; 77.5% of the sample fall within ±1 SD around the mean. You would expect 68% of the sample to fall within ±1 SD, so this dataset includes more participants than would be expected with normally distributed data.
   2.2. Scores would range from 17 to 37; 81% of the sample fall within ±2 SD around the mean. You would expect 95% of the sample to fall within ±2 SD, so this dataset includes fewer participants than would be expected with normally distributed data.
3. Full calculations are given in the online resources.
   3.1. Boys: mean = 26, variance = 66.86. Girls: mean = 25.25, variance = 14.79.
   3.2. The smallest variance is 14.79 in the girl's condition. Four times this is 59.16 (4*14.79 = 59.16). The variance in the boy's condition is 66.86, which is greater than 59.16, and therefore more than four times the size of the variance in the girl's condition. This means that there is evidence of heterogeneity of variance in this dataset (different variances), and the assumption of homogeneity of variance has been violated.
   3.3. A non-parametric test would need to be used as the parametric assumption has been violated.

Chapter 14: Do my data fit the expected frequencies? Chi squared

Brief answers to study questions

Remember that your hypothesis must be two-tailed. They could be written in various ways, but must all be two-tailed..

1. Chi squared goodness of fit with three categories (documentary, drama, reality TV).
2. 2 (sex) x 3 (programme type) chi squared test of association.
3. The variable that has already been designed has two levels: original recipe or new and improved recipe. You could add any relevant variable, as long as the data collected provides frequencies within categories. This would be analysed using a 2 (recipe) x X (your variable) chi squared test of association.

Brief answers for additional dataset

The chi squared analysis was significant (χ^2 (2, N = 60) = 10.31, p < .010). In the no teddy condition, no help was offered more often than would be expected by chance, whereas immediate help was offered less often than chance. In the teddy condition, no help was offered less often than would be expected by chance, whereas immediate help was offered more often than chance. For those offering delayed help, observed frequencies were similar to expected frequencies. (Go to the online resources for full answers, including the fully worked calculations.)

Chapter 15: Are there differences between groups or conditions? Wilcoxon and Mann-Whitney U

Brief answers to study questions

1. Yes, the answers to all three of the questions are exactly the same!
    1.1. 7
    1.2. 7
    1.3. 7
2. The significance for each analysis would be:
    2.1. Significant with $p < .020$.
    2.2. Not significant.
    2.3. Significant with $p < .002$.
3. In a full write up you should also use descriptive statistics to interpret the direction of the difference. I've added these in, using the median, to show how an interpretation could be written up. Your exact wording could be quite different, and that is fine.
    3.1. The Mann-Whitney U showed a significant difference in addictive personality scores between addicts and non-addicts ($U = 9$, $p < .050$), with higher addiction scores for addicts (median = 85) than for non-addicts (median = 62).
    3.2. Addiction scores were higher before the treatment (median = 88) than after the treatment (median = 72), and a Wilcoxon signed rank test revealed that this was a significant reduction ($W = 16$, $p < .002$).

Brief answers for additional dataset (Mann-Whitney U)

A Mann-Whitney U analysis showed that the two groups differed significantly ($U = 5$, $p < .050$), with a median spend of £36 in the no scent condition and a median spend of £61 in the scent condition. (Note, this analysis assumes a two-tailed hypothesis. Go to the online resources for full answers, including the fully worked calculations.)

Brief answers for additional dataset (Wilcoxon signed rank test)

Analysis using a Wilcoxon signed rank test showed a significant improvement in memory ($W = -5$, $p < .005$), as scores were lower before the neurorehabilitation (median = 15) than afterwards (median = 17.5). (Note, this analysis assumes a one-tailed hypothesis. Go to the online resources for full answers, including the fully worked calculations.)

Chapter 16: Is there a relationship between two variables? Spearman's correlation

Brief answers to study questions

1. Don't forget that df = $n-2$. The critical values are:
    1.1. .466
    1.2. .521
    1.3. .425

2. The *p* values should be:
   2.1. *p* = < .020
   2.2. Not significant
   2.3. *p* = < .010
3. The exact wording of the interpretation may vary, but you need to mention two things: if the result is significant or not, and if it is, then interpret the direction of the relationship (positive or negative).
   3.1. There is a significant positive correlation between the two variables (r_s (15) = .523, $p < .050$).
   3.2. There is a significant negative correlation between the two variables (r_s (22) = −.644, $p < .001$).
   3.3. There is no significant correlation between the two variables (r_s (28) = −.359, $p > .050$).

Brief answers for additional dataset

The social support variable has tied ranks, and therefore the Pearson's equation should be used on the rank scores to analyse the relationship between social support and cold likelihood. Neither the hugs variable nor the cold likelihood variable have tied ranks, and therefore Spearman's correlation can be used to examine this relationship. Both of the analyses below assume a two-tailed hypothesis. Go to the online resources for full answers, including the fully worked calculations.

There is no significant correlation between social support and cold likelihood (r (5) = −.709, $p > .050$).

There is a significant negative correlation between hugs per week and cold likelihood (r_s (5) = −.786, $p > .025$). This shows that the more hugs a person has, the less likely they are to develop a cold.

Chapter 17: Which statistical test should I use?

Brief answers to study questions

Full explanations for each of these answers are given in the online resources.
1. Correlation, possibly linear regression
2. Independent *t* test
3. Chi square test of association
4. One-way ANOVA
5. Repeated *t* test
6. Wilcoxon

Chapter 18: Moving beyond the basics of research and analysis: how do I understand more complicated research designs?

Brief answers to study questions

1. Anxiety and different interventions design:
   1.1. There would be 10 *t* tests. The contrasts would be: control vs placebo, control vs prescribed, control vs alternative, control vs CBT, placebo vs prescribed, placebo vs

alternative, placebo vs CBT, prescribed vs alternative, prescribed vs CBT, alternative vs CBT.
- **1.2.** Bonferroni corrected alpha would be α = .005 (.050/10 = .005).
- **1.3.** There are a number of ways you could write this hypothesis, but the key thing is that it is two-tailed. So it must specify that conditions will vary, but not where the differences would be.
- **1.4.** Again, many hypotheses could work here, but they would have to be one-tailed, so you would specify where you think differences would lie and where scores would be higher or lower.

2. You could have suggested many, many different IV2s and DVs in this exercise. The important thing is that you really thought about how the scores changed for control and clinical groups, and whether the two groups scored the same, or whether one group scored higher or lower.
   - **2.1.** No interaction: Answer given in the chapter.
   - **2.2.** Interaction 1: Here, in condition X people with depression needed to score higher than controls. Looking at the difference from X to Y, scores need to decrease for people with depression and increase for controls so that controls now score higher than participants with depression.
   - **2.3.** Interaction 2: In this example both groups scores exactly the same in condition X, but the change to condition Y shows that scores decrease for those with depression and increase for participants in the control group.
   - **2.4.** Interaction 3: Again, both groups should score the same in condition X, but in this example participants in the depression group score exactly the same in condition Y, whereas scores increase markedly in condition Y for participants in the control group.

3. As this is a design task, it isn't possible to give you exact answers! But for each study you should have two confounds, one continuous variable and one binary categorical variable, and you should have a directional prediction for each one.

Index

abstract 44, 294
academic dishonesty 18
active deception 13, 294
alpha (α) level 102, 294
    Bonferroni correction 268
    chi square goodness of fit 223
    chi square test of association 227
    controversies 287
    familywise error rate 154
    independent *t* test 136-7
    Mann-Whitney *U* test 236
    one-way independent measures ANOVA 162-3
    Pearson's correlation 186, 187
    planned and post hoc contrasts 269
    power analysis 290
    problems 103
    repeated *t* test 147, 148
    Spearman's correlation 252-3
    Wilcoxon signed rank test 241-2
alternative hypothesis 294
    see also experimental hypothesis
American Psychological Association (APA)
    chi square goodness of fit 224
    chi square test of association 227
    confidence intervals 289
    effect sizes 139, 149, 164-5, 287
    ethical guidelines 10-11
    independent *t* test 137, 138, 139
    Mann-Whitney *U* test 237, 238
    one-way independent measures ANOVA 163, 164-5
    p values 103, 287
    Pearson's correlation 188, 189
    presenting research 55
        statistics 56, 57
        writing style 55, 56
    psychological research papers
        references 53, 57, 58-9
        structure 43, 44, 48, 49
    repeated *t* test 148, 149
    Spearman's correlation 253
    tables and figures 105
    Wilcoxon signed rank test 242
analysis of covariance (ANCOVA) 267, 277-8, 294
analysis of variance (ANOVA) 294
    advanced experimental designs 267-77
    breaking down a significant effect 268-9, 272
    checking whether data are normally distributed 214
    effect size 288
    parametric assumptions 207
    wider thinking about 165
    see also one-way independent measures ANOVA
analytical pluralism 79, 294
ANCOVA (analysis of covariance) 267, 277-8, 294
anonymity 15, 18, 294
    qualitative research 72
ANOVA *see* analysis of variance
APA *see* American Psychological Association
appendices 47, 53, 294
averages *see* central tendency

bar charts 285-6
bell curve *see* normal distribution
beta (β) value 294
    linear regression 196
    multiple regression 280
between groups variance 294
    see also experimental variance
between participants design *see* independent measures design
bias
    critical thinking 65
    experimental design 122-3
    internal validity 33
    opportunity sampling 38
    qualitative research 71, 74
    running a research study 40
    Thematic Analysis 74
    volunteer sampling 38
bimodal dataset 83
binary categorical variable 281-2, 294
binary outcome variables 283
Bonferroni correction 268, 269, 272, 294
British Psychological Society (BPS) 3-4
    ethical guidelines 10, 16

carryover effects 122
categorical data/variable (frequency/nominal data) 23, 209, 260, 294
    binary 281-2, 294
    chi square test 121, 216, 219

    logistic regression 283
    misused in correlational studies 173-4, 189
    non-parametric analysis 25
    regression 281-2
    three or more categories 282
categorical design 27, 28, 260, 294
    choice of statistical test 260-1
categorical variable *see* categorical data/variable
causal relationship 294
    correlational studies 175, 178
    experimental design 30, 31, 113
    not implied by correlation 31
    quasi-experimental design 115
    randomized control trials 124
    regression analysis 178
central tendency 82, 83-6, 294
    presenting findings 105
change scores *see* difference scores
chi square 219, 229-30
    critical values table 314
    effect size 288, 290
    typical uses 228-9
    see also chi square goodness of fit; chi square test of association
chi square goodness of fit 219-20, 221, 294
    assumptions 228
    calculating and interpreting 221-5
    choice of 261
    following chi square test of association 228
chi square test of association (chi square test of independence) 216, 294
    assumptions 228
    calculating and interpreting 225-8
    categorical research designs 28
    choice of 260-1
    experimental designs 121, 220-1
children
    ethical considerations 15-16
    reading age as co-variable 25-6
choice of statistical test 259, 264-5
    categorical design 260-1
    correlational design 263
    experimental design 262-3
    flow charts 260, 261
    what type did you use? 259-60
    which test next? 264

INDEX

codes 76-7, 294
Cohen's d 288, 294
   independent t test 138
   repeated t test 149-50
Cohen's f^2 201-2, 294
complex regression models 282-3
confidence intervals (CIs) 289-90, 294
confidentiality 15, 18, 294
   qualitative research 72
confounding variables 25-7, 294
   ANCOVA 277-8
   correlational designs 175-7
   critical thinking 64-5
   discussion section, of psychological research paper 52
   experimental design 120-2
   hierarchical regression 282
   independent t test 145
   internal validity 33
   linear regression 198
   repeated t test 145
construct validity 32, 294
   critical thinking 65
content validity 32, 294
continuous score/variable 294
   choice of statistical test 262, 263
   correlational designs 30-1, 173, 174, 189
   dependent variables 114
   independent t test 121, 129
   linear regression 193
   logistic regression 283
   one-way independent measures ANOVA 153
   Spearman's correlation 247
control groups 294
   experimental design 124
   randomized control trials 124-5
control variables (co-variables/mediating variables) 25, 120, 294
   ANCOVA 277-8
   correlational designs 176
   partial correlation 278-9
   running a research study 39
   selecting and thinking about 26-7
convergent validity 32, 294
   running a research study 39-40
correlation 171, 278, 294
   checking whether data are normally distributed 214
   homoscedasticity 212
   motto 173-4, 263
   parametric assumptions 207
   regression analysis 192, 197
   strength of 181, 182
   see also Spearman's correlation

correlational design 27, 30-1, 171, 178-9, 260, 295
   advanced 278-86
   causality 175
   choice of statistical test 261, 263
   confounding variables 175-7
   graphing data 285-6
   predictive models 177-8
   relationships 171-2
   running a research study 39-40
   variables 173-4
   see also Pearson's correlation
counterbalancing 121-2, 295
co-variables 295
   see also control variables
covariance 183-4, 295
Cramer's V 290
critical thinking
   about psychological research 49, 64-5
   in publishing process 66
critical values 295
   chi square goodness of fit 223, 224
   chi square test of association 227
   independent t test 136, 137
   Mann-Whitney U test 236, 237
   one-way independent measures ANOVA 162-3
   p values 101, 288
   Pearson's correlation 186, 187-8
   repeated t test 147-8
   Spearman's correlation 252-3
   tables 309-18
   Wilcoxon signed rank test 241-2
Cronbach's alpha 35-7, 40, 295
crossover effects 122, 295
   factorial ANOVAs 274
cross-sectional designs 116-17, 295

data 22, 295
   analysis 118-19, 127
   types 22-4
debriefing 12, 295
   deception 13
   protecting participants from potential harm 14
   in psychological research paper 48
   sheets 16, 17
deception 13, 295
   in psychological research paper 48
deductive 69, 295
degrees of freedom (df) 104-5, 295
   chi square goodness of fit 223, 224
   chi square test of association 227
   independent t test 135-6, 137, 138

Mann-Whitney U test 237
one-way independent measures ANOVA 156-7, 163
   example 160, 162
one-way repeated measures ANOVA 271
Pearson's correlation 187, 189
presenting in psychological research paper 56, 57
repeated t test 147, 149
Spearman's correlation 252, 253
Wilcoxon signed rank test 242
demand characteristics 123, 295
dementia patients, ethical considerations 16
dependent variables (DVs) 29, 231, 295
   choice of statistical test 262, 263
   examples 114
   experimental design 114
   independent t test 129, 130, 133
   one-way independent measures ANOVA 153, 158, 165
   repeated t test 142, 143, 145
descriptive statistics 82, 295
   central tendency 83-6
   checking whether data are normally distributed 213-14
   dispersion 86-91
   independent t test 137-8
   Mann-Whitney U test 237
   non-parametric statistics interpreted with 216
   one-way independent measures ANOVA 164
   presenting 105-6
   in psychological research paper 48-9, 50
   repeated t test 148
   Wilcoxon signed rank test 242
Design (and Analysis) section, of psychological research paper 48, 295
designing an experiment see experimental design
difference scores 239, 240, 241
Digital Object Identifiers (DOIs) 59
Disclosure Barring Service (DBS) check 15
Discourse Analysis 74, 295
discriminant (divergent) validity 32, 295
   running a research study 39-40
Discussion section, of psychological research paper 50-2, 54, 55, 295
dishonesty, academic 18

dispersion 82, 86-91, 295
    presenting findings 105
distribution 92-5, 295
divergent validity *see* discriminant (divergent) validity
double blind design 123, 125, 295
dummy variable modelling 282

ecological validity 33-4, 295
effect sizes 9, 103, 287-90, 295
    advantages 288-9
    confidence intervals 289-90
    independent *t* test 138-9
    linear regression 201-2
    non-parametric statistics 290
    one-way independent measures ANOVA 164-5
    Pearson's correlation 188
    power analysis 290
    repeated *t* test 149-50
enter method of regression 282
error variance 295
    see also random variance
ethical approval 11, 295
    applying for 16
    deception 13
    psychological research paper 47
    research process 6
    running a research study 40
ethical considerations 6, 10-18, 295
    control groups in randomized control trials 125
    in psychological research paper 48
    qualitative research 71-2
    research process 6
ethical guidelines 10-11, 16, 295
Ethics Committees 11, 13, 16
expected frequency 295
    chi square goodness of fit 220, 221
        example 222, 223
    chi square test of association 229
        example 226, 227
    Yate's correction 228
experimental design 27, 29-30, 113, 127-8, 260, 295
    advanced 267-78
    causality 30, 31
    choice of statistical test 261, 262-3
    conditions 119-20
    confounding variables 120-2
    cross-sectional 116-17
    data analysis 118-19, 127
    decisions 117-19
    describing your variables 113-14
    graphing data 285-6
    hypotheses 125-7

independent 115-16, 117
longitudinal 116-17
non-manipulable independent variables 114-15
non-parametric statistics 231-2
parametric assumptions 207, 209
pitfalls 120-3
random variability and bias 122-3
repeated measures 115, 116, 117
treatments and interventions 123-5
experimental hypothesis (alternative hypothesis) 8-9, 100, 295
experimental design 125-6
    Type I Error 101
    Type II Error 101
experimental variance (between groups/model variance) 88, 90-1, 92, 103, 105, 295
    ANCOVA 277-8
    experimental design 118
    independent *t* test 130-2
        example 135
    one-way independent measures ANOVA 154-5, 156, 157-8
        example 160, 161
    repeated *t* test 142-3, 144-5
        example 147
explained variance
    advanced experimental designs 267
    factorial ANOVAs 276
    one-way repeated measures ANOVA 270
external validity 33, 295
extraneous variables *see* confounding variables; control variables
Eysenck Personality Questionnaire - Revised, Addiction Scale 39

F ratio 296
    critical values tables 310-12
    factorial ANOVAs 276
    multiple regression 280
    one-way independent measures ANOVA 155, 156, 157-8
        example 161, 162, 163
factor analysis 279, 283-5, 296
factorial ANOVA 272-7, 296
    independent design 267, 272-3
    mixed design 267, 272-3
    repeated design 267, 272-3
falsifiable 10, 296
familywise error rate 153-4, 296
    Bonferroni correction 268, 269
fatigue effects 117, 122-3, 296

figures 105-6
    complex analyses 285-6
    in psychological research paper 49, 53
focus groups 70, 296
    possible harm 72
    Thematic Analysis 76
frequency 296
frequency data 296
    see also categorical data/variable

goodness of fit, chi square *see* chi square goodness of fit
Google 60, 61
Google Scholar 61
graphs *see* figures
Grounded Theory 73, 296

heterogeneity of variance 211-12, 296
    Mann-Whitney *U* test 232
hierarchical regression 279, 282, 296
histograms 210, 296
    checking whether data are normally distributed 212-13
homogeneity of variance 211-12, 247, 296
    checking 214
    one-way repeated measures ANOVA 270
homoscedasticity 212, 296
hypotheses 6, 8, 296
    chi square goodness of fit 220, 221
    correlational designs 172
    experimental (alternative) *see* experimental hypothesis
    experimental design 125-7
    hierarchical regression 283
    independent *t* test 133
    Mann-Whitney *U* test 234
    null *see* null hypothesis
    one-tailed *see* one-tailed hypothesis
    Pearson's correlation 184
    psychological research papers 54
        Discussion section 50
        Introduction section 45
    and qualitative research questions, comparison between 70
    research process 6
    stepwise regression 283
    testing 7-10
        possible outcomes 100-1
    two-tailed *see* two-tailed hypothesis
    Wilcoxon signed rank test 240

INDEX

independence of observations 208-9, 296
   Mann-Whitney U test 232
   Wilcoxon signed rank test 232
independent experimental designs
   choice of statistical test 262, 263
   homogeneity of variance 211
independent measures design 29, 115-18, 232, 296
   advantages and disadvantages 117, 119
   random variance 119
   randomization 121
   see also one-way independent measures ANOVA
independent measures t test 129, 139-41, 232, 296
   calculating and interpreting 132-8
   checking whether data are normally distributed 214
   choice of 261, 263
   comparison with repeated t test 142-3, 144, 145, 148, 149
   effect sizes 138-9
   experimental design 121
   interpreting and writing up 137-8, 139
   limitations 268
   logic behind the 130-2
   non-parametric equivalent *see* Mann-Whitney U test
   significance 135-7
independent variables (IVs) 29, 231, 296
   choice of statistical test 262, 263
   examples 114
   experimental design 113-14
   factorial ANOVAs 272-7
   independent t test 129, 130, 133
   non-manipulable 114-15
   one-way independent measures ANOVA 153, 158, 165
   one-way repeated measures ANOVA 271, 272
   repeated t test 142, 143, 145
indexing services 61-3
inductive 69, 296
inferential statistics 296
   independent t test 137-8
   presenting 105-6
   in psychological research paper 48
   repeated t test 148
   significance 82-3, 99-105
information sheets 11, 16-17
informed consent 11-12, 296
   anonymity and confidentiality 15
   deception 13
   forms 16, 17
   protecting participants from potential harm 14
   in psychological research paper 48
   right to withdraw 14
   vulnerable groups 15-16
intelligence 39
interaction effects 273-6, 296
intercept 194-6, 296
   example 199-201
internal consistency 35-7, 40, 296
internal validity 33, 34, 40, 296
Interpretative Phenomenological Analysis (IPA) 73-4, 296
inter-rater reliability 34, 296
   critical thinking 65
   qualitative research 71
   running a research study 40
interval data 24, 247, 296
   correlational designs 30, 31, 189
   dependent variables 114
   mean 85
   parametric analysis 25, 209
intervention experiments 123-5
interviews 70, 296
   Thematic Analysis 76
Introduction section, of psychological research paper 44-6, 54, 55, 296

Kolmogorov-Smirnov test 212
kurtosis 93, 94, 95, 296

latent variables 284
leptokurtic distribution 94, 95, 296
levels of measurement 296
Levene's test 214
Likert scales 217, 296
line graphs 285
line of best fit 171-2, 296
   correlational designs 285
   linear regression 193-6, 199-201
   Pearson's correlation 180-3, 184, 187
   slope and intercept 193-5, 199-201
linear regression 31, 177-8, 192, 202-4, 278, 297
   choice of 261, 263
   effect sizes 201-2
   example 197-201
   line of best fit 193-6
   terminology 193
logistic regression 279, 283, 297

longitudinal designs 116-17, 124, 297

McNemar test 228
main effect 273, 274, 275-6, 297
manifest variables 284
manipulation 231, 297
   experimental design 29, 113-14
Mann-Whitney U test 216, 231-3, 242-6, 297
   calculating and interpreting 234-8
   choice of 261
   critical values tables 315-16
   effect size 288, 290
   logic behind the 233-4
   z score 242-3
matching participants 119, 121, 297
Materials section, of psychological research paper 47, 297
mean 297
   advantages and disadvantages 86
   calculation 84-6
   checking whether data are normally distributed 213
   confidence intervals 289-90
   independent t test 129, 130, 131
   effect sizes 138-9
   example 133, 134, 137-8
   linear regression 199, 200
   Mann-Whitney U test 237-8
   and non-parametric data 216
   normal distribution 93
   one-way independent measures ANOVA 158, 163
   presenting findings 56, 105
   repeated t test 146, 148, 149, 150
   z scores 95-9
mean squares (MS) 156, 157, 160-1, 297
measuring variables 21-7
   confounding variables 25-7
   operationalising variables 22
   parametric and non-parametric analysis 24-5
   types of variables and data 22
median 297
   advantages and disadvantages 86
   calculation 84
   Mann-Whitney U test 237, 238
   non-parametric data 216
   normal distribution 93
   Wilcoxon signed rank test 242
mediating variable 297
   see also control variables
meta-analysis 287

INDEX

methodology 21, 40-2
  measuring variables 21-31
  research designs 27-31
  running a research study 39-40
  selecting and recruiting participants 37-8
  validity and reliability 31-7
Methods section, of psychological research paper 46-8, 53-4, 55, 297
mixed methods 69, 79-80, 260, 297
mode 297
  advantages and disadvantages 86
  calculation 83-4
  normal distribution 93
model variance 297
  see also experimental variance
multimodal dataset 84
multiple regression 279-80, 281-2, 297

naturalistic 68, 297
negative correlation/relationship 172, 297
  Pearson's correlation 180-1, 183
  Spearman's correlation 247
negative skew 94, 210, 297
nominal data 297
  see also categorical data/variable
non-normal distributions 93-5, 297
non-parametric statistics 25, 189, 207, 217-18, 297
  choice of 262
  effect sizes 103, 290
  equivalents of parametric tests 216
  how they work 214-16
  interpreting with descriptive statistics 216
  median 84
  need for 216-17
  z scores 242-3
  see also Mann-Whitney U test; Wilcoxon signed rank test
normal distribution 91-3, 247, 297
  alpha level 102
  area under the normal curve 303-8
  checking whether data are normally distributed 212-14
  one- and two-tailed hypotheses 126-7
  parametric analyses 210
  z scores 95-9
null hypothesis 8, 9, 100, 297
  experimental design 125

Type I Error 101
Type II Error 101
null hypothesis significance testing (NHST) 7-8, 100, 297
  controversies 287
  problems 103

observational studies 70, 297
  and informed consent 12
observed frequencies 297
  chi square goodness of fit 220, 221
  example 222, 223
  chi square test of association 229
  example 226, 227
one-tailed hypothesis 8-9, 297
  correlational designs 172
  experimental design 125-7
  independent t test 133
  linear regression 193
  Mann-Whitney U test 234, 237
  normal distribution 126-7
  Pearson's correlation 184, 186, 187
  planned contrast 269
  psychological research papers 54
  Spearman's correlation 249, 252
  Wilcoxon signed rank test 240, 241-2
one-way independent measures ANOVA 153, 267
  calculating and interpreting 158-63
  problem 163-4
  choice of 261, 262
  effect sizes 164-5
  familywise error 153-4
  logic behind the 154-8
  stages 155-8
  summary table 156
  example 159, 160, 161
one-way repeated measures ANOVA 267, 269-72
operationalising variables 22, 39, 297
opportunity sampling 38, 297
  critical thinking 65
  running a research study 40
ordinal data 23-4, 209, 297
  choice of statistical test 263
  median 84
  non-parametric analysis 25, 189
  Wilcoxon signed rank test 238
outcome variables 297
  binary 283
  hierarchical regression 282
  linear regression 177-8, 263, 278
  example 197, 198, 199, 200

  line of best fit 193, 194, 195
  regression equation 195-6
  logistic regression 283
  multiple regression 279-80
  regression analysis 177-8, 193
  regression with categorical variables 281
  stepwise regression 283
outliers
  Mann-Whitney U test 237
  mean 85-6
  median 84, 86
  range 89

p value 297
  chi square goodness of fit 223-4
  chi square test of association 227
  controversies 286-8
  factorial ANOVAs 276
  independent t test 138-9
  linear regression 201-2
  Mann-Whitney U test 237, 238
  multiple regression 280
  one-way independent measures ANOVA 163, 164-5
  Pearson's correlation 187, 188, 189
  presenting in psychological research paper 56, 57
  problems 103
  repeated t test 149-50
  reporting 102-3
  Spearman's correlation 253, 254
  statistical significance 101-3
paired design *see* repeated measures design
papers *see* psychological research papers
parametric assumptions 91, 207-12, 232, 297
  choice of statistical test 262, 263
  violations 212-14
parametric statistics/tests 25, 207, 232, 297
  choice of 262
  effect sizes 103
partial correlation 278-9, 297
partial eta squared 288, 297
  one-way independent measures ANOVA 164-5
  and R^2 value 201
participant information sheets 11, 16-17
participant selection and recruitment 37-8
  critical thinking 65
  psychological research paper 47
  qualitative research 71
  running a research study 40

INDEX

participants 56, 297
Participants section, of psychological research paper 46-7
passive deception 13, 298
Pearson's correlation 180-1, 189-91, 279, 298
   calculation and interpretation 184-8, 189
   choice of 261, 263
   effect size 188, 288
   logic behind a 181-4
   non-parametric equivalent *see* Spearman's correlation
   regression analyses 197, 198, 201
   tied ranks 247-8
   variables which can't be used for a 189
peer review 65-6, 298
Phi 290
pilot study 123, 298
placebo group 121, 298
plagiarism 18
planned contrasts 268-9, 272, 298
platykurtic distribution 94, 95, 298
pluralism 79
   analytical 79, 294
population 37, 289, 298
positive correlation/relationship 172, 298
   Pearson's correlation 180-1, 183, 186
   Spearman's correlation 247, 251, 252, 254
positive skew 93, 94, 210, 298
   ranked scores 215
possible/potential harm 298
   protecting participants from 14
   qualitative research 71-2
post hoc contrasts 268-9, 272, 298
potential harm *see* possible/potential harm
power 290
power analysis 290-1, 298
practice effects 117, 122-3, 298
predictive models
   correlational designs 177-8
   linear regression 194-6
predictor variables 298
   hierarchical regression 282
   linear regression 177-8, 263, 278
      example 197, 198, 199, 200
      line of best fit 193, 194, 195
      regression equation 196
   logistic regression 283
   multiple regression 279-80
   regression analysis 177-8, 193
   regression with categorical variables 281-2

stepwise regression 283
presenting research 55-60
   chi square goodness of fit 224-5
   chi square test of association 227-8
   descriptive and inferential statistics 105-6
   ethical considerations 18
   independent t test 137-8, 139
   Mann-Whitney U test 237-8
   one-way independent measures ANOVA 163, 164-5
   Pearson's correlation 188, 189
   regression analysis 201
   repeated t test 148-50
   Spearman's correlation 253-4
   Wilcoxon signed rank test 242
primary sources 298
   finding 60
   referencing 57-8
Procedure section, of psychological research paper 48, 298
PsychInfo 61
psychological research papers 43, 66-7
   critical thinking 49, 64-5
   finding 60-3
   hourglass structure 54-5
   presenting 55-60
   publication process 65-6
   structure 43-54
   writing 54-5
   writing style 50, 55-6
Pub Med 61
published research
   advanced correlational designs 278-86
   advanced experimental designs 267-78
   basics 266-7
   issues and debates in statistical analysis 286-91
publishing process 65-6

qualitative research/methods/approach 68, 80-1, 260, 298
   comparison with quantitative methods 68-9
   data sources 70
   ethics 71-2
   methodological issues 71-2
   pluralism and mixed methods 79-80
   reliability 71
   sampling 71
   types 72-9
   validity 71
quantitative data 22-4
quantitative research/methods/approach 68, 260, 298

   comparison with qualitative methods 68-9
   mixed methods 79-80
   statistical analysis 82
quasi-experimental design 115-16, 298
   choice of statistical test 263
   matching participants 121
quotes, in psychological research papers 56

r value 180-1, 184, 298
   critical values table 313
   example 185-8
   negative 188
   regression analyses 198
R^2 value 298
   linear regression 197-9, 201
   multiple regression 280
r^s statistic 318
random sampling 37-8, 298
random variance (error/residual/within groups variance) 87, 88, 90-1, 92, 103, 104, 298
   advanced experimental designs 267
   ANCOVA 277-8
   experimental design 118-19, 122-3
   factorial ANOVAs 276
   independent t test 130-2, 135
   one-way independent measures ANOVA 154-5, 156, 157-8, 160, 161
   one-way repeated measures ANOVA 270
   Pearson's correlation 183
   repeated t test 142-3, 144-5, 147
randomization 120-1, 122, 298
randomized control trials (RCTs) 124-5, 298
range 89, 298
ranked scores 214-16, 298
   choice of statistical test 263
   Mann-Whitney U test 233-4, 234-5, 238
   Pearson's correlation 247
   Spearman's correlation 247-50
   tied 247-50
   Wilcoxon signed rank test 239, 240
ratio level data 24, 247, 298
   correlational designs 30, 31, 189
   dependent variables 114
   mean 85
   parametric analysis 25, 209
Raven's Progressive Matrices 39
reading age 25-6
recruitment of participants *see* participant selection and recruitment

references 57–60, 298
 body of report 57–8
 Discussion section 51–2
 list of 52, 58–60
reflexivity 74
regression analysis 177, 298
 checking whether data are normally distributed 214
 complex models 282–3
 describing variables in a 178
 effect size 288
 enter method of regression 282
 hierarchical regression 279, 282
 homoscedasticity 212
 parametric assumptions 207
 stepwise regression 279, 282, 283
 see also linear regression
regression equation 195–6
related design *see* repeated measures design
relationship 298
 correlational designs 171–2
 Spearman's correlation 247
reliability 31–2, 34–7, 298
 critical thinking 65
 qualitative research 71
 running a research study 39
repeated measures design 92–30, 115, 116, 117–18, 232, 298
 advantages and disadvantages 117, 119
 choice of statistical test 262, 263
 counterbalancing 121–2
 independence of observations 208–9
 intervention experiments 124
 McNemar test 228
 one-way repeated measures ANOVA 269–72
 randomized control trials 124
 sphericity of variance 212
 Wilcoxon signed rank test 239
repeated *t* test 142, 150–2, 232, 298
 calculating and interpreting 145–9
 checking whether data are normally distributed 214
 choice of 261
 comparison with independent *t* test 142–3, 144, 145, 148, 149
 effect sizes 149–50
 interpreting and writing up 148–9
 logic behind the 142–5
 non-parametric equivalent *see* Wilcoxon signed rank test
 one-way repeated ANOVA 272

significance 147–8
 and sphericity 212, 272
replications 5–6, 33, 298
research designs 27
 see also categorical design; correlational design; experimental design
research papers *see* psychological research papers
research process 5–7
research question 70, 298
residual values 299
 chi square goodness of fit 222, 224
 chi square test of association 226, 227, 228
residual variance *see* random variance
Results section, of psychological research paper 48–50, 54, 55, 299
right to withdraw 14, 299
 vulnerable groups 16

sample 37, 289, 299
sample size 299
 checking whether data are normally distributed 214
 chi square test 228
 confidence intervals 289
 and effect size 288
 importance 103–4
 non-parametric tests 242
 null hypothesis significance testing 103
 p values 287
sampling
 opportunity *see* opportunity sampling
 qualitative research 71
 random 37–8, 298
 stratified 38, 299
 systematic 38, 299
 volunteer 38, 300
scatterplots 171–2, 285–6, 299
 Pearson's correlation 180–1
 strength of correlation 182
Science Direct Scopus 61
scientific method 9–10, 299
search engines 60–1
secondary source 299
 limitations 60
 referencing 57–8
selection of participants *see* participant selection and recruitment
semi-structured interview 70, 299
Shapiro-Wilks test 212
significance 82–3, 99–105, 299
 presenting findings 105

statistical *see* statistical significance
testing 126–7
 presenting in psychological research paper 56
 see also null hypothesis significance testing
simple linear regression 299
 see also linear regression
skewness 93–4, 210, 299
 Mann-Whitney *U* test 237
 median 84
 ranked scores 215
slope 194–6, 299
 example 199–201
Social Learning Theory 7
Spearman's correlation 216, 247, 254–5, 299
 calculating and interpreting 250–4
 choice of 261, 263
 effect size 288, 290
 and tied ranks 247–50
sphericity 212, 270–2, 299
split-half reliability 35, 299
standard deviation 299
 calculation 89–90, 91
 checking whether data are normally distributed 213
 confidence intervals 289
 independent *t* test 137–9
 normal distribution 92, 93
 one-way independent measures ANOVA 158, 163
 presenting findings 56, 105
 repeated *t* test 146, 148, 149, 150
 z scores 95–7, 99
standard normal distribution 93, 299
statistical analysis 82–3, 106–9
 central tendency 83–6
 descriptive statistics 83–91
 dispersion 86–91
 distributions in datasets 91–5
 inferential statistics 99–105
 presenting 105–6
 z scores 95–9
statistical significance 99–100
 alpha level 102
 breaking down a significant effect in an ANOVA 268–9
 chi square goodness of fit 223–4
 chi square test of association 227
 degrees of freedom 104–5
 effect sizes 103
 factorial ANOVAs 276
 independent *t* test 129, 135–7, 138
 Mann-Whitney *U* test 233–4, 236–7, 238

INDEX

statistical significance (*Cont.*)
  one-way independent measures ANOVA 154, 162-3, 164
  p values 101-3, 287
  Pearson's correlation 186-8, 189
  repeated *t* test 147-8, 149
  sample size 103-4
  Spearman's correlation 252-3
  Wilcoxon signed rank test 239, 241-2
statistical symbols and conventions 301-2
statistics, presenting in psychological research paper 56-7
stepwise regression 279, 282, 283, 299
stratified sampling 38, 299
subjective nature of qualitative research 69, 299
Sum of Products (SP) 199-200
Sums of Squares (SS) 155-6, 157, 299
  effect sizes 164
  example 159-60
systematic sampling 38, 299

t statistic 299
  critical values table 309
  independent *t* test 131-8
  multiple regression 280
  negative 137
  repeated *t* test 147
t test
  choice of 262
  comparison with ANOVA 155, 156-7
  comparison with Pearson's correlation 181
  effect size 288
  familywise error 153-4
  independent *see* independent measures *t* test
  parametric assumptions 207
  repeated *see* repeated *t* test
tables 49, 53, 105-6
test-retest reliability 35, 40, 299
test statistic 259, 299
testable 10, 299
Thematic Analysis 72-3, 74-5, 299
  phases 74-9
  themes 77-9, 299
theories 7, 8, 299
title, of psychological research paper 44
transcription of data 76
treatment evaluation 123-5
two-tailed hypothesis 8-9, 299
  chi square goodness of fit 220, 221
  correlational designs 172
  experimental design 125-7
  linear regression 193
  Mann-Whitney *U* test 234, 236, 237
  normal distribution 126-7
  one-way independent measures ANOVA 158, 162
  Pearson's correlation 184
  post hoc contrast 269
  psychological research papers 54
  repeated *t* test 145, 147
  Wilcoxon signed rank test 241
Type I Error 100, 101, 299
  alpha level 102
  chi square goodness of fit 223, 224
  chi square test of association 227
  degrees of freedom 104-5
  familywise error rate 154
  independent *t* test 136-7, 268
  one-way independent measures ANOVA 162-3
  p values 101-2
  Pearson's correlation 187
  repeated *t* test 148
  Spearman's correlation 252
Type II Errors 100, 101, 299

unpaired design *see* independent measures design
unstructured interview 70, 299

validity 31-4, 299
  critical thinking 65
  qualitative research 71
  running a research study 39
variability 291, 299
  ANCOVA 277-8
  factorial ANOVAs 276-7
  independent *t* test 129-32
  one-way repeated measures ANOVA 270-2
  Pearson's correlation 181-4
  repeated *t* test 142-5, 147
  sources 87-9
  understanding 86-9
variables 21, 299
  correlational studies 173-4
  measurement *see* measuring variables
  operationalising *see* operationalising variables
  parametric assumptions 209
  types 22-4
variance 300
  calculation 89-90, 91
  experimental (between groups/ model variance) *see* experimental variance
  heterogeneity *see* heterogeneity of variance
  homogeneity *see* homogeneity of variance
  homoscedasticity 212
  independent *t* test 129
  linear regression 197-9
  one-way independent measures ANOVA 154-5, 156, 157-8
    example 160, 161
  random (error/residual/within groups variance) *see* random variance
  repeated *t* test 142-3
  sphericity 212
volunteer sampling 38, 300
vulnerable groups 15-16

Web of Knowledge 61
Wikipedia 60, 61
Wilcoxon signed rank test 216, 231-2, 238, 242-6, 300
  calculating and interpreting 240-2
  choice of 261
  critical values table 317
  effect size 288, 290
  logic behind the 239
  z score 242-3
withdrawal from study *see* right to withdraw
within groups variance 300
  see also random variance
within participants design *see* repeated measures design
writing psychological research papers 53-4
  see also presenting research
writing style 50, 55-6

x-axis 300
  linear regression 193, 194
  normal distribution 91

Yate's correction 228
y-axis 300
  linear regression 193, 194
  normal distribution 91-3

z scores 95-9, 300
  comparing studies 95
  effect size 290
  looking at scores and distributions 95-7
  non-parametric tests 242-3
  problems 97-9
  relevance to psychological statistics 99
  table 303-8